£40
As seen

ENGLISHMEN AND JEWS

ENGLISHMEN AND JEWS

Social Relations and Political Culture
1840–1914

David Feldman

YALE UNIVERSITY PRESS
NEW HAVEN AND LONDON
1994

Set in Baskerville by Best-set Typesetter Ltd., Hong Kong
Printed and bound in Great Britain by Biddles Ltd., Guildford and Kings Lynn

Library of Congress Catalog Card Number: 94–60013

ISBN 0–300–05501–3

A catalogue record for this book is available from the British Library.

To My Parents

Contents

Acknowledgments

This book has been a long time in preparation. Concluding it brings many pleasures and one of them is the opportunity to acknowledge the contributions of at least some of those individuals and institutions who have helped me along the way.

As a research student I received financial assistance from the Economic and Social Research Council, YIVO Institute for Jewish Research, Gonville and Caius College, Cambridge and the Association of Jewish ex-Servicemen. Without the support I received thereafter from Churchill College, Cambridge, where I was elected to a Research Fellowship, it would have been impossible for me to write this book. Later, at Christ's College, Cambridge and the University of Bristol I enjoyed the support and encouragement of colleagues as I strove to finish it. I am also grateful to the Henry M. Jackson School of International Studies at the University of Washington, Seattle, where I enjoyed a fruitful six months as a Stroum Research Fellow in Jewish Studies.

Archivists, librarians and the staff of other institutions enabled me to consult material in their care. I would especially like to mention the help I received from staff at Cambridge University Library, the Library of the London School of Economics and Political Science, the British Library Newspaper Division at Colindale, the Greater London Record Office, the Anglo-Jewish Archives, the Federation of Synagogues, the Jewish Board of Deputies and the YIVO Institute for Jewish Research in New York.

Teachers, scholars and friends have helped sustain this project with a supply of advice, criticism and encouragement. The origins of this book lie in my doctoral thesis which was supervised by Gareth Stedman Jones. His advice and his example have been formative influences, not only in my time as a research student but also in the years since then. In the early stages of my research I was fortunate to be able to turn to Chimen Abramsky for guidance on aspects of

Jewish history and to Bill Fishman for induction in the history of the East End of London. Barry Supple was one of the examiners of my doctoral thesis and in this role he raised some important questions which I have attempted to answer here.

I owe a great debt to the members of the London History Group, which met regularly through the early 1980s and, in particular, to Jennifer Davis, Jim Gillespie, Tom Jeffrey and Susan Pennybacker. Our meetings at the time and our conversations since inform this book. I would also like to acknowledge warmly the importance of many discussions with Peter de Bolla, Rajnarayan Chandavarkar and David Crew. On particular points I was able to benefit from the expertise of Jonathan Zeitlin, David Cesarani and Bryan Cheyette.

Stefan Collini, Todd Endelman, Margot Finn, David Sorkin and Miles Taylor, all responded generously to requests to read parts of the manuscript: I learned a great deal from their many thoughtful comments. I owe a particular debt to Miles Taylor who gave me the benefit of his knowledge of the history of patriotism in nineteenth century Britain. Many of these chapters were also read by Linda Pollock and burnished by her corruscating criticism. At short notice Lawrence Goldman made time to read the entire manuscript and his commentary on it was invaluable. I would also like to acknowledge the advice of Jay Winter and Paula Hyman: both read the manuscript for Yale University Press and their suggestions helped me to bring this project to a conclusion. After so much generous and excellent advice it is inevitably the case that any errors that remain are my responsibility alone.

Some parts of chapters 11, 12 and 14 of this book first appeared in two essays: 'The Importance of Being English: Immigration and the Decay of Liberal England', in D. Feldman and G. Stedman Jones eds., *Metropolis London: Histories and Representations since 1800* (London, 1989) and 'Jews in London, 1880–1914', in R. Samuel ed., *Patriotism: The Making and Unmaking of British National Identity* (London, 1989). I am grateful to Routledge for permission to reproduce this material.

On final acknowledgment remains to be made – to my wife Naomi Tadmor. She has contributed to this book in innumerable ways. I only hope that some of her clear thinking has found its way into this text. Certainly, she has changed my life both as an Englishman and a Jew.

Glossary of transliterations from Yiddish and Hebrew

aliyos	ritual participation in reading of the Torah (q.v.).
arbayter	worker.
Ashkenazim	Jews of Central or East European origin.
balebatim	householders.
Beth Hamedrash	place for the study of sacred literature, often attached to a synagogue.
dayan	judge; a member of a Jewish court.
droshe	sermon.
get	Jewish bill of divorce.
goy	non-Jew, can be perjorative.
haskalah	the enlightenment movement in the Jewish world.
herem	a rabbinical ban or excommunication.
hesped	a funeral oration.
kashrut	Jewish dietary laws.
kehila	Jewish community, can have an institutional sense.
khazan	cantor.
khevra	association or society.
kheyder pl. *khadorim*	a small traditional Jewish religious school, literally a room.
kosher	food prepared according to the Jewish dietary laws.
landsmanshaftn	association of immigrants from the same town or district.
landslayt	people from the same town or district.
luftmensh	person without a fixed occupation.
maged	a popular religious preacher.
maskil	an adherent of the *haskalah* (q.v.).
melamed pl. *melamdim*	teacher, particularly in a *kheyder* (q.v.).
mikvah	ritual bath.
mitzvos	religious commandments.
Sephardim	Jews of Spanish descent.
shechita	slaughter of animals according to Jewish law.
shtetl	township.
Talmud	the body of teaching that comprises the theory and prescriptions of Jewish Oral Law adumbrated by

generations of scholars in centres of Jewish learning in Babylon and Palestine, dating from the first
half of the third century to the end of the fifth
century.

Talmud Torah	traditional elementary school for Jewish learning.
tsukunft	future.
Yom Kippur	Day of Atonement.

In general, transliterations from Yiddish follow the YIVO system set out in
Max Weinreich's dictionary. Hebrew transliterations are taken from the
Encyclopaedia Judaica. There are, however, exceptions. These occur where
the spelling or language of historical actors differed from those set out by
modern authorities. Readers should also be aware that the Yiddish and
Hebrew languages hold many words in common. Where such words have
arisen in this text I have tried to adopt the transliteration most appropriate
to the historical context. Exceptions arise when to have done so would have
entailed more than one transliteration of the same word.

List of Abbreviations

ADC	Aliens Defence Committee.
AF	*Der Arbayter Fraynd.*
AST	Amalgamated Society of Tailors.
AJA	Anglo-Jewish Association.
BBL	British Brothers League.
col.	references to *Hansard* are to column numbers.
GLRO	Greater London Record Office.
JBD	Jewish Board of Deputies.
JBG	Jewish Board of Guardians.
JC	*Jewish Chronicle.*
LBYB	Leo Baeck Year Book.
LCC	London County Council.
MTIA	Master Tailors Improvement Association.
PP	Parliamentary Papers.
q.	question (used when citing material from the proceedings of Royal Commissions and Parliamentary Select Committees).
PRO	Public Record Office.
RCAI	Royal Commission on Alien Immigration.
SDF	Social Democratic Federation.
TJHSE	Transactions of the Jewish Historical Society.

Introduction

)

Between 1830 and 1914 the Jewish minority in England underwent a double transformation. The first part was legal and political. At the beginning of the period all public offices were closed to professing Jews. They were debarred from Parliament and from civic office and were disqualified from any employment connected to the administration of justice. In the civil sphere, Jews were obstructed from entering professions which demanded a Christian oath: most branches of schoolteaching, medicine and the Bar were closed to them and, for the same reason, Jews were ineligible to take degrees or hold any office at Oxford and Cambridge Universities.[1] Between 1830–71 these political and civil disadvantages were erased. Reform came piecemeal, but the combined effect of limited and particular measures was momentous. Above all, this was the case in public life, where hitherto the Jews' exclusion had been total. The relation of Jews to the state was cast anew.

The second part of the transformation was demographic. As a result of immigration from Eastern Europe, the Jewish population, which had numbered just sixty thousand in 1880, grew dramatically to reach three hundred thousand by 1914.[2] This was a revolution in quality as well as quantity. An influx of poor Russians and Poles saturated a predominantly middle-class and anglicised Jewish population. By the 1890s the immigrants had radically altered the occupational and cultural profile of Jews in England.

Englishmen and Jews explores these two phases of transformation. At one level it addresses some of the broad questions arising from the history of the Jewish presence in England. To what extent did

1. H.S.Q. Henriques, *The Jews and the English Law* (Oxford, 1908) provides an unsurpassed account of the Jews' legal position from their resettlement to the early twentieth century.
2. H. Pollins, *Economic History of the Jews in England* (London, 1982), p. 131.

English society accept or reject the Jewish minority within it? How did the collective identity and collective interests of the Jewish minority change during this period? And, bearing on each of these issues, what was the impact of immigration? At another level, this book sets out to contribute to more wide-ranging reinterpretations of both English and Jewish history in the period. It strives to do so by studying both in conjunction. By showing that some of the concerns of both English and Jewish history were intricately connected this study aims to promote new perspectives on both. Let us begin, however, by elaborating upon some of the themes which arise from the Jewish presence in England.

Jews were expelled from England by an edict of 1290. With this act Edward I closed a century of royal spoliation and popular persecution. But since their resettlement in the seventeenth century, those Jews who lived in England were comparatively fortunate – in their capacities as Jews, at least. Initially, they did not enjoy the same rights as the sovereign's Christian subjects but their disabilities were not as extensive as those which afflicted Jews elsewhere in Europe and they arose in a different way. In general, Jews were not disadvantaged expressly because they were Jews but because they were not members of the Church of England. Most of their disadvantages arose in the same way as those which burdened Catholics and Protestant Dissenters.[3] In pre-Revolutionary France, and in late eighteenth-century Holland, Austria and in the German states, by contrast, Jews were subject to bodies of law which applied to them specifically and which, for instance, determined their rights to settle or follow particular occupations. In these states Jews had no general claim to residence or toleration.[4] Not only were the Jews' disabilities lighter in England but their removal presented an issue that was less combustible than was the case, for instance, in Germany.[5] Following emancipation, Jews in England were disturbed neither by anti-Semitic political parties, as was the case in Germany and Austria, nor by an anti-Semitic movement such as the one in France which

3. There were two significant exceptions. First, there is doubt over whether Jews were legally entitled to own land and, second, Jews until 1830 were unable to engage in retail trade in the City of London: Henriques, *The Jews and the English Law*, pp. 191, 199–201.
4. J. Katz, *Out of the Ghetto: The Social Background to Jewish Emancipation, 1770–1870* (New York, NY edn, 1978), pp. 9–19.
5. T. Endelman, 'The Englishness of Jewish Modernity in England', in J. Katz, ed., *Towards Modernity: The European Jewish Model* (New York, NY, 1987), p. 241, makes this point. For another contrast between England and other countries, see M. Salbstein, *The Emancipation of the Jews in Britain* (Rotherford, NJ, 1982), p. 44. C. Roth's classic text, *A History of the Jews in England* (Oxford 3rd edn, 1964), is an extended essay and paean to the contrast: see especially p. 270.

crystallised around and developed through the Dreyfus affair.[6] On the contrary, in England it had been possible for a converted Jew – Disraeli – to become the leader of the Conservative Party and Prime Minister.

This is a happy story. To the extent that it is accurate it will require some explanation. But the explanation which has been given hitherto – namely, that England was blessed with a peculiarly powerful tradition of liberalism – appears less persuasive in view of the research of the last two decades. Nineteenth-century liberalism is no longer portrayed solely as the secular, tolerant and principled creed that we find celebrated, for instance, in John Morley's biography of Gladstone.[7] More often than not, it is now seen to have been driven by Christian theology, by Gladstone's populist appeal to the mass electorate, and by fractious interest groups.[8] If this was the case, then the relation of liberalism to the Jews is due for reassessment.

Indeed, there is reason to doubt whether the conventional narrative of Jewish history presents the entire story. Jewish emancipation in England was by no means precocious. Altough the changes it required were less far-reaching than elsewhere in Europe, emancipation in England was preceded by Jewish equality in the United States, France, Holland and some German states. The removal of Jewish disabilities in England was one aspect of the changing relation between Church and state in the forty years following the repeal of the Test and Corporation Acts in 1828. These Acts, which, in theory, debarred non-Anglican Protestants from membership of corporations or from holding office under the Crown, had fallen into desuetude before their repeal.[9] More significant than their removal was the admission of Catholics to Parliament in 1829. With this

6. P. Pultzer, *The Rise of Political Anti-Semitism in Germany and Austria* (New York, NY, 1964); R. Levy, *The Downfall of Anti-Semitic Political Parties in Imperial Germany* (New Haven, CT, 1975); S. Wilson, *Ideology and Experience: Anti-Semitism in France at the Time of the Dreyfus Affair* (East Brunswick, NJ, 1982).

7. A turning point in the historiography was the publication in 1966 of J.R. Vincent, *The Formation of the English Liberal Party, 1857–68* (London).

8. *Ibid*; D.A. Hamer, *Liberal Politics in the Age of Gladstone and Rosebery* (Oxford, 1982); J. Parry, *Democracy and Religion: Gladstone and the Liberal Party, 1867–75* (Cambridge, 1986); R. Brent, *Liberal Anglican Politics: Whiggery, Religion and Reform 1830–41* (Oxford, 1987); H.C.G. Matthew, ed., *Gladstone Diaries*, vol. ix (Oxford, 1986), 'Introduction'.

9. Nevertheless, the grievances of Dissenters – most notably, the compulsory payment of rates to the Church of England and the imposition of religious tests at Oxford and Cambridge Universities – were not satisfied before a Jew took his seat in the House of Commons: Church Rates were abolished in 1868, the last University Tests went in 1871.

measure the relation of the state to religion began a process of decisive change. Following Catholic emancipation, and the abandonment of the exclusively Protestant constitution, the ideal of the
union of Church and state gave ground before the grievances
of non-Anglicans and, in particular, those of Protestant nonconformists.[10] Nevertheless, this was a slow process, and the state had
to undergo a radical alteration before it was able to contain the
Jewish minority on equal terms. Jewish emancipation was part of,
and contributed to, the decomposition of the confessional state in
England. Its tardiness suggests that Jewish integration was attended
by more friction than is often allowed.

Moreover, the mid-nineteenth-century reforms which brought
Jewish equality do not mark the end of the story. Jewish emancipation redefined the relation of Jews to the state, but the state underwent further changes after Jews entered Parliament. From the 1880s
governments assumed an increasingly proactive role in social relations and there were demands, from the political right as well as the
left, for their functions to be extended radically. If the state was to
assume a greater responsibility for the well-being of the people,
would its embrace extend to Jews and immigrants? It will be fruitful
to ask whether it was not only the confessional state but the growth
of the collectivist state as well that faced a Jewish problem.

The evolution of Jewish religious and cultural practices and communal institutions in the context of English society forms one part of
a process that encompassed the Jews of West and Central Europe.
After the mid-eighteenth century, as Jews emerged from their separate legal, social and cultural existence, non-Jewish society became
an increasingly significant environment for them. Growing numbers of Jews embraced the non-Jewish world, or aspects of it. For
many of them political emancipation was connected to programmes
of religious, educational and institutional reform designed to revise

10. G.F.A. Best, 'The Protestant Constitution and its Defenders', in R. Robson, ed.,
     Ideas and Institutions of Victorian England (London, 1967); J.C.D. Clark, *English
     Society, 1688–1832* (Cambridge, 1985), pp. 383–420; G.I.T. Machin, *Politics and
     the Churches in Great Britain, 1832–68* (Oxford, 1987). In 1840 Jews were far
     from the only group in England disadvantaged on religious grounds. It was
     only in 1835 that Dissenters were no longer required to undergo an Anglican
     marriage ceremony. But Oxford and Cambridge Universities remained closed
     to them, and non-Anglicans were bound to pay a Church Rate for the upkeep
     of the parish church. Moreover, over the next decades the grievances of
     nonconformists were to find new fields. As the state began to fund public
     education, nonconformists fought to prevent any national or local taxes from
     being used to support Church education. It is important, therefore, to under-
     line the centrality of arguments over the relation of state and religion in the
     ideological composition of liberalism in Victorian England.

the content and boundaries of Jewish affiliation.[11] Many Gentiles, too, hoped that once the Jews' civil and political disabilities were removed so also their 'exclusive spirit' would disappear.[12] Which sorts of Jewish identification were legitimate and which should be discouraged was a recurrent point of debate, both within Jewry and between Jews and non-Jews.

Jewish identification was a matter of changing practice as well as a point of debate. Understanding and explaining these changes has become a central concern in recent Jewish historiography. The term 'acculturation' has been used to address this problem. It denotes an accommodation to non-Jewish standards that was less complete than assimilation, in which Jewish religion or culture was not renounced. The term has gained currency as an historiography which regarded the history of emancipated Jewry through the lens of the Holocaust and the establishment of the state of Israel has been reassessed. From the standpoint of the first post-war generation of historians, European Jewry had been engaged in a hopeless pursuit of acceptability and, to this end, had compromised its Jewish inheritance. We are now offered a more positive and nuanced evaluation of Jewish history between the French Revolution and the rise of Nazism.[13]

This different description – that the period was one in which Jewish communities and culture changed rather than degenerated – has also produced a different explanation of cultural change. A number of historians have turned to the concept of modernisation. Influenced by the assumptions of functionalist sociology, they see change as an adaptation to modern society; new conditions – urbanisation, industrialisation, the wider circulation of people and knowledge – inevitably elicited new patterns of behaviour. Relations of institutional and social power are relegated in importance.[14] This

11. For an unsurpassed survey see Katz, *Out of the Ghetto.*
12. For example, I. Abrahams and S. Levy, eds., *Macaulay on Jewish Disabilities* (Edinburgh, 1910), p. 31.
13. On German-Jewish historiography see D. Sorkin, 'Emancipation Assimilation: Two Concepts and their Application to German-Jewish Historiography', *LBYB,* 1990, especially pp. 22–8. Examples of the more positive assessment are *idem, The Transformation of German Jewry, 1780–1840* (Oxford, 1987); P. Hyman, *From Dreyfus to Vichy: the Remaking of French Jewry* (New York, NY, 1979); for a survey of this literature see T. Endelman, 'The Legitimization of Diaspora Experience in Recent Jewish Historiography', *Modern Judaism,* May 1991, pp. 195–209.
14. For example, S. Lowenstein, 'The Pace of Modernization of German Jewry', *LBYB,* 1976, pp. 41–56; T. Endelman, *The Jews of Georgian England* (Philadelphia, Pa, 1979); S. Zipperstein, *Jews of Odessa* (Stanford, Calif., 1985); *idem,* '*Haskalah,* Cultural Change and Nineteenth-Century Russian Jewry', *Journal of Jewish Studies,* Autumn 1983, pp. 191–207.

view contrasts with other approaches to cultural history which have
been influential during the last two decades. These see culture as
a field in which power is exercised. In this regard one has only to
think of the very different but equally influential work of Edward
Thompson and Michel Foucault.[15] But there is an interesting equivo-
cation in the way Jewish historiography has taken up the concept
of modernisation. For while the idea is often used as a window on
to the field of Jewish social and cultural history, the transition
from tradition to modernity in Jewish history is generally defined in
political terms: as the erosion of Jewish communal authority by
the state so that the Jewish community lost the degree of political
autonomy it once enjoyed.[16] It is a definition which may prompt us
to investigate what the relation was between political power and
cultural change. The direction of historical work in other fields as
well as this ambiguity within recent Jewish historiography suggests
that the place of power relations in modern Jewish cultural history is
in need of re-examination. The English case is a particularly perti-
nent case through which to do this since, in mid-Victorian England,
it has been argued, Judaism developed in a benign environment in
which external pressure to adjust Jewish practice to English norms
was notably weak.[17]

Immigration from Eastern Europe added a new dimension and
a new dynamic to the problems I have been discussing. First, the
period of large-scale Jewish immigration broadly coincided with the
state's growing concern with the physical and material well-being of
the people. The immigrants were interpolated within debates on the
problems of the labour market, 'sweated' working conditions and
overcrowded and insanitary housing. In this way the Jewish problem,
as it was perceived in England, changed fundamentally. At the start
of the twentieth century it inspired legislation designed to restrict
Jewish immigration specifically: the Aliens Act of 1905, which was
also the foundation for modern immigration law. Thus immigration
plus collectivism had far-reaching consequences for the relation of
Jews to the state.

Second, the immigrants challenged the shape of Anglo-Jewish
religious, cultural and political life as it had developed during
and after emancipation. The temper of the immigrants' orthodox

15. See for example E.P. Thompson, *Customs in Common* (London, 1991); M.
   Foucault, *The History of Sexuality*, vol. i (Harmondsworth, 1981).
16. See J. Katz, 'Introduction', in Katz, ed., *Towards Modernity*, pp. 1–2; M. Meyer,
   'Modernity as a Crisis for Jews', *Modern Judaism*, May 1989, pp. 152–3; E.
   Lederhendler, *The Road to Modern Jewish Politics: Political Reconstruction and the
   Jewish Community of Tsarist Russia* (New York, NY, 1989), p. 8.
17. This last point is discussed in more detail below: pp. 25–7.

Judaism was both an embarrassment and a rebuke to Anglo-Jewry. The radical secularism of anarchists and socialists, as well as the doctrine of class conflict they presented to the greatly enlarged Jewish working class, issued a challenge from a different direction. If there is reason to reconsider both the history of Jewish integration in England and the history of the Jews themselves, then the consequences of Jewish immigration will figure largely in both projects.

Immigration had a third consequence, which adds a new theme to this discussion: it vastly increased the size of the Jewish working class. It did so in the sense that immigration increased the number and also the proportion of manual workers within the Jewish population in England. It also did so in the sense that, for the great majority of immigrants, emigration to England either confirmed a proletarian status they had already encountered or was the occasion of their entry to the ranks of manual waged labourers. In England Jewish workers comprised a far larger portion of the Jewish population than was the case in Eastern Europe.

The conjuncture of the particular designation 'Jewish' with the universal connotations of the term 'proletarian' raises the question, 'How Jewish is Jewish history?' Can the history of the Jewish minority contribute to our understanding of the non-Jewish majority and, conversely, can the history of the majority add to our understanding of Jewish history? These are questions whose purchase is not restricted to the case of Jewish workers. Any account of Jewish history should consider whether figures in the past were acting as Jews or as members of other collectivities: whether it is more enlightening and appropriate to understand the behaviour and attitudes of Jewish workers, bankers or women as Jews or as figures within these other social categories. Contextual questions of this sort, and the disagreements that surround them, are not unique to Jewish history. But problems of contextualisation are particularly evident when we deal with the history of Jews in the post-emancipation period as, increasingly, a group which had lived a separate social existence interacted with the non-Jewish world.

In the case of Anglo-Jewish history this question has been answered in two distinct ways. On one side, historians writing in a tradition of Jewish historiography have examined the experience of Jews as Jews. They explore the particularity of the Jewish past revealed in the history of communal institutions, in the quest for political and civil equality, in patterns of religious and cultural identification, and in the particular qualities of the Jews' economic and social behaviour. In this spirit, Lloyd Gartner describes his history of *The Jewish Immigrant in England* as 'Jewish history with an

English background'.[18] The distinction between Gentiles and Jews is the principle of social differentiation which underpins such an enquiry. A second group of historians question the Jewishness of Jewish history. This need not take the form of a Marxist interpretation, but in the case of Anglo-Jewish historiography it has done so, reflecting the influence of Marxism in English social history.[19] For these writers Jewish history presents a particular example of broader social processes which are defined by class interests.[20]

The history of Jewish immigrants and, above all, their history as workers, brings this divide sharply into focus. One body of research regards the immigrants as a group apart from English workers, uncomfortable with their proletarian status and forever striving to move up the social ladder and out from the class of wage earners. But another interpretation rejects this view and replaces it with a history in which class and class-consciousness were the determining features of economic and social life.[21] This controversy marks a division between historians of Jewish exceptionalism and historians who attempt to recuperate Jewish history for a general interpretation already in place. One approach does not necessarily deny the existence of the context which the other privileges but, rather, it seeks to establish a hierarchy of significance. In both traditions the returns on studying Jewish history are slim indeed. In one version it is *sui generis* and, except as a curio, of no general interest; in the other, it merely confirms 'truths' that were known at the outset.

The problem here does not lie with one interpretation or another but with a conception of history they hold in common. Both sorts of interpretation try to locate an axis of interaction which generates collective interests and identities. In one case this is the difference between Jews and Gentiles, in the other it is class relations conceived in a broadly Marxian fashion. In this way, both interpretations greatly reduce the range of social relations in which Jews

18. L. Gartner, *The Jewish Immigrant in England, 1870–1914* (London, 1973 edn), p. 12.
19. Away from the confines of Anglo-Jewish history C. Goldscheider and A. Zuckerman, *The Transformation of the Jews* (Chicago, Iu, 1984) is an example of a non-Marxist interpretation.
20. For example, B. Williams, *The Making of Manchester Jewry, 1740–1875* (Manchester, 1985).
21. Two studies at either extreme of the controversy are Gartner, *The Jewish Immigrant* and J. Buckman, *Immigrants and the Class Struggle: The Jewish Immigrant in Leeds 1880–1914* (Manchester, 1983). The debate is discussed further in the introduction to Part Two of this study. A useful summary of the debate can be found in T. Endelman, 'English Jewish History', *Modern Judaism*, February 1991, pp. 94–5.

were engaged, and which could generate collective interests and identities. They continue to do so even when they seek to balance Jewish and class imperatives.[22] These interpretations do not necessarily ignore social relations arising from differences between the sexes, or skill, length of residence in England, social geography, mother-tongue, piety and politics but, at best, they subsume them within a more fundamental social relation, or see them as inherently less significant. Yet these interactions cannot be reduced to class and Jewish interests. On the contrary, they contained the potential either to fragment them or to establish other patterns of interest. Relations to the means of production or the differences between Gentiles and Jews were but two of the social relations animating social experience. Accordingly, one aim of this book is to uncover the diverse social relations whch structured the lives of Jewish immigrants and to analyse their determinants. If, in the face of this diversity, some Jews did come to identify their interests as class interests, or if they aligned themselves as Jews, this is more remarkable than has been acknowledged.

Indeed, it is important for us to question in what sense these collectivities existed. The relation of social experience to the ways groups define their collective interest has been subject to a good deal of reconsideration in the last decade. As the field of social history developed it was customary for ideologies and institutions, which claimed to represent collective interests, to be analysed as reflections of those interests as social forces. In recent years, however, some historians have begun to conceive of discources and institutions as the elements that defined social relationships, and through which the babble of experience was given shape and content. Among the problems analysed in this way have been the origins of the French Revolution, the emergence of the Chartist movement, the development of trade unionism and the growth of feminism. Scholars have suggested that since, in complex societies, interests can be defined in many ways, according to many principles of differentiation, the manner they are defined is negotiated discursively and institutionally.[23]

Equally significant, a growing body of historical research has shown how the past meanings of terms such as 'working class', 'the

---

22. For an attempt to do this, in a work that was very significant in opening up the subject, see W.J. Fishman, *East End Jewish Radicals, 1875–1914* (London, 1975).
23. G. Stedman Jones, 'Rethinking Chartism', in *idem, Languages of Class* (Cambridge, 1983); K. Baker, *Inventing the French Revolution* (Cambridge, 1990); J. Zeitlin, 'From Labour History to the History of Industrial Relations', *Economic History Review*, May 1987, pp. 159–84; D. Riley, *Am I that Name?* (Basingstoke, 1988).

people' or '*sans-culottes*', which have been used by historians to refer to objective social groups, emerged from a context of political debate. The terms had different meanings that changed over time and were continually disputed.[24] Their availability to historians as decisive social categories is open to doubt. If this much is accepted, the corollary is that even the most fundamental collective interests and identities may be contingent. If an interest can be defined, it can be redefined or can even be abandoned.

In relation to the present study this suggests that when we find people in the past aligning themselves as Jews, or workers or immigrants, this cannot merely be seen as a reflection of a unified social experience or a crystallised cultural identity, because potentially these people could have identified their collective interests in various different ways. It is necessary even to be sceptical of assumptions regarding the referents of terms such as 'Jew' or 'worker'. It is important to attend to the different meanings given to them. Through terms such as these, different institutions and movements claimed the affiliation of historical actors. The competing claims of these terms demanded choices from their audiences and offered opportunities to them. The historical interests of Jews or workers, therefore, cannot be defined independently of the way they were interpreted by the actors themselves, within the range of choices available to them at particular moments. As I shall suggest, the conflicting interpretations of the Jewish immigrants – their characterisation as exceptional individualists and as class-conscious workers – reflect nothing so much as a conflict that took place in the past between immigrant radicals and Anglo-Jewish philanthropists over how the immigrants' interests and identities should be conceived. But the historians have instated one or other of these arguments as representations of reality when, more accurately, they were two of the most significant attempts to shape it.

This discussion can lead to a new view of the contribution which the history of the Jewish minority can make to our understanding of English history. It does so by directing attention to the ways in which collectivities and interests are defined. For just as historians have been concerned to establish the ways in which Jews were similar or different to Gentiles, so too were contemporaries. Debate and

24. H. Cunningham, 'The Language of Patriotism, 1750–1914', *History Workshop Journal*, Autumn 1981, pp. 8–33; Stedman Jones, 'Rethinking Chartism'; M. Sonenscher, 'The *sans-culottes* of the Year II: Rethinking the Language of Labour in Revolutionary France', *Social History*, October 1984, pp. 301–28.

reflection on Jews in Victorian and Edwardian England constantly developed around points of comparison. Logically, attempts to capture the Jews' distinguishing qualities presupposed a standard to which the Jews were compared, from which they were distinguished or to which they were assimilated. These comparisons were sometimes implicit but on many occasions they were clearly stated. Among other characterisations, Jews were presented as religious obscurantists and as the collective incarnation of Ricardo's 'economic man'. Religious pedantry was compared to Christian spirituality, and economic individualism was contrasted to the custom-bound and union-oriented preferences of the English working man. In part, it was through comparison with the Jews that some versions of the Christian community and the English working class were constituted. Discourse on Jews was never about Jews alone. When we find these discussions concerned with the nature of the Jews' difference we need to ask the question 'different from what?'.[25]

The two collectivities to which the Jews were assimilated or from which they were differentiated most persistently were the nation and the working class. Let us take the case of the nation. In the pages that follow I deal specifically with the nation as a political idea. Clearly, this does not exhaust the topic. There is also, for example, a developmental history to national integration. As Linda Colley persuasively argues, the growth of systems of transport and communication, the wider circulation of newspapers and magazines, a more mobile population, the experience of war and the threat of invasion, promoted greater 'national consciousness' in Britain after 1750.[26] But while this growth enabled men and women to conceive of the national community in new ways, it did not determine how they would do so. It is these visions and accounts of the nation which this book addresses, and which the example of the Jews does much to illumine.

The nation was a recurrent presence in political argument in Victorian and Edwardian England. The national community was envisioned variously as Protestant, Christian, freeborn, imperial and so on; its boundaries and characteristics were labile and contested, they were not simply a reflection of an actual nation. It is no coincidence, for example, that the opponents of the Boer War

25. An exploration of this theme in a different context can be found in S. Aschheim, *Brothers and Strangers: The East European Jew in German and German Jewish Consciousness* (Madison, Wisc., 1982).
26. L. Colley, 'Whose Nation? Class and National Consciousness in Britain, 1750–1850', *Past and Present*, November 1986, pp. 100–3.

between 1899–1902 were known as 'Little Englanders', for they were no less patriotic than the jingo enthusiasts for war considered themselves to be. For one group, love of nation was conceived in terms of imperial grandeur; for the other, it was in a native political tradition apparently endangered by military adventurism.[27]

The history of the nation and of patriotism have received growing attention over the last decade or so.[28] In particular 'patriotism' and 'national consciousness' have been examined both as the cohesive force which eased social division and social conflict in the late eighteenth and late nineteenth centuries and as the currency through which class identities or anxieties were expressed.[29] This work has drawn attention to the language of patriotism and of national identity in nineteenth-century political argument. But the political significance of these vocabularies have been seen as secondary. Rather, there has been a tendency to regard them as instruments wielded in conflicts which really concerned class interests and identities. The idea of the nation itself has been relegated in importance. Other scholars have looked at the cultural dimensions of Englishness and, in particular, at the emergence of a self-consciously national culture in the late nineteenth and early twentieth centuries.[30] Their interpretations have focused more directly on contests over national identity as a subject for investigation in their own right. But they have drawn attention away from consideration of the nation as a political community. This omission, as well as the focus on class, is understandable. It reflects the ways in which the creation of this national culture was not connected, as it was in Europe, with national revolutions and with a radical discontinuity in the history of the state. Nevertheless, in British history too the debate on the nation had a political significance.[31] Here too the nation was one way

---

27. This is discussed in more detail below: pp. 264–7.
28. See R. Samuel, ed., *Patriotism: The Making and Unmaking of British National Identities* (London, 1989), 3 vols.
29. Best, 'The Protestant Constitution'; Cunningham, 'The Language of Patriotism'; Colley, 'Whose Nation? Class and National Consciousness in Britain', pp. 97–117; F. Harcourt, 'Disraeli's imperialism: A Question of Timing', *Historical Journal*, March 1980, pp. 87–110; R. Price, 'Society, Status and Jingoism: The Social Roots of Lower Middle-Class Patriotism', in G. Crossick, ed., *The Lower Middle Class* (London, 1977), pp. 89–112.
30. C. Baldick, *The Social Mission of English Criticism, 1848–1932* (Oxford, 1983); R. Colls and P. Dodd, eds., *Englishness: Politics and Culture 1880–1920* (Beckenham, 1986); S. Collini, *Public Moralists, Political Thought and Intellectual Life in Britain 1850–1930* (Oxford, 1991), chapter 9.
31. This is brought out in M. Taylor, 'John Bull and the Iconography of Public Opinion in England *c.*1712–1929', *Past and Present*, February 1992, pp. 93–128.

of expressing the community which was seen to join government and people.[32]

At a number of points, men and women confronted the question of what the Jews' relationship to the nation should be: whether they could be accommodated within it or whether they presented an anomalous and alien element. At different times, the answers people gave determined whether they would support or oppose the claims of professing Jews to sit in Parliament, whether they would bar poor East European Jews from entering the country and whether, once in the country, the immigrants would be eligible for help from the state in the form of national insurance contributions. In this way attempts to deal with the Jews' legal and political integration revealed and, in part, shaped conceptions of the nation. Attitudes did not merely reflect beliefs and solidarities that were already in place; indeed, conceptions of the nation were constituted and developed, in part, through the ways men and women confronted the Jewish issue. By illuminating this history of the nation, the Anglo-Jewish past has a significant contribution to make to our understanding of English history. It is not my contention that the history of nineteenth-century political argument has to be rewritten in terms of a debate over national identity. But I do suggest that this debate was more pervasive than has been acknowledged. By examining this debate it will be possible to re-examine the development of political culture and government in Britain.

This interactive view of English and Jewish history works in two directions, leading to a reconsideration of the latter as well as the former. For example, it has been usual to organise the history of attitudes to Jews around the theme of anti-Semitism or, more rarely, of philo-Semitism. Several historians have asked whether individuals, institutions or movements in modern Britain were anti-Semitic, and if so, in what degree, and why.[33] They have uncovered political currents and anti-Jewish stereotypes which had been little acknowledged. They have demonstrated that anti-Semitism in modern England was not a European import but was substantially home-produced. But, as these scholars amply demonstrate, in England

32. The United Kingdom was, and remains, a multi-national state. The focus of this book, however, is on its dominant, English component. Of course, many Englishmen habitually failed to distinguish between England and Britain. On British identity see K. Robbins, *Nineteenth Century Britain: Integration and Diversity* (Oxford, 1988); L. Colley, *Britons: Forging the Nation, 1707–1837* (London, 1992).

33. In the case of Britain see C. Holmes, *Anti-Semitism in British Society 1876–1939* (London, 1979); T. Kushner, *The Persistence of Prejudice: Anti-Semitism in British Society during the Second World War* (Manchester, 1989); G. Lebzelter, *Political Anti-Semitism in England 1918–39* (London, 1978).

between the mid-nineteenth and mid-twentieth centuries, the category of anti-Semitism brings together disparate phenomena from
many times and places. It brings together elements from the political
right and left, from elite and from mass culture, and from institutionalised discrimination and personal dislikes. Conventionally,
these phenomena are united by examining them from the point of
view of their relevance to the Jewish minority.[34] But it is possible to
regard them from a different vantage point. Attitudes to Jews, I have
suggested, were predicated upon perceptions of the Jews' similarity
or difference to collectivities such as the nation or the working class.
These attitudes, then, not only emerged from traditions of hostility
to Jews but also from a context of political debate and social interaction which extended beyond the case of the Jewish minority. If the
Jewish problem erupted within this larger arena, then we need to
adopt a more dynamic understanding of the political and cultural
meanings of anti-Jewish attitudes for those who held them.

This suggests that we can advance our understanding of attitudes
to the Jews by taking not the standpoint of the Jewish minority but
that of the Gentile majority whose deeds and utterances we are
examining. We need to shift the initial historical question away from
the problem of why men and women objected to the Jews, to the
question of what they meant when they were doing so. Some
historians of European anti-Semitism have already followed this
path.[35] In the case of England the answers will lead beyond the
phenomenon of anti-Semitism and attitudes to the Jews, towards a
consideration of those collectivities in English society which strove to
accommodate the Jewish presence as well as those which aspired to
exclude it.

It is not only the history of attitudes to Jews but the history of the
Jews themselves which can benefit from an interactive view of Jewish
and non-Jewish history. In fact, the idea that Jewish history must be
placed in its different national contexts has become a commonplace
in recent years among historians interested in the ways Jewish culture and identity changed in the period of emancipation.[36] However,
the national context too often has been regarded as a given, as the

---

34.   For an example of an attempt to treat the history of anti-Semitism in general
      in this way see S. Ettinger, 'Jew Hatred in its Historical Context', in S. Almog,
      ed., *Anti-Semitism through the Ages* (Oxford, 1988), pp. 1–12, especially, pp. 9–
      12.
35.   See for instance G.L. Mosse, *Germans and Jews* (New York, NY, 1970); S. Volkov,
      'Anti-Semitism as a Cultural Code', *LBYB*, 1978, pp. 25–46.
36.   See for example J. Katz, 'Introduction', in Katz, ed., *Towards Modernity*, pp. 1–
      12; and on Anglo-Jewry, T. Endelman, 'The Englishness of Jewish Modernity',
      ibid, pp. 242–3.

scenery against which Jewish history is acted out. But once we see that the idea of Englishness itself was open to differing interpretations then the history of the Jews' accommodation to it can be conceived in new ways. For in crucial respects, what sort of a collectivity the Jews were joining was a matter of debate, among Jews as among non-Jews. To the historians of acculturation we might ask, 'acculturating to what?' Jews were not approaching English culture and society in general but particular collectivities and cultures within it. If this was the case, then the history of cultural change must attend to both sides of the interaction: the national contexts of Jewish history had a more dynamic role than has often been allowed.

Inevitably, some important topics remain beyond the scope of these pages. For example, comparatively little attention is given here to the history of Jewish women. Recent work by other scholars and work currently in progress, however, will make good this omission.[37] The economic history of mid-Victorian Jewry is dealt with much less extensively than the economic history of the period during and immediately after the major waves of immigration. The reason for this particular focus is that in the earlier period the problem of Jewish integration was discussed primarily in relation to a set of constitutional and theological controversies. The Jews' ability to turn a bargain to their advantage was an abiding theme in mid-Victorian culture but it was not until after 1880, with the arrival of thousands of poor immigrants, that Jews attracted extensive notice as figures in labour and housing markets as well. The emphases of these pages follow and investigate the changing contours of contemporary debate.

Moreover, *Englishmen and Jews* develops its chosen themes while also focusing on certain geographical limits. The book's geographical focus is on London. This emphasis is not arbitrary. Throughout the period covered by this book at least one half of English Jews lived in the capital, and London accommodated a similar proportion of the Jewish immigrants who came to the country between 1880–1914.

---

37. See E. Umansky, *Lily Montago and the Advancement of Liberal Judaism* (New York, NY, 1983); R. Burman 'The Jewish Woman as Breadwinner. The Changing Value of Women's Work in a Manchester Immigrant Community', *Oral History*, Autumn 1982, pp. 27–39; *idem*, 'Women in Jewish Religious Life: Manchester 1880–1930', in J. Obelkevich, L. Roper, R. Samuel eds., *Disciplines of Faith: Studies in Religion, Politics and Patriarchy* (London, 1987), pp. 37–54; *idem*, 'Jewish Women and the Household Economy in Manchester, 1890–1920', in D. Cesarani ed., *The Making of Modern Anglo-Jewry* (Oxford, 1990), pp. 55–78; L.G. Kuzmack, *Woman's Cause: The Jewish Woman's Movement in England and the United States, 1881–1933* (Columbus, Ohio, 1990); L. Marks, ' "Dear Old Mother Levy's": The Jewish Maternity and Side Room Helps Society 1895–1939', *Social History of Medicine*, April 1990, pp. 61–88.

This demographic concentration meant that, at a national level, public debate on Jews as a social phenomenon, whether as *parvenus* or as paupers, invariably became a debate on the Jews of London. In some important respects the history of Jews in the capital was different and, therefore, possibly not representative of Anglo-Jewry in general and should not stand in for the whole. For instance, the political context of Jewish integration in Liberal Manchester was very different from that of the capital, which grew increasingly Conservative after the 1860s. In Leeds the demographic impact of Jewish immigration was more dramatic than in London.[38] More generally, the communal and social structure of provincial Jewish communities, relatively distant from the overweening influence of Anglo-Jewish grandees, did not mirror that of London. But nevertheless London remained throughout this period the centre for Jewish life in England, as well as the focus of debate and the fount of government policy concerning the Jews.

What follows, then, is not a comprehensive account of Anglo-Jewish history between 1840–1914, nor can this study attempt to cover all of the many and diverse relations between Englishmen and Jews. Rather, this book has some major thematic concerns. First, it sets out to examine the nature of Jewish integration in Victorian and Edwardian England. In this regard it focuses, above all, on the relation of Jews to the nation and to the institutions which comprised the state. Second, it examines the changing forms of collective identity and collective interest which Jews in England fashioned for themselves. Specifically, this study analyses the religious, associational and political aspects of Jewish acculturation. Third, the following pages examine closely the history of Jewish immigration. In particular, they analyse the economic, social and political history of Jewish immigrants and of the greatly enlarged Jewish working class.

These themes, however, are not equally present in all parts of this book: different sections deal with them and stress them in different ways. The first section deals with the politics of Jewish integration in the emancipation and immediate post-emancipation periods. It also considers the changing appearance of the Jews' collective identity in these years: it is concerned both with the Jews' relation to the state and with their acculturation. The subject matter of the second section is very different. The focus shifts from politics and culture to the economy and society. The chronological framework changes as well. The second section deals with the period after 1880 and focuses on Jewish immigration, on the social conditions and social relations in the East End of London and on how Jewish immigrants struggled to

38. Buckman, *Immigrants and the Class Struggle*, p. ix.

achieve a measure of economic security. The subject matter of the first two sections merge and contribute equally in the third and final section of this study. In part this section deals with the history of the Jews' relation to the state and the nation, and the history of acculturation in the years between 1880 and 1914. In other words, the issues presented in the first section are now followed to the decades of immigration. However, these chapters also deal with the history of politics and associational life in the Jewish East End. In this respect, they develop the history of Jewish immigration and of the Jewish East End begun in the second section.

In treating the themes of Jewish emancipation and Jewish immigration within a single study, this book will enable us to ask what the relationship was between the two. Inevitably it raises the question of whether there were important continuties between the decades of emancipation and immigration. As we shall see, it also raises the question of whether there were significant causal connections between the nature of Jewish integration in England following emancipation and the history of politics and acculturation among Jewish immigrants after 1880.

What follows attempts to take a broad view of the history of the Jewish presence in England. It strives to draw together the institutional, social and economic history of the Jews with the political, religious and social history of England between 1840–1914. Its intention is to bring Jewish history and English history to bear on each other in illuminating exchanges. By seeing each in the context provided by the other it aims to bring new insights to both.

PART 1

Jews and the Nation, 1840–80

Introduction

In 1851 there were roughly 35,000 Jews in England and Wales; 20,000 were concentrated in London alone. Settlements of Jews in other towns were small. Communities ranging in size from a few score to a few hundred were scattered the length of the country from Gateshead to Penzance. The largest were in Liverpool and Manchester, whose Jewish populations were about 2,500 and 1,100 respectively, and Birmingham, which contained fewer than 1,000 Jews. The fastest-growing Jewish centre, however, was Leeds. At mid-century, Leeds contained fewer than 100 Jews, but by the end of the 1870s this figure had reached 2,250. This remarkable growth was caused by immigration from Eastern Europe. Even before the mass immigration which began in 1881–2, there was a steady influx of Jews to nineteenth-century England, from Germany and Holland initially and, after 1840, from Russia and Poland. In 1883 Joseph Jacobs, the folklorist, statistician and historian, estimated that during the previous 23 years, 12,000 Jews from Russia and Poland and 7,000 German Jews had entered the country.[1]

In 1851, surveying British Jews, the Reverend John Mills judged that just one half of London's Jews were 'lower class'.[2] Three decades later, Jacobs made a more detailed estimate of the social composition of London Jewry. But the image he too delivered was of a disproportionately middle-class population. Jacobs suggested that metropolitan Jewry contained a narrow band of 15 per cent of

1. V.D. Lipman, *Social History of the Jews in England, 1850–1950* (London, 1954), pp. 9, 22–6; *idem, A History of Jews in Britain since 1858* (Leicester, 1990), pp. 12–16; B. Williams, *The Making of Manchester Jewry, 1740–1875* (Manchester, 1985), p. 176; A.R. Rollin, 'Russo-Jewish Immigrants in England before 1881', *TJHSE*, 1968, pp. 202–13; C.C. Aronsfeld, 'German Jews in Victorian England', *LBYB*, 1962, pp. 312–29. Many of the German Jews in London were, in a cultural sense, Polish Jews and had emigrated from Prussian-controlled Poland.
2. J. Mills, *British Jews* (London, 1853), p. 257.

families who enjoyed annual income of over £1,000 and, at the other end of the scale, 24 per cent whose income was below £100. But the solidly middle-class group living off an income of between £200 and £1,000 each year was by far the largest and comprised 42 per cent of the capital's Jews and a further 20 per cent, with an income of between £100 and £200, were placed precariously above the Jewish working classes. The London middle class was large by national standards but even in this milieu Jews were over-represented.[3]

Throughout these middle decades of the century the East End remained the primary place of settlement for the capital's middle-class Jews. But in growing numbers they drifted away from East London, and just like their Christian counterparts they contributed to the growth of new suburbs: spreading west in the 1830s and '40s to Finsbury Square, Islington, Bloomsbury and Marylebone, and still further to 'Tyburnia' – Bayswater – in the 1860s, and from there to Lancaster Gate, and in the last three decades of the century, north to Maida Vale and Kilburn.[4]

The biases of the London economy were also reproduced among the Jewish population. Its dynamism was based on the service sector and, to a lesser extent, the manufacture of consumer goods.[5] The greatest part of London's wealth was generated by the trade of the port and by the City's central importance for banking, insurance, lending and brokerage on a national and international scale. The demand for services and luxury goods was sustained by the concentration of government and fashionable society. Jews were integrated within this larger pattern of economic activity. The wealthiest prospered as merchant bankers, members of Lloyds, bullion dealers and stockbrokers in the City. Apart from the towering presence of N.M. Rothschild and Sons, in 1845 D.M. Evans noted other 'influential City-houses, represented by Hebrews connected with money and stock exchange affairs, and which, though following, in some degree, behind the Rothschilds, are nevertheless firms of note –

---

3.   J. Jacobs, *Studies in Jewish Statistics* (London, 1891), pp. 10–17; In London as a whole, semi-skilled and unskilled workers, a conservative categorisation of those earning less than £100 in a year, comprised 31 per cent of the male working population in 1861 and 34 per cent in 1891: G. Stedman Jones, *Outcast London: a study in the Relationship between Classes in Victorian Society* (Oxford, 1971), tables 13 and 14, p. 381.

4.   V.D. Lipman, 'The Rise of Jewish Suburbia', *TJHSE*, 1968, pp. 78–103.

5.   C.H. Lee, 'Regional Growth and Structural Change in Victorian Britain', *Economic History Review*, August 1981, p. 450. Whereas service employment accounted for 13.1 per hundred of the population over the economy as a whole in 1841, in London and Middlesex the figure was 21.7 per hundred.

the Goldsmids, the Mocattas, the Cohens, the Raphaels and the Montefiores. They are all wealthy firms'.[6] Jews also thrived in the several levels of trade and exchange: as wholesale merchants and shippers, for example. Jacobs found 600 Jewish merchants were mostly 'in a small way of business'.[7] Away from the port, Jews were active as general dealers supplying costermongers, shopkeepers, street sellers, and a falling number travelled as pedlars and old clothes men.[8] Alongside the decline of itinerant trading, Jews increasingly found work in manufacturing. In some of the luxury trades Jews weighed heavily. By 1880, among those listed in directories, they accounted for between 34 and 44 per cent of all meerschaum pipemakers, ostrich feathermakers, furriers and diamond merchants. In consumer trades with wider markets, such as cigar, clothing and jewellery manufacture, in which much larger numbers of Jews were engaged, collectively they commanded a less significant proportion of the trade.[9]

A Jewish population is not the same thing as a Jewish community. The extent to which the Anglo-Jewish population constituted a Jewish community depended solely on voluntary association. By contrast, in both France and Germany, for a significant part of the nineteenth century, the Jewish communities, the *consistoire* and the *Gemeinde*, were statutory organisations to which all Jews were affiliated.[10] However, in Britain, since Jewish disabilities arose negatively – they were disadvantaged as non-Anglicans or non-Christians rather than specifically as Jews with few exceptions, the state did not need to recognise Jews as such.[11] The absence of statutory recognition in Britain meant that structures of communal authority and cohesion had to be manufactured entirely by Jews themselves.

In London between 1830–70 Jewish communal institutions were consolidated and reformed. These changes were directed by an elite drawn from a small group of very wealthy families, connected by

6. D.M. Evans, *The City; or the Physiology of London Business* (London, 1845), pp. 104, 186.
7. H. Pollins, *Economic History of the Jews in England* (London, 1982), p. 107.
8. *Ibid*, chapters 5–7.
9. Lipman, *Social History of the Jews in England*, p. 80.
10. D. Englander, 'Anglicized not Anglican: Jews and Judaism in Victorian Britain', in G. Parsons ed., *Religion in Victorian Britain*, vol. i (Manchester, 1988), p. 246. P.C. Albert, *The Modernization of French Jewry* (Hanover, NH, 1977); I. Schorsch, *Jewish Reactions to German Anti-Semitism, 1870–1914* (New York, NY, 1972).
11. The laws regarding marriage and divorce were exceptions: C.H.L. Emanuel, *A Century and a Half of Jewish History* (London, 1910), pp. 26–7.

business interests and by marriage, as well as by their role in communal governance.[12] Synagogues, for instance, were constituted by a three-tier structure of status and affiliation. This differentiated between members who had sole or prior claim on honorary offices, seat holders who rented their places annually, and the remainder.[13] At the summit of communal authority were representatives of leading banking and broking dynasties: Moses Montefiore headed the Jewish Board of Deputies (JBD), Lionel Louis Cohen presided over the Jewish Board of Guardians (JBG), created in 1859 to coordinate the relief of the metropolitan Jewish poor, while Louis Cohen and Anthony de Rothschild dominated the United Synagogue, a combination of the major London *ashkenazi* congregations established in 1870.

From the mid-1830s the JBD claimed authority over secular matters. Above all, this was the case after 1835 and the appointment of Moses Montefiore as President. The origins of the Board can be traced back to 1760, but in the 1820s it remained 'informal, exclusive and limited to the major metropolitan synagogues'.[14] Change came in 1836 when the Board adopted its first constitution and opened itself to deputies from congregations outside London. At the same time it arrogated to itself the task of representing the Jews of Britain 'in all matters touching their political welfare'.[15] This claim appeared to receive immediate validation when, in the same year, the Marriage Act allowed the Board to regulate Jewish marriages for the state: the Board received statutory recognition as the body competent to record marriages and ensure they were performed 'according to the usages of the Jews'.

Using this power, the JBD refused to certify David Wolf Marks, the minister of the breakaway, reform-minded West London Synagogue of British Jews, as a fit person to celebrate marriages, claiming that his congregation was not a synagogue. In its treatment of the West London Synagogue the majority commanding the JBD aligned itself completely with the Jewish ecclesiastical authority – the Chief Rabbi. Given the voluntary character of the Jewish community, rabbinical authority had particular significance. The voluntary basis of Jewish affiliation meant that religious pluralism endangered not only traditional patterns of worship and observance but the possibility of a coherent Jewish community as well. The ecclesiastical supremacy of

12. T. Endelman, 'Communal Solidarity among the Jewish Elite of Victorian London', *Victorian Studies*, Spring 1985, pp. 494–5.
13. Lipman, *Social History of the Jews in England*, pp. 41–2.
14. I. Finestein, 'Anglo-Jewish Opinion during the Struggle for Emancipation', *TJHSE*, 1959–61, p. 113.
15. Emanuel, *A Century and a Half of Jewish History*, p. 23.

the Chief Rabbi was the counterpart to the secular supremacy of the JBD.

From the early nineteenth century the rabbi of the Duke's Place congregation in the City, Rabbi Solomon Hirschell, was regarded as the foremost Jewish religious authority in Britain and the Empire. But his pre-eminence was informal. The status of his successor was more certain. Nathan Marcus Adler took office in 1845 following his election by twenty congregations from throughout the country and he rapidly consolidated his position by issuing his *Laws and Regulations for all the Synagogues in the British Empire* in 1847.[16] In Britain, Adler uniquely allowed only himself to carry the title of 'Rabbi', and claimed authority over all Jewish religious questions.

One other institution should be mentioned at this point. The Anglo-Jewish press presented the Jewish world in England and elsewhere to its readers. Because Jewish affiliation was voluntary the press was particularly significant for the way it enabled English Jews to perceive themselves as members of a Jewish community. This was in addition to its more obvious role in mediating relations between the communal leaders and the mass of affiliating English Jews. Other Jewish newspapers came and went but throughout this period, for those Jews able to read English, it was the *Jewish Chronicle* pre-eminently that performed these functions. The newspaper first appeared in 1841 but still more important was its revival in 1844. By 1847 it was appearing weekly.[17]

*

Between 1830–71 the legal framework of Jewish life in England underwent a process of fundamental change. Most famously, in 1858 Lionel de Rothschild became the first professing Jew to sit in the House of Commons. The great jurist A.V. Dicey wrote that the admission of Jews to Parliament was but one example of concession 'to the demand of dominant liberalism for the extension of religious and civic equality'.[18] This early twentieth-century verdict has been reinforced by more recent historians. They too have located Rothschild's victory as one moment in the triumph of liberalism.

16. C. Roth, 'The Chief Rabbinate of England', in I. Epstein, E. Levine and C. Roth, eds., *Essays in Honour of the Very Rev. Dr J.H. Hertz* (London, 1942), pp. 371–84.
17. Unfortunately this study was completed before the publication of David Cesarani's new history of the *Jewish Chronicle*. I have had to rely on *The Jewish Chronicle 1841–1941: A Century of Newspaper History* (London, 1949).
18. A.V. Dicey, *Lectures on the Relation between Law and Public Opinion on England during the Nineteenth Century* (London, 1905), p. 343.

This larger victory is conceived as the extension of universalist principles of rights or of the doctrine of utility.[19] In this light, the process of Jewish emancipation has been aligned with the wider advance
of causes such as religious toleration and the extension of the right
to vote.[20] Many have argued that Jews in Britain were the happy
beneficiaries of the related strengths of liberalism and capitalism.
Cecil Roth, the doyen of Anglo-Jewish historiography, regarded the
opposition to religious disabilities from the 1830s as a reflection
of the opinions of 'the now dominant middle class', and this verdict
has been reinforced by later historians.[21] Not surprisingly this interpretation translates easily into Marxian terms. Bill Williams con-
curs that Jewish emancipation was an expression of 'bourgeois
power' and 'middle-class liberalism'.[22] The history of Jewish emancipation in Britain has been contrasted with its history in other
European nations; above all with Germany. Where capitalism was
less developed, where the bourgeoisie less dominant, where liberalism was weak, there Jewish emancipation was more fiercely
opposed.[23]

Two other arguments are easily aligned with this characterisation
of Jewish emancipation. The first is that anti-Semitism was a feeble
weed in the garden of England. Most recently, in a series of important books and articles, Todd Endelman has used the perspectives of
social history to broaden and reinforce the established lines of interpretation. He argues that antipathy to Jews in the mid-nineteenth
century 'lacked political resonance' and 'did not erupt into an anti-
Jewish campaign'. And while 'substantial prejudice and insensitivity'
remained, there was no 'broadly based opposition to the entry of

19. A. Gilam, *The Emancipation of the Jews in England, 1830–60* (New York, NY,
     1980), pp. 150–1; U.R.Q. Henriques, *Religious Toleration in England, 1783–
     1833* (London, 1961), pp. 203–4.
20. See for example A.V. Dicey, *Lectures on the Relation between Law and Public
     Opinion*, p. 343; Henriques, *Religious Toleration*, pp. 191, 201–2; Gilam, *The
     Emancipation of the Jews*, p. 1.
21. C. Roth, *A History of the Jews in England* (3rd edn, Oxford, 1964), p. 253.
     According to Henriques the Jews' acquisition of civil and political rights was
     borne on 'the rising tide of middle-class liberalism': Henriques, *Religious Tol-
     eration in England*, pp. 191, 201–2; M.C.N. Salbstein, *The Emancipation of the Jews*
     (East Brunswick, NJ, 1982), p. 39.
22. B. Williams, 'The Anti-Semitism of Tolerance: Middle-Class Manchester and
     the Jews, 1870–1900', in A.J. Kidd and K.W. Roberts, eds., *City, Class and
     Culture: Studies of Social Policy and Cultural Production in Victorian Manchester*
     (Manchester, 1985), pp. 74–5.
23. T. Endelman, 'The Englishness of Jewish Modernity', in J. Katz, ed., *Toward
     Modernity: The European Jewish Model* (New York, NY, 1987), pp. 237–43. This
     also echoes the nineteenth-century view: see J. Jacobs, 'The Typical Character
     of Anglo-Jewish History', *TJHSE*, 1896–8, pp. 138–40.

Jews into English society'.[24] The second argument is that the religious and cultural history of Anglo-Jewry developed in a benign environment, and so Jews came under little suasion to reform their religious and cultural practices. The weakness of anti-Semitism and the quality of English liberalism removed any pressing need for change: Endelman argues, 'because the course of emancipation in England was relatively smooth – at least by comparison with Germany – most Jews felt little pressure to renounce traditional beliefs'.[25]

Evidently, we possess an internally coherent and broad-ranging interpretation of Jewish history in mid-nineteenth-century England. It hinges on its view of liberalism. This is the basis for its understanding of emancipation, the absence of anti-Semitism and the nature of religious and cultural change within Anglo-Jewry. Even revisionist historians who have suggested that liberalism in England generated its own hostility to the Jews – by demanding that Jews efface their identities as Jews to win acceptance as individuals – continue to characterise liberalism as a universalist, bourgeois creed, concerned with the rights of individuals.[26] But it is this shared reconstruction of liberalism and Jewish emancipation which, I want to suggest, is open to question. In the next chapter I propose a different characterisation of the debate on Jewish emancipation. Having done so, I shall move on to reconsider both the history of hostility to Jews and the Jews öwn religious and cultural development in mid-nineteenth-century England.

24. Endelman, 'The Englishness of Jewish Modernity', pp. 237–9; *idem*, 'English Jewish History', p. 100; *idem, The Jews of Georgian England, passim.*
25. Endelman, 'The Englishness of Jewish Modernity', p. 242; *idem*, 'English Jewish History', p. 101. Once again, these assessments are informed by comparisons to the history of Jewish integration elsewhere in Europe. Nevertheless, there is a more nuanced view in *idem, Radical Assimilation in English Jewish History, 1656–1945* (Bloomington Indiana, 1990), p. 209. On the general point, see too C. Roth, 'Conclusion', in Roth, *A History of the Jews in England*, p. 270, on the 'process of Anglo-Jewish history . . . consolidating itself slowly but surely, and never outstripping public opinion'.
26. Williams, 'The Anti-Semitism of Tolerance'. This echoes analyses of the ambivalence of German Liberals on the Jewish issue. On this see R. Rurup, 'German Liberalism and the Emancipation of the Jews', *LBYB*, 1975, pp. 60–1.

Chapter 1

Jewish Emancipation and Political Argument in Early Victorian England

Christian institutions and the Christian nation

Until the 1880s, at the very least, the country's constitutional arrangements – the privileges of the Crown, the House of Lords, and the national Church in the face of claims made on behalf of the Commons, the electorate, the disenfranchised and religious dissenters – continued to provide the stuff of radical political argument. The defence of established institutions or their reform in the face of new conditions was a perennial concern of the governors. In this way, Jewish disabilities – whether to maintain, reform or abolish them – were inserted within the decisive conflicts of mid-nineteenth-century British politics. The excitement they generated and the tenacity with which they were defended derived from this larger context.

At the heart of the campaign for the Jews' political and civil equality was the claim that professing Jews should be able to enter Parliament. As all acknowledged, the Jewish minority was too small to compel Parliament to open its doors. For non-Jews, therefore, the issue of Jewish disabilities was primarily symbolic. In 1849, when Lionel de Rothschild attempted to take his seat in the House of Commons by swearing on the Old Testament, Lord Stanley, son of the then leader of the Conservative Party, noted that 'the acrimony of feeling elicited by the controversy bears no proportion to its practical importance. Every Whig or Radical seemed to think every Conservative a bigot, and the Conservatives treated the arguments of their opponents as if they had been insults to Christianity.'[1] Debate rapidly and repeatedly leapt to formulations of principle. One supporter of Jewish disabilities observed, 'the arguments were so very

---

1. J. Vincent, *Disraeli, Derby and the Conservative Party: Journals and Memoirs of Edward Henry, Lord Stanley 1849–69* (Hassocks, 1978), p. 29.

few, and the ground so very limited and so frequently traversed'.[2]

As Stanley suggested, it was common for supporters of Jewish emancipation to present the dispute as a conflict between reason and prejudice. According to the pro-Jew *Weekly Dispatch*, the arguments brought forward by the opponents of emancipation amounted to 'a diarrhoea of words, terminated by a flatulent explosion of windbags'.[3] Less colourfully, in 1853, the Prime Minister, the Earl of Aberdeen, contemplating his conversion to the Jewish cause, attributed his former opinions to 'a remnant' of 'prejudice'.[4] This change of mind bore the impress of a progessive theory of history. In 1845, *The First Report of Her Majesty's Commissioners for Revising and Consolidating the Criminal Law* expressed its view that 'the ancient laws affecting Jews arose out of institutions of a barbarous period, equally opposed to good policy, justice and humanity'.[5] Likewise, the *Christian Reformer or Unitarian Review* presented the opponents of Jewish relief as 'a union of sectarian bigotry and feudal intolerance'.[6]

Historians too have been impressed by the anachronistic and prejudiced quality of opposition to Jewish emancipation.[7] In view of the outcome of the struggle this perspective has something to recommend it. But one consequence has been that the arguments of the losers have not received the same attention they were given by contemporaries. Nevertheless, we should consider the protest made by Sir Frederick Thesiger, and echoed by many others: 'I am aware that those who take the part of opposition to this measure must expect to be assailed by charges of timid and narrow-minded intolerance and bigotry. I am not aware that I am actuated by such motives.'[8] Rejecting the charge of prejudice, Thesiger promoted a vision of national exclusivity by striving to sustain the Christian character of the nation. Voices such as this are significant, not least because we shall not understand the case made in favour of Jewish emancipation unless we grasp the discursive context within which it was made. It would be a mistake to believe that the terms under which Jews acquired civil and political equality can be read off from theories of natural rights or of utility. The Jews' supporters were not

2. *Hansard*, 3rd series, XCVI, col. 221, 7 February 1848.
3. *Weekly Dispatch*, 13 February 1848, p. 73.
4. *Hansard*, 3rd series, CXXVI, col. 755, 29 April 1853.
5. *The First Report of Her Majesty's Commissioners for Revising and Consolidating the Criminal Law*, PP 1845, XIV, p. 22.
6. *Christian Reformer or Unitarian Review*, August 1848, p. 506.
7. A. Gilam, *The Emancipation of the Jews in England, 1830–60* (New York, NY, 1980), p. 1; U.R.Q. Henriques, 'The Jewish Emancipation Controversy in Nineteenth-Century Britain', *Past and Present*, July 1968, pp. 131–5.
8. *Hansard*, 3rd series, XCVIII, cols. 606–7, 4 May 1848.

enunciating an ideal-typical modern liberal creed but were engaged in a political argument.

Indeed, it is difficult to find the supporters and opponents of Jewish emancipation arguing that at root the struggle was one over 'liberalism'. The term was largely ignored by supporters of Jewish relief. In contrast, some militant opponents of Jewish relief were happy to address the question of liberalism unequivocally; none more so than the Conservative and evangelical Henry Drummond. But here liberalism was not identified as a doctrine of utility or rights but of free thought.

> It had been said that . . . [Jewish relief] would complete the triumph of Liberalism – that it would remove the last remnant of bigotry from the statute-book. Yes, it would be the triumph of Liberalism; but what was Liberalism? The anatagonist and opponent of religion. Religion was the principle which taught man to reverence God. Liberalism left a man at liberty to make from his imagination, his own God, and taught him to despise the dogmata of the Church. Liberalism taught a man to deny what the Church told him – that everything that was called God, but the God incarnate, was a false God. Liberalism was just egotism, it led every man to seek his own interest and of no other person. . . . The French Revolution was the triumph of Liberalism.[9]

Similarly, an anti-emancipationist pamphleteer defined the views he opposed as 'liberalism' because, he alleged, to those who upheld them it was 'a matter of most perfect indifference whether the country is Christian, Jewish or absolutely Heathen'. Against this tendency, he was struggling to maintain the 'Christian National Church'.[10] But, as this quotation indicates, the argument over liberalism dealt not only with the rights and privileges of individuals but also with the collectivity to which they belonged. It is necessary to turn to that debate to understand the basis on which Jews received political equality.

Jews entered political controversy on the shirt-tails of Dissenters and Catholics. Progress for Dissenters, in fact, confirmed the Jews' exclusion from the political nation. The price of Conservative acquiescence in repeal of the Test and Corporation Acts was a new religious test: the Oath of Abjuration had now to be taken 'on the true faith of a Christian'. It is not certain whether this was framed with the intention of excluding Jews but it was passed in full knowledge that

9.   *Hansard*, 3rd series, XCV, col. 1380, 17 December 1847. On pre-millenarian evangelicalism see B. Hilton, *The Age of Atonement: The Influence of Evangelicalism on Social and Economic Thought, 1795–1865* (Oxford, 1988), pp. 10–19.

10.   C. Archer, *The Lords and the Jews* (London, 1857), pp. 3–4.

it would have this effect.[11] Nevertheless, the progress of religious toleration led some prominent Jews to raise with the Conservative government, and with Whig sympathisers, the question of whether the Jews also would be relieved from their disabilities.[12] The issue lingered unresolved in British politics for three decades. Between 1830 and 1858 fourteen bills were introduced which attempted to remove parliamentary disabilities. All but the first of these were accepted by the House of Commons and all those that won a majority in the lower House were rejected by the House of Lords.

At times the issue became the focus of political debate and party conflict. Above all, this was the case in the early months of 1848. Following the election of Lionel de Rothschild to the House of Commons as a representative of the City of London, and before the revival of Chartism and revolution in Paris diverted the attention of radicals, petitions supporting Jewish relief gathered over two hundred and fifty thousand signatures. Rothschild presented himself at the Table of the House in December 1847 but his refusal to swear a Christian oath prevented him from taking his seat. On 16 December the Whig Prime Minister Lord John Russell who, like Rothschild, represented the City of London, introduced a bill which, had it passed into law, would have enabled Jews to sit in Parliament.[13] The excitement and controversy stimulated by Russell's bill was due, in part, to the novelty of the situation. Rothschild was the first Jew to be elected to Parliament, and his election converted Jewish emancipation from a high-minded cause of more theoretical than practical import to a pressing issue of the political moment. This was the first time, moreover, that Jewish relief had been proposed by the prime minister of the day, a development which greatly alarmed the opponents of emancipation.[14] Rothschild's name, his magnificent wealth, his reputed power within the world's financial markets, and accusations that his electoral success had been bought, added drama to the conflict: could Parliament withstand the claims not only of Jews in general but of this particular Jew?

But if these considerations added a sensational quality to Russell's Bill, the political moment was also significant and helps us to explain why the argument over Jewish emancipation reached a climax ten years before Rothschild was able to take his seat. On the one side,

11. Gilam, *The Emancipation of the Jews*, pp. 72–3.
12. *Ibid*, pp. 72–5.
13. Thus other Jewish disabilities would have remained. In this respect Russell's Bill was more moderate than earlier attempts to reform the Jews' legal position. Roth suggests that it is for this reason that opposition to the bill was so fierce: C. Roth, *A History of the Jews in England* (3rd edn, Oxford, 1964), p. 260.
14. *Hansard*, 3rd series, XCV, col. 1,250, 16 December 1847.

radical expectations were not limited to the cause of free trade. Stimulated by the repeal of the Corn Laws in 1846 and the consequent break-up of the Conservative Party, their goals extended to a further assault on Anglican privilege – the abolition of Church Rates and all state grants for elementary education – and to the extension of the authority of the Commons and the electorate.[15] The *Weekly Dispatch*, a habitually robust voice of metropolitan Dissent and anti-clericalism, illustrates the way in which Jewish disabilities provided an issue through which these aspirations could be focussed and conflated. Supporting Rothschild's claims, the newspaper assailed the Church as 'a dead wall to progress', and cited Anglican opposition not only to repeal of the Test and Corporation Acts and Catholic emancipation but also to the 'untaxing of the people's bread and the free intercourse of nations'.[16] The Jews' emancipation would insert the thin end of the wedge, 'rifting the oak of fanaticism and bigotry . . . let us get the Jew introduced into Parliament first and all the rest will follow'.[17]

Similarly, the supporters of Jewish disabilities endowed Russell's Bill with portentous significance. Twenty years before the 1847–8 debates on Jewish relief, the unity of Church and state had stood unaltered if not unchallenged. The formal acknowledgement in 1828 that the one-Church state had dissolved was followed rapidly and more alarmingly in 1829 by the collapse of the Protestant state. To some Conservatives the exclusively Christian state appeared as a last ditch in which to defend a religious requirement for the discharge of political duties. In this sense, the argument over Jewish disabilities concerned Jews only incidentally. For Henry Drummond 'the intense interest which the discussion of this question excited did not regard the Jews, but the Established Church'.[18] For other Conservative protectionists such as George Bankes and John Plumptre,

15.　G.I.T. Machin, *Politics and the Churches in Great Britain, 1832–68* (Oxford, 1987), pp. 183–92.

16.　*Weekly Dispatch*, 9 January 1848, p. 13; For other instances of this conflation of economic and religious questions see D. Fraser, *Urban Politics in Victorian Britain* (Leicester, 1976), p. 242.

17.　*Weekly Dispatch*, 9 January 1848, p. 13. Likewise, the Unitarian *Eclectic Review* took a portentous view of the legislation: 'Conceal it as we may, the Jewish Disabilities Bill, now before Parliament contemplates a more marked invasion of our national prejudices than any recent act of the legislature. . . . The Christianity of the legislature is to be abandoned, at least in any such sense as it has hitherto been maintained, and those who deny the obligation of our faith, and deem the Messiah an imposter, are to be admitted to our legislature and to become framers of our laws.' 'The Jewish Disabilities Bill', January–June 1848, pp. 360–1.

18.　*Hansard*, 3rd series, XCV, col. 1,379, 17 December 1847.

as well as a Peelite such as Viscount Drumlanrig, the real issue was whether or not there should be any religion of the state, and whether Parliament was to be a Christian legislature 'believing Christ to be their only Saviour and Redeemer' or, instead, they were to admit men who looked on Him as an imposter.[19] Opponents of Russell's Bill warned repeatedly that admitting the Jew would open the way to the 'Hindoo', the 'Parsee' and the 'votary of Boodh'. Despite the Prime Minister's denials, his opponents repeatedly accused him of endangering the Christian character of government.[20]

In the spring of 1848, when the protectionists were in disarray, the Jew bill was the one measure on which almost all of them were able to agree.[21] Betrayal by the Conservative leaders in 1845 over the grant to the Catholic seminary at Maynooth, and the threat to state religion signalled by the radicals' triumph in 1846, left the legislature's exclusively Christian composition a barrier whose defence was not only a point of principle but one that had become strategically crucial.

The defence of Jewish disabilities expressed an hierarchical as well as a religious vision of political authority. Symptomatic of this was that whereas many supporters of Jewish emancipation presented the Jews as 'fellow-citizens', almost without exception their opponents placed them, and everyone else, as subjects.[22] The High Tory position was set forward in the House of Commons by Sir Robert Inglis. He scorned the emancipationist argument that men had rights and that Jews were having theirs denied to them. 'Power is no man's right,' he explained, 'it is distributed by the state to each.'[23] The constitution punished Jews no more than it did other groups, such as copyholders, who did not qualify for the franchise. To admit Jews would be a step on the road to binding a people and sovereign without sacred oaths. In a similarly juridical vein, Charles Ewan Law argued that the Crown derived its title by connection with the Church – a connection under threat once the Christian character

19. *Hansard*, 3rd series, XCV, cols. 1,304, 1,321, 1,376–7, 1,379, 16–17 December 1847.
20. Contemplating Russell's Bill, W.J. Conybeare claimed 'the principle, which is to receive its final triumph and complete development in a Judaizing parliament, is that the end of government has nothing to do with religion or morality': 'Jewish Disabilities', *Quarterly Review*, September 1847, pp. 526–7.
21. R. Stewart, *The Politics of Protection* (Cambridge, 1971), p. 135.
22. In one telling instance, Charles Law, an opponent of emancipation, mistakenly quoted Sir Charles Romilly, a supporter, as having spoken of 'subjects' when, in fact, the word he used had been 'citizens': *Hansard*, 3rd series, XCV, col. 1,359, 17 December 1847.
23. *Ibid*, 1,252.

of the legislature was attacked.[24] If the notion that Jews had rights
was bogus, prudence dictated the necessity of Christian oaths. The
experience of France demonstrated the terrible consequence of
depriving institutions of their sanctity.[25]

Jewish emancipation endangered the political community as well
as constitutional legitimacy and stability. For Inglis, the admission of
Jews to the nation would damage its integrity irreparably. The merits
and demerits of Jews were not his main concern. To be sure, he felt
bound to comment on the 'still subsisting and indissoluble nationality of the Jews'. But his point was not simply that Jews could never be
a part of the English nation: rather, their admission to Parliament
would undermine the nation's distinguishing quality. Christianity,
he maintained, was 'the foundation of their national glory', and
'never since England was a nation has it been anything other than
Christian making its acts and oaths reflect a Christian character'.
Inglis took on the historical theme, conceding that he would allow
new countries to establish a constitution without Christian obligations; 'but I resist it here; I deny your right to introduce these
doctrines here: for here is Christian England – here we have a
Christian constitution – here we all profess ourselves at least to be
Christians'.[26] A shared Christian history, enshrined in the country's
laws and institutions, and producing a shared community among
governors and governed, was appealed to by many others. In this
way, among high Tories, the debates over Jewish disabilities provided occasions to affirm their vision of England as an hierarchical
and Christian nation.[27]

But it was not only protectionists and high Tories who linked the
stability of political institutions to the exclusive Christian integrity
and foundation of those institutions.[28] Peelites and free trade Conservative MPs divided heavily in favour of retaining Jewish disabilities
in 1847–8.[29] Sir Frederic Thesiger predicted 'the greatest violence to

24. *Ibid*, 1,357.
25. *Ibid*, 1,370; *Hansard*, 3rd series, XCVI, cols. 241, 474, 7 February 1847, 11
     February 1847.
26. *Hansard*, 3rd series, XCV, col. 1,258, 16 December 1847.
27. *Hansard*, 3rd series, XCVI, cols. 265–6, 7 February 1848.
28. The situation is complicated by the position of two of the most prominent
     protectionists – Bentinck and Disraeli – who supported Russell's Bill. But in
     this they were out of step with their followers and, in consequence, Bentinck
     resigned his position as leader. 'The great protectionist party has degenerated
     into a 'No Popery; No Jew League,' he complained: Machin, *Politics and the
     Churches*, p. 194.
29. One historian reports that of 72 free trade Conservatives who voted on the
     second reading of the Jewish Disabilities Bill, 43 opposed it and 29 voted in
     favour: J.B. Conacher, *The Peelites and the Party System, 1846–52* (Newton

the religious sentiments and feelings of the nation, if the House admitted Jews by removing the requirement of a Christian oath'. Thesiger was Attorney-General in Peel's ministry of 1845–6 and again under Derby in 1852, and finally as Lord Chelmsford was appointed Lord Chancellor in 1878. To him the emancipationist doctrine that 'the Christian electors of this Christian nation have the right to choose whom they liked as their representative' was unconstitutional because it misunderstood the mechanism of parliamentary representation and its role in constituting the nation. Citing Burke, he explained that Members of Parliament represented national not local interests. Consequently, not only electors in a particular constituency 'but the entire nation had an interest in the person chosen and had a right to determine if he was duly and properly qualified to sit in Parliament'.[30] Parliament represented the nation, not in the sense of reflecting its will but, rather, of determining its character. A pamphlet written by the Oxonian clergyman Robert Kennard, which he dedicated to Thesiger, provides a lengthy elaboration of the same argument. The maintenance of national Christianity did not depend upon the 'private convictions and personal character of its individual members', but 'the principles on which they in their collective capacity profess to act'.[31] It followed that electors had no rights to claim. 'The entire nation' alone, which was to say its institutions, determined whether anyone was a fit and proper person to legislate. In this way the nation's identity was not determined 'solely or even principally from the fact that the majority of its members are Christians', but by its institutions. In this respect, Christianity was 'the vital and essential and fundamental principle of our system'. Jews could be members of a Christian society but not make laws for it; they were in the country but not of the nation.[32] 'As a nation we are Christians, because we have a Christian Government and a Christian Legislature, and because that Government and Legislature have hitherto been bound indissolubly to the faith and life of Christ.'[33]

There were varieties of resistance to Russell's Bill. But at their centre was a common opposition to surrendering national Christianity. Jewish disabilities appeared to constitute the last line of defence

Abbott, 1972), W.D. Jones and A.B. Erikson in *The Peelites 1846–59* (Ohio, 1972), p. 95, give slightly different figures. They found that the Peelites opposed relief by 31 to 14, and the miscellaneous Conservatives by 30 to 14.

30. Thesiger was speaking in the 1853 debate on Jewish disabilities: *Hansard*, 3rd series, CXXV, cols. 80–1, 11 March 1853.
31. R.B. Kennard, *The Admission of Jews into Parliament* (London, 1855), p. 18.
32. *Ibid*, pp. 81–4.
33. *Ibid*, p. 19.

for a vision of the state in which religion, the nation and the authority of established institutions were all connected. What united the varieties of resistance to Russell's Bill was not only their view of political legitimacy and the nation rooted in Christianity but the combination of this with a hierarchical understanding of legitimate political authority. The character of the nation as a Christian nation followed from the character of the established institutions of the state. The Jew's inability to swear a Christian oath demanded by Parliament disqualified them from that institution and placed them beyond the parameters of the nation.

Jewish emancipation and English liberties

Beyond all doubt conditions for Jews changed significantly and for the better in mid-nineteenth-century Britain. Increasingly, Jews were able to enjoy the same rights and privileges as others, and gradually they ceased to endure disadvantage as a result of their failure to embrace Christianity. In this way it is easy for us to recognise a liberal process in Jewish emancipation: restrictions which disadvantaged Jews collectively were removed and they were to take part as individuals in the political life of the nation. But it is difficult to match this view with the contours of political debate as they took shape in the 1840s and 1850s. It would be easier to do so if the vindication of Jewish disabilities could be dismissed as reaction and prejudice; it would then seem to follow that the Jews' supporters were spokesmen for individual freedom and reason. But as we have seen, opposition to Jewish relief was expressed primarily in terms of a view of the inter-relation of Christianity, the nation and political authority. It is not surprising, then, to find supporters of the Jews' equality engaging with these arguments and, moreover, presenting their own case not only as a defence of the rights of individuals but also of their own idea of the nation.

The most significant politician to identify himself with the Jewish cause was Lord John Russell, the most celebrated was Thomas Babington Macaulay. Both were historians as well as statesmen, though their stature in the two fields was scarcely comparable. Yet their common activities are notable since it was through an account of the national past that the Whigs furnished themselves with a political heritage and sought to explain and vindicate their political practice. The Whigs' justification of their attempt to repeal Jewish disabilities was underpinned by their understanding of English history.[34] When they argued for the admission of Jews to Parliament,

---

34. J.W. Burrow, *A Liberal Descent* (Cambridge, 1981), Part 1.

Russell, Macaulay and others promoted a theory of constitutional authority and an image of national identity radically different from the one advanced by anti-emancipationists.

Speaking in 1847 in support of the Jewish Relief Bill he had introduced, Lord John Russell claimed the question was not one of seeking favour for the Jews but one of right.

> I place this question upon the simple and as I think solid ground that every Englishman is entitled to all the honours and advantages of the British constitution. I state further that religious opinions ought of themselves be no disqualification or bar to the enjoyment of those advantages. I found my motion upon the declaration that the laws of England are the birthright of the people of England.[35]

In part, Russell was dealing with the issue of civil and religious equality. He claimed for propertied men the right to participate in politics regardless of the way they worshipped, in a manner we associate readily with the traditional picture of nineteenth-century liberalism. But this argument was interwoven with an equally significant concern with the nature of the collectivity to which the individuals belonged. The rights he sought to extend to the Jews were not only natural rights but, as he said, the rights of Englishmen.

This was an argument from the mainstream of Whig political thinking. As John Burrow has demonstrated, in the first decades of the nineteenth century a Whig consensus emerged on the nation's political history, expounded by Russell and Macaulay among others. In particular, they aimed to defend the claims of the seventeenth-century parliamentarians in their struggle with the Crown and to establish the early nineteenth-century Whigs as the true inheritors of that legacy. Theirs was a history characterised by its affirmation of the existence of constitutional rights, stemming from the twelfth and thirteenth centuries, from the Magna Carta and the early Parliaments. 'Its essential character was clear: monarchy was limited, the sovereign was below the law; kings could not tax, or legislate without Parliament.'[36] To Russell, freedom appeared to be 'nobly characteristic of the English nation'.[37] The constitution, however, was capable of growth and adaptation in the face of new conditions. This contrasted with the view of those radicals who imagined themselves engaged in a struggle to recover a Saxon democracy which had been usurped by the Norman invasion, and also with the opinions of Conservatives for whom the constitutional settlement of 1688–9 was

35. *Hansard*, 3rd series, XCV, col. 1,236, 16 December 1847.
36. Burrow, *A Liberal Descent*, p. 33.
37. *Ibid*, p. 30.

sacred and to be fought for to its last remaining letters. To the Whigs, 1688 represented one constitutional adjustment, inventing as well as conserving forms of government, and the Reform Act of 1832 was another. The revolution had introduced principles of natural right into the constitution but these lay alongside, they did not supersede, the place accorded to the rights of Englishmen. In this emphasis on the liberties of propertied individuals, and on the constitution's adaptability in the face of 'opinion', the nation's heritage was vested in and determined by the people as well as its institutions. Indeed, within this scheme the role of the Whigs was to act as the self-appointed aristocratic interpreters of 'opinion' who would manage the adaptation of the constitution to new conditions.[38]

These claims and assumptions powerfully informed the arguments brought in favour of the Jews' legal equality. Because the Englishness of English history was bound to the idea of individual liberties protected by the law, the language of rights, the argument for Jewish emancipation constituted an argument about the nation as well as the individual. As the Earl of St Germain put it: 'In England, all natural-born subjects had the same legal rights.' Similarly, Lord Brougham's support for the Jews became a lecture on 'the doctrine of the constitution'.[39]

Even Macaulay's writings and speeches in support of Jewish relief, which eschewed an appeal to 'rights', were nevertheless informed by a sense of national history; the English past both justified Jewish relief and made demands on its beneficiaries. The 'sense of the privileged possession by Englishmen of their history' encased in Macaulay's *History of England* has been explored by John Burrow.[40] This same concern underpinned Macaulay's opposition to Jewish disabilities. His most significant statements on the subject were made early in his career and in the history of the controversy: an essay published in the *Edinburgh Review* in 1831 and a speech in the House of Commons in 1833. But his opinions did not change. In 1858, newly ennobled, Macaulay informed Russell that he would not speak on the question, explaining that years earlier he had exhausted all he had to say.[41]

The coincidence of Macaulay's essay and speeches with the reform

38. J. Burrow, *Whigs and Liberals: Continuity and Change in English Political Thought* (Oxford, 1988), pp. 70–1.
39. *Hansard*, 3rd series, XCVIII, cols. 1,382, 1,404–5, 25 April 1848. The doctrine was flexible, so that in some mouths English rights became British: *Hansard*, 3rd series, XCV1, col. 272, 7 February 1848.
40. Burrow, *A Liberal Descent*, p. 93.
41. G.P. Gooch, ed., *The Later Correspondence of Lord John Russell*, vol. ii (London, 1925), p. 228.

crisis provides a helpful way to approach his opinions on the Jews' disabilities: both issues involved constitutional adjustments and both were understood in relation to the tendencies of social development and the traditions of the constitution. For Macaulay, the reform crisis of 1831–2 demonstrated the potentially calamitous consequences of a system of representation which failed to reflect the development of commerce and the progress of society.[42] Jewish disabilities, so far as he was concerned, were the cause of a further imbalance – although in this case the maladjustment was absurd rather than dangerous. For while Jews were denied a share in political power, their commercial power was enormous. The result was a sham.

> In fact, the Jews are not now excluded from political power. They possess it; and as long as they are allowed to accumulate large fortunes they must possess it. . . . What power in civilised society is so great as that of the creditor over the debtor? If we take this away from the Jew we take away the security of his property. If we leave it to him, we leave him a power more despotic than that of the king and all his cabinet.[43]

But Macaulay's comments were not confined to this sort of pragmatism. He was also concerned with the political community to which individuals, whether freeholders or Jews, would join. The national past recounted and celebrated by Macaulay was a history of constitutional continuity and progress. In his 'Essay on Jewish Disabilities' this led Macaulay to address the question of whether Jews were able to develop feelings of 'patriotism' and cease to prefer 'their sect to their country'.[44] He did not dismiss the question of the Jews' capacity for 'patriotism' as contemptuously as he treated the anti-emancipationist's passion for Christian government. On the contrary, he took care to demonstrate that Jews as well as Christians could become good Englishmen.

> The feeling of patriotism, when society is in a healthful state springs up by natural and inevitable associations in the hands of citizens who know that they owe all their comforts and pleasures to the bonds that unite them in one community. But under a partial and oppressive government, these associations cannot acquire that strength which they have in a better state of things. Men are compelled to seek from their party that protection which they ought to receive from their country, and they, by a natural

42. B. Fontana, *Rethinking the Politics of Commercial Society: The Edinburgh Review 1802–32* (Cambridge, 1985), p. 149. See too Burrow, *A Liberal Descent*, p. 43.
43. I. Abrahams and S. Levy, eds., *Macaulay on Jewish Disabilities* (Edinburgh, 1910), p. 25.
44. *Ibid*, p. 28.

consequence, transfer to their party that affection which they ought
otherwise to have felt for their country.[45]

Here was an argument that would be repeated on numerous occasions by the Jews' supporters. Macaulay claimed that in the light of
their past treatment by England – 'like a stepmother' – there was no
reason to conclude that Jews, with fair dealing, could not be made
Englishmen altogether.

But here was an ambiguity, for although 'patriotism' was produced by a political relationship – the interaction between the state
and individuals – its absence among Jews was evidence of their
'exclusive spirit'.[46] In other words, the Jews' want of 'patriotism' was
not merely a negative, an empty space waiting to be filled by a true
appreciation of the patrimony of English institutions: it was seen to
extend to their behaviour in the large space between the synagogue
and political life – to the clannishness of their social relations. This
left open the question of how the Jews might have to reform themselves in order to be seen as 'patriots'. Macaulay did not pursue the
question but, in time, others did.

Within Russell's arguments for Jewish relief there was a more
substantial ambiguity. The English nation envisioned by Russell, and
which the Jews would join, remained a Christian community. This
becomes clear if we look at Russell's historical sociology. The Whig
historians faced the task of explaining the vitality of English liberty
in the face of the nation's power and increasing wealth. For
Macaulay this had not been difficult, since he embraced an explanation based on the sociology of the Scottish enlightenment, which
regarded liberty and opulence as compatible.[47] However, a different
sociology, one drawn from Machiavelli and Harrington, predicted
that the two were not compatible; as the history of Rome commonly
was taken to demonstrate.[48] Russell accounted for the vigour of
English liberty by emphasising the public-spiritedness of a Christian
people. In his introduction to the 1821 edition of *English Government
and Constitution* Russell proposed that 'the excellence of English
government does not consist in the law only but in the spirit and
good sense of the nation'.[49] Speaking on the occasion of the third
reading of the 1848 Jewish Relief Bill, Russell answered his Conserva-

45. *Ibid*, p. 28.
46. *Ibid*, p. 31.
47. Burrow, *A Liberal Descent*, p. 46.
48. *Idem, Whigs and Liberals*, pp. 114–16.
49. R. Brent, *Liberal Anglican Politics: Whiggery, Religion and Reform, 1830–41*
     (Oxford, 1987), p. 53.

tive critics by reaffirming his belief 'that religion ought to influence us in the smallest of our domestic affairs and in the highest of our legislative duties'. It was the want of Christianity, he explained, which had permitted 'corruption' in ancient states and republics in proportion to the advance of civilisation within them, and it was the force of Christianity in public affairs that would save modern nations from the same fate.[50] Thus it was possible for Russell to deny that the entry of Jews to Parliament would threaten its Christianity. In contrast to his Tory opponents, who relied on oaths and institutions, it was not 'the fag end of a declaration' that would guarantee good government according to Christian principles, he told Parliament: it must depend on 'the general opinion of the country'. He was, however, confident that this would remain forever Christian.[51]

But the question might arise, if the nation was Christian, would Jews always be able to find a place within it? For Russell as well as for Macaulay, one image of the nation lay in the heritage of individual liberty; it was located in the relation between an individual and the state. The argument did, however, go beyond this at times to encompass a collective identity located in the people as a whole.

By the end of 1847 it was not only Whigs such as Russell for whom the future of Christianity in British political life would rest on the rock of 'opinion'. This can be seen even in the case of an emancipationist as reluctant and new-found as William Ewart Gladstone. In 1847 Gladstone supported Jewish relief for the first time. It was his first public retreat from the doctrines expressed in 1838 in *The State in its Relations with the Church* in which he presented national religion as 'the vivifying and ennobling principle of all national life'. The state was to be the expression of this national conscience.[52] It was a vision which, for Gladstone, perished with the Maynooth grant. But his response, unlike that of his fellow representative for Oxford University, Sir Robert Inglis, was not to dig another trench and defend the Christian constitution against encroachment from the Jews. To do so would have been to place too high a value on the common Christianity which the constitution now upheld, admitting groups such as Unitarians. Gladstone valued Anglicanism too highly to take this step. The process of reform had gone so far, he explained in the debate on the second reading of Russell's bill, that 'the constitution . . . has altogether ceased to require of us the recognition of any fixed body of Christian truths as an indispensable

50. *Hansard*, 3rd series, XCVIII, col. 662, 4 May 1848.
51. *Hansard*, 3rd series, XCV, col. 1,238, 16 December 1847.
52. Cited in H.C.G. Matthew, *Gladstone 1809–74* (Oxford, 1986), p. 63.

element of fitness for legislative duties'.[53] National religion could no longer provide the basis of a political community determined from above. In his response to critics at Oxford University, Gladstone wrote: 'for what I thought the true principle of national religion I stood, until no man stood by me. Nor would it have been time to retire had a standard been ordained for national religion *without relation to the elements of which the nation was composed.*'[54] It was not possible, he argued, to protect the Christianity of the nation through compulsion and 'repression'. Nevertheless, Russell's Bill would lead to a de-Christianising of Parliament only in the most formal sense. Parliament, he was pleased to say, would remain Christian in substance because the nation would remain a Christian nation.[55]

Evidently, supporters of Jewish emancipation were arguing about whether the legislature should discriminate between individuals on the basis of their religious beliefs *and* about the nature of the community to which those individuals belonged. But there were significant differences among them. These could be expressed, for example, in the willingness of speakers to use the terminology of 'citizenship' and 'rights' and the meanings given to these terms. We have already noticed their use by Russell and others. But their absence from the speeches of Gladstone and Peel was also significant. For them it was appropriate to refer to Jews as 'subjects' who would be admitted to the 'privileges' enjoyed by other subjects of the British Crown.[56]

Another distinction lay between the Whigs and more radical supporters of emancipation. Although Russell and other Whigs spoke of rights, for them 'opinion' and the electorate were only two of the forces weighing on the complex mechanism of political adjustment. For radical supporters of emancipation, however, arguments dealing with the rights of the popular element in the constitution were inseparable from claims asserting the legitimacy of the electorate as the ultimate political authority. The City radical Raikes Currie, speaking in support of Lionel de Rothschild in the name of 'the

---

53. It had ceased to do so with the admission of Unitarians. He probably agreed with his tractarian friend James Hope, who wrote to him, 'Better have the legislature declared what it really is – not professedly Christian, and then let the Church claim those rights and that independence which nothing but the presence of Christianity can entitle the Legislature to withhold from it.' Cited in P. Knockes, 'Pusey and the Question of Church and State', in P. Butler, ed., *Pusey Rediscovered* (London, 1983), p. 283. See too P. Butler, *Gladstone, Church, State and Tractarianism: A Study of his Religious Ideas and Attitudes, 1809–59* (Oxford, 1982), pp. 133–7.
54. Machin, *Politics and the Churches*, p. 194 (emphasis added).
55. *Hansard*, 3rd series, XCV, cols. 1,290, 1,302–3, 16 December 1847.
56. *Hansard*, 3rd series, XCVI, col. 520, 11 February 1848.

matter-of-fact citizens of London', gave a more determining status to 'citizenship' and to the 'people of England': 'An obstinate resistance on the part of the Lords to the now emphatically declared will of the people of England, would soon open another question, far more pregnant with danger to themselves than the recognition of the right of the Hebrew people to enjoy equal civil privileges with their Christian neighbours'.[57] For W.J. Fox, MP for Oldham – a veteran of the Anti-Corn Law campaign, who supported disestablishment and the ballot – the issue 'concerned much more nearly the civil disabilities of Christians than it did Jews': namely, the rights of the electors of the City of London freely to choose their representative.[58] This estimate of the conflict, as one between electors and established institutions, was shared by radical supporters of Jewish emancipation. The removal of Jewish disabilities was foreseen as a significant step towards shifting the balance of the constitution. This movement, it was imagined, would be one not only towards an electorate of free-choosing individuals but also towards the electorate as constituting the nation.

Since the early eighteenth century, political opposition had presented itself as the patriotic defence of liberties endangered by corrupt government.[59] This continued to be the case even as the social composition of radical politics shifted: radicalism pitted the people against privilege, the nation against the monopoly of political power enjoyed by narrow and selfish interests.[60] The Lords' rejection of Russell's bill in May 1848 by 163 votes to 128 provoked the *Weekly Dispatch* to a polemical display of rage and first principles.

> Repeal rages in Ireland, and Chartism threatens Britain. . . . It is at such a time when Government has the greatest difficulty to preserve the very order of society, that the two institutions of the Peerage and the Priesthood, the most odious to the people, have the rash folly to throw down a challenge to the whole nation, to try whether a country's will or a Lord's veto is strongest. . . . This is no longer a struggle between a Jew and a

57. *The Christian Reformer or Unitarian Review*, August 1849, pp. 506–7.
58. *Hansard*, 3rd series, XCV, cols. 1,267–8, 16 December 1847.
59. Q. Skinner, 'The Principles and Practice of Opposition: The Case of Bolingbroke versus Walpole', in N. McKendrick, ed., *Historical Perspectives: Studies in English Thought and Society in Honour of J.H. Plumb* (London, 1974), pp. 93–128.
60. H. Cunningham, 'The Language of Patriotism, 1750–1914', *History Workshop Journal*, Autumn 1981, pp. 8–23; G. Stedman Jones, 'Rethinking Chartism', in *Idem, Languages of Class* (Cambridge, 1983), pp. 102–4; M. Taylor, 'The Meaning and Context of Patriotism in the Middle of the Nineteenth Century', unpublished paper (1987), pp. 31, 39.

nobility. The City of London has been insulted – the popular will has been made of no account – two Estates of the realm have been made to succumb to the crotchets of the third – the whole country is at issue with a handful of rent-consumers, tax-eaters and shovel hats – one, and that the least popular and most insignificant branch of the Estates of the realm, is at issue with the rest, and the question is now distinctly to be put to the nation, 'Which is to yield?'[61]

The differences between Whig and radical supporters of Jewish relief were given a theatrical expression in the course of the campaign for emancipation. In July 1851 another Jew, David Salomons, standing on a platform advocating an extension of education, of the suffrage and the ballot, was elected to Parliament in a by-election at Greenwich. Unlike Rothschild, Salomons did attempt to take his seat without swearing the oaths in the prescribed form. His forcible removal from the House was proposed by Lord John Russell and seconded by Sir Robert Inglis – a vivid demonstration of the limits Russell placed upon the rights of electors when faced with the opposition of established institutions. For the Whigs, the balance of interests to be represented within the constitution included the Lords temporal and episcopal, and to force them to alter their decision on an issue such as this would unbalance the constitution rather than the opposite.[62] However, to the *Weekly Dispatch*, the debacle of Salomons' attempt to take his seat appeared as an attempt to deprive 'the common people of England' of their rights as well as the Jews. The answer was not to mollify the Lords but to overcome their resistance with a display of popular opinion. 'To your tents, O Israel. To the hustings and the polling booth John Bull', was the rallying cry uniting the cause of the Jewish minority with the English nation. And for a radical such as John Bright the battle was one incident in a larger conflict in which the people of the country had wrested the rights of citizenship from 'a powerful and dominant church' and 'a powerful ruling class'. The community of the nation was to be guaranteed by the patriotism, meaning the public-spiritedness, of the people.

61. *Weekly Dispatch*, 4 June 1848, p. 277.
62. The Duke of Argyll, a Whig who favoured 'leaving constituents free to exercise their judgement as to the religion of their Members', nevertheless felt that the Prime Minister's zeal in seeking to put the question again in the same parliamentary session was 'unjustifiable to express so distinctly disrespect for the deliberate opinion of the House of Lords' once that House had rejected the Jewish Disabilities Bill. Likewise, in 1857, the Chief Justice, Lord Campbell, a supporter of Jewish emancipation, urged Russell not to introduce Jews to the Commons by resolution. 'It would be a bare-faced attempt by one house to make laws against the wish of the other without the consent of the Crown.' Gilam, *The Emancipation of the Jews*, pp. 99, 107–8, 116.

He should like some clean sweep to be made of these oaths, and that they should regard each other as he believed they were, as patriotic citizens of their country come there [the House of Commons] to do that which was their duty to their country, and not binding themselves in the slightest degree by these antiquated forms of asseveration.[63]

The combination of the terms 'patriotic' and 'citizens' was significant and indicates further how the struggles to remove Jewish disabilities became occasions to prescribe a new relation between the government, the nation and the people. Among radicals, just as for Whig supporters of Jewish emancipation and for Tory opponents, the argument was not only one about the rights of individuals: it was concerned also with the nature of the collectivity which united the government and the people. The republican echoes of patriotic citizenship indicated a vision of the nation which the Whigs repudiated.[64] A motion that Salomons should withdraw from the House, although passed by a majority of 150 votes, was opposed by 81 Members of Parliament.[65] And it was this same combination of radicals who unsuccessfully urged Russell to challenge the House of Lords' resistance by making Jewish relief an issue of confidence or by pressing the Commons to pass a resolution in defiance of the Lords.[66]

Finally, in 1858, the resistance of the House of Lords was overcome. At first sight it is paradoxical that this victory was achieved during a period of Conservative government. But, crucially, the ministry was a minority one. The Prime Minister, the Earl of Derby, believed a conflict between Lords and Commons over Jewish relief would seriously endanger the government's chances of survival.[67] Moreover, in these circumstances it was easier for radicals and even Lord John Russell to threaten that the Commons would resolve to alter its oaths independently and act in defiance of the Lords. Faced by a minority Conservative government, this move was less likely to appear an imprudent attack on a balanced constitution by a Whig ministry and more as a challenge to Conservative-sponsored reaction and prejudice. In December 1857 Russell introduced yet another Oaths Bill and duly in April 1858 the Lords neutered it by removing

63. G.B. Smith, *The Life and Speeches of John Bright*, vol. i (London, 1881), pp. 329–30.
64. Burrow, *Whigs and Liberals*, chapter 2.
65. More detailed accounts of this episode can be found in Salbstein, *The Emancipation of the Jews*, pp. 179–87; Gilam, *The Emancipation of the Jews*, pp. 102–6.
66. Gilam, *The Emancipation of the Jews*, pp. 115–16, J. Bright, *Speeches* (London, 1868), vol. i, pp. 487–96.
67. A. Hawkins, *Parliament, Party and the Art of Politics in Britain 1855–9* (London, 1987), p. 149.

the clause relating to Jews. Liberated by the political conjuncture, the bill's supporters threatened that the Commons would proceed unilaterally. It was at this point that Derby stepped towards a compromise solution to avert a constitutional crisis. Thus it was on 5 July 1858 that the House of Lords passed Lord Lucan's bill which allowed either House to modify the oaths it required members to take.

Accordingly, eleven years after he had first been elected to the House of Commons by the electors of the City of London, and after he had been re-elected on four subsequent occasions, Lionel de Rothschild was allowed to swear the Oath of Abjuration omitting the words 'on the true faith of a Christian'; he took his seat in Parliament.[68] But this was only a partial victory. Rothschild had been admitted in the first instance on an *ad hominem* basis, and until the parliamentary oaths were altered Jews sat in the Commons 'not by absolute right but by sufferance'.[69] Moreover, the House of Commons was able to take this moderate step only by agreeing to the compromise that each House of Parliament could determine separately the oath to be taken by a Jew. The Lords continued to insist 'that the denial and rejection of that Saviour whose name each House of Parliament daily offers up to its collective prayers for the Divine blessing on its counsels, constitutes a moral unfitness to take part in the legislation of a professedly Christian community'.[70] It was not until 1866 that the Parliamentary Oaths Act introduced a form of words for both Houses which required a conscientious speaker to believe in God but made no particular demands beyond this.[71]

The Parliamentary Oaths Act of 1866 signalled the virtual end of one phase in the politics of Jewish integration. Jewish and non-Jewish members of both Houses of Parliament henceforth swore the same oath on either the New Testament or the Old.[72] The Act's passage coincided with the revival of the issue of parliamentary reform. It is easy to see the two Acts as connected – one a relatively minor, the other a major, extension of political liberties. Moreover,

68. The Oath of Abjuration was required of all Members of Parliament along with the Oaths of Supremacy and Allegiance. The Oath of Abjuration had been introduced in 1701 to discover 'Popish recusants' supporting the claims of the former House of Stuart: *First Report for Revising and Consolidating the Criminal Law*, p. 43. Apostates such as Benjamin Disraeli and David Ricardo encountered no legal objection to their becoming Members of Parliament.

69. *Hansard*, 3rd series, CLXXXI, col. 456, 13 February 1866. The words were those of Sir George Grey, the Home Secretary, introducing the Parliamentary Oaths Bill of 1866.

70. *Hansard*, 3rd series, CLI, col. 1,255, 12 July 1858.

71. The last major disability suffered by Jews was removed in 1871, when religious tests for entry to Oxford and Cambridge Universities were abolished.

72. It was Roman Catholics, not Jews, who caused most controversy in 1866.

locating the history of Jewish emancipation within this narrative reveals an inescapable aspect of the politics of Jewish integration in Britain. Jewish emancipation, assuredly, was a step within a larger process extending civil and political liberties through society. In this sense, Shaftesbury was correct to fear that having first conceded a Protestant Parliament, and then a Christian Parliament, members would eventually have to fight for a male Parliament.[73] But, as we have seen, the argument over the Jews' status concerned the nature of the community they might join as well as the extension of individual liberty. The different sides in the emancipation debate were engaged in an argument not only about the particular issue but also, more generally, about the nature of English national identity. Jewish emancipation was an episode in the history of nationalism as well as of liberalism in England. For Jews this would prove very significant. It meant that they were not merely acquiring as individuals the same rights as other citizens, it also meant they were being allowed access to a positive community – the nation.

73.   *Hansard*, 3rd series, XCV, col. 1,278, 16 December 1847.

Chapter 2

Rabbinism, Popery and Reform

Jewish reform and evangelical Christianity

The view that Jewish emancipation was one moment in the ascent of liberal individualism has left its mark on interpretations of religious and cultural change among Jews in early Victorian England. For it is the supposed absence in England of any national ideologies producing religious, cultural or racial standards to which the Jews had to conform which underpins the prevailing assessment of Jewish acculturation. But if, indeed, Jewish emancipation was concerned not only with establishing the rights of individuals but also with promoting and realising one account of national identity, then our understanding of Jewish cultural and religious change may also have to be revised.

In this chapter I examine, in particular, the dynamic of religious change among English Jews. From this perspective I analyse their attempts to adapt to the temper of early Victorian society. One theme will be the ways in which Jews attempted to negotiate the competing claims generated by Judaism, on one side, and by the state, on the other. The debate on Jewish emancipation brought into question both the exercise of authority within the Jewish community and the content of Judaism. The claims made on behalf of rabbinical law to legislate for areas of practice such as marriage and divorce trespassed on spheres which normally were regulated by the state, not by a voluntary and autonomous agency. The hope for national restoration, expressed regularly in Jewish prayers, could be seen to conflict with the campaign for complete integration within the English nation. These connections between a movement for religious reform and the project of political emancipation were clear to Moses Montefiore, for one, whose enthusiasm for political equality cooled as a result. In 1837 he wrote, 'I am most firmly resolved not to give up the smallest part of our religious forms and privileges to obtain civil rights.'[1] Others disagreed. But the debate on religious change, within Anglo-Jewry and outside of it, was not a straightforward function of emancipation. Religious controversy also possessed its own dynamic.

Although nominally orthodox, the general temper of religious observance among mid-Victorian Jews was relaxed. Synagogue attendance was thin. In 1851 on census sabbath only 24 per cent of London Jews were found in a metropolitan synagogue.[2] The Jewish middle classes generally maintained principles of *kashrut* and sabbath observance but, with the exception of a rigorous minority, the detail of observance was neglected and most Jews took a wide view of the sorts of activity allowed on the sabbath.[3] Even the observant were noted for their ignorance of Jewish literature and learning by German standards. As for the rest, the *Jewish Chronicle* complained, 'the great majority of our English brethren are in general ignorant of the principles and great truths of our Holy religion. The majority of the mass follow the customs and observances of our faith because forsooth their fathers did so before them.'[4] Yet occasional attendance was commonplace, particularly on high holydays. Among 'street Jews', Henry Mayhew claimed, indifference to religion was normal. But on his own evidence attitudes were more complex. He reported an interview with a Jewish boy who had no formal connection with the Jewish community. Nevertheless, the lad would not eat pork, and became aggressive when he mistook the pioneer social investigator for a Christian missionary.[5]

The men who established the West London Synagogue of British Jews in 1842 were driven, in part, by their desire to halt the march of 'indifferentism'. Four years later, seeking to justify their innovations in the face of anathematisation by the leaders of orthodoxy, the

1. Cited in I. Finestein, 'The Uneasy Victorian: Montefiore as Communal Leader', in S. and V.D. Lipman, eds., *The Century of Moses Montefiore* (Oxford, 1985), p. 52.
2. V.D. Lipman, *Social History of the Jews in England, 1850–1950* (London 1954), p. 36.
3. S. Singer, 'Orthodox Judaism in Early Victorian London' (Yeshiva University PhD, 1981), p. 217; *idem,* 'Jewish Religious Thought in Early Victorian London', *Association for Jewish Studies Review,* Fall 1985, pp. 181–210. I am greatly indebted to Singer's pioneering work in this field, and this chapter seeks to build on his important argument regarding the bibliocentricity of reform currents among orthodox Anglo-Jewry.
4. *JC,* 19 September 1851, p. 393.
5. H. Mayhew, *London Labour and the London Poor* (New York, NY, 1968 reprint), vol. ii, pp. 122–3. Moreover, even when contact with the community had been slight over a whole lifetime there was identification with the community through death, since it was through the synagogue that rights to a Jewish burial were purchased or, if necessary, a pauper burial was provided.

synagogues' representatives claimed they had established their place of worship in response to gathering irreverence which they attributed to the 'antiquated mode of synagogue worship'.[6] The leaders elaborated their principles in August 1841, in a letter written by a number of them to the Elders of Bevis Marks – the Spanish and Portuguese congregation. In most respects they dwelt on the need to improve the synagogue's devotional character and 'preserve proper decorum during the performance of Divine Worship'. At the West London Synagogue, services were to begin at a later hour than was customary, to enable members and their families to assemble before worship commenced, and they were to be abridged – divested 'of those portions which are not strictly of a devotional character' – to permit 'that solemn and devout attention without which prayer is unavailing'.[7]

If the form of the service was seen to be one cause of religious apathy, ignorance was another. Beyond the emphasis on 'decorum', therefore, the secessionists announced that 'religious discourses delivered in the English language, will form a part of the service on every Sabbath and Holiday' in order to 'familiarise the rising generation with the great principles of our holy faith'. Most radical of all, however, the members of the West London Synagogue celebrated festivals on a single day only instead of, as was customary, treating two days as a holiday. 'It is not the intention of the body of which we form a part', wrote the secessionists, 'to recognise as sacred, days which are evidently not ordained as such in scripture.'[8] In this way the new synagogue challenged the authority of rabbis to legislate for Jewish religious practice.

The origins of the new congregation extended beyond its members' opinions on ritual, liturgy and custom. There was, for example, a demographic aspect to its formation. The growing population of wealthy Jews living in the West End of London required a local synagogue which the East End congregations refused to provide, fearing this would diminish their own membership, wealth and status.[9] More narrowly, the new synagogue was a family affair. Of the twenty-four founder members the *Sephardim* were dominated by the Mocattas and the *Ashkenazim* by the Goldsmids: families which had had business connections for more than fifty years. Moreover, for some of its members at least, the new congregation was intended to challenge temporal as well as ecclesiastical authority. The campaign for Jewish emancipation and the articulation of communal authority

6. *JC*, 20 February 1846, p. 80.
7. C. Roth, ed., *Anglo-Jewish Letters, 1158–1917* (London, 1938), p. 282.
8. *Ibid.*
9. Lipman, *Social History of the Jews in England*, p. 15.

were closely interwoven. The most prominent supporters of Jewish emancipation were drawn from the elite. And it was the members of this group who had most to gain from political equality.[10] For I.L. Goldsmid, a bullion broker and one of the leading campaigners for Jewish emancipation, who was increasingly frustrated by the JBD's cautious approach to political emancipation, and who declined to serve on the Board in 1839 having been elected to it, the formation of the West London Synagogue provided a forum through which to challenge the Board's claims to monopolise communal representations to the government. In consequence, in 1845, when the government was preparing a measure to remove some of the Jews' disabilities, Peel was approached by a delegation from the JBD and by a group led by Goldsmid, drawn in part from members of the West London Synagogue. Whereas the five deputies assured the Prime Minister they would be content with a measure of relief confined to the municipal sphere, Goldsmid's delegation insisted they would be satisfied with nothing short of full emancipation.[11] It was clear that the West London Synagogue intended to challenge the disposition of temporal as well as ecclesiastical authority within Anglo-Jewry.

Many orthodox Jews also favoured measures of religious reform, even though they did not ally themselves with the West London Synagogue. The development of this broad reform movement within Anglo-Jewry was more than a programme of change dragged forward by the momentum of some Jews' political aspirations. In fact, programmes of synagogue reform preceded the emergence of Jewish emancipation as a political question. Although the Jewish communal debate interacted with the cause of the Jews' political equality at many points, it went beyond this issue and reflected on the Jews' integration in English society in a wider sense.

Attempts to reform the appearance of the synagogue service had recurred from the 1820s. The service was customarily an occasion for the display of wealth and receipt of honours which also served to maintain the synagogue finances. In his history of the Great

10. However, as Abraham Gilam has demonstrated, the less wealthy majority of the Jewish population was not as indifferent to the cause as once was believed. In January 1848 the Jewish Association for the Removal of Civil and Religious Disabilities succeeded in gathering nine hundred supporters at a mass meeting. The Jewish elite, however, did not encourage a policy of agitation which trespassed upon its monopoly of representation: A. Gilam, *The Emancipation of the Jews in England, 1830–60* (New York, NY, 1980), pp. 58–62; *JC*, 4 February 1848, p. 415; *ibid*, 28 July 1848, p. 618.

11. R. Liberles, 'The Origins of the Jewish Reform Movement in England', *Association of Jewish Studies Review*, 1976, pp. 121–50; Gilam, *The Emancipation of the Jews*, pp. 93–4.

Synagogue, the primary London congregation, Cecil Roth describes how 'every person summoned to the Reading of the Law was not only expected, but at that time also compelled, to make an offering or offerings on behalf of the synagogal funds and charities for the "well-being" of those of his relatives and acquaintances whom he desired to honour'. Particular mention had to be made of the presiding officers of the synagogue and of the Chief Rabbi.[12]

In the course of the 1820s some synagogues introduced pulpit addresses in English and placed a limit on the number of monetary offerings that could be read out during prayers. But the men who went on to form the West London Synagogue were not alone in supporting further change. In 1841 C.K. Salaman, in an address to other members of the Western Synagogue, criticised features of the service and accused others of promenading 'as in an exchange for merchants'. He complained of an absence of decorum more generally – the chatter of the congregants and their children, the movements of members to and fro throughout the service, the 'frivolous' tunes to which prayers were sung – and that as a result the service did not excite any 'divine emotions'.[13] The following year some members of the Great Synagogue brought forward a set of proposals to revise the service, which was based upon a similar list of complaints.[14]

The men who favoured change were also, with some notable exceptions such as Moses Montefiore and Louis Cohen, the men of 'wealth and influence' in London Jewry. Their opinions were in harmony 'with the great majority of the Jewishly committed community', despite some resistance from a minority of rigorous conservatives who were drawn largely from the less wealthy middle classes and poorer elements of the Jewish population.[15] Moreover, as Nathan Adler asserted his authority the orthodox reformers won a great deal of what they wanted. The new Chief Rabbi's *Laws and Regulations* placed great emphasis on decorum: infants below the age of four were excluded from services and older children were to be supervised by their parents; milling around and conversations during services were prohibited, loud responses by the congregation were

12. C. Roth, *The Great Synagogue, 1690–1940* (London, 1950), pp. 250–1.
13. A. Barnett, *The Western Synagogue through Two Centuries* (London, 1961), pp. 182–3.
14. They wanted the abolition of monetary offerings, sermons in the English language, prayers to be recited by a choir or in unison but not by individuals at their own pace, shorter services and a later start to services to enable families to assemble before they commenced: Singer, 'Orthodox Judaism in Early Victorian London', p. 133.
15. *Ibid.*, pp. 138, 207; *JC*, 25 October 1844, p. 12.

forbidden, the public sale of *mitzvos* was discontinued and a limit placed on the recitation of monetary offerings. Adler also introduced a division to the service on sabbaths and holidays to allow worshippers who did not want to commence prayers at eight in the morning to assemble two or three hours later. He discouraged the cacophony which arose from individuals reciting prayers at their own pace, and congregants were encouraged to utter their prayers in unison or together with a male choir.[16]

Where did the ideas informing the direction and content of reform come from? In general, the emergence of a separate Reform movement, as well as reforming tendencies within orthodoxy, have been seen by historians as part of the Jews' response to 'modernity': in particular, to the development in eighteenth-century Europe of universal, inclusive conceptions of humanity. This influenced Jewish life through the conduit of the *haskalah* – the Jewish enlightenment – whose devotees emphasised the universalist aspect of the teachings and doctrines of Judaism and relegated the significance of its particularistic rituals and observances.[17] But as Endelman has shown, the ideological programmes of the *haskalah* had little impact on Anglo-Jewish history.[18] How, then, should we explain the English development?

One answer can be suggested by placing the debates taking place inside Anglo-Jewry in the context of religious argument in society more widely and, in particular, in relation to a critique of Judaism. Christian critiques of Judaism were not novel, of course. But the desire of many Jews to take a full part in British society and politics was more recent, as was the prospect that this might be possible. Moreover, in the battle to determine what the long-term consequences would be of the great constitutional reforms of 1829 and 1832, the contending forces of evangelicalism, tractarianism and liberal Anglicanism, within the Anglican establishment, and nononformity, outside of it, ensured that religion and politics drew close in early Victorian public life.[19] In these circumstances criticisms

16. Singer, 'Orthodox Judaism in Early Victorian London', p. 148. T. Endelman, 'The Englishness of Jewish Modernity', in J. Katz, ed., *Towards Modernity: The European Jewish Model* (New York, NY, 1987), p. 236; *JC*, 26 June 1846, p. 161.

17. J. Katz, *Out of the Ghetto: The Social Background to Jewish Emancipation, 1770–1870* (New York, NY edn, 1978), pp. 130–6; M. Meyer, *Response to Modernity: A History of the Reform Movement in Judaism* (Oxford, 1988), pp. 13–17.

18. Endelman, 'The Englishness of Jewish Modernity', p. 226.

19. G.I.T. Machin, *Politics and the Churches in Great Britain, 1832–68* (Oxford, 1987); Brent, *Liberal Anglican Politics: Whiggery, Religion and Reform, 1830–41* (Oxford, 1987); B. Hilton, *The Age of Atonement: The Influence of Evanglicalism on Social and Economic Thought, 1795–1865* (Oxford, 1988) P. Toon, *Evangelical Theology, 1833–56: A Response to Tractarianism* (London, 1979), p. 203.

of the Jewish religion possessed a powerful resonance for both non-Jews and Jews.

For some evangelicals, Judaism and the Jews had a special significance. Whereas the first generation of evangelicals had believed the millennium would be achieved through preaching the Gospel, from the late 1820s faith in prophetic interpretation led growing numbers to expect it imminently. The London Society for Promoting Christianity among the Jews was established in 1809 as an interdenominational mission but in 1815 it narrowed to a purely Anglican basis. In the 1820s it attracted the energies of pre-millenarians in particular, whose messianism and literal reading of Old Testament prophecy led them to place special emphasis on the conversion of the Jews.[20]

In its early years the Society's activities were directed chiefly towards Jews living in Eastern and Central Europe and in the Ottoman empire. But in 1829 it began more actively to seek converts in London. These changes were accompanied by a considerable increase in support: between 1820–30 the Society's annual income averaged £12,687; by 1840–50 this figure had reached £30,020. Many thousands were raised by annual dues of just £1.[21] A mission house was established in the capital, and also the Jews' Operatives Converts Institution in Bethnal Green. According to the Society's official historian, W.T. Gidney, the years between 1830–50 were 'the palmy days in the entire history of the London mission'. But the return in souls was modest: between 1843–9 just 180 baptisms were recorded.[22]

The Society's principal worker in London was Alexander McCaul; no marginal figure, McCaul became Professor of Hebrew and Rabbinical Literature at King's College, London in 1841 and was offered the bishopric in Jerusalem when it was established in the same year.[23] He had spent most of the 1820s working among Jews in Poland and returned permanently to work for the Society in London in 1831. Gidney judges 'no one ever rendered higher services to the Society than McCaul'.[24] Between 1832–6 he delivered a series of addresses to Jews at Saturday evening conferences and these formed

20.   D.W. Bebbington, *Evangelicalism in Modern Britain: A History from the 1730s to the 1980s* (London, 1989), pp. 76–7, 81–3, 88–9.
21.   M. Scult, *Millenial Expectations and Jewish Liberties: A Study of Efforts to Convert the Jews in Britain up to the Mid-Nineteenth Century* (Leiden, 1978), pp. 100, 125.
22.   W.T. Gidney, *The History of the London Society for Promoting Christianity among the Jews from 1809–1908* (London, 1908), pp. 216–7. On the Society's more vigorous and visible activity in London see *ibid*, pp. 158–61.
23.   P. Greaves, 'The Jerusalem Bishopric, 1841', *English Historical Review*, July 1949, p. 344. McCaul turned down the bishopric, arguing that it should be occupied by a 'son of Abraham'.
24.   Gidney, *The History of the London Society*, pp. 158–9.

the basis for his weekly pamphlet *Old Paths.* In 1837 they were published as a single volume. Over ten thousand copies were distributed in the first year of publication. Subsequently, it was translated into Hebrew, French and German, while a second English edition appeared in 1846, and McCaul's analysis was further repeated with slight variations in the political and literary reviews.[25] In 1838 he followed *Old Paths* with *Sketches of Judaism and the Jews,* a collection of articles he had written for the *British Magazine* between 1834–8.

McCaul contrasted Judaism as he found it in the Bible with the religion he saw practised by the Jews. *Old Paths* was published with the informative subtitle '*Or a Comparison of the Principles and Doctrines of Modern Judaism with the Religion of Moses and the Prophets.*' McCaul aimed to prove that Christianity was the faithful continuation of the writings of Old Testament, and Judaism 'a new and totally different system, devised by designing men and unworthy of the Jewish people'.[26] The faith had been corrupted by rabbis and their instrument had been the oral law. Indeed, 'rabbinism' was a favoured term for Judaic practice. According to this view, as A.A. Cooper (later to become Lord Shaftesbury) wrote in the *Quarterly Review,* 'Talmudical learning and the power of the Rabbis, the depositories of it, are the ultimate object of Jewish discipline.'[27] Faced with what they saw as a powerful class of priests who claimed to interpret the Bible for the people and who had generated an elaborate ritual sustained by tradition, one for which there was no literal sanction in scripture, these men found in 'rabbinism' the same evils evangelicals habitually found in 'popery'. McCaul introduced his *Sketches of Judaism and Jews* by explaining that

> From the dispersion to the latter end of the last century, rabbinism prevailed universally amongst the Jewish nation with the exception of the one small sect of the Karaites. If asked to give a concise yet adequate idea of this system, I should say it is Jewish Popery: just as Popery may be defined to [sic] by Gentile Rabbinism. Its distinguishing feature is that it asserts the transmission of an oral or traditional law of equal authority with the written law of God, at the same time, that, like Popery, it resolves tradition into the present opinions of the existing Church.[28]

25. A. McCaul, *The Old Paths: Or a Comparison of the Principles and Doctrines of Modern Judaism with the Religion of Moses and the Prophets* (London, 1846 edn), p. vii; Gidney, *The History of the London Society,* p. 217; A.A. Cooper, 'State and Prospects of the Jews', *Quarterly Review,* January 1839, pp. 166–92; 'Present State and Prospects of the Jews', *Fraser's Magazine,* September 1840, pp. 253–74.
26. McCaul, *The Old Paths,* p. 645.
27. Cooper, 'State and Prospects', p. 182.
28. McCaul, *Sketches of Judaism and Jews* (London, 1838), p. 2; see too the comments in *Fraser's Magazine,* 'Present State and Prospects of the Jews', p. 261.

In a similar fashion, at a meeting of four thousand supporters assembled in the capital to celebrate the London Society's thirty-fifth anniversary in 1843, Lord Ashley, who would become the Society's President in 1848, placed its claims for support on the ground that 'it is essentially an association of Protestants'. 'It is founded upon Scripture and not upon tradition. It loves antiquity, but it is the antiquity of the Bible. It is hostile to Popery and all her allies, and all her affiliations. Every blow they dealt at Rabbinism is a blow at Popery itself and all the various ramifications of the system.'[29] Anti-popery was a more potent force than any hostility to Jews in mid-nineteenth-century Britain. Inevitably, for militant Protestants, Catholicism was a more significant opponent. However, this primary opposition did not deflect attention away from Judaism. Instead, it could provide the terms within which the Jewish religion was understood.[30]

Judaism was not regarded by conversionists as wholly a negative force. Most obviously, as the precursor and foundation of Christianity it was not without value. Indeed, the Jews' survival as a people, their success in resisting a descent into barbarism, despite eighteen hundred years of exile, and their isolation from the peoples around them, was attributed to their attachment to their religion. Even 'rabbinism' had its positive aspect, for it had encouraged a love of education among Jews, albeit one 'calculated far more to sharpen than to enrich the understanding'.[31] Indeed, it was the double-sided and paradoxical aspect of the Jewish condition which held a special attraction for these evangelicals. The Jews were 'princes in degradation', 'sublime in misery', 'a people chastened but not wholly cast off'.[32] Both their decline and survival were confirmations of Christian truth.

For McCaul and the others, the Jews' errors, rooted in the quality of the Jewish religion, were highlighted by comparison with Protestant Christianity.[33] Judaism was not a vital religion, it was a faith without engagement: 'the rabbinical Jew fulfils a commandment, and thinks he consequently lays up a portion of merit'.[34] But the limitations of Judaism were different from those of Roman Catholicism for, whereas the latter reflected a perversion of Christianity, the former remained in a condition of pre-Christian stasis.

29. *Jewish Intelligence*, June 1843, p. 186.
30. Endelman, 'The Englishness of Jewish Modernity', p. 238, suggests Catholics provided an 'alternative' object of contempt.
31. Cooper, 'State and Prospects', pp. 181–2; McCaul, *Sketches of Jews and Judaism*, pp. 3–16; 'Present State and Prospects', *Frasers Magazine*, p. 256.
32. *Ibid*, pp. 253–4; Cooper, 'State and Prospects', p. 191.
33. McCaul, *The Old Paths*, p. 652.
34. 'Present State and Prospects', *Frasers Magazine*, p. 259.

The incapacity of Judaism for development, its incompatability with any conception of progress or improvement, was the counterpart to its neglect of spirituality. The stranglehold of the oral law meant that 'a Rabbinical Jew of the present day, as he exists in Poland or Palestine, conveys a tolerably accurate idea of what the Jews were centuries ago'.[35]

In his *Sketches of Judaism*, McCaul did not doubt that in England 'the system' of Judaism was petrified.[36] Yet, with some contradiction, he did acknowledge the existence of a dynamic element within Judaism and alluded to the moves towards reform. By 1846, when *Old Paths* entered its second edition, McCaul responded enthusiastically to the formation of the West London Synagogue. The new congregation had renounced a great deal of what he found objectionable and was testimony to the influence of his book. Similarly, he welcomed the development of the Jewish Reform movement in Germany.[37]

At first sight, McCaul's claims to have influenced the development of Reform Judaism in England may seem far-fetched. The *Jewish Chronicle*, for example, a newspaper which supported both conciliation with the West London Synagogue and reform within the orthodox community, was also bitter in its attacks on the conversionist system of 'fraud and imposition'.[38] In April 1847, at the same time as it deprecated the 'dross' of 'modern Rabbinism', the *Jewish Chronicle* denied it was relaying the opinions of the 'traducers of the Talmud'.[39] Naturally, it was to the reformers' disadvantage if they were identified as the conversionists' parrots. This was particularly the case since 'conversion-mongers', such as Sir Robert Inglis, Lord Ashley and Sir Robert Newdegate, were among the die-hard anti-emancipationists in the House of Commons who would sooner have de-Judaised Rothschild than de-Christianised Parliament.[40] But support for the London Society from a number of leading anti-emancipationists seemed only to render the need to refute its arguments all the more pressing.[41] The parallels between the conversionists and the reformers are too striking to ignore and if it

---

35. McCaul, *Sketches of Judaism*, p. 2. See too the comments in 'Present State and Prospects', p. 261.

36. McCaul, *Sketches of Judaism*, chapter vii. McCaul supported emancipation, however.

37 McCaul, *The Old Paths*, p. vii; others also expressed their hope that the decline of talmudism opened a way through which Jews might be led to recognise Jesus Christ as the Messiah: 'Present State and Prospects', pp. 261–3.

38. *JC*, 22 February 1850, p. 154.

39. *Ibid*, 16 April 1847, p. 113.

40. *Blackwood's Magazine*, December 1847, p. 724; *Hansard*, 3rd series, CXVI, 372–5, 1 May 1851.

41. *JC*, 15 June 1848, p. 286; *ibid*, 22 February 1850, pp. 153–4.

is implausible to see reform as an embrace of McCaul and the London Society it was, in great measure, a response to them and the critique of Judaism they offered.

The minister of the West London Synagogue, David Marks, explained his religious opinions, in part, as an attempt to preserve Judaism from external attack. In the face of the assault on rabbinical authority being made by the London Society, he argued that the best strategy was to 'rest our hopes and form our observances upon the laws of God alone'.[42] He made the same point more guardedly in a sermon delivered at the consecration of the synagogue: 'As Israelites, who have the glory of God at heart, we feel the importance of averting the evil blow, which ignorance and misconception cannot fail to strike at our hallowed institutions, especially in days, whose peculiar character it is, to submit every system to the severity of critical scrutiny.'[43] Indeed, there is evidence that Marks consulted McCaul when formulating the innovations at the West London Synagogue.[44] In abolishing customs, such as the second day of holidays, and prayers and references to angels and demons which had no scriptural basis, these reforms made at the West London Synagogue certainly appeared to answer evangelical criticism.[45] When he preached on the occasion of the synagogue's consecration Marks underlined the point: 'it is the spirit of the ritual to which we should have our attention directed, more than to any set form in which it is presented to our senses'.[46] Indeed, at times the full weight of the evangelical critique was adopted by the Jewish reformers in the course of their lengthy feud with the leaders of orthodoxy. In 1854 Marks gave a course of four lectures the title of which disclosed its anti-rabbinical message: *The Law is Light: A Course of Four Lectures on the Sufficiency of the Law of Moses as the Guide of Israel.* In the first of these addresses Marks set out to remonstrate with 'a large class of our Jewish brethren, who receive unconditionally, the rabbinical system as a whole'. More particularly he criticised the vindication of that system presented by Nathan Adler, the Chief Rabbi, in which

---

42. Cited in Meyer, *Response to Modernity*, pp. 172–3.
43. D.W. Marks, *Sermons Preached on Various Occasions at the West London Synagogue of British Jews* (London, 1851), p. 11.
44. B.-Z. Lask Abrahams, 'Emanuel Deutsch of "The Talmud" Fame', *TJHSE*, 1969–71; p. 56.
45. For a more comprehensive survey of the changes made, see M. Meyer, *Response to Modernity*, p. 173. Meyer also comments suggestively on the importance in England of the evangelical attack on Judaism. See too Singer, 'Orthodox Judaism in Early Victorian London', pp. 82–3.
46. D.W. Marks, *The Law is Light: A Course of Four Lectures on the Sufficiency of the Law of Moses as the Guide of Israel,* (London, 1854), p. 43.

Adler had defended the necessity for and the authority of rabbinical interpretation of the law: 'A doctrine like this, which is so boldly asserted in the sermon of the Reverend Rabbi, may well startle us, and induce us to question whether instead of listening here to the voice of Judaism, we are not having rehearsed to us the substance, though in a different phraseology, of the theology of Rome.'[47]

Equally striking was that the substance of the evangelical assault was reproduced within the ranks of Anglo-Jewish orthodoxy and provides one context in which Adler's reforms were encouraged and received. (The Chief Rabbi himself, who arrived in Britain from Hanover in 1845, was less touched by this context.) The *Jewish Chronicle* was the mouthpiece for familiar laments on the standard of decorum. In part this was seen as a question of manners and modernity; a matter of the sorts of behaviour appropriate among Jews now that they enjoyed a large measure of toleration. Persecution explained and excused much in traditional practice that now seemed unacceptable. 'That loud tumultuous, unrestrained and unharmonious clamour of their prayer, so offensive and disgusting to us, to them was natural and genuine, it was the immediate and adequate expression of their souls, filled with sorrow and oppression.'[48] When C.K. Salaman lectured the Western congregation on the need to improve their services, he asked his audience 'to remember that we are living in the nineteenth century and in England – the most civilised and enlightened country in the world'.[49] But even this concern with modernity may be seen in the light of the incapacity for development ascribed to Judaism and the Jews; observance of the minutely detailed rabbinical system had left Jews much as they had been centuries before. 'Rabbinism in our age is an incongruity,' the *Jewish Chronicle* claimed. The newspaper's prescription was 'to cut off the excrescences' which had grown around the law.[50]

The reasons for the turn to more decorous forms of worship went beyond a felt need to conform to modern manners. It encompassed a desire to find within Judaism a religion of the heart, and in this it echoed clearly the evangelical impulse. Consider, for example, this *Jewish Chronicle* editorial on devotion in the synagogue.

Devotion in the general acceptation of the term signifies a condition of the mind, in which our senses and our feelings are absorbed in communication with the Supreme Being – a state of emotion produced by involuntary agency; a panting desire and an arduous longing to pour out our

47. *Ibid*, p. 8.
48. *JC*, 26 June 1846, p. 161.
49. Barnett, *The Western Synagogue*, p. 184.
50. *JC*, 18 August 1848, p. 641.

thoughts before our heavenly Creator, to whom we entirely *give up* our-selves, and to whose worship we resign for a time our powers and faculties.[51]

Obstacles to this state of abandonment had to be purged from the service. Even within orthodoxy some of the traditional functions of the rabbinate were open to criticism from reformers who strove to nurture a Judaism of the spirit. When, in 1847, the Chief Rabbi prohibited the use of rice for food during Passover and forbade baking *matzos* on the middle days of Passover, the *Jewish Chronicle* attacked 'the numberless and thickly twined fences with which mod-ern rabbinism has hedged in the true law of God'. The sacred law had to be distinguished from the 'dross' with which it had become alloyed.[52]

Similar analyses can be found outside the pages of the press, in texts produced by orthodox Jews.[53] Moses Angel, the headmaster of the Jews' Free School and the single most significant figure in Anglo-Jewish religious and secular education in the nineteenth century, possessed impeccable orthodox credentials but he too felt bound to answer the commonplace critique of Judaism.

> Judaism has come to be entirely misunderstood. It was been universally described as a thing of obsolete forms and customs – as incompatible with progress – as the associate of a low standard of morality – as the obstacle preventing the approach to heaven rather than the ladder reaching thither – that the world has grown to believe what few have taken the trouble to contradict.[54]

In defending Judaism, Angel distinguished 'the spirit of the law . . . from the shroud in which it has lain entranced'.[55] He too com-prehended the religion's degeneration as a consequence of a history that had come to an end, requiring Jews themselves to adapt to a new era. Hitherto, in the face of persecution, 'all that the Jew owned to invoke the future was the religion which had attached him to the past'. It was the rabbi who bore and transmitted these traditions. But in the transformed climate of toleration and enlightenment these same institutions became 'frequently unnecessary, sometimes objectionable'.[56]

If certain sorts of Jewish expression were encouraged, others were

---

51. *Ibid*, 10 July 1846, p. 173.
52. *Ibid*, 16 April 1847, p. 113.
53. See for example C. Montefiore, *A Few Words to the Jews by One of Themselves* (London, 1853), pp. 26–8.
54. M. Angel, *The Law of Sinai and its Appointed Times* (London, 1858), p. iii.
55. *Ibid*, p. vi.
56. *Ibid*, p. 178.

not, as the pre-history of the Anglo-Jewish seminary, Jews' College, illustrates. The development of an Anglo-Jewish ministry capable of presenting the truths of Judaism in a form appropriate to nine-teenth-century conditions was thought to be an immediate need by the founders of the West London Synagogue, who promised weekly English language sermons, and also by many within the orthodox synagogues, including the Chief Rabbi.[57] The absence of an 'Anglo-Jewish pulpit' had political implications too, as the *Jewish Chronicle* pointed out in 1849: 'we are anxious to attain full emancipation: and would it not be a disgrace if we were told by our Christian opponents that the Jews of England are so ignorant that they cannot find a lecturer in their community'.[58] For his part, Adler was anxious to establish a seminary which could produce a corps of teachers able to give instruction in English and he issued a circular which proposed that such a college should be created.[59] In January 1852 a public meeting was organised to raise funds for the planned seminary and day school. Yet for lack of funds neither one was opened until 1855. At the first meeting, of the Anglo-Jewish notability only Moses Montefiore attended.[60] For so long as Adler's scheme threatened to establish a college connected to the *Beth Hamedrash* – the traditional house of study and a location rich in its association with beards, gaberdines, the ghetto and Talmudic learning – it did not receive support from the community's notables. When Jews' College finally was established, Hebrew was taught there to an elementary level only and classics and general literature were included within the cur-riculum.[61] This outcome suggests religious change did not develop independently of the need to legitimise the persistence of Judaism in the face of a Christian society in which the religion, according to the *Jewish Chronicle*, was 'decried as petrification, incapable of all development, condemned by reason'.[62]

The Jews' neglect of the 'spirit' was open to wide interpretation, and evangelicalism, although the dominant influence was not the only one. The *Jewish Chronicle* repeatedly mourned the poverty of Anglo-Jewish literary life. Charlotte Montefiore regretted the neglect of the arts among English Jews: the absence of painters, poets, musicians and sculptors. It was easy to see the materialism of the

57. *JC*, 19 September 1851, p. 393; *ibid*, 19 December 1851, p. 84.
58. I. Harris, *History of Jews' College* (London, 1906), p. vi.
59. Adler voiced his concern 'that among the numerous clerical offices of the united congregations in this Empire some are vacant and only a few are held by Englishmen': Harris, *History of Jews' College*, p. vii.
60. *JC*, 9 January 1852, p. 105.
61. Singer, 'Orthodox Judaism in Early Victorian London', pp. 201–5.
62. *JC*, 13 September 1861, p. 4.

Jews' religion and the materialism of their worldly activities as reflecting each other: 'The lives of most of us are devoted to a vain ambition, to the acquisition of money, more and more money, or they are chilled by a profound religious apathy.'[63] As Israel Finestein has remarked, elevating 'the social and cultural level of the poorer ranks of the Jewish tradesmen and manual workers became something of an obsession with the emancipationists'.[64] The middle classes too were seen to be in need of improvement in the same direction. Accordingly, in 1845 the Jews' and General Literary and Scientific Institution was inaugurated – a Jewish equivalent of the mechanics' institutes which had been established more widely in the 1820–30s.[65]

Thus it would be mistaken to present evangelicalism as the only influence on the programmes of religious and cultural reform being promoted within Anglo-Jewry at this time. For some such as I.L. Goldsmid the political context appears to have been the most significant. The connections between religious reform, intellectual improvement and the project of political emancipation were made by representatives of the West London Synagogue. When they saw Peel in 1845 they placed before him 'certain facts connected with the advancement of British Jews in the several branches of letters and science, in the different learned professions, as well as in the improvement of the worship of the synagogue, during the last few years; and thus to induce him to originate, or to support in the next Session of Parliament, a bill for full and complete emancipation'.[66] It is, perhaps, no coincidence that the financial failure of the Jews' and General Institution, a result of its diminishing attraction to wealthy patrons, coincided with the achievement of political emancipation.[67]

But notwithstanding this recognition that the influence of evangelicalism did not stand alone, the parallels between religious reform and the evangelical critique of Judaism are impressive. Several historians have pointed to the impact of evangelicalism beyond the ranks of those who formally aligned themselves with the movement.[68] In many respects Jews resisted evangelical theology just

63. Montefiore, *A Few Words to the Jews*, p. 29.
64. I. Finestein, 'Anglo-Jewish Opinion During the Struggle for Emancipation', *TJHSE*, 1964, pp. 125–6.
65. Cited in A. Barnett, 'Sussex Hall: The First Jewish Venture in Popular Education', *TJHSE*, 1955–9, p. 68.
66. Cited in Liberles, 'The Origins of the Jewish Reform Movement in England' p. 139.
67. Barnett, 'Sussex Hall', p. 78.
68. Most recently Hilton, *The Age of Atonement*: see especially pp. 26–35.

as they resisted Christianity more generally. The idea of vicarious atonement, for example, the belief that faith in Christ's atonement on the Cross prepared the way for redemption and salvation, could have no place in Judaism. The connected emphasis on depravity and sinfulness and the need for constant vigilance against temptation, likewise, seems not to have been reproduced in the Jewish context. This is not surprising. The evangelical emphasis on sin, pain, punishment and temptation, Hilton suggests, was an attempt 'to reconcile the evil and suffering, which after 1789 were felt to dominate the world, with the continuing existence of a powerful and loving God'.[69] But the Jews' experience of discrimination and persecution and their martyrological rendition of their own history meant that these were not novel problems to them. Indeed, for those Jews eager to attain civil and political equality the legacy of the French Revolution was not entirely negative. By the 1830s, the majority of the Anglo-Jewish upper and middle class looked upon the revival of political reform in Britain as a movement likely to create a polity more rich with opportunity for Jews rather than one fraught with danger. But if these aspects of evangelicalism did not 'take', it is possible to highlight striking parallels elsewhere; above all in the emphases on 'unmysterious' forms of worship and a vital religion of the heart.

These parallels raise questions concerning what the relation was between Jewish cultural change and English society in this period. One response may be to argue that the parallels were fortuitous and distract attention from an autonomous Jewish pattern of development – the influence of the more advanced Jewish reform movements in Germany, for example.[70] But although the developments in Germany were well reported in the Anglo-Jewish press they were not seen to be fit for emulation. The German example was regarded as a recipe for dissolution by those pressing for change in orthodox congregations. Proposals such as moving the sabbath to a Sunday or that Jews should cease to circumcise male babies, the *Jewish Chronicle* complained, 'strike at the root of our holy religion', these changes were not reforms but 'inroads'.[71] Equally significant, these reforms were not contemplated by the powers at the West London Synagogue. In all but their decision to dispense with some customary holidays, the doctrinal innovations of Reform Judaism in Britain were notably moderate. Belief and hope in the Jews' eventual

69. *Ibid*, p. 17.
70. B. Williams, *The Making of Manchester Jewry, 1740–1875* (Manchester, 1976) pp. 259–60; L. Wolf, 'The Queen's Jewry', in C. Roth, ed., *Essays in Jewish History by Lucien Wolf* (London, 1934), pp. 318–19.
71. *JC*, 29 November 1850, p. 57.

restoration were not denied as they were in Germany, and there was no suggestion that Hebrew should be replaced as the language of worship or that the sabbath should be changed to Sunday.[72] In Britain, reformers wedded themselves to the word of the Bible. This limited their innovations but it also led them to abolish the second day of festivals for which there was no scriptural authority; something beyond the agenda of European reform.

This particular programme of change reflected the force in Britain of a bibliocentric critique of Judaism. In Germany Old Testament criticism was more radical and more precociously influential among Protestants than in Britain. Inevitably, in that context, a Reform movement which dealt with the *Talmud* only would have provided a less respectable basis for a revised Judaism. It is possible to suggest that the differences between the Jewish Reform movements in Britain and the German states were influenced strongly by the different critiques of Judaism developed in the two contexts. Whereas in Germany scholars 'adopted philosophically oriented views of religion and theology that led them to propose radical reconstructions of the history of Israelite religion based upon source criticism', in Britain they accepted 'the general reliability of the history and religion of Israel' presented in the Hebrew Bible.[73] In Britain it was the evangelical bibliocentric attack on Judaism that was loudest and most persistent before 1860.

If the changes in early Victorian Judaism reflected the influence of evangelicalism, rather than the Jewish reforms in Germany, it remains for us to offer some suggestion of how that influence worked. Endelman, rejecting the view that English Reform Judaism was simply a pale reflection of continental developments, has argued that Anglo-Jewry's concern with 'decorum' was a reflection of the desire of wealthy Jews to conform to 'English' or 'Anglican' norms of conduct and bibliocentric religion. The reforming movement, he argues, stemmed from a drive for social acceptance which, moreover, was achieved with relative ease. This is an interpretation which emphasises choice to the exclusion of any pressure which privileged some options above others. It is a history of change with its politics

72. *Ibid*, 28 November 1845, p. 27, for Marks' sermon on Israel's restoration.
73. J. Rogerson, *Old Testament Criticism in the Nineteenth Century: England and Germany* (London, 1984), pp. 9, 219. On the influence of Protestant values in Germany see A. Altmann, 'The New Style of Preaching in Nineteenth-Century Germany', in Altmann, ed., *Studies in Nineteenth-Century German Intellectual History* (Cambridge, Mass., 1964), pp. 65–116; M. Meyer, 'Christian Influence in Early German Reform Judaism', in C. Berlin, ed., *Jewish Bibliography, History and Literature* (New York, NY, 1971), pp. 289–304.

left out and fits well with the accepted, benign view of Jewish integration in England.[74] But at the very least we can see that it is based on
two misconceptions. First, the reformers' obsession with 'decorum'
has been treated as if it were simply a question of manners – hence
of social acceptance – but this is to miss many of its early Victorian
resonances. Manners, embarrassing and acceptable, were seen to
carry the freight of ghetto tradition and emancipated modernity.
These connections followed from the association of traditional
Judaism with a system of ritual and rabbinism which not only made
it *appear* incongruous but which also stunted the development of a
vital and personal religion. Second, the view that English or even
Anglican religiosity offered a single model to which Jews might try to
make Judaism approximate turns a blind eye to the differences
which divided the Church of England internally and separated
it from Protestant nonconformity and Roman Catholicism. Had
nakedly social considerations been uppermost for Jews, with shots
flying in so many directions, it would have been difficult to know
which camouflage to adopt.

The theological distinctions within the Church of England are significant because it was the evangelicals alone who could be described
as 'bibliocentric'. But it was the evangelicals also who were active
conversionists – it was they who financed and otherwise supported
the London Society for the Promotion of Christianity among the
Jews – and it was they who published elaborate critiques of contemporary Jewish practice on bibliocentric principles. In this light, if
Jewish reform was, indeed, an attempt to render the religion more
'bibliocentric', the drive for acceptability which this represented was
more defensive and intellectually more elaborate than has been
acknowledged. The arguments generated by the reform tendency
represented an attempt to revise Judaism in the face of criticism
from inside and outside of Jewry which counterposed degenerate
'rabbinism' to a religion of the 'spirit'. Internal reform was a
response to criticism from the non-Jewish world. The dominant
answer to the charges of 'rabbinism' was to fall back on the Bible and
to cleanse the synagogue of those elements which contradicted not
only the norms of Victorian decorousness but which also offered the
impression that Jews attended synagogue for any purpose other than
prayer and spiritual elevation.

74. Endelman, 'The Englishness of Jewish Modernity', pp. 231–8; see too D.
Englander, 'Anglicized not Anglican: Jews and Judaism in Victorian Britain',
in G. Parsons ed., *Religion in Victorian Britain*, vol. i (Manchester, 1988), p. 258.

Jewish authority, the Jewish religion and Jewish nationality

The reform controversy threw into question the practice of authority within the Jewish community. The conflict between on one side the JBD and the Chief Rabbi, and, on the other, the West London Synagogue, presented in sharp relief the question of whether a Jewish community which existed solely on a voluntary basis should create an effective centralised structure of communal and ecclesiastical authority.[75] A united Jewish community depended on the existence of institutions which could plausibly claim to represent it and were able to marginalise challenges to that position. But while the threat of religious reform pushed in one direction the desire for political emancipation pulled in another. The claims of rabbinical law and its enforcement could undermine the campaign for political equality. Even in their capacities as Jews, members of the Anglo-Jewish elite were subject to conflicting claims and interests.

As we have seen, within the ranks of orthodoxy, reformers used similar arguments to those called upon by leaders of the West London Synagogue. Moreover, the changes undertaken within orthodoxy took much of the ground away from the new congregation. Reforms similar to those initiated at West London were introduced, with the exception of the two which contradicted the oral law. These changes help account for the fact that in Britain an institutionally distinct Reform Judaism was a feeble affair.[76] The breakaway in London was followed in the next three decades by the formation of only two other Reform congregations in Britain, in Manchester in 1856 and Bradford in 1873. The force of the independent movement cannot account for the hostility of the institutional response to it. Yet the official response to the new

75. But although founded upon voluntarism, the potency of communal authority greatly depended upon the state. The pre-eminent position of the Jewish Board of Deputies and the Chief Rabbi were successfully established in this period, not least through the powers granted by the 1836 Marriage Act. Threats to those positions were successfully marginalised and contained, but not to the extent that some had hoped. One reason was that the government would not allow itself to be used as a tool of the Jewish authorities. In 1856 an Act of Parliament which enabled a group of twenty householders to appoint a marriage secretary allowed the West London Synagogue to circumvent the opposition of the Board. Fourteen years later, the Home Secretary balked at writing the powers of the Chief Rabbi into the Act of Parliament creating the United Synagogue: Lipman, *Social History of the Jews in England*, p. 64.

76. The creation of two branch synagogues in the West End of London by the Great Synagogue and Bevis Marks in 1853 and 1855 removed some of the pragmatic reasons which may otherwise have driven Jews away from orthodoxy.

congregation was severe. In January 1841 a *herem* – a ban – was placed on the new congregation and its members. The following month this was reinforced by the JBD's refusal to certify Marks as a secretary fit to register Jewish marriages. Under the Chief Rabbinate of Nathan Adler, for a time the full extent of the *herem* was imposed, including a prohibition on marriages between members of the two congregations.[77]

This uncompromising reaction may have been stimulated by the more radical developments in religious reform among German Jews as well as the actions of the West London Synagogue. Additionally, there was the possibility that the new synagogue would present itself as a rival and more radical political representative of Jewish interests.[78] But what fundamentally was at stake was the status of rabbinical authority within Anglo-Jewry. This was made clear in 1842 in the response of the Anglo-Jewish ecclesiastical authorities, led by Rabbi Solomon Hirschell, whose manifesto to the Jewish public reminded them of their claim that 'whoso rejecteth the authority of the oral law, opposeth thereby the holy law handed down to us on Mount Sinai, by Moses the servant of the Lord'.[79] Adler, when he became Chief Rabbi, insisted no less adamantly on the authority of the oral law. 'If human laws required interpretation, how much more must divine law,' he claimed when preaching at the Hambro Synagogue during Passover 1847.[80] The lay leadership of Anglo-Jewry supported Adler. Indeed, without undermining the claim of the JBD to represent Anglo-Jewry it was bound to do so. Without the authority of the rabbinate over the synagogues, uniting their congregations within a single religious community, the authority of the lay leaders would have had no foundation. As a result, among the more reform-minded orthodox congregations there was a contradiction between their opposition to 'rabbinism' and their support for rabbinical authority. The *herem* was not accepted universally by orthodox congregations who, nevertheless, did not want to repudiate the communal and religious establishment.[81]

A more urgent source of contradiction was that rabbinical author-

77. Wolf, 'The Queen's Jewry', pp. 323–7. In 1849 the ban was moderated so that it would apply to the West London congregation but not to its individual members.

78. Liberles, 'The Origins of the Jewish Reform Movement', pp. 135–50.

79. Roth, ed., *Anglo-Jewish Letters*, p. 287.

80. *JC*, 28 April 1848, p. 517. See too N. Adler, *The Jewish Faith: A Sermon Delivered in the Great Synagogue, Duke's Place* (London, 1848), pp. 12–13.

81. At the Western Synagogue there was no desire to alter 'sacred observances' but many members questioned the religious intolerance of the Chief Rabbi. Montefiore was informed that the *herem* could not be read there without internal division: Barnett, *The Western Synagogue*, pp. 180–2.

ity could be an embarrassment in relation to other goals pursued by English Jews, political equality above all. The role of rabbinical authority in producing a degree of Jewish unity had to be balanced against the way in which strict interpretation of rabbinical law might inhibit legal equality.[82] The emancipationists' pleas for religious toleration appeared incongruous when set alongside the Chief Rabbi's declaration of the *herem*. The leaders of the West London Synagogue seized on this and issued the following appeal:

> We ask whether you can continue, as boldly as you have heretofore done, to claim from your fellow citizens an exemption from tyrannical attempts upon your conscience, whilst you concur in, or calmly permit, endeavours of a similar character towards a minority of your co-religionists, brethren in country, in race and in faith?[83]

In early 1846, when the Chief Rabbi imposed a religious test before permitting a religious ceremony between an applicant and a member of the West London Synagogue, he was accused, in an obvious reference to the emancipation controversy, of imposing an act of abjuration.[84]

This argument came to a head in 1853 when supporters of the West London Synagogue made the *herem* an issue in the elections to the JBD and succeeded in having four of their number elected. A decision had to be taken on whether these representatives were eligible to take their seats: whether members outside of orthodoxy would be recognised at the Board notwithstanding the *herem*. The controversy was a parallel to, or a parody of, the argument over the admission of Jews of Parliament: the question was whether or not a body could impose religious tests on representatives elected to it or whether the electors' decision was paramount.

The first meeting of the Board following the elections broke up, abandoned by its president, Moses Montefiore, when 'a scene of the most undescribable uproar' was created by the four trying to take their seats.[85] At the next meeting on 18 August 1853, Louis Cohen proposed the Board should exclude members of a place of worship 'which does not conform in religious matters to the ecclesiastical authorities'. He was opposed by the leading emancipationists in the communal elite, including Lionel de Rothschild and David Salomons. Salomons, echoing the debate over the Jews' entry to Parliament, stood by the right of an elected deputy to his seat

82. On this see I. Finestein, 'An Aspect of Jews and English Marriage Law during the Emancipation', *Jewish Journal of Sociology*, June 1965, pp. 3–22.
83. *JC*, 20 February 1846, p. 83.
84. *Ibid*, 23 January 1846, p. 66.
85. *Ibid*, 2 September 1853, pp. 380–1.

regardless of his opinions and the latter, likewise, argued 'it mattered not to what [sic] synagogue he belonged, but having been elected he was entitled to his seat'. Rothschild accused the conservatives of 'popery'. In enquiring into the religious opinions of an elected deputy their proposal was 'inquisitorial'.[86] At a later meeting he was more explicit: 'He had every respect for the ecclesiastical authorities, but he was not going to be led by them as by a Catholic priest. They might be, and no doubt were, very learned men but they had no right to inquire of him whether he kept one day or two days of the festivals'.[87] The issue was settled at a meeting of the Board on 23 November. The conservatives had grown militant and refused to recognise the four deputies as members of the same faith as themselves: the West London Synagogue 'had formed a religion which was quite contrary to the customs of Israel'.[88] When the vote was taken it was indecisive: twenty-three on each side. Moses Montefiore's casting vote went to the exclusionists. He had satisfied himself that the Board was entitled to ensure that men nominated by their synagogues possessed the necessary qualifications to take their places. As if this formulation was not a sufficient parallel to the emancipation debate, the Queen's Council whose opinion Montefiore sought was the Burkean opponent of Jewish emancipation, Sir Frederick Thesiger.

The meeting was significant not only for its outcome but also for the way it revealed a division which supplemented the conflict between those who placed the greatest emphasis on political emancipation or on communal authority: one between religious orthodoxy and Jewish nationality. One deputy, H.T. Louis, urging conciliation, warned the conservatives: 'You will inflict a wound on our people that will take an age to heal, in this bitter unnatural strife. You will have Jew against Jew, synagogue against synagogue. But united and at peace, what good can we not achieve, not alone to our people here but to our race throughout the world.'[89] For some Jews, then, the idea of communal unity was not only an expression of rabbinical authority and religious orthodoxy. It also reflected the sense in which many Jews in England continued to regard themselves as part of a Jewish nation as well as the English nation. It was a sense of a common history, located in their religion, which bound Jews across countries and continents in the present, as well as through time, and which joined them in their expectation of restoration, however distant in time that would be. This was reflected

86.   *Ibid*, 16 September 1853, pp. 400–2.
87.   *Ibid*, 9 December 1853, p. 80.
88.   *Ibid*, 9 December 1853, pp. 80–1.
89.   *Ibid*.

in the significance placed on Hebrew as the sacred language, the justifications of which focused on secular as well as religious meanings. Hebrew was 'our inheritance, our religion, our nationality... the witness of our brightest glory as of our deepest shame, it is indissolubly bound up with our very existence'.[90] In England none of the reformers considered replacing Hebrew with the vernacular, just as they did not contemplate erasing from their prayers the hope for restoration. The significance of Hebrew in the present was expressed most clearly by the *Jewish Chronicle*.

> The whole house of Israel calls to his God in *one* language and *one* sense, as if it were the voice of *one* person. In the sacred halls of worship we give each other a sign of recognition that we are of *one* Faith, *one* Spirit, *one* Hope, children of *one* Father. The national sounds carry us irresistibly back to our native home and petty differences vanish in fervent longing for that native home.[91]

Of course, what was meant by Jewish nationality has to be reconstructed historically, just as the same must be done to elucidate the contemporary meanings of the English 'nation' or 'patriotism'. With the exception of a minority of Jews who opposed emancipation on the ground that it was incompatible with the prayer for the coming of the Messiah and the restoration of Israel, English Jews professed to find no conflict between their nationality as Jews and their claims for political equality. In an editorial on 'the nationality of the Jews', the *Jewish Chronicle* explained that by this it referred to 'our Jewish spiritual nationality'.

> There is a nationality in our adherence to the faith of our fathers . . . there is a nationality in the benign feeling of charity which animates the greater part of our co-religionists; and there is lastly, a nationality in our strict observance of a code of morals which makes it incumbent upon us to contribute, as much as it is in our power, to the welfare and happiness of our fellow-men.[92]

In the last chapter it was seen how the idea of the nation in Britain in the 1840s–'50s was principally a political construct. It was centred on a relation between the individual and the state that was taken to guarantee a range of indigenous freedoms, rather than upon the people themselves and their culture. The demands for conformity in these circumstances were narrow. It was this culturally attenuated construction of the nation that provided a space in which the ideal

90. *Ibid*, 5 December 1851, p. 65.
91. *Ibid*.
92. *Ibid*, 4 August 1848, p. 625.

of 'spiritual nationality' could flourish, and even the religious reformers did not seek to erase the signs of the Jews' 'spiritual nationality'. But, on the other side, the march of reform reflected the force
of a critique of traditional Judaism which received its most forceful
expression, but not its only one, among evangelical conversionists.
English Protestantism and the philo-Semitic strain within it have
been widely thought of as an element which encouraged the Jews'
integration.[93] At the very least, we must recognise that these same
aspects of Protestantism were deeply ambivalent. In a sense, conversionists venerated Jews but they set the terms of a debate which
set normative Judaism decisively on the defensive. The pattern of
reform in Britain, both in and out of orthodoxy, developed from the
constellation of pressures on English Jews and the opportunities
open to them. In general, the path of religious and cultural change
among Jews in England reflected the particular inflection of pressures on Jews, not their absence.

Religious change within early Victorian Anglo-Jewry has been
presented as one reflection of the desire of wealthy Jews for social
acceptance. In this way the history of cultural change has been
divorced, first from the need to legitimise the persistence of Judaism
in the face of a Christian state and society in which the religion was
subject to a swingeing critique and, second, from the articulation of
communal authority. By giving due weight to conflicts between Jews
and Gentiles as well as those within Jewry, it has been possible to
indicate the extent to which Jewish interests were fragmented and
contested. The claims of religious orthodoxy, communal authority,
political emancipation and Jewish nationality each generated their
own and, at times, incompatible imperatives.

93. For example, T. Endelman, *The Jews of Georgian England, 1714–1830* (Philadelphia PA, 1979), pp. 50–85.

Chapter 3
Dimensions of Difference

The ambiguities of emancipation

Any analysis of Jewish integration in English society must take account of aversion to the Jews, hostility to them, and those moments when such antipathy had a political significance. By the late 1870s groups which had once supported Jewish equality were, at best, divided on the Jewish issue. In these years it was not Conservative peers, prelates and backwoodsmen who were the propagators of a broadly disseminated critique of the Jews. In Chapter Four I examine the 'Judaeophobia' of the years 1876–80. In the present chapter, as a preparation, I draw out the ambiguities inherent within Jewish emancipation and specify the influences in mid-Victorian society and culture which gathered and burst into signicance in 1876. Taken together, these two chapters present an analysis and reassessment of attitudes to Jews and Judaism in mid-Victorian political culture.

There were three main sources of instability inherent within Jewish emancipation. First, the political context which governed the debate on Jewish integration was dynamic. The Parliamentary Oaths Act of 1866 did not announce a conclusion to the politics of Jewish integration but the moment at which it entered a new phase. As the Jewish question died within one context it re-emerged in another marked by the extension of the franchise in 1867. Captured by Disraeli, the extension of the franchise was more extensive than would have been the case under Gladstone's superintendence. The 1867 Reform Act increased the size of the electorate by 89 per cent.

I have argued that Jews were granted political rights not only as men but as Englishmen. Jews were not joining a political society comprised of atomised individuals but a positive community – the nation. The liberalism for which parliamentary reform signalled a great advance, and the entry of Jews to Parliament a minor but significant step forward, was not only the individualism whose next demand was the secret ballot, it expressed also an attempt to re-define the national community in terms of its citizenry as well as the country's institutions. In the new situation, marked by the agitation for and achievement of a second Reform Act, the liberal ideology of the nation acquired new dimensions.

The Liberal and radical supporters of Jewish emancipation had located the idea of the nation in a set of liberties guaranteed to the individual and wrung from an oppressive monarchy. They had given some attention to the basis in civil society of these liberties; whether this was conceived to have been Christianity, as Russell claimed, or the 'patriotism' discussed by Macaulay. But for some Liberal intellectuals the prospect of the wider franchise led to a greater emphasis on these historical and cultural bonds of national-ity which underpinned the relationship between the rulers and the people.

The connections between representative government and a wider franchise and nationality had been elaborated by John Stuart Mill in his *Considerations on Representative Government*, published in 1861. According to Mill the common sympathies of nationality are gener-ated by race and descent, language and religion, geographical limits and, above all, 'the possession of a national history and consequent community of recollections'.[1] 'Where the sentiment of nationality exists in any force, there is a *prima facie* case for uniting all the members of the nationality under the same government, and a government to set themselves apart. This is merely saying that the question of government ought to be decided by the governed'.[2] But Mill also believed also that representative institutions were almost impossible to maintain in a country composed of different nationali-ties. In these cases 'without fellow-feeling . . . the united public opinion, necessary to the working of representative government cannot exist'. The solution to diversity was for the inferior to be absorbed by the more advanced. Mill's reflections indicate the way in which the extension of representative government was accom-panied by an idea of the nation which was more far-reaching cultur-ally and antipathetic to cultural diversity.[3]

The leading mid-nineteenth-century historians of medieval Eng-land also demonstrate this turn. John Burrow has found in the work of E.A. Freeman, William Stubbs and J.R. Green 'the patriotic and

---

1. J.S. Mill, *Considerations on Representative Government* (London, 1861), p. 287.
2. *Ibid*, p. 289.
3. *Ibid*, pp. 289–90.

populist impulse to identify the nation and its institutions as the collective subject of English history, which made the new historiography of early medieval times an extension of, filling out and democratising, older Whig notions of continuity'.[4] It was an approach which distinguished these historians from earlier Whig practitioners such as Macaulay and also from the example of Ranke in Germany. Green told Freeman, 'Now Ranke looks fairly enough, for one who is not an Englishman, and has done good in bringing out the foreign and foreign-policy side of things; but for one who is an Englishman and sees from his very boyhood things in a light which Ranke could not see them, the Ranke point of view is a very inadequate and miserable one' – the reason being that it was 'national feeling' which produced the 'impulses' making history.[5]

This connection of the nation to civil society can also be seen in the writing of another historian, Goldwin Smith, who was to become a prominent and persistent critic of the Jews. In his analysis of 'The Experience of the American Constitution', which he wrote in 1866 for *Essays on Reform*, he claimed 'a step, though but a step, has been made towards the realisation of that ideal community, ordered and bound together by affection instead of force'. The experience of the United States was an important model for those who contemplated the effects of reform in Britain. Smith reported that in the United States 'instead of individual greatness, you have the greatness of a nation; instead of a king and his subjects, you have a community; instead of loyalty, patriotism and attachment to the common good'.[6]

These responses to the reform agitation and the 1867 Act held dangers for Jews. If the nation was identified with its populace and its national feeling, then demands for conformity might extend beyond the Jews' incapacity to swear an oath 'upon the true faith of a Christian' and touch more widely on their ability to identify with the texture and traditions of national life. For members of the liberal intelligentsia such as Goldwin Smith and Bernard Cracroft the components of patriotism broadened to encompass the ties of social and cultural intercourse. Here for example is Cracroft on aristocratic privilege and want of patriotism: 'They have a common freemasonry of blood, a common education, common pursuits, common ideas, a common dialect, a common religion. . . .'[7] There was a potential for

4. J.W. Burrow, *A Liberal Descent* (Cambridge, 1981), pp. 227, 287.
5. See the letters he sent to E.A. Freeman on 30 August 1878 and 20 November 1878 and published in the L. Stephen ed., *Letters of J.R. Green* (London, 1901), pp. 476–7.
6. Goldwin Smith, 'The Experience of the American Constitution,' in *Essays on Reform* (London, 1867), pp. 218, 238.
7. B. Cracroft, 'Analysis of the House of Commons in 1867', in *Idem, Essays Political and Miscellaneous*, vol. i (London, 1868), p. 100.

the critique of the aristocracy as a separate caste within the state, tending to its own interests and not to the public good, to be applied to the Jews. Indeed, by the late 1870s Goldwin Smith was asking the question 'Can Jews be Patriots?'[8]

The Reform Act, moreover, strengthened a challenge to Anglo-Jewry from another direction. It doubled the number of non-conformist MPs.[9] This newly empowered force demanded that state policy should be moralised and regenerated by militant noncon-formity; by a combination of Protestantism and the people.[10] In the 1840s an exclusivist Christian politics was located chiefly among Conservatives expounding an hierarchical interpretation of political authority and of the nation. Over the next two decades, as non-conformists sought to infuse policy with a mix of populist Christian-ity and constitutional radicalism, a different version of national identity was expressed by the most powerful element within popular Liberal politics. By the late 1870s some nonconformist divines were attributing Disraeli's immoral and un-Christian statecraft to his Jewish origin. The idea of the nation to which the Jews had been admitted was dynamic and this was one reason why Jewish emancipa-tion did not bring the problem of Jewish integration to a close.

The second source of instability in Jewish emancipation was that support for the Jews' equality did not require a positive view of the Jewish minority and this also contributed to the instability of emancipation. It was perfectly compatible, for instance, with a stereotype of the Jew as usurious and clannish. In many cases, sup-port for the Jews was contingent and depended upon the particular political question at issue. If the issue changed then so too might the appearance of the Jewish question. As we have seen, a crucial point in Macaulay's argument supporting Jewish emancipation was that 'property is power' and that since the Jews already possessed the substance of power it was absurd to refuse them its garb. In delineat-ing the realities of the Jews' power Macaulay drew on an image of the Jew as financier and source of covert influence which, had it come from an opponent of Jewish emancipation, many historians would have categorised as anti-Semitic.

> The Jew may govern the money market, and the money market may govern the world. The minister may be in doubt to his scheme of finance till he has been closeted with a Jew. A congress of sovereigns may be forced to summon the Jew to their assistance. The scrawl of the Jew on the back of a piece of paper may be worth more than the royal word of three kings or

8. G. Smith, 'Can Jews be Patriots?', *Nineteenth Century*, May 1878, pp. 875–97.
9. Parry, *Democracy and Religion: Gladstone and the Liberal Party, 1867–75* (Cambridge, 1986), p. 39.
10. *Ibid*, p. 28.

the national faith of three new American republics. But that he should put Right Honourable before his name would be the greatest of national calamities.[11]

The article Macaulay wrote on Jewish disabilities in the *Edinburgh Review* was produced in response to a request for assistance by some Jews. 'I would gladly serve a cause so good,' he wrote to the editor.[12] Nevertheless, the Jews' champion was uncomfortable if kept too long in company with his protégés. Through his membership of the Anti-Slavery Society, Macaulay knew I.L. Goldsmid. In June 1831 he was invited to a ball at the Goldsmids'. The experience proved disagreeable. He wrote to his sister: 'the company was not such as we exclusives think quite the thing. There was a little too much St Mary Axe about it – Jewesses by dozens and Jews by scores.' He made his excuses but once home he could not sleep: 'the sound of fiddles was in mine ears, and gaudy dresses, and black hair, and Jewish noses were fluctuating up and down before mine eyes'.[13] What Macaulay thought of the Jews depended on the context and the question.

The *Weekly Dispatch*, despite its enthusiastic support for Jewish emancipation, at the same time headed court reports with titles such as 'More Jew Scoundrels – Inciting A Youth To Rob His Employer.' The implication, of course, was that there was a connection between the crime and the perpetrator's identity as a Jew. Jews protested that Christian miscreants were not pointed out in the same way. It might be suggested that we are presented in these examples with a distinction between political and social prejudice. But what was defined as political was not fixed. What one day may have been a social question may have appeared in altogether a more political light on another. An extension of what was politically significant undermined the stability of Jewish emancipation in the 1860s and '70s. In this respect, a significant dichotomy lay between what some emancipationists thought of Jews as victims of Anglican and aristocratic privilege on one side, and as actors within the economy, on the other.[14] The image of the Jew as financier could lead radicals into political opposition to Jewish influence, as *Reynold's Newspaper* illustrates in its commentary on Salomons' attempt to enter the Commons.

11. I. Abrahams and S. Levy, eds., *Macaulay on Jewish Disabilities* (Edinburgh, 1910), pp. 25–6.
12. T. Pinney, ed., *The Letters of Thomas Babington Macaulay*, vol. i (Cambridge, 1974), pp. 262, 311.
13. *Ibid*, vol. ii, pp. 34–6.
14. See for example F.D. Maurice, 'Thoughts on Jewish Disabilities', *Fraser's Magazine*, November 1847, p. 624.

We should like to see such men excluded by the people; not on the grounds of religious faith, or on account of their refusal to take a trumpery oath, which, in fact, means nothing; but simply because we believe the trading system of Moses and Co. is more than sufficiently represented already by Christians in the House of Commons. . . . We know that the Peers – the only obstacle to the passing of a tolerant measure for emancipating the Hebrew race – can only be turned from their obstinacy by a powerful and popular expression of public opinion. This could not be arrived at for the behoof of an Austrian loan-monger or a partner in the monstrous sweating establishment of Moses and Co.[15]

In its tendency to reduce the historical question to one of whether an individual was for or against the Jews, a contrast between 'tolera-tion' and 'anti-Semitism' allows no space for more complex sets of attitudes. The opinions of some of the Jews' best-known supporters had more than one dimension.

Although the case for the Jews' emancipation had been argued in terms of a discussion of their status as a religious minority it was also true that perceptions of Jews went beyond this definition. Here was a third cause of ambiguity in the post-emancipation years. The pieties of the emancipation argument were contradicted by everyday perceptions of what sort of a minority the Jews were. Jews were widely identified, and identified themselves, as something more than a just a religious minority. Sometimes, the terminology of race was used to describe and explain this.

Confusion over the compass of Jewish identity surfaced widely in the 1850s and '60s: in Charles Dickens' portrait of Fagin, for example. The novelist wrote to a Jewish correspondent explaining he had not intended to slight Judaism. 'Fagin . . . is called "the Jew" not because of his religion but because of his race. . . . I make men-tion of Fagin as the Jew because he is one of the Jewish people and because it conveys that kind of idea of him which I should give my readers of a Chinaman by calling him Chinese.'[16]

Yet the supporters of Jewish emancipation claimed recurrently that Jews were Englishmen. In 1853 Sidney Herbert wondered 'if a man professing the Jewish creed is not an Englishman, to what country does he belong?' He addressed the Tory anti-emancipation-ists: 'you exclude him, you say, on account of his nationality, his origin and his race; but if that be true, and if you say there is an inherent nationality about the Jews – about his race and about his

15. See too *The Examiner* on Rothschild's loans to Austria, cited in the *JC*, 11 September 1852, p. 401.
16. C. Roth, ed., *Anglo-Jewish Letters, 1158–1917* (London, 1938), p. 306.

origin why do you not exclude a converted Jew?'[17] But Herbert's query could not have been innocent of Disraeli's position as leader of the Conservative Party in the House of Commons. It was an attempt to embarrass the Tories. Disraeli was, of course, a converted Jew, and in 1848 he had spoken in favour of admitting Jews to Parliament. Herbert's jibe was ambiguous and played on the perception that Disraeli was, indeed, in some sense, still a Jew, even though the logic of his own argument would have denied this. But was Disraeli's Jewish parentage of any significance or had his baptism, at the age of thirteen, cleansed him of its mark? Disraeli's own writings had emphasised the historical significance of race. His apologia for the 'Jewish race' in *Tancred*, *Sidonia* and his memoir of Lord George Bentinck, had encouraged the view that bonds between Jews far exceeded the ties between Christian dissenters. No race elevated and ennobled Europe so much as the Jews, Disraeli wrote in 1852, and their endurance despite persecution served to prove 'that a superior race shall never be destroyed or absorbed by an inferior'.[18]

As the Jews' emancipation made clear, confusion over what a Jew was did not present an insurmountable barrier to their political equality. But, in the face of a political argument which claimed that Jews were just another group of religious nonconformists, it led to ambiguity and controversy. In the third quarter of the century, the spectacular commercial and social success of wealthy Jews prompted some observers to dwell upon the origins and causes of what was distinctively Jewish about the English Jews. Ideas concerning race offered them the tools with which to do so.

The ascendancy of the Jews

Jews were disproportionately well represented among the nation's very wealthy. Between 1870–9 they accounted for 14 per cent of all British non-landed millionaires.[19] With few exceptions these great fortunes were accumulated in finance: from the closely linked activities of merchant banking and stock exchange dealing. In the third quarter of the century the City of London provided the backing to lay down railways, raise buildings and prop up governments on every continent. It was the clearing house for a massive outflow of

17.   *Hansard*, 3rd series, CXXV, 102–3, 11 March 1853.
18.   B. Disraeli, *Lord George Bentinck: A Political Biography* (London, 1852), pp. 492, 495; see too P. Smith, 'Disraeli's Politics', *Transactions of the Royal Historical Society*, 1987, pp. 83–5.
19.   W.D. Rubinstein, 'Jews among Top British Wealth Holders, 1857–1969', *Jewish Social Studies*, January 1972, pp. 73–84.

capital. The average net outflow of British savings into overseas assets tripled in the 1850s, it doubled in the 1860s, and from the 1870s to the First World War the average doubled again. No nation has ever devoted so great a proportion of its national income to capital formation abroad.[20] Much of this investment went into social overheads; massive projects in transport and communications generally undertaken by governments or by joint-stock companies whose borrowings were guaranteed by governments. Between 1860–79, over 150 government loans were raised in London to a nominal value of over £720 million.[21]

The firm of N.M. Rothschild and Sons was the most spectacular example not only of Jewish eminence in the City but of the City's first place in international finance. Between 1818–32 it was solely responsible for 38 per cent of the value of loans to foreign governments contracted in London and had a share in a further 12 per cent.[22] In 1845 they were acknowledged as 'decidedly the greatest people on the 'Change'.[23] Subsequently the market became more competitive and the leading firm more conservative. Between 1860–76 over 50 houses issued more than £700 million in loans to foreign governments. But even in these years Rothschilds were sole agents for loans of £110 million and joint agents for a further £130 million.[24]

Below the Rothschilds in importance in the market, in wealth prestige and notoriety were other prominent Jewish firms which entered the London market in the third quarter of the century. Stern Brothers and Bischoffsheim and Goldschmidt came to public notice floating government loans and company promotions in the 1860s.[25] Other Jewish firms which established themselves in London

20. M. Edelstein, *Overseas Investment in the Age of High Imperialism* (London, 1982), pp. 3, 18, 20; P.L. Cottrell, *British Overseas Investment in the Nineteenth Century* (London, 1975), p. 27; L. Davis and R.A. Huttenback, *Mammon and the Pursuit of Empire, 1860–1912* (Cambridge, 1986), pp. 37–8.
21. Some of this was raised at a discount, some took savings from overseas, but British investors contributed £320 million. These figures exclude the £160 million raised for the Indian governments and for railway companies, nor does it include £230 million raised for companies operating abroad: E.V. Morgan and W.A. Thomas, *The Stock Exchange; its History and Functions* (London, 1962), p. 88.
22. Barings as well as Rothschilds were 'market leaders' in nineteenth-century merchant banking but Rothschilds were 'well ahead of their rivals throughout this period': S.D. Chapman, *The Rise of Merchant Banking* (London, 1984), p. 17.
23. Evans, *The City; or the Physiology of London Business* (London, 1845), pp. 104, 186.
24. R. Davis, *The English Rothschilds* (Durham, NC, 1983), pp. 30–40.
25. Chapman, *The Rise of Merchant Banking*, p. 45; P. Emden, *Money Powers of Europe in the Nineteenth and Twentieth Centuries* (London, 1937), p. 259.

were Speyers in 1861, Erlangers in 1870 and Lazard Brothers in 1876–7, while Seligman Brothers arrived via the United States, during the American Civil War. Additionally, there were City firms of Anglo-Jewish origin, whose leading members were more likely to take part in Anglo-Jewish communal government – Louis Cohen and Sons, Raphael Raphael, and Samuel Montagu and Co. These firms concentrated on business of a different type. The latter two were specialists in arbitrage. Montagu's 'exposition of a situation which might involve not only "triangular" but even "quadrangular" arbitrage operations was an intellectual treat', his obituarist in *The Times* recorded.[26] Cohen and Raphael had begun their businesses as stockbrokers but movement between this secondary market and the primary market of banking was not unusual. After his death Louis Cohen was remembered as 'unquestionably one of the shrewdest and boldest operators who ever opened a jobbing book. . . . He possessed that instinctive grasp of men and markets which is so characteristic of the Jewish financier.'[27]

Firms were connected by ties of marriage as well as business; between the Rothschilds and Cohens and the Cohens and Montagus, for example.[28] This cousinhood represented the pinnacle of Jewish commercial achievement but its numbers were supplemented by a growing contingent who prospered less dramatically in the City. The Stock Exchange expanded rapidly as its business boomed and Jews were disproportionately numerous among its growing membership. In mid-century there were 864 members of the Stock Exchange; by 1877 the figure had risen to 2,000, 5 per cent of whom where Jews.[29]

It was members of the metropolitan elite who invested in imperial and overseas securities in the late nineteenth century.[30] The connections brought a minority of Jews to social prominence. Writing under the pseudonym of 'A foreign resident', T.H.S. Escott, the editor of the *Fortnightly Review*, surveyed society in London. It was composed of 'a chaotic congerie of sets', but he found that among the 'smart' set 'the Israelites are the Lords paramount'. More gener-

26. Cited in J. Camplin, *The Rise of the Plutocrats* (London, 1978), p. 65.
27. G.D. Ingall and G. Withers, *The Stock Exchange* (London, 1904), p. 37.
28. See Y. Cassis, *Les Banquiers de la City à l'Époque Edouardienne* (Geneva, 1984), pp. 256–63.
29. Morgan and Thomas, *The Stock Exchange*, p. 140; Pollins, *Economic History of the Jews in England* (London, 1982), p. 108.
30. Davis and Huttenback, *Mammon and the Pursuit of Empire*, pp. 211–16. The activities of the Jewish bankers and brokers thus aligned them with that 'amalgam of rentier money, service employments and the remnants of landed society which came together to form the new upper class after 1850': P.J. Cain and A.G. Hopkins, 'Gentlemanly Capitalism and British Expansion Overseas II: New Imperialism, 1850–1945', *Economic History Review*, February 1987, p. 2.

ally, he found, 'English society once ruled by an aristocracy is now dominated by a plutocracy. And this plutocracy is to a large extent Hebraic in its composition. There is no phenomenon more noticeable in society than the ascendancy of the Jews.' The development reflected both the power of money and the influence of the Prince of Wales who, Escott wrote, 'regards the best class of Jews with conspicuous favour'.[31] Escott published his analysis in 1885, but the fabulous wealth of a few Jews, the Rothschilds above all others, their presence at fashionable Mayfair parties and in the Prince of Wales' circle, was already apparent in the 1870s.[32]

Henry Labouchere's newspaper *The Truth* found the Jews' commercial and social visibility in mid-Victorian London, and the ways in which their qualities as Jews informed this prominence, hard to reconcile with a definition of them as a religious minority only. It took the opportunity afforded by the marriage of Hannah de Rothschild to Lord Rosebery to ponder and answer the question, 'When it is incidentally said of a Jew that he is a Jew, what is meant?'

> They are essentially speculative; their fondness for making money is only equalled by their love of spending it, and their mania to gamble with it. . . . Left entirely to himself the Jew would succumb to the Anglo-Saxon. He holds his own, and elbows the Anglo-Saxon out of his way, by the support, which he finds in the corporate cohesion that distinguishes his race.[33]

Issuing houses, stockbrokers and jobbers possessed a repertoire of skills to stimulate demand for securities in a market increasingly congested with stock.[34] On occasions a fraudulent prospectus was issued. This was the case, for example, when Bischoffsheim and Goldschmidt encouraged the public to invest in a £15 million loan to construct a 'ship railway' in Honduras. The loan failed and the ensuing scandal led to an investigation by a House of Commons Select Committee into the issue of foreign loans. The Committee singled out the finance house for special criticism, suggesting 'a remedy ought to be found in the tribunals of the country'.[35] *The Economist* prescribed culture to tame the 'intense vitality and recklessness' of the commercial man which 'quite as much as any mere

31. A foreign resident [T.H.S. Escott], *Society in London* (London, 1885), pp. 86–7.
32. P. Magnus, *King Edward the Seventh* (London, 1964), p. 106; R. Davis, *The English Rothschilds*, pp. 113–15; R.F. Foster, *Lord Randolph Churchill; a Political Life* (Oxford, 1981), p. 30.
33. *The Truth*, 21 March 1878, p. 375.
34. *The Economist*, 23 March 1875, p. 362.
35. L. Jenks, *The Migration of British Capital to 1875* (London, 1963), p. 292.

thirst for wealth, leads him into operations extending beyond the scope of his legitimate means'.[36] The faults of the Jewish financier could be imputed from this humanist critique of commercial life. In 1879 George Eliot deprecated 'the predominance of wealth-acquiring immigrants whose appreciation of our political and social life must often be as approximate or as erroneous as their delivery of our language'.[37] But this is a theme rightly more often associated with Anthony Trollope. Acquisitive, socially ambitious Jews who inevitably fail as 'gentlemen' recur in his novels: Joseph Emilius in *The Eustace Diamonds* and *Phineas Redux*, published in 1873 and 1874 respectively, and Ferdinand Lopez in *The Prime Minister*, which appeared in 1876.[38] Most famously, in *The Way We Live Now* Trollope satirised the deficiencies of character and culture which he saw in the power of commerce and the plutocracy. Their vices were concentrated in the figure of the monstrous swindler Melmotte, who may or may not have been Jewish, though his wife certainly was. Melmotte's supremacy reflected a sickness in society which extended beyond a few wealthy Jews but, nevertheless, their prominence was one symptom of decline in social and public life. Thus Samuel Cohenlupe MP was responsible for Melmotte's City affairs and ran off with company funds. Whatever doubts surrounded Melmotte's origins, those of Ezekial Breghert, Georgina Longstaffe's suitor, were plain. 'The man was absolutely a Jew' but also 'the leading member of the great financial firm of which he was the second partner'. Planning his honeymoon to follow an August wedding he exclaimed, 'Vy not my dear? ve would have our little holiday in Germany – at Vienna [sic]. I have business there, and know many friends.' Breghert's grotesque accent, his gross materialism and his ignorance of the rudiments of European political geography personified the transgressions of the Jewish *parvenu*.

Christianity without Judaism

Victorians confronted the problem of relating their 'civilisation' to others. The growth of anthropology reflected the interest in comparisons with contemporaneous civilisations.[39] Commentary on

---

36. *The Economist*, 19 June 1875, p. 722.
37. G. Eliot, 'The Latest Hep, Hep, Hep', *Impressions of Theophrastus Such* (3rd edn, Edinburgh 1879), p. 346.
38. On Trollope, I am indebted to Bryan Cheyette for allowing me to read and use material from the second chapter of his forthcoming study *Constructions of the 'Jew' in English Literature and Society: Racial Representations, 1875–1945* (Cambridge, 1993).
39. This theme is explored centrally in G. Stocking, *Victorian Anthropology* (Chicago, Ill., 1987).

Judaism took this discussion in another direction, exploring the relation between Victorian civilisation and its antecedants. These discussions bore on opinions of contemporary Jews as well as ancient Israelites.[40]

Historians have drawn attention to a recoil from evangelical doctrines in mid-Victorian England. They have highlighted the growing emphasis on the Incarnation rather than the Atonement in Anglican thought from the 1850s. Jesus, increasingly, was portrayed as 'noble exemplar rather than primarily as saviour'. The decades 1860–80 were 'the heyday of incarnational thought' as it was taken up first by Anglicans and then by nonconformists.[41] The decline of evangelicalism was connected to a decline in the religious authority of the Hebrew Bible. In a society in which sermons and religious tracts outsold novels this was particularly significant.[42]

The evangelical milieu had produced a sweeping critique of Jewish religious practice. But at the same time as they condemned 'rabbinism', conversionists venerated the Old Testament and retained a special sympathy for the Jews, in view of the role the chosen people had once played in the divine scheme and the part they were destined to play in the future. Evangelical theology placed a high value on the Hebrew Bible but, increasingly, the Judaism of the Old Testament was presented as a religion of prohibition and punishment, and the possession of a particular people, not a universal religion of love and moral liberty. Within the evangelical tradition the constant backsliding and disobedience of Israel had a universal significance: it illustrated the fallen nature of humankind which led inevitably to divine punishment. Theological liberals now portrayed this process in educational and progessive terms 'as the painful grasping of truths not easily learnt'.[43] It was a phase which had been superseded. In this new context, Judaism was still portrayed as a religion whose development had been arrested. But this was now a matter of essentials, not the outcome of rabbinical corruption. The nature of Judaism's deficiency also altered, in parallel to the changing emphasis of Christian belief. Though 'rabbinism'

40. On this see S.S. Prawer, *Israel at Vanity Fair: Jews and Judaism in the Writings of W.M. Thackeray* (Leiden, 1992), pp. 4–5.

41. B. Hilton, *The Age of Atonement The Influence of Evangelicalism on Social and Economic Thought, 1795–1865* (Oxford, 1988), pp. 298–303, 332–7; D. Bebbington, *Evangelicalism in Modern Britain: a History from the 1730s to the 1980s* (London, 1989), pp. 144–5.

42. On the intense and extensive religious life of Mid-Victorian Britain, see G. Parsons, 'Victorian Religion: Paradox and Variety', in *idem*, ed., *Religion in Victorian Britain*, vol. i (Manchester, 1988), pp. 4–7.

43. T. Rogerson, *Old Testament Criticism in the Nineteenth Century: England and Germany* (London, 1984), p. 212.

was still criticised, the religion was convicted less often of ritualism which barred Jews from a personal apprehension of religious truth. Instead, the focus of criticism became the attenuated and highly particularised, racial, understanding of God's love found in the Hebrew Bible. The tendency among educated Anglicans was now to stress the rupture between Judaism and Christianity.

Liberal theology in England pre-dated the 1850s–'60s. The first nineteenth-century High Church commentator to propose a fully developed theory of the progressive character of revelation, and hence of the inadequacy for Christians of revelation in the Hebrew Bible, was the Oxford scholar John Davison, whose *Discourses on Prophecy* was published in 1824.[44] In the 1830s–'40s, Liberal Anglican writers such as Thomas Arnold, H.H. Milman and F.D. Maurice had treated the biblical narrative of the Jews historically. They did not doubt the authenticity of the Old Testament as revelation but argued that the lessons it held were comprehensible only as the word of God adapted to the level of civilisation of the people to whom He had spoken. In his *History of the Jews*, published in 1829, Milman wrote as follows:

> God, who in his later revelation, appeals to the reason and the heart, addressed a more carnal and superstitious people chiefly through their imagination and their senses. The Jews were in fact more or less barbarians, alternately retrograding and improving, up to the 'fulness of time' when Christianity, the religion of civilised and enlightened men, was to reveal in all its perfection the nature of the benficient Creator and the offer of immortality through the redemption of our blessed Saviour.[45]

It followed that the great religious truths disclosed to the Israelites – the unity and omnipotence of a universal God – had to be disentangled from the ways in which an uncivilised nation had been taught these lessons. While the authenticity of the Old Testament was affirmed, its authority was relegated.

For Thomas Arnold, the supercession of the Old Testament by the New was compounded by the supercession of the ancients by the moderns. In his inaugural lecture as Regius Professor of Modern History at Oxford, in 1841, Arnold defined modern history as the biography of living nations, the beginning of which could be traced to the fall of the Western Empire and the dark period following it. At this time the four components of modern nations – race, language, institutions and religion – were fused. Modern history took the

---

44. P. Corsi, *Science and Religion. Baden Powell and the Anglican Debate, 1800–60* (Cambridge, 1988), pp. 24–5.
45. Cited in D. Forbes, *The Liberal Anglican Idea of History* (Cambridge, 1952), p. 76.

achievements of Rome, Greece and Israel, and melded them with a new race – the German race – changing 'the character of whole mass'.[46] Arnold subscribed to the orthodoxy that civilisation advanced as the achievements of eastern peoples were developed to a higher level by western races. Left to itself, the East was able to produce only Judaism. From this vantage point, the nineteenth-century Jew was an anomaly; a remnant of the ancient order unblended with either the German race or the Christian religion.[47]

By the mid-1850s liberal theology had progressed well beyond an Oxonian minority. The claims of the liberal Anglicans were reinforced by geologists whose findings could be used to question literal interpretations of the six-day creation, the flood and, as a result of the fossil remains of extinct species, the idea of a purposeful creation.[48] In 1852 the *Westminster Review* was brought under the editorship of the publisher John Chapman and became a forum in which religious orthodoxy was challenged and the proponents of scientific naturalism were given a pulpit.[49] It was a place where radical German theology received sympathetic criticism. Gerald Parsons has argued that the bitter conflicts which surrounded biblical criticism in the 1850s–'60s were not due to the fact that the ideas were new but that they were gaining ground.[50]

One indication of the new climate was the publication in 1857 of Baden Powell's *Christianity without Judaism*. The arguments in this volume were not novel; the book presented a development of articles first published in 1848 in *Kitto's Journal of Sacred Literature*. But encouraged and emboldened by the appreciative reception given to this sermons and addresses, not least in 1856 at Kensington Palace, Baden Powell published an amplified and accessible version of his ideas.[51] Baden Powell was Professor of Geometry at Oxford. But he was a philosopher and theologian as well as a scientist. *Christianity without Judaism* was a precription intended to save Christianity from the 'superstition and fanaticism' which followed from a literal reading of the Old Testament.[52] His immediate targets

46. T. Arnold, *Introductory Lectures on Modern History* (London, 1843), pp. 25–7.
47. See his letter of 16 May 1835 to Archbishop Whately, in A.P. Stanley ed., *The Life and Correspondence of Thomas Arnold*, vol. ii (London, 1844), pp. 33–4.
48. G. Parsons, 'Biblical Criticism in Victorian Britain: From Controversy to Acceptance?', in G. Parsons, ed., *Religion in Victorian Britain*, vol. ii (Manchester, 1988), p. 244.
49. J.R. Moore, 'The Crisis of Faith: Reformation versus Revolution', in G. Parsons, ed., *Religion in Victorian Britain*, vol. ii, pp. 226–7.
50. Parsons, 'Biblical Criticism', pp. 244, 249.
51. Corsi, *Science and Religion*, p. 6; B. Powell, *Christianity without Judaism* (London, 1857), p. vi.
52. *Ibid*, p. 15.

were evangelicals of all denominations but Judaism was necessarily disparaged in his attempt to establish the integrity of Christianity by detaching it from 'Mosaism'.

Baden Powell argued that discrepancies with 'physical truth' found in the Old Testament were 'wholly peculiar to the Mosaic religion, with which Christianity has, however, been too commonly mixed up and confounded.'[53] He understood the specific character of 'the Judaical scriptures' in relation to the role Jews had played in the religious and moral education of mankind. 'In fact, the Mosaic institution was mainly directed to putting down and *destroying* the superstitions to which the Israelites had become attached in Egypt, and by the introduction of an elaborate ceremonial, to wean them from that idolatry to which they were so prone, but which the law denounced with its severest penalities.'[54] Accordingly, the Old Testament did not contain a universal religion or a truthful account of the physical world. Rather, it was composed of 'successive revelations, systems, covenants, laws . . . adapted to the ideas of the age and the condition of the parties to whom they were vouchsafed'.[55] He found a religious system which did not distinguish between ceremonial and moral duties, in which good conduct was enforced by laws and prohibitions, and which sanctioned the *lex talionis* – 'that most perfect idea of retributive justice to the uncivilised mind'.[56] Thus neither the science nor the morality of the Old Testament had a universal significance; they were the possession of a particular people. Circumcision, the prohibition of intermarriage, exclusive usages and ceremonies were all designed to separate the people of Israel as a people chosen for a particular divine purpose: 'the Law throughout is a series of adaptations to them and their national character and position'.[57] In *Christianity without Judaism* Baden Powell gave only the most elaborate formulation of a widespread reassessment of the relation of the Old Testament to Christianity and Victorian civilisation.

In 1860 the publication of *Essays and Reviews* gave an expression to liberal theology which became both notorious and celebrated. Contributors such as Benjamin Jowett and William Temple presented an interpretation of the Hebrew Bible in which the Israelites underwent a progressive education. Aspects of the texts that were unpalatable to modern Christians could, in this way, be cast aside by them. Temple's essay, 'The Education of the Human Race', presented the

53.   *Ibid*, p. 5.
54.   *Ibid*, pp. 19–20.
55.   *Ibid*, p. 86.
56.   *Ibid*, pp. 93, 103–6.
57.   *Ibid*, p. 102.

Old Testament as analagous to the childhood of the human race, a period in which the Mosaic system taught the law rather than the freedom of conscience which characterised the higher stage of Christianity.[58] John William Colenso's study of *The Book of Joshua and the Pentateuch Critically Examined*, the first volume of which appeared in 1862, went a step further, arguing that the Pentateuch was in important respects inaccurate as history, and that parts had been composed long after the time of Moses. By exposing inaccuracies and evidences of composition it would become clear, Colenso hoped, that the Old Testament could not literally be the word of God. If accepted, his biblical criticism meant it was no longer necessary to believe in God as a 'bloodthirsty tyrant' who required, for example, the slaughter of all the male Midianites.[59]

Aspects of Victorian Hellenism reinforced the declining authority of the Hebrew Bible and Judaism among many mid-Victorian intellectuals. George Eliot commented that her contemporaries 'hardly know that Christ was a Jew. . . . I find men educated at Rugby supposing that Christ spoke Greek.'[60] The counterpart to revulsion from aspects of the Hebrew Bible was to discover the origins of Victorian civilisation among the ancient Greeks. The most celebrated Victorian Hellenist, Matthew Arnold, included in his *Culture and Anarchy*, published in 1869, a systematic comparison of 'Hebraism' and 'Hellenism'. The former represented 'conduct and obedience', the latter freedom of spirit and intellect.[61] Hellenism embodied spontaneity, Hebraism constraint; both aimed at the perfection of man, and western history oscillated between the two. Arnold saw both as necessary, for with the Greeks Hellenism was premature; with them 'the indispensable basis of conduct and self-control' was absent. Its provision was the achievement of Hebraism. But the innovation of the Old Testament was perfected in the New, which substituted for law and prescription 'that inspiring and affecting pattern of self-conquest' offered by Jesus Christ'.[62] Arnold's characterisation of Hebraism clearly drew on the commonplaces of Liberal theology.

> The discipline of the Old Testament may be summed up as a discipline teaching us to abhor and flee from sin; the discipline of the New Testament, as discipline teaching us to die for it. As Hellenism speaks of thinking

58. Rogerson, *Old Testament Criticism*, pp. 191, 210–16.
59. *Ibid*, chapter 16.
60. F.M. Turner, *The Greek Heritage in Victorian Britain* (New Haven, CT, 1981), p. 72.
61. M. Arnold, *Culture and Anarchy* (London, 1869), pp. 142–97.
62. *Ibid*, pp. 147, 153–4.

clearly, seeing things in their essence and beauty, as a grand and precious feat for man to achieve, so Hebraism speaks of becoming conscious of sin of awakening to a sense of sin as a feat of this kind.[63]

In some respects Arnold used 'Hellenism' and 'Hebraism' as metaphors for rival forces in human history and through them he attacked contemporary targets. His strictures on the limits of Hebraism were a commentary on nonconformity. Hebraism expressed the conventional morality, mechanism and materialism that Arnold conceived as the root of 'anarchy'. But Hebraism was also being discussed in terms of a real past. Seeking to press his argument and to demonstrate why in England there should be a turn to the values he invested in Hellenism, the tension between the literal and metaphorical in Arnold's use of his two terms slipped decisively towards the former as culture was returned to nature.

> Science has now made visible to everybody the great and pregnant elements of difference which lie in race, and in how signal a manner they make the genius and history of an Indo-European people vary from those of a Semitic people. Hellenism is of Indo-European growth; and we English, a nation of Indo-European stock, seem to belong naturally to the movement of Hellenism.[64]

Arnold's writing was informed by the commonplace distinction between Aryans and Semites. Discussions of Aryanism in these years did not produce a coherent body of racial thought.[65] But this does not mean they were insignificant. The terminology of race, however imprecise, did promote the belief that cultural differences could be located in nature.[66] The vague but pervasive concept of race when confronted with the endogamy of contemporary Jews connected them with the ancient Israelites. It provided critics with a theory which allowed them, if they chose, to draw connections between the ethical shortcomings of biblical Israelites and those of the modern Jews. Bernard Cracroft, who applauded Jewish emancipation, complained nevertheless that they continued practices such as 'the barbaric rite of circumcision', on account of their continued belief in the 'plenary and verbal inspiration of the Old Testament'. This, he observed, was something which 'the great bulk of intelligent men

---

63. *Ibid*, p. 153.
64. *Ibid*, p. 162. In the 1830s and '40s the theory that Greek civilisation had Aryan, European, not Egyptian origins became a new orthodoxy: see M. Bernal, *Black Athena; the Afroasiatic Roots of Classical Civilization*, vol. i (London, 1987), pp. 281–336.
65. On the leading theorist, the philologist Friedrich Max Muller, see Stocking, *Victorian Anthropology*, pp. 58–9; Turner, *The Greek Heritage*, pp. 104–12.
66. N. Stepan, *The Idea of Race in Science: Great Britain 1800–1960* (London, 1982), p. xx.

throughout Europe' had abandoned.[67] The Victorian intellegentsia aimed its volleys at the ancient Israelites but some fell on modern Hebrews.

Race, theology and politics

The emergence of a Jewish plutocracy, the advance of the idea of 'race' and of incarnational theology did not necessarily give rise to anti-Jewish polemic. For a London doctor, J.H. Stallard, for instance, these elements were combined with a different purpose, namely criticism of the poor law. In 1867 he published *London Pauperism among Jews and Christians.* The Jews' social ascent was noted by Stallard. Moreover, he believed the Jews, though no better or worse than any one other group, did possess peculiar and uniform racial characteristics. The Jew was sober, clean, speculative in his business dealings and placed a high value on family life.[68] Stallard's main concern, however, was to compare the system of poor relief administered by the Jewish Board of Guardians with 'the repressive system of the English'. He contrasted the all but penal discipline of the work-house and the poor law guardians' aim of maximising prevention by minimising relief with the investigation of individual cases and the compassion practiced at the Jewish Board of Guardians. There 'every man in health is treated as an honest man until he is proved contrary. Everything is done to sustain the self-respect of those who apply.'[69] Stallard was contributing to a critique of the poor law which resulted, in 1869, in the formation of the Charity Organisation Society.[70] The shortcomings of the poor law guardians' administrative treatment of paupers were expressed in terms of the ideal of a Christian society modelled on Christ's own life.

> Where is the trace of that noble religion which we desire to carry to every corner of the earth? Here under the very shadow of its temple, the poor lie neglected and forgotten. The very object of religion seems entirely changed. The great Exemplar spent his life in visiting the sick and doing good; but we seek heaven for ourselves and leave the sick and poor to the tender mercies of the official system.[71]

67. B. Cracroft, 'The Jews of Western Europe', *The Westminster Review*, April 1863, p. 466.
68. J. Stallard, *London Pauperism amongst Jews and Christians* (London, 1867), pp. 10–11.
69. *Ibid*, p. 140.
70. On this see G. Stedman Jones, *Outcast London: a Study in the Relationship between Classes in Victorian Society* (Oxford, 1971), chapter 13.
71. Stallard, *London Pauperism*, p. 85.

There was a double-edged quality to Stallard's praise for the JBG. The example of the Jews, of all people, was held up to shame Christians into recognising how far they were from 'harmony with the life and teaching of Christ'.[72] Nevertheless, Stallard drew a flattering picture of London Jewry while employing many of the ideas we have discussed in this chapter: the social prominence of the Jews, their racial separateness, and the importance of Christian love over a presumption of sin.

However, the themes of race, theology and the Jews' commercial success were drawn together to reach a radically different conclusion by the historians Goldwin Smith and E.A. Freeman. In an essay published in the *Contemporary Review* in February 1878 Goldwin Smith proposed that it had been a mistake to regard Judaism as a species of religious nonconformity: 'Judaism like the whole circle of primitive religions of which it is a survival is a religion of race.'[73] The essay provoked a response from Hermann Adler, and Smith published a more elaborate version of the same argument in *Nineteenth Century* in May of the same year.[74] The Old Testament, Smith argued, presented an imperfect monotheism.

> The victories of the Jewish people over their national enemies were the triumphs of Jehovah over the gods of the nations, just as the victories of the Greeks over the barbarians were triumphs of Zeus and Athene. It is true that the Jewish conception of the Deity is already showing its superiority and its tendency gradually to rise and broaden into a real monotheism, while the service of Jehovah, although largely national and ceremonial, is also most strikingly and exceptionally moral. Still the Jehovah of the Jews is a Jewish Deity. He has sworn a special covenant with the forefathers of the tribe. . . . The age was one of universal war and conquest; the expulsion of the Canaanites by the Jews was in all probability the substitution of a more moral for a less moral civilisation: still these breathings of a ruthless partiality belong most distinctly to the tribal era. To the civilised heart and conscience such precepts are not known. They emanate not from the father of all men but from the Jehovah of the Jews.[75]

Jews continued to demonstrate the tribal fundamentals of their religion by refusing to proselytise, by treating intermarriage as a sort of apostasy and by the 'primeval rite' of circumcision, a mark of tribal separation – whereas baptism constituted 'a rite of

72. *Ibid*, p. 305.
73. G. Smith, 'England's Abandonment of the Protectorate of Turkey', *Contemporary Review*, February 1878, p. 617.
74. H. Adler, 'Can Jews be Patriots?' *Nineteenth Century*, April 1878, pp. 637–46; G. Smith, 'Can Jews be Patriots?', *Nineteenth Century*, May 1878, pp. 875–87.
75. *Ibid*., pp. 879–80.

humanity'.[76] Judaism represented the highest level attained by tribal religion, but it was Christianity, and its declaration of the universal fatherhood of God and the universal brotherhood of man, which had signified 'the close of tribalism and the advent of humanity'.[77] In this way Goldwin Smith drew on developmental interpretations of the Old Testament, comparative mythology and the doctrine of race to reach a view of Judaism that allowed him to conclude a '*genuine*' Jew 'is not an Englishman or Frenchman holding particular theological tenets: he is a Jew, with a special Deity for his own race. The rest of mankind are to him not merely people holding a different creed, but aliens in blood.'[78]

The political dangers arising from this were rendered more acute by the strength of Jewish influence in 'the money world', and the power this brought with the increase of national debts.[79] Goldwin Smith, as we noted earlier in the chapter, greeted the Reform Act of 1867 as an opportunity to establish within the nation a stronger sense of community and attachment to the common good. Speaking at Sheffield he expressed his hope that 'government shall henceforth not be the government of a class or of a balance of classes but of the nation'.[80] But though he had been prominent in campaigns for religious equality in the 1850s and '60s he was now dismayed that the 'ruling motives of the Jewish community' were not the same as those which activated 'patriotic Englishmen'.[81]

Similarly, E.A. Freeman entertained a vision of the nation which not only expressed a set of constitutional arrangements but the language, religion and traditions of the people as well. For Freeman, nationality was a consequence of 'race'. Democracy signified a restoration of the nation's Saxon heritage and, in this way, national history took its place within a broader, Teutonic, past which, in its turn, was located within a still wider Aryanism.[82] Freeman's concept of race was rooted in philology not physiology. It was a generous view not restricted by blood ties or notions of physical purity. For while he believed that the common root of the Indo-European languages indicated a common race, the ties of language were reinforced and modified by the imprint of culture. In this way the Indian element of Aryanism could be cast away. It was Europe – its Teutons,

76. *Ibid*, pp. 876–7, 879–83.
77. *Ibid*, p. 879.
78. *Ibid*, p. 876.
79. *Ibid*, p. 875; Smith, 'England's Abandonment of the Protectorate of Turkey', p. 618.
80. Cited in E. Wallace, *Goldwin Smith, Victorian Liberal* (Toronto, 1957), p. 146.
81. Smith, 'Can Jews be Patriots?', p. 875.
82. J. Burrow, *A Liberal Descent*, pp. 171–2, 225.

Slavs and Celts – which possessed not only a community of languages but a shared classical and Christian heritage; 'a common civilisation, a common morality, a common possession of political and intellectual instincts.'[83]

There were limits to the inclusiveness of Freeman's community of race, and the case of the Jews revealed one such limit. In 1877 Freeman addressed this problem. The Jews provided a stark example of the way in which culture, in this case religion, worked upon race. The tenacity with which they clung to their nationality was the distinguishing characteristic of their history since the Babylonian captivity. Jews illustrated the capacity of religion to preserve national purity. As a result, even after the Jew had been relieved from medieval oppression 'something of his old historical position still clings to him.' The feeling between Jews of different countries was more than the commonality felt between co-religionists.

> It is more than the feeling which a Christian or a Mussulman has for other Christians or Mussulmans as such. It is a distinctly national feeling. It is a feeling not only for professors of the same creed, but for men of the same nation. Here the doctrine of race may indeed come in its fulness. The Jew must be very nearly or absolutely, a pure race, in a sense in which no European nation is pure. The blood remains untouched by conversion, it remains untouched even by intermarriage.[84]

The Jews, their nationality underscored by religious particularity, had been shown to be unassimilable to the wider European family of Christian nations.

There were theological and political aspects to all this, Freeman added, though he declined to enter into them in the same article. But his readers would have had no difficulty in catching the political implications of his remarks. The essay was published in the midst of the Eastern Crisis which dominated British foreign policy between 1876–8. Goldwin Smith, however, did not hold back from explaining why he had examined the relation of religion to race among Jews. 'When we see that England is being drawn into a war, which many of us think would be calamitous, and that Jewish influence . . . is working in that direction (as people on every side are saying that it is), we . . . note the presence of a political danger.'[85]

83. *Ibid*, pp. 189–91; E.A. Freeman, 'Stray Thoughts on Comparative Mythology', *Fortnightly Review*, November 1870, pp. 536–48; C.J.W. Parker, 'The Failure of Liberal Racialism: The Racial Ideas of E.A. Freeman', *Historical Journal*, December 1981, pp. 825–46.
84. E.A. Freeman, 'The Jews in Europe', *Historical Essays*, 3rd series, vol. i (London, 1879), p. 230.
85. Smith, 'Can Jews be Patriots?', p. 875.

The writings of Goldwin Smith and E.A.Freeman bring together several of the strands discussed in this chapter. Both writers were influenced by the broader conception of the nation which developed in relation to parliamentary reform. Both writers, too, found the definition of the Jews as a religious minority, commonplace within emancipation propaganda, to be unsatisfactory. Both turned towards a categorisation of Jews as a 'race'. In doing so, Goldwin Smith drew on biblical criticism and the attempt to separate Christianity from its Jewish inheritance. The practices and beliefs of Victorian Jews were thus attacked through their biblical forbears but this was mixed with an assessment of their contemporary power. The Jews' prominence in the financial world gave them opportunity to turn their tribal loyalty to good account. Freeman took a different route: he focused on a philological theory of Aryanism. But he too was concerned with the relation of Jews and Judaism to the antecedents of Victorian civilisation. Like Goldwin Smith, he concluded that Judaism lay outside this heritage.

It is clear that trends in theology and in thinking about race tended to devalue Judaism and draw lines more starkly between Jews and non-Jews. The ascendency of Jews in finance could encourage adverse commentary about Jews in England. But as the comparison between Stallard on one side and Freeman and Smith on the other suggests, whether they did so or not and, still more, whether they came together in an elaborate critique of Jews and Judaism, was not determined by the presence of a number of Jewish *arrivistes* or by fashions of intellectual life in themselves. To understand the conditions in which they were used to produce such a critique we must turn to the politics of the 1870s.

Chapter 4

Disraeli, Jews and the English Question

Bulgarian atrocities and Jewish sympathies

Between 1876–80 many nonconformists, radicals and Liberal intellectuals – groups which had supported the Jews claims during the struggle for emancipation – associated themselves with a critique of Judaism and criticism of Jews. Many of Disraeli's opponents found the key to the Prime Minister's actions in his Jewish origins and 'oriental' sympathies. More generally they scrutinised the motives and questioned the patriotism of English Jews. We need to account for this transformation of the Jewish issue in British politics. Political historians have taken the view that Disraeli's Jewish origins presented an unpleasant and opportune stick with which some of his opponents chose to beat him. Historians of Anglo-Jewry have seen the attacks as a brief and narrowly based episode in the history of anti-Semitism.[1] But criticism of Disraeli and the Jews was more widespread and its meanings more complex than has been acknowledged; certainly, it signified antipathy to Jews but it also signified more than this. Just as the argument over the Jews' political status before emancipation turned on contending visions of the nation, so too the reappearance of the Jewish question reveals a fierce debate over the meaning of patriotism between contending doctrines of national identity.

The 1867 Reform Act required politicians to address voters in new ways and in doing so it led some Conservative figures to promote more populist images of the nation. In the short term, the Conserva-

1. R.T. Shannon, *Gladstone and the Bulgarian Agitation, 1876* (London, 1963), p. 200 finds the anti-Semitic aspect of the agitation to have been 'superficial'. R. Blake, *Disraeli* (London, 1966), p. 604 notices 'an unpleasant streak of anti-Semitism' in the attacks on Disraeli but he does not pursue the theme. C. Holmes, *Anti-Semitism in British Society, 1876–1939* (London, 1979), pp. 11–12 devotes little space to the episode.

tive Party gained little from parliamentary reform. In 1868 it was defeated yet again in a general election. But in the medium term the outlook was more favourable. The Liberal government moved in directions which caused disunity in the party and alarmed moderate sections of the electorate. In the field of foreign policy, Gladstone eschewed bravura and brinkmanship, in self-conscious contrast to Palmerstonian precedents, and emphasised the concert of European powers and international law as tools of diplomacy.[2] The government's reforming ambitions appeared more far-reaching than they were, in part on account of the support it received from radicals such as Charles Dilke and Joseph Chamberlain, who flirted with republicanism in England following the creation of the French Republic in September 1870.[3] These were the circumstances in which Disraeli sought to reinstate the Conservative Party as the political embodiment of national ideals. Speaking in November 1867, he presented the Tory Party as 'the national party of England'. He drew an opposition between national and philosophic systems of reform: the former giving full weight to 'the manners, the customs, the laws and the traditions of a people', the latter built on 'abstract principles and arbitary and general doctrines'.[4]

This comparison, between Conservative and Liberal identities, was drawn more elaborately in Disraeli's better-known speeches delivered at Manchester and at the Crystal Palace in April and June 1872. Disraeli identified the Conservative Party with the preservation of the constitution, in contrast to the war waged on the country's institutions by the Liberal government.[5] The doctrine of the constitution, moreover, was not focused on the principle of individual liberties – as was the case in Whig and radical versions – but on the nation's institutions and, in the first place, the monarchy. Disraeli promoted the Sovereign's exercise of personal influence and professed himself thankful for a system of government which placed supreme power above the partisanship of parties, classes and factions. He went on to defend the principle of a hereditary second chamber and the union of Church and state.[6]

Disraeli's formulations of Conservative principles in 1872 con-

2. H.C.G. Matthew, *Gladstone* (Oxford, 1986), pp. 180–8.
3. W.M. Kuhn, 'Ceremony and Politics: The British Monarchy, 1871–2', *Journal of British Studies*, April 1987, pp. 133–62.
4. Blake, *Disraeli*, p. 482.
5. T.E. Kebbel, *Selected Speeches of the Late Right Hon. the Earl of Beaconsfield*, vol. ii (London, 1882), pp. 491, 502.
6. *Ibid*, pp. 492–505.

tained more than resistance to constitutional change.[7] After 1867 an emphasis on institutions was no longer a sufficient basis upon which to define the political nation. Disraeli enunciated a more populist Conservatism alongside his defence of the country's institutions. This was present in the Manchester speech but it was developed more fully two months later at the Crystal Palace. The Conservative Party was identified as national – one drawn 'from all the numerous classes in the realm' – and the Liberals' programme of reform was stigmatised as anti-national, a foreign creed which not only attacked the institutions of the country but also made 'war on the manners and the customs of the people of this country'.[8] Those institutions, as 'the embodied experiences of a race', were connected to the people, indeed were an expression of them.[9] The empire too was called upon to express the connection of the people to the country's institutions.

> [The 1867 Reform Act] was founded on a confidence that the great body of the people of this country were 'Conservative'. When I say 'Conservative' I use the word in its purest and loftiest sense. I mean that the people of England, and especially the working classes of England, are proud of belonging to a great country, and wish to maintain its greatness – that they are proud of belonging to an Imperial country, and are resolved to maintain if they can, their empire – that they believe, on the whole, that the greatness and the empire of England are to be attributed to the ancient institutions of the land.[10]

The comments on empire were vague. The modern trend among historians has been to highlight the absence from these speeches of any practical programme of progressive Conservatism combining imperialism and social reform. But the speeches did announce a consistent and self-conscious formulation of 'Conservative principles' – the title of the Manchester address. They had a rhetorical function in the transformed polity. Disraeli offered a choice between an 'England modelled upon Continental principles' and an imperial future which expressed national institutions and 'the sublime in-

7. That this is all it did contain seems to be the implication of P.R. Ghosh in 'Style and Substance in Disraelian Social Reform', in P. Waller, ed., *Politics and Social Change in Modern Britain* (Oxford, 1987), pp. 66–8. But Ghosh is surely right to restore the importance of the constitution to our understanding of political controversy around the figure of Disraeli in the later 1870s: see *idem*, 'Disraelian Conservatism: A Financial Approach', *English Historical Review*, April 1984, p. 292.
8. Kebbel, *Selected Speeches*, vol. ii, p. 524.
9. The phrase in quotation marks was uttered at Manchester but there too it was in a passage linking institutions, empire and the people: see *ibid*, p. 506.
10. *Ibid*, pp. 527–8.

stinct of an ancient people'. But this attempt to capture the language of national identity inevitably came into conflict with another ideological tradition – namely, the identification of patriotism with disinterested attachment to the common good, and of the nation with a set of hard-won freedoms guaranteed to its people. As we have observed, this version of the nation was being extended in a populist direction as Liberal intellectuals and nonconformists hoped that the extended franchise would enable them to work towards a remoralised polity; one that would suppress personal interest, through an appreciation of the bonds of community in civil society or through the realisation of a Christian government.[11] This was the immediate polemical context in which the Jewish question was revived.

The specific issue which precipitated the revival of the Jewish question was the crisis of the Turkish empire between 1875–8 and what British policy towards it should be. Before turning to the debate on the Jews, therefore, we must first set out the nature of the crisis and the way it impinged on British interests. In July 1875 the Turks were confronted by an uprising in Hercegovenia which spread rapidly to Bosnia. The revolts were driven by Christian, nationalist sentiment in the face of rule by a foreign, Moslem empire. Fighting continued through the first half of 1876 and at the end of April insurrection spread to Bulgaria. On June 30 Serbia and Montenegro, supporting the rebellions, declared war on Turkey. Although an armistice between the Turks and Serbs was in place from 31 October 1876 this did not signal an end to the crisis. A conference of the great powers was convened at Constantinople in December 1876 to consider the future of the Turkish empire, in the hope of forcing reforms upon it. Lord Salisbury was the British special ambassador to the conference. With good reason, he departed anticipating 'seasickness, much French and failure'.[12] The conference broke up on 20 January 1877 having failed to persuade Turkey to accept foreign supervision of its rule in Europe. Three months later, Russia unilaterally declared war with the stated aim of enforcing a set of minimum requirements on the Ottoman empire.

The traditional purpose of British policy in the Eastern Question

---

11. John Parry has observed, 'despite their differences . . . radical nonconformists, positivists, academic radicals and leading working-men shared much in common and, in particular, an ethical vision: most of them hoped, by radicalising the liberal conscience, and by using it to diminish privilege, to work towards an ideal state of material and spiritual class harmony': *Democracy and Religion: Gladstone and the Liberal Party, 1867–1875* (Cambridge, 1986), p. 29.
12. G. Cecil, *Life of Robert Marquis of Salisbury*, vol. ii (London, 1921), p. 9.

– the future of the Ottoman empire in Europe – was to sustain Turkish rule. The collapse of the Ottoman empire, it was feared, would allow Russian expansion in Asia as well as Europe; it would open the way for Russia to menace British rule in India and threaten access to the eastern Mediterranean. Although Britain had acted with the European powers at Constantinople, Russia's unilateral declaration of war altered the situation. The British government's response was to declare its neutrality on three conditions: namely, that Constantinople was not occupied, the Dardanelles remained open, and Egypt was not attacked. The Russian advance, however, gave rise to the possibility that the first two conditions would be violated. After the fall of Plevna on 10 December 1877 Russian forces were able to move towards Constantinople. These events formed the diplomatic and military background to the first phase of criticism of Disraeli and of Jews during the Eastern Crisis: a phase which extended until December 1877, when the prospect of war with Russia began to alter the terms of polemic.

On 23 June 1876 the leading Liberal newspaper, the *Daily News*, published an account of massacre, rape and destruction perpetrated by a Turkish irregular militia, the *bashi-bazouks*, on helpless Bulgarian Christians. It claimed that twenty-five thousand innocents had been killed.[13] The news transformed public debate over what British policy should be. By the beginning of September a massive public agitation had formed, mobilised by metropolitan high churchmen and provincial nonconformists. Hundreds of meetings were held not only to express outrage at the atrocities but to demand the removal of British support from Turkey, independence or self-government for Bosnia and Bulgaria, and reparations and relief for Turkey's Christians.[14] Nonconformists were the most prominent group in the agitation. Radicals and trade unionists were also well represented, though as groups they were less unanimous.[15] This outbreak of mass indignation induced Gladstone to emerge from retirement and place himself at the head of the agitation. His pamphlet *The Bulgarian Horrors and the Question of the East* sold over two hundred thousand copies in the four weeks following its publication on 6 September.

Disraeli's view of the Eastern Question as a problem of diplomacy

13. The real number of dead was about half the figure reported: Blake, *Disraeli*, p. 592.
14. R. Millman, *Britain and the Eastern Question, 1875–8* (Oxford, 1979), p. 527 (footnote). On the agitation see Shannon, *Gladstone and the Bulgarian Agitation*.
15. Some radicals, such as Dilke, were unwilling to side with Russian autocracy: *ibid*, p. 22. On the social composition of the agitation: *ibid*, pp. 147–52.

was flexible. He was prepared to accept partition of Turkey so long as Britain took a leading role in determining the terms of division.[16] But he responded to the domestic aspect of the Eastern Question – the agitation – with insouciance. He diminished the atrocity stories and, further, he cast doubt on the motives of 'designing politicians' – meaning Gladstone – who took advantage of the 'sublime sentiments' of the English people. Disraeli appeared to deny both the role of moral seriousness and of public opinion in forming foreign policy. In their place he elevated 'our duty . . . to maintain the empire of England' and 'the permanent interests of this country'.[17]

The atrocities agitation challenged this basis of conduct: moral considerations were to determine the direction of British policy. Revulsion from Disraeli's doctrine of empire and interest produced E.A. Freeman's notorious denunciation of the government, made at the National Convention on the Eastern Question in London on 8 December 1876: sooner than 'uphold the integrity and independence of Sodom . . . perish the interests of England, perish our dominion in India, rather than we should strike a blow or speak a word on behalf of right against wrong'.[18] Opposing the doctrine of national interest, the agitation called on the government to align British policy with the cause of Christianity against Islam, humanity against barbarism, and with liberty against tyranny.[19]

Parliament was not in session between August and February. In these months especially, anti-Turks could make extravagant constitutional claims for 'opinion', and it was acknowledged that the press played a crucial part forming 'opinion'.[20] The agitation press claimed to speak for the nation and claimed constitutional force for this assertion. The *Daily News* called for policy to be conducted 'in harmony with national feeling'.[21] The claim to speak for the 'nation' was more than an assertion that the majority supported the agitation. A particular version of the national political tradition was being called into service. In early October, the Hyde Park Demonstration Committee sent a message to the Serbian government expressing, as

16. Millman, *Britain and the Eastern Question*, pp. 167–8.
17. W.F. Moneypenny and G.E. Buckle, *The Life of Benjamin Disraeli, Earl of Beaconsfield*, vol. vi (London, 1920), p. 48.
18. Though Freeman added 'the path to India does not lie by Constantinople': R. Seton Watson, *Gladstone, Disraeli and the Eastern Question* (London, 1935), pp. 112–13. See too E.A. Freeman, 'The English People in Relation to the Eastern Question', *Contemporary Review*, February 1877, p. 498.
19. J.O. Johnston, *Life and Letters of Henry Parry Liddon* (London, 1904), p. 206; H.J. Leech, ed., *The Public Letters of John Bright* (2nd edn, New York, NY, 1969), pp. 17–18; Shannon, *Gladstone and the Bulgarian Agitation*, p. 61.
20. See for example *The Nonconformist*, 20 September 1876, p. 942.
21. *Ibid*, 27 September 1876, p. 966; *Daily News*, 10 November 1876, p. 4.

British citizens, sympathy with their struggle for national independence. It recalled that their own forefathers had secured liberty and security of life and property through suffering, rebellion, persecution and revolution and saw the Serbs engaged in the same fight.[22] According to *The Nonconformist* it was the voice of the nation enfranchised by the 1867 Reform Act that was now seeking to assert its powers and moralise the polity: 'Now, when the extended suffrage had placed political power to an unexampled extent in the hands of the people . . . the issues of good and evil involved are too vast for any to abstain.'[23] The movement saw itself as the voice of English liberty as well as Christian policy.

Inevitably, the question arose of why the government and, above all, why Disraeli – since it was well known that the Cabinet was divided – was pursuing a policy that was un-Christian, inhumane and contrary to the nation's ideals. Here Disraeli's Jewish origins provided a plausible and, to some, a compelling explanation. From the high churchman Liddon to *The Nonconformist* we find the belief that the Turks' crimes, their 'stagnation in evil', reflected their distance from Christianity.[24] At the National Convention Gladstone confided that the occasion signified 'pre-eminently a Christian revolution'.[25] In this light, the Prime Minister's indifference to the massacre of Christians seemed full of meaning. Cannon Liddon wrote to Madame Novikoff that 'as long as Lord Beaconsfield is Prime Minister we are not safe. His one positive passion is that of upholding Asiatics against Europeans – non-Christian Asiatics against Christian Europeans.'[26]

This view received its fullest expression in spring 1877 in E.A. Freeman's *The Ottoman Power in Europe. The Nonconformist* described the work as 'masterly'. The historian J.R. Green enthused, 'it makes a fearful Bulgarian massacre of my Lord Beaconsfield'.[27] Freeman's

22. *Ibid*, 4 October 1876, p. 2. John Kennedy, speaking at Stepney Meeting House in January 1878, addressed the servitude of the Turks' subject peoples: 'Now I ask, is it for Englishmen, Christian Englishmen to do aught to perpetuate such a yoke. There are echoes from Runnymeade and Marston Moor, from Bannockburn and Bothwell Bridge that cry out "Forbid"! In the name of all that is best and noblest in English history, "Forbid"!': *ibid*, 9 January 1878, p. 28.
23. *The Nonconformist*, 17 October 1877, p. 1,046.
24. Johnston, *Henry Parry Liddon*, p. 222; *The Nonconformist*, 14 November 1877, p. 1,150.
25. W.T. Stead, *The MP for Russia: Reminiscences and Correspondence of Madame Olga Novikoff* (London, 1909), vol. i, p. 293.
26. *Ibid*, p. 364.
27. *The Nonconformist*, 7 February 1877, p. 134; L. Stephen, ed., *Letters of John Richard Green* (London, 1901), p. 459.

main argument was that the Turk was essentially oriental and in Europe his presence was 'something which supplies a never-failing stock of difficulties and complications'.[28] But British policy, under Disraeli's influence, did not acknowledge this reality: 'while Lord Derby simply wishes to do nothing one way or the other, Lord Beaconsfield is the active friend of the Turk'. His policy was but one local example of an alliance that ran through Europe. All over the continent, Freeman claimed, 'the most fiercely Turkish part of the press is largely in Jewish hands. It may be assumed everywhere, with the smallest class of exceptions, that the Jew is the friend of the Turk and the enemy of the Christian.'[29] The alliance originated within the Turkish empire, where the law pressed more lightly on Jews than Christians and where Jews served the empire. Freeman drew on theories of race to argue that despite the differences between the Jews of the East and West 'blood is stronger than water, and Hebrew rule is sure to lead to a Hebrew policy'.[30] Likewise, a common oriental identity determined that 'the Turk and the Jew are leagued against the Christian'.[31]

> No one wishes to place the Jew, whether Jew by birth or by religion, under any disability as compared with the European Christian. But it will not do to have the policy of England, the welfare of Europe, sacrificed to Hebrew sentiment. The danger is no imaginary one. Every one must have marked that the one subject on which Lord Beaconsfield, through his career, has been in earnest has been whatever has touched his own people. A mocker about everything else he has been utterly serious about this. . . . His zeal for his own people is really the best feature in Lord Beaconsfield's career. But we cannot sacrifice our people, the people of Aryan and Christian Europe, to the most genuine belief in Asian mystery. We cannot have England or Europe governed by a Hebrew policy.[32]

The private correspondence and comments of the agitation's leaders turned repeatedly to discuss Disraeli as an 'oriental' and a 'Jew'. Freeman's letters are spattered with denunciations of 'the Jew's policy' and 'the Jew government'.[33] But even in this case,

---

28. E.A. Freeman, *The Ottoman Power in Europe; its Growth and Decline* (London, 1877), p. xvii.
29. *Ibid*, p. xx. See also H.H. Jenkins, *Breakers Ahead! Or the Doomed Ship, the Determined Captain, and the Docile Crew: A Review of Lord Beaconsfield's Policy* (Birmingham, 1878), especially pp. 6–7. Jenkins claimed to have dedicated the pamphlet to Gladstone 'by permission'.
30. Freeman, *The Ottoman Power*, p. xx.
31. *Ibid*.
32. *Ibid*, pp. xviii–xix.
33. W.R.W. Stephens, *The Life and Letters of Edward A. Freeman*, vol. ii (London, 1895), pp. 138–44; Stead, *The MP for Russia*, vol. i, pp. 333–6.

where the anti-Jewish comments were most full of personal loathing, the remarks reveal more than hatred of the Prime Minister and a low view of Jews. A venerable narrative of anti-Semitism was only one context in which these comments were made. In defining and castigating Disraeli as a Jew his critics also affirmed the Christian principles which the Prime Minister's actions and speeches seemed to challenge. At the same time, they offered an explanation for this challenge. Disraeli's Jewish identity placed him outside those traditions of self-conscious Christian morality which informed the anti-Turk agitation.[34]

Gladstone held a similar view. The basis of Disraeli's behaviour and interest in the Eastern Question and, following from this, the attitude of Jews more widely, was something which exercised Gladstone in 1876–7. 'He [Disraeli] is not quite such a Turk as I had thought', Gladstone wrote to the Duke of Argyll in August 1876; 'what he hates is Christian liberty and reconstruction'.[35] The key to this, he suspected, was 'Dizzy's crypto-Judaism. . . . The Jews of the East bitterly hate the Christians who have not always used them well.' At the start of January 1877 he wrote to Granville, 'he [Disraeli] may be willing to risk his government for his Judaic feeling, the deepest and truest now that his wife has gone, in his whole mind'.[36] These were not light, unconsidered remarks. Gladstone was the most prolific Homeric scholar of the Victorian period, and although his commentaries were not widely accepted they provide another instance of the action of the ancient Greek heritage upon the Judaic. F.H. Turner has argued that 'Gladstone's interpretation of the Jewish messianic mission thoroughly denigrated the possible contributions of Hebraism to the more general secular development of human culture. . . . By allowing the history of the Old Testament to pertain exclusively to human salvation, Gladstone made the natural achievements of the Greeks appear prescriptively adequate for temporal life'.[37] Indeed, Gladstone's version of Hellenism and the Hebraism evinced in Disraeli's novels is one further dimension to their rivalry.

These concerns reached the public domain after Leopold Gluckstein sent Gladstone a copy of his pamphlet 'The Eastern Question and the Jews'. Gladstone's response was published widely in the newspapers. He wrote: 'I have always had occasion to admire

34. Freeman wrote to W.T. Stead complaining, 'the duty and honour of the nation are being spoiled by the Jew': *ibid*, p. 343.
35. J. Morley, *Life of Gladstone*, vol. ii (London, 1903), p. 551.
36. A. Ramm, *The Political Correspondence of Mr Gladstone and Lord Granville*, vol. i (Oxford, 1962), p. 28.
37. Turner, *The Greek Heritage in Victorian Britain* (New Haven, CT, 1981), p. 169.

the conduct of English Jews in the discharge of their civil duties, but I deeply deplore the manner in which what I may call Judaic sympathies, beyond as well as within the circle of professed Judaism, are now acting on the question of the East.[38] In part this was a reference to Disraeli, in part to information Gladstone had been sent by Liddon claiming that two-thirds of the leading articles written in the Vienna daily press were written by Jews.[39] But it was also due, in part, to the pattern of Anglo-Jewish sympathies. It was certainly the case that prominent English Jews, with some few exceptions, were unmoved by the agitation in the autumn of 1876.[40] The *Jewish Chronicle* conceded that fierce discrimination against Jews in Roumania and the milder disadvantages in Serbia left English Jews mistrustful of Slav nationalism and Slav feelings for justice and religious liberty.[41] Most significantly, so far as perceptions were concerned, the most ardently Turkophile newspaper, the *Daily Telegraph*, was owned by a Jew, Edward Levy-Lawson.[42]

Gladstone's letter caused a great stir among English Jews. Abraham Benisch, who in 1875 had sent Gladstone a copy of his volume *Judaism Surveyed*, requested and was given an interview to explain to him the position of English Jews.[43] The Reverend A.L. Green remonstrated with Gladstone in the pages of the *Daily News*. The newspaper tried to defuse the quarrel. It did not believe Jews were actuated by their Judaic sympathies, nor did it believe that Gladstone had intended to suggest such a thing. But Gladstone had a voice of his own. In his interview with Benisch he once again lamented that 'Judaic sympathies' within and beyond the Jewish community should lie with Turkey.[44] Similarly, in a letter to the Liverpool Jewish Literary and Debating Society, he regretted that Jewish sympathies over Bulgaria were not assisting the cause of their civil and religious equality in the 'Christian states of Turkey'.[45]

38. The letter is reproduced in L. Glückstein, *The Eastern Question and the Jews* (London, 1876), p. 23.
39. Johnston, *Henry Parry Liddon*, p. 209.
40. The Jewish Liberal MPs Arthur Cohen and Serjeant Simon were among the exceptions. On Jewish sympathies in general see G. Alderman, *The Jewish Community in British Politics* (Oxford, 1983), pp. 36–8.
41. *JC*, 20 October 1876, p. 450.
42. S. Koss, *The Rise and Fall of the Political Press in Britain*, vol. i (London, 1981), pp. 200–3.
43. *Daily News*, 13 October 1876, p. 6; *ibid*, 14 October 1876, p. 2; *ibid*, 16 October 1876, p. 3; *ibid*, 17 October 1876, p. 3; *JC*, 3 November 1876, p. 486.
44. He was able to meet the accusation that his concern for the Christians in the East exceeded his concern for persecuted Jews by stating that he wanted equal rights for Turkish subjects irrespective of race or creed.
45. *JC*, 3 November 1876, p. 486; *ibid*, 10 November 1876, p. 499.

Disraeli's support for the Ottoman empire was thus presented as a reflection of the indelible influence of his Jewish origins which left him insensitive to Christian feeling. And Jews more widely were seen to place the particular interests of their co-religionists above sympathy with the suffering of eastern Christians.

The idea that British policy was being subverted to Jewish interests was elaborated in Labouchere's newspaper *The Truth* in November 1877 in an argument which aligned the interests of the government with those of Jewish bondholders: 'These conspirators are powerful, influential, and wealthy, and they have their organs in the press.' The aim of the war would have been 'the continuance of Semitic rule in Europe, not in the interests of England, but on account of affinity of race and feeling between the Jews and the Turks'.[46] In fact, the interest of bondholders in the Ottoman presence in Europe varied depending on the sort of stock they held.[47] But it was undoubtedly the case that the City was a source of strong support for Disraeli in 1876–8 and, not without reason, was regarded as a place where Jews were prominent. The suspicion that Semitic financiers had an unwarranted and selfish influence on government policy was intensified by the connections between the government and the Rothschild firm.[48]

The accusations brought by *The Truth* expressed not only hostility to Jewish influence but also to other, selfish and, in this sense, 'unpatriotic' interests within the polity. The impermeability of the plutocracy to considerations of the public good was a lesson drawn by Freeman and Gladstone during the agitation on the Eastern Question.[49] The ascendancy of the Jews was often perceived to be one facet of the rise of the plutocracy. Within a search for sinister interests, the Jewish component of the plutocracy seemed to call for particular attention. The indifference of most Jews to the Bulgarian

---

46. *The Truth*, 22 November 1877, p. 620.
47. H. St-C. Cunningham, 'British Public Opinion and the Eastern Question' (University of Sussex D. Phil, 1969), pp. 198–201.
48. The £4 million the government had needed for the purchase of the Suez Canal in November 1875 was raised by Disraeli in the form of a loan from N.M. Rothschild and Sons, obviating the need to recall and consult Parliament; the money was provided at an immodest rate equivalent to 13 per cent per annum: Blake, *Disraeli*, pp. 581–4. During the Eastern Crisis the Rothschilds' unrivalled intelligence network had been placed at the government's disposal. The head of the firm, Nathan, was described by Granville as 'a red hot Turk': Ramm, *The Political Correspondence*, vol. i, pp. 64–5; On the exchange of information see G.A. Knight, 'The Rothschild-Bleichroder Axis in Action: An Anglo-German Co-operative, 1877–8', *LBYB*, 1983, pp. 43–59.
49. Freeman, 'The English People in Relation to the Eastern Question', p. 503; Stephens, *E.A. Freeman*, pp. 164–5; Stead, *The MP for Russia*, vol. i, p. 356.

horrors could be interpreted as another selfish and particular interest overriding considerations of civilisation and humanity. Having achieved their own emancipation, Jews were accused of turning their backs on the aspirations of other oppressed minorities.

'A grotesque foreign accident in our English history'

Disraeli's indifference to English liberties and constitutional traditions was a subordinate issue during 1876–7. In this period it was the idea of a Christian and humane foreign policy which directed the critique of Disraeli's statecraft. But from December 1877 the constitutional theme became increasingly significant. The attack on the Prime Minister's foreign policy and his apparent preparedness to engage Britain in a war with Russia was connected to claims that he was eroding constitutional freedoms at home. This was the ground on which the 'Judaeophobe' opposition to the government took new forms. Before examining these in detail, however, we must first set out the context of policy and polemic from which they emerged.

The advance of Russian troops through the Balkans in late 1877 and January 1878 left the British government divided. In November Disraeli complained to the Queen that 'in a Cabinet of twelve there are seven parties or policies'.[50] The Prime Minister's own view was bullish. He wanted to threaten Russia with intervention. On 17 December he persuaded the Cabinet to recall Parliament and, when it reassembled in January, the government succeeded in adding an extra £6 million to the army and navy estimates. Russia's sinister silence on the terms it would impose on Turkey, as well as Whig sympathy for a policy of conditional neutrality, inhibited the opposition. Only ninety-six Liberals voted against the estimates on 7 February.

Between mid-February and the end of April 1878 war between Britain and Russia seemed an imminent danger.[51] The terms imposed on the Turks at the Treaty of San Stefano and signed on 3 March only increased the likelihood of conflict. So far as the British government was concerned the Treaty included a host of objectionable features, notably the creation of an enlarged Bulgaria – which it was assumed would be a Russian client – and Russian gains in Asiatic Turkey. The government continued to strike threatening poses, apparently risking war to induce an amendment of the Treaty. The reserves were called up and arrangements made to move troops from India to the Mediterranean.

50. Seton Watson, *Disraeli, Gladstone and the Eastern Question*, p. 286.
51. Blake, *Disraeli*, p. 639.

Towards the end of April Russian policy changed direction; something which owed a great deal to intrigue in St Petersburg and Austro-Hungarian disquiet, as well as bluster in London.[52] The way was clear for the negotiations which culminated in Disraeli's triumphant return in July from the Congress of Berlin. 'Big Bulgaria' was diminished, and although Russia would not relinquish its acquisitions in Asia, British honour and strategy were satisfied by the acquisition of Cyprus from the Sultan, as 'a strong base of arms' in the eastern Mediterranean, in return for an undertaking to defend the Turkish empire in Asia.

The domestic consequence of these events was that, whereas towards the end of 1877 the government had seemed almost paralysed by internal dissension, Disraeli's policy of brinkmanship not only won through but he and Salisbury returned from Berlin to be feted and honoured. At a banquet in Knightsbridge, Salisbury celebrated their success, not only at the Congress, but also over 'a loud-mouthed diplomacy struggling in another direction out-of-doors'.[53] Within opposition circles, the rising image of Disraeli in 1878 as a Semitic and dictatorial aberration within national history took shape at this moment of the Prime Minister's greatest popularity. Initially, at least, it was a response to political failure.

The recall of Parliament on 19 December 1877 stimulated petitions and public meetings whose aim was to mobilise opinion in favour of peace.[54] The agitation was different from the movement of autumn 1876. The preceding year the aim had been to induce Britain and the other great powers to intervene and impose reforms on Turkey. The agitation of December and January 1877–8 had the simpler object of maintaining British neutrality and keeping the country out of a war with Russia. It was also the more wide-ranging movement of protest. Nonconformists, who had provided the backbone of the Bulgarian agitation, were still more involved in the mobilisation of peace opinion and the movement also reached more deeply into the working classes.[55] The hope of the movement was that by its vociferous action it would strengthen the 'peace party' in the Cabinet and restrain Disraeli.[56]

52. Millman, *Britain and the Eastern Question*, pp. 425–7.
53. G.C. Thompson, *Public Opinion and Lord Beaconsfield, 1875–80*, vol. ii (London, 1886), p. 482.
54. Cunningham, 'British Public Opinion and the Eastern Question', pp. 134–5.
55. *Ibid*, 'British Public Opinion and the Eastern Question', pp. 137, 142. Of 1,576 petitions sumitted to Parliament opposing the vote of credit, 1,157 were from nonconformists: *ibid*, p. 146. Cunningham, 'The Language of Patriotism', *History Workshop Journal*, Autumn 1981, p. 23, suggests the peace agitation had more support among working men than had the Bulgarian agitation.
56. *Daily News*, 12 January 1878, p. 4; *ibid*, 19 January 1878, p. 4.

The government's apparent determination to risk war despite 'the nation's' clamour in favour of neutrality stimulated dire constitutional speculations within the peace movement. In early January the *Daily News* found England was in a position that 'our fathers and ourselves until a few years ago would have thought impossible'. The country had spoken clearly in favour of peace and neutrality but its wishes had been disregarded. The newspaper reflected, 'the nation is suffering just such misfortunes as would befall it if a conspiracy against its peace and honour were existing in the highest regions of the state'. The country was not permitted to know whither it was being led. This was a policy of 'Asiatic concealment which Englishmen abhor'.[57] Talk of 'conspiracy' and 'Asiatic concealment' was symptomatic of the direction the analysis would take.

In December the Queen had signalled her support for Disraeli's policy by lunching with him at Hughenden, the Prime Minister's country house – only once before had she taken such a step and that had been forty years earlier when Lord Melbourne was in office. The coincidence of the war scare and the Queen's visit with the publication of the third volume of Theodore Martin's *Life of the Prince Consort* provided additional material for constitutional alarms. The book was understood to have been written under the Queen's influence, as a vindication of her dead husband. Its account of the origins of the Crimean War was hostile to Russia; a point of view which accorded well with the Queen's own attitude to Russia in 1877–8. Further, the volume 'contained strong indications of a leaning to the doctrine of personal government in foreign affairs'.[58] *The Nonconformist* denounced the currency of theories 'about the relation of the Crown to the country which are utterly irreconcileable with sound constitutional practice'.[59] These would not have mattered but for the political juncture at which they arose: the Queen had become an Empress and Lord Beaconsfield articulated political theories 'more suited to Mordecai at the court of Ahasuerus than to the Prime Minister of England'.[60] The radical riposte to the biography in turn drew a reply in April in the *Quarterly Review* from W.J. Couthorpe. The journal's reputation as the fount of Tory doctrine gave the essay particular significance.[61] Couthorpe asserted that the Queen should have 'a large personal share in the control of our foreign policy', because of her knowledge of international

---

57. *Ibid*, 5 January, 1878, p. 4.
58. Thompson, *Public Opinion and Lord Beaconsfield*, vol. ii, p. 433.
59. *The Nonconformist*, 16 January 1878, p. 51.
60. *Ibid.*
61. Seton Watson, *Disraeli, Gladstone and the Eastern Question*, pp. 397–8.

affairs but also because 'her interest is beyond all comparison greater than that of any other single Englishman; and may even be compared with that of the nation itself'.[62] But the nation was precisely what the peace agitation claimed to represent.

Criticism of the Sovereign rebounded on Disraeli. H.C.G. Matthew notes that 'Gladstone shared the non-Tory alarm that, first, Disraeli was acting as the Queen's minister, and second, that there were threats to Cabinet control of foreign policy through the intervention of the court'.[63] These fears acquired greater substance in April 1878. The secret dispatch to Malta of 7,000 Indian troops was finally announced on 17 April once Parliament was in recess. The *Daily News* warned: 'It can by no means be regarded as accidental that these things have taken place concurrently with the assertion of strange and un-English doctrines concerning the personal authority of the Sovereign, a subject most unnecessarily forced upon the public by court biographers and panegyrists'.[64] The opposition claimed the manoeuvre, by enlarging the imperial forces without parliamentary consent, endangered English liberties. It breached Parliament's financial control over the number employed in the British army, and through this, in Gladstone's words, it undermined Parliament's 'restraint upon the foreign policy, especially the war policy, of the Executive Government'.[65] The Whigs, who were happy to struggle to sustain English liberties, if not peace, joined in with the criticism of the government's conduct.[66]

The opposition press made connections between these discrete incidents and linked them to 'foreign' influences within the government. Writing in the *Edinburgh Review*, W.N. Massey found the unconstitutional views of the Prince Consort and the *Quarterly Review* exemplified in the way Indian forces had been called to Europe. Significantly, Massey dwelt on the indigenous character of the constitution. The damage done to the constitution was attributed to Disraeli, rather than to the Cabinet as a whole. The Prime Minister's genius and ambition placed him in a line of great statesmen such as Godolphin, Walpole, Chatham and the Younger Pitt, and enabled him to dominate the Cabinet 'on all the great lines of policy'. But unlike his illustrious predecessors, his 'dazzling qualities are not

62. W.J. Couthorpe, 'The Crown and the Constitution', *Quarterly Review*, April 1878, p. 298.
63. H.C.G. Matthew, ed., *The Gladstone Diaries*, vol. ix (Oxford, 1986), p. liv.
64. *Daily News*, 9 May 1878, p. 4.
65. Thompson, *Public Opinion and Lord Beaconsfield*, vol. ii, p. 444.
66. T. Jenkins, *Gladstone, Whiggery and the Liberal Party, 1874–86* (Oxford, 1988), pp. 66–7.

those of an English statesman'.[67] *The Nonconformist*, contemplating the prospect of Indian troops' being called to Europe, perceived 'the rapid development of an Imperial policy inconsistent with the constitutional traditions of the English race'.[68] The charge of 'imperialism' referred primarily to the effects of foreign policy upon domestic freedoms. It was the antithesis of English constitutionalism. In 1886 George Carslake Thompson defined it as 'an exaltation of the military side of the State together with a corresponding depression of parliamentary institutions'.[69] The outcome of the Berlin Congress – the acquisition of Cyprus and the agreement to defend Turkish despotism in Asia – seemed to confirm this trend; Britain's provocation of wars in Afghanistan and South Africa within the next six months – matters in which Disraeli was, in fact, the victim of disobedient colonial administrators – appeared to illustrate its continuation.[70]

Imperialism led to the decline of political liberty and civic virtue. *The Nonconformist* identified the Prime Minister's policy as one which followed 'Imperialistic theories which will place us alongside the great military powers of Europe', and in doing so commit the country to maintain an enlarged army to this end. The analogy to Rome was quickly drawn. There, 'lust of conquest made a standing army the chief need of the Empire, destroyed the civic patriotism of the Republic, made despotism inevitable, and personal interests supreme'.[71] In this light Disraeli's fondness for the rhetoric of empire was alarming. J.G. Ashworth in his biographical poem 'Imperial Ben' rhymed as follows:

67. W.N. Massey, 'The Constitution and the Crown', *Edinburgh Review*, July 1878, pp. 262–94. In the same journal, Henry Reeve complained that the ministry's actions were outside 'the old traditions of the British constitution'. In transferring power from Parliament to the Crown and from the Crown to the first minister, Disraeli's policy was likened to that of Strafford and Bolingbroke: H. Reeve, 'England in the Levant', *Edinburgh Review*, October 1878, pp. 558–93.
68. *The Nonconformist*, 22 May 1878, p. 505.
69. Thompson, *Public Opinion and Lord Beaconsfield*, vol. i, pp. 40–2; *ibid*, vol. ii, p. 448. See too R. Koebner and D. Schmidt, *Imperialism: The Story and Significance of a Political Word* (Cambridge, 1964), chapter 1.
70. Blake, *Disraeli*, pp. 658–74.
71. *The Nonconformist*, 5 June 1878, p. 558. And likewise Gladstone, in his third Midlothian speech, affirmed, 'Nothing can be more fundamentally unsound, more practically ruinous, than the establishment of Roman analogies for the guidance of British policy. What gentlemen was Rome? Rome was indeed an imperial state . . . but a state whose very basis it was to deny equal rights, to proscribe the independent existence of other nations. That gentlemen, was the Roman idea.' W. Gladstone, *Midlothian Speeches 1879* (Leicester, 1971), p. 129.

Imperialism will never do
Where Cromwell, Hampden, had a birth
Our fathers' spirit doth imbue
Their children all the world-wide through
And well they know its worth

Imperialism! What is it, save
Presumptuous arrogance and pride? –
A monstrous self-love that would crave
All for its own of good and brave
Self-crowned, self-deified.[72]

How was the revival of an idea so un-English and un-Christian as the idea of empire, in both its domestic and foreign aspects, to be explained? The connection between despotism and the orient was a common theme. Henry Reeve dwelt on Disraeli's oriental imagination, exemplified by the Queen's assumption of the title 'Empress of India' in 1876. This was the badge of 'the oriental character of the British monarchy' and of the supremacy of Asia over Europe – a favourite theme of Disraeli's novels.[73] An anonymous pamphlet, *Peace or War! An Indictment of the Policy of the Government*, described the ministry's foreign policy as one that sighed for 'universal empire'. It was summed up as 'our modern Anglo-Israelitish-Caeserism'.[74]

A lengthier assessment of the influence of Disraeli's Jewishness was made by Henry Dunckley in November of the same year, in an essay on 'The progress of personal rule'. He made the familiar charge that Disraeli was 'imperialising the constitution' and brought forward the usual evidence to support it. The connection between Empire and the erosion of liberties was highlighted by the use of the Indian Treasury to bring Indian troops to Malta in April 1878. In evading the need for a vote of credit from Parliament, Dunckley claimed, the principle had been established that 'any number of Asiatics can be brought almost within sight of our shores preparatory to a whiff of grapeshot in Westminster'.[75] Disraeli's aim was 'to restore the monarchy to the position it occupied in the days of Charles the First'; to 'establish the ascendancy of Jacobitism under the House of Hanover'.[76] The general reason for his consistent

72. J.G. Ashworth, *Imperial Ben* (London, 1879), p. 75.
73. Reeve, 'England in the Levant', p. 559.
74. Anonymous author, *'The Eastern Crisis', Peace or War! An Indictment of the Policy of the Government* (London, 1879), pp. 2–3.
75. H. Dunckley, 'The Progress of Personal Rule', *Nineteenth Century*, November 1878, pp. 798, 802.
76. *Ibid*, pp. 792, 795, 802.

attempt to undermine liberty was that he was not truly English. His ideas were 'foreign to the English temperament'.[77] This had dire consequences. Whereas Tories, Whigs and radicals were united by 'the same vein of English sentiment', with Disraeli as Prime Minister 'Englishmen might almost imagine they were living in another land.'[78]

Disraeli's foreignness was marked by his race and religion. He was 'a Jew by birth and a Christian by accident'. This meant that he had no appreciation of the ecclesiastical and theological questions at the heart of 'modern history': 'the seventeenth century must be a sealed book to him . . . the blood of our martyrs has no sanctity in his eyes'.[79] In its place he exhibited the preference of the 'Asiatic mind' for 'absolute monarchy tempered by sacerdotalism'.[80]

Disraeli's own writings of the 1840s and early 1850s, in which he celebrated the monarchy and the Jewish 'race', comprised a treasure trove of evidence for arguments such as these. Writing in the *Fortnightly Review* in April 1878, F. Harrison Hill, surveyed Beaconsfield's career and observed that 'Judaism and Jews have been thrust by him with an almost unnecessary pertinacity into English politics and literature. The consciousness of his race and their faith seems never to escape him.'[81] If Disraeli's novels and thinking on Jewish emancipation had enabled him to combine national Christianity and Hebraism to his own satisfaction many others remained unpersuaded. The conceit of Alfred C. Shaw's pamphlet *The Book of Benjamin*, which aped the style of the King James Bible, underscored the point in its content as well as its form. According to *The Book of Benjamin*, when the nations of Europe witnessed Parliament's support for Beaconsfield's foreign policy, 'they laughed one to another, and said: Behold how Benjamin of Israel doth lead leviathan – even John Bull – with a hook, and doth make him go wheresoever it pleaseth him.'[82]

John Bull appears elsewhere in these writings. On the front of a pamphlet titled *Squire Bull and his Bailiff Benjamin*, the former is represented as a rotund gentleman, complete with side whiskers and top hat, driving away Benjamin who appears like one of *Punch's*

77. *Ibid*, pp. 790, 794.
78. *Ibid*, p. 795.
79. *Ibid*, pp. 792–3.
80. *Ibid*.
81. F. Harrison Hill, 'The Political Adventures of Lord Beaconsfield', *Fortnightly Review*, part i, April 1878, p. 486.
82. A.C. Shaw, *The Book of Benjamin* (London, 1879), p. 27. Shaw's pamphlet was sufficiently popular to run into 7 editions and for him to publish a sequel, *The Second Book of Benjamin* (London, 1880).

cringing, dirty, Jewish, old clothes men. The pamphlet concludes with the Squire informing Ben that 'you have acted as if you were dictator of this island and people are beginning to tremble for their rights'.[83] Elsewhere, John Bull lectures Ben that he had better cease his 'flattery and palaver' and do as he is told, or else retire and invest his savings 'in the establishment of an old clothes shop in some suitable back street'.[84] The presence of John Bull underlines the point that caricature and polemic focused on Disraeli was generating two stereotypes: an image of the Jew but also an image of English political traditions which were brought sharply into focus by the Jews' distance from them.

The causes of the Jews' unassimilability could be understood in two ways: one pursued the opposition of Judaism to Christianity, the other focused on the operation of race. In practice, the two themes can often be found together within single pamphlets, articles and speeches. It was in T.P. O'Connor's biography of Beaconsfield – first published in 1879 and which ran into eight editions over the next six years – that the idea that Christian morality and English liberties were being subverted to the working of Jewish power received its most vivid treatment. Here the themes of race and religion were mixed promiscuously as O'Connor opposed the interests of 'the Jewish race' to the 'policy of Christendom'. The extraordinary unanimity of European Jews in the Eastern Question arose from their preference for the Turks' 'contemptuous toleration' above Russian oppression, and the Jews' bond with Mohammedans against Christians – their common enemy. The key to understanding Disraeli's policy was that 'he treated the whole question from the standpoint of the Jews'.[85] This was a specific instance of the determinations of theology and race.

> Every genuine Jew . . . bows down within the recesses of his heart before his own people, as still, if not the chosen of God, yet as immeasurably supreme among men; and other nations are but the mushroom nations, whose fathers were barbarians when Judea was the land of civilization. I am not blaming the Jews for feeling thus. The feeling is most natural. The Jew *can* look back to a more glorious past; and it is the more natural that he should feed his imagination on the glories of that past, because of the position to which the rise of Christianity has reduced his race. I am only pointing out

83. Anonymous author, *Squire John Bull and his Bailiff Benjamin: A Political Allegory* (London, 1879), p. 14.
84. Anonymous author, *Ben's Dream about the 'Schemers of Philistia' and 'Ishmael's Noble Sons' with my Lord John Bull's Rude Remarks* (London, 1878), pp. 11–12.
85. T.P. O'Connor, *Lord Beaconsfield* (London, 1879), pp. 607–9.

how this feeling operated on the mind of Lord Beaconsfield when dealing with the affairs of the English people.[86]

But though it was 'natural' for him to do so, in imposing a Jewish policy Disraeli violated traditions of English and Christian liberty. In the East he consigned 'a million Christians to the most degrading slavery' while at home 'we, under the spell of our Oriental dictator were taught to trample our representative institutions under foot'.[87]

However, the mix between race and religion in most texts was not equal. A Congregationalist preacher such as William Crosbie complained that Beaconsfield was 'English neither in blood nor in sympathy' but the core of his sermons on 'the Beaconsfield policy' and on 'Christian patriotism' dealt with the need to conduct policy on Christian principles and asserted the nation's Christian identity.[88] Beaconsfield's actions were 'out of the line of the noblest traditions of English citizenship' and not since the Stuarts had the arbitrary and personal element been so forceful in government. Crosbie rehearsed a litany of the insults to Parliament offered by Disraeli but he also asserted, 'the spirit of genuine Patriotism is not dead in England'.[89] This patriotism was essentially Christian. 'The Bible *is* the secret of England's greatness. The vital element in her progress; the marrow of her strength; the palladium of her liberties; the condition of the guardianship of omnipotence; the source of the charm, and of the terror, and of the trust which England's name heretofore inspired.'[90]

What began as an attack on Disraeli ultimately reflected on all Jews. Beaconsfield possessed only an 'artificial, manufactured sense of God', not the deep sense felt by Bright and Gladstone in the present and Cromwell in the past. He was a Jew, 'and his mind is infected with the ideas of his race'. In particular, Jews had looked forward to the coming of the Messiah with expectations of temporal glory. 'They thought they would become the supreme political, military and IMPERIAL power in these latter days.' Beaconsfield's policy was but 'a vulgar parody of the ancient Jewish dream'.[91]

In place of this 'diseased excrescence' Crosbie hoped to erect a

86. *Ibid*, pp. 613–14.
87. *Ibid*, pp. 663, 671.
88. See W. Crosbie, *The Beaconsfield Policy: An Address* (London, 1879), p. 3, for comments on Disraeli's blood; also E. Paxton Hood, *The Beaconsfield Sermon, No. 2, Act the Citizen* (Manchester, 1879), p. 16.
89. Crosbie, *The Beaconsfield Policy*, pp. 3–4.
90. W. Crosbie, *The Situation of Public Affairs from the Standpoint of Christian Patriotism* (London, 1879), p. 6.
91. Crosbie, *The Beaconsfield Policy*, pp. 13–14.

nation whose Christian character flowed from the people to its leaders and institutions. It was not the alliance of Church and state that rendered a nation Christian (as the opponents of Jewish emancipation had claimed). 'A nation is Christian only when the units and the families which compose it are Christian, and when its laws are Christian, and when its prevailing tone is Christian, and when its dealings and relationships with other nations are based on Christian principles and pervaded by the Christian spirit.'[92] The nonconformists of England and Gladstone, who had prevented Disraeli from dragging the country into a war with Russia to prop up Turkish despotism, were the embodiments of active Christian citizenship and patriotism.[93]

Doctrines of race and historical development were preferred by Liberal intellectuals whose more secular sense of the development of English liberty promoted an analysis of the problem in these terms. In the last chapter we noted the ways in which Goldwin Smith and E.A. Freeman appropriated such ideas. But they were diffused far more widely than this. To Frank Harrison Hill, whose lengthy assessment of 'the political adventures of Lord Beaconsfield' ran into four parts in the *Fortnightly Review* in the spring and summer of 1878, the man was 'a grotesque foreign accident in our English history'.[94] One feels, he suggested, that the man had come from another world, 'and that he is to be judged the law of his domicile, wherever that may be, rather than by the rule according to which Englishmen pass moral sentence upon eachother'.[95] This world was Jewish and oriental. His policy in the Eastern Question was more 'the product rather of an erratic Oriental imagination than of a European intelligence'.[96]

As in the essays of Goldwin Smith, the sustained use of 'race' ensured that although Disraeli was the main subject of attack, criticism was not limited to him. It extended to Jews more generally. Disraeli's success was one part of a widespread phenomenon: 'in administration, in finance, and in journalism, Jewish influences notoriously guide and shape English politics'.[97] Hill referred to the work of the French Semitist Ernest Renan. According to Renan,

92. Crosbie, *The Situation of Public Affairs*, p. 9.
93. A similar project was expressed in two sermons delivered in November 1878 by the Rev. E. Paxton Hood: *The Beaconsfield Sermon, Preached at Cavendish Street Chapel, 18 November, 1878* (Manchester, 1879) idem, *The Beaconsfield Sermon, No. 2, Act the Citizen.*
94. F. Harrison Hill, 'The Political Adventures of Lord Beaconsfield', part iv, *Fortnightly Review*, August 1878, p. 269.
95. *Idem,* 'The Political Adventures of Lord Beaconsfield', part i, pp. 477–8.
96. *Idem,* 'The Political Adventures of Lord Beaconsfield', part iv, p. 268.
97. *Idem,* 'The Political Adventures of Lord Beaconsfield', part i, pp. 482–92.

'The Semitic race is to be recognised almost entirely by negative characteristics. It has neither mythology, nor epic, nor science, nor philosophy, nor fiction nor plastic arts, nor civil life; in everything there is a complete absence of complexity, subtlety or feeling, except for unity. It has no variety in its monotheism.'[98] As a result Jews were able to display a remarkable adaptability in the societies to which they had been transplanted. It was this which explained the prominence of 'Hebrew gentlemen' in Parliament and in the press, 'singing the national anthem and patriotic melodies to an amused and excited audience who have shouted and banged their glasses, and have believed in the[ir] spontaneity and disinterestedness and genuine British feeling'.[99] This was only a superficial alteration, however, and Disraeli was but the foremost example of his own doctrine of the determining significance of race.[100] Thus, whether it was framed primarily in terms of race or religion, the attack which focused on Disraeli was not restricted to him. As his misdeeds were attributed to his Jewish origins, the criticisms inevitably extended to Jews in general.

Jingos and Jews

Unlike the Bulgarian agitation in the autumn of 1876, the peace movement of December and January 1877–8 faced vociferous opposition, from a counter-agitation urging the government to adopt a strong policy against Russian aggression. Its centres were towns in the west Midlands, Lancashire and above all London.[101] Seton Watson's judgement was that 'rarely, if ever, has opinion been so keenly roused, and so deeply divided, on a question of foreign policy' as in January 1878.[102] This conflict was carried on daily in the press and in pamphlet literature but also at public meetings, in the music halls and on the streets. By the end of January peace meetings were being broken up and the agitation was curtailed.[103] It was a conflict between contending definitions of patriotism and of the nation's true identity. Speaking at the Guildhall in

---

98. Cited in M. Bernal, *Black Athena; the Afroaslatic Roots of Classical Civilisation*, vol. i (London, 1987), p. 346.
99. 'The Political Adventures of Lord Beaconsfield', part i, p. 481.
100. On this see too A. Boyle, *The Sympathy and Action of England in the Late Eastern Crisis and What Came of Them* (London, 1878), p. 11.
101. H. Cunningham, 'Jingoism in 1877–8', *Victorian Studies*, June 1971, pp. 429–53.
102. Seton Watson, *Disraeli, Gladstone and the Eastern Question*, p. 272.
103. It revived in the spring but without its earlier vigour and strength of numbers. Cunningham, 'British Public Opinion and the Eastern Question', pp. 184–6.

November 1877, Disraeli answered 'cosmopolitan critics, men who are the friends of every country save their own', who criticised his policy as selfish: 'My Lord Mayor,' he responded, 'it is as selfish as patriotism.'[104]

The phenomenon at the centre of the aggression against the peace movement was 'jingoism'. In *The Book of Benjamin* A.C. Shaw satirised its emergence. 'And in those days there arose a new sect in England. And they made unto themselves a God and called him Jingo and worshipped him and all his deeds; and they loved the Turks. And the name of the sect was Jingo and their temple was called Music Hall, and they assembled in great numbers to sing lewd songs and praise their God.'[105] The term 'Jingo' was taken by the peace movement from the music hall song, made famous by the Great MacDermott:

> We don't want to fight
> But by Jingo if we do
> We've got the ships, we've got the men,
> We've got the money too.[106]

The chorus from which it was taken formed part of just one of several anti-Russian songs popular in the music halls during the winter of 1877–8, and its notoriety may have been due to the way it captured the mood of support for a foreign policy which was seen by its adherents as unsentimental, proud and defensive. A pamphlet titled *What are we Going to Fight for?* echoed the attitude of the song when it stated, 'we dislike Russia for her blasphemies, her falsehoods, her deceptions, her robberies and her brutalities . . .', but for none of these was England going to declare war. 'England will fight in self-defence if Russia dares to extend her aggression to what England has defined as her interest.'[107]

Here was a view of the Eastern Crisis which repeated the terms in which it had been presented by Disraeli at the Guildhall in November 1876. Having said that 'Peace is essentially an English policy,' Disraeli asserted England's preparedness for war if her interests were threatened.

---

104. Moneypenny and Buckle, *The Life of Benjamin Disraeli*, vol. vi, p. 192.
105. Shaw, *The Book of Benjamin*, pp. 22–3.
106. H. Broadhurst, *Henry Broadhurst MP: The Story of his Life* (London, 1901), p. 80; Thompson, *Public Opinion and Lord Beaconsfield*, vol. i, p. 59.
107. Anonymous author, *What are we Going to Fight for? This Question Considered and Answered Liberally and Conservatively and on Radical Grounds* (London, 1878), pp. 14, 15; see too Anonymous author, *The Decline of the British Empire?* (London, 1878), pp. 1–2.

If she enters into a conflict in a righteous cause – and I will not believe that England will go to war except for a righteous cause [cheers] – if the contest is one which concerns her liberty, her independence, or her Empire, her resources, I feel, are inexhaustible. [Loud cheers] She is not a country that, when she enters into a campaign, has to ask herself whether she can support a second or third campaign. [Cheers] She enters into a campaign which she will not terminate till right is done.[108]

What Beaconsfield uttered at the Guildhall, the Great MacDermott performed at the music hall.[109]

The ministry's opponents faced the problem of the apparent success of the government's diplomacy and war-like gestures and the popularity this brought. In October 1878, writing in the *Edinburgh Review*, Henry Reeve complained that Disraeli's policy, 'like the Caeserism of the French empire . . . is all the more despotic for being founded on a broad popular basis'.[110] Here was an apprehension, common to many Liberal intellectuals, of the dangers of too broad a franchise. Henry Dunckley too feared Disraeli was using 'vast numbers of people but poorly provided with political knowledge, and with no party antecedents' to pursue his own anti-parliamentary goals.[111] 'Jingoism' was the evidence feeding these worries.

Indeed, the Second Reform Act shaped perceptions of the pro-government demonstrations and music hall rumbustiousness. These were regarded as new and dangerous phenomenon, and historians have followed this lead. But crowds proclaiming support for the government and monarchy, and loathing of foreigners were not unprecedented. What was novel was the way in which a Conservative leader addressed them and the fact that many of them were now enfranchised.[112] The peace movement portrayed the 'jingos' as representatives of an unintelligent, sub-political class manipulated by the interests supporting the war party.[113] Some Liberals, however,

108. Cited in Thompson, *Public Opinion and Lord Beaconsfield*, vol. ii, p. 96.
109. See too Disraeli's speech at the Guildhall in November 1878, *The Times*, 11 November 1878, p. 10. The Prime Minister's ability to speak to the jingos 'in their own language' was acknowledged by his colleagues: Cecil, *Robert Marquis of Salisbury*, vol. ii, p. 288.
110. Reeve, 'England in the Levant', p. 561.
111. H. Dunkley, 'The Progress of Personal Rule', *Nineteenth Century*, November 1878, pp. 785–808; G. Smith, 'A Word for Indignation Meetings', *Fortnightly Review*, July 1878, p. 97.
112. On an earlier manifestation see L. Colley, 'The Apotheosis of George III: Loyalty, Royalty and the British Nation, 1760–1820', *Past and Present*, February 1984, pp. 94–129.
113. *Daily News*, 1 February 1878, p. 5; *Nonconformist*, 6 February 1878, p. 122.

appreciated that the challenge of 'jingoism' was more substantial and that it constituted an eager response to Disraeli's vision of an imperial England. It had to be contested, not merely dismissed. They sought to discredit Tory patriotism by revealing the Judaic goal at the core of Disraeli's policy. One pamphleteer protested at Disraeli's 'spurious patriotism': 'He is sailing the ship under false colours, and he has cajoled the crew into believing that the proud Union Jack floating at the peak is the joint property of the Turk and the Jew.'[114] O'Connor hammered the point in a cameo describing Disraeli's triumphant return from the Congress of Berlin. He portrayed the aged, ninety-five-year-old Moses Montefiore coming out to meet him.

> By that small scene the meaning of this apotheosis of Lord Beaconsfield by a Christian people is written in letters of light. That day represented the triumph, not of England, not of an English policy, not of an Englishman. It was the triumph of Judea, a Jewish policy, a Jew. The Hebrew, who drove through these crowds to Downing Street, was dragging the whole of Christendom behind the juggernaut car over the rights of Turkish Christians, of which he was the charioteer.[115]

As well as discrediting Tory patriotism, the peace agitation claimed 'true patriotism' for itself. In July 1878, in the wake of Disraeli's return from Berlin, the *Daily News* pronounced:

> That which ought just now to be the 'imperial instinct' and 'imperial patriotism' of every genuine Englishman – if such pompous words could ever be properly employed to describe anything true and patriotic – is the wish to recover for England that right of parliamentary self-government which we all believed until the other day that constitutional principles, if not technical rules, secured to her.[116]

This was a theme addressed also by William Crosbie in 1879, who identified three types of patriot. First, there were the 'true patriots who desire to see the nation's character and the nation's life, and all the nation's doing conformed to the Bible'. But these were opposed by the 'patriots of the MUSIC HALL': 'The greatness in which they believe is the greatness of the terrier or the bulldog type. They will shout themselves hoarse in praise of that greatness, and in denunciation of moral greatness.' Third, these were joined by 'patriots of the IMPERIALIST type': 'the patriots who range themselves so obsequiously under the Beaconsfield banner, and who cultivate alliances

---

114.   Jenkins, *Breakers Ahead!*, p. 12.
115.   O'Connor, *Lord Beaconsfield*, p. 672.
116.   *Daily News*, 23 July 1878, p. 65; see too *The Nonconformist*, 17 July 1878, p. 705.

with the patriots of Music Hall'. With an eye to the coming election, Crosbie concluded, 'the hour is approaching when the English people will have to decide as to the various types of patriotism. The arbitrament is with them.'[117] As Gladstone travelled to Scotland for his Midlothian campaign of 1879 he addressed a crowd in similar terms, telling them it was upon their exertions 'as true Britons and true patriots' that he depended to place the country 'in hands more competent to guide them with honour and with safety than those to which they are now entrusted'.[118]

The emergence of jingoism has been taken to signal a decisive moment at which the 'language of patriotism' was captured by the 'right' in British politics.[119] However, an image of the nation rooted in a set of indigenous freedoms remained a powerful presence in political argument. In the short term, its force was revealed by the Liberal victory in the general election of 1880 and Gladstone's triumphant Midlothian speaking tours in 1879 and 1880. Indeed, the force of Gladstone's popularity compelled the Whigs to accept him as Prime Minister after the general election.[120] Rather than indicating the victory of an imperial vision of the nation, the fierce battle fought over Disraeli's foreign policy and constitutional practice reflected the adjustment of Conservative and Liberal politicians, and of large numbers of their supporters, to political conditions after 1867.

Between 1876–80 popular opposition to Disraeli expressed an attempt to establish a vision of the nation which extended well beyond the relation of individuals to the state; it now scrutinised their religious life and social relations. This had been imminent in the franchise extension of 1867 as the radicals of the 1860s – nonconformists, academics and working men – hoped the extended franchise would enable them to work towards a more harmonious political community – by diminishing the role of the self-interested aristocracy.[121] During the Eastern Crisis and after it, for some Liberal intellectuals and nonconformists, the Jews, their bonds and their influence seemed to explain why the moral and political returns on 1867 were so slender. At the heart of the matter were traditions of liberty and humanity, located in the nation's culture and religious

117. Crosbie, *The Situation of Public Affairs*, pp. 10–12.
118. Gladstone, *Midlothian Speeches*, p. 19.
119. Cunningham, 'The Language of Patriotism', p. 23.
120. T.A. Jenkins, 'Gladstone, the Whigs and the Leadership of the Liberal Party, 1879–80', *Historical Journal*, June 1984, pp. 337–60; Ghosh, 'Disraelian Conservatism', p. 292, mentions the neglect by historians of the fundamental constitutional grievances in the 1880 election.
121. Parry, *Democracy and Religion*, p. 29.

life, which lay beyond them and beyond Disraeli in particular. The part of Christianity within these traditions went far in explaining why they were alien, but so too did the eastern character of Judaism and the operation of race. The Jews' behaviour between 1876–80, whether looked at from the point of view of their commercial, religious or race interests, appeared as a clear example of selfishness – of an absence of 'patriotism'.

Antipathy to Jews and censure of Judaism had a much stronger presence in mid-Victorian political culture than has been acknowledged. But we need to reassess the significance of anti-Jewish feeling as well as its strength. The Judaeophobia of the late 1870s did not signify the failure or the antithesis of that liberalism for which Jewish emancipation was a signal victory; rather, it was its extension. These years saw the development of articulations of national identity which two and three decades earlier had been used to justify Jewish equality. The critique of Disraeli and the Jews underlines both the centrality of contending conceptions of national identity in English political culture and also their pivotal significance in the politics of Jewish integration. The Bulgarian agitation and its aftermath was an attempt to fulfil the radical promise of 1867 and establish the government as a disinterested expression of a moralised and Christian nation. It went beyond an attack on Disraeli as an individual and laid open to question whether the particular interests and bonds of Jews placed them outside the parameters of the national community. The Jews' critics reformulated in populist terms the idea of a Christian polity and nation which had been confronted a generation earlier in the arguments of the anti-emancipationists. This drew out an ambiguity at the heart of the politics of Jewish emancipation. Non-conformist clergymen and radicals had been staunch supporters of the Jews' political equality. But whereas for most Jews emancipation was an end in itself, for their supporters it was but one step towards a moralised polity. In these circumstances, in view of their allegiances in the Eastern Crisis, and in view of Disraeli's behaviour, the Jews could appear no longer as the victims of aristocratic and Anglican privilege but as a self-interested and powerful minority.

Chapter 5

The Contradictions of Emancipated Jewry

Jewish apologetics

The political and religious culture of mid-Victorian England was changing and divided. It did not permit a single, stable resolution to the problem of Jewish integration. No sooner had Jews achieved civil equality and attempted to reform their religious services than the terms of criticism shifted and they faced new challenges in theology and in politics. In this chapter I examine the ways Jews responded to these new challenges.

The 'Judaeophobia' of the late 1870s alarmed English Jews. Communal leaders and Jewish writers struggled to present the claims of Judaism and the ties between Jews in ways that would be acceptable in English society. They repudiated the charges that Jews could not be patriots and that they were indifferent to the universal claims of humanity. In October 1877, for instance, the *Jewish Chronicle* explained that Jews tended to favour the Turks in their war with Russia not because they were 'Turkophile' but because they were 'Russophobe'. Their preference was not born from antipathy to 'Christianity or Aryanism' but from the fact that Jews received better treatment from Turks than from eastern Christians. At the end of 1877 'atrocities' committed against Jews in Bulgaria were broadcast triumphantly as confirmation of this point. Nevertheless, the *Jewish Chronicle* insisted, Jews would not have been influenced by their fear of Slavic Christians had they not been convinced it was also in harmony 'with the true interests of humanity and the well-being of those Christian populations whom Russia professes to have come to liberate'. A religious or race war, such as the one pursued by Russia, would encourage fanaticism and lead to yet further massacres.[1] Jews

1. *JC*, 5 October 1877, p. 9; on anti-Jewish violence in Bulgaria see *ibid*, 16 November 1877, p. 9.

not only tried to establish grounds on which the interests of humanity and Jewry were complementary: they also loudly protested their concern for the well-being of England. The *Jewish Chronicle* portrayed its readers as patriots without peer. Hermann Adler protested: 'Granted that eighteen hundred years ago our ancestors dwelt amid the vine-clad hills of Judaea, is that any reason why we should be less solicitous for the glory and interest of the empire we now inhabit?'[2]

In 1871 British Jews established an organisation – the Anglo-Jewish Association (AJA) – whose purpose was to defend Jewish interests throughout the world.[3] The AJA illustrates the way in which English Jews attempted to reconcile, in the words of Serjeant Simon, one of the founders, 'a bond of brotherhood among the scattered fragments of our race' with the demands of citizenship and patriotism.[4] At a programmatic level this was done by disavowing any 'political' aim.[5] The connection of race was understood to be 'natural' and 'simply the expression of kinship and family attachment'. To the *Jewish Chronicle*, it was harmless because among Jews there was no racial policy, unlike among the Slavs, Teutons and Greeks.[6]

But in practice this was difficult to sustain. Representing the cause of religious and political liberty for oppressed Jews necessarily impinged on the business of politics and the affairs of state. It could lead Jews into conflict with the goals of the government or opposition. At a rhetorical level, therefore, there were consistent attempts to erase these tensions by matching Jewish interests with the pieties of national ideology. The President of the AJA, Baron de Worms, spoke at a meeting held in the North London Synagogue in June 1878 when he aligned the aims of the Association with the fundamentals of English constitutional theory.

> The object of this Association is, in a word, the defence of the liberty of Jews when assailed . . . the defence of the civil liberty which accords to every man his post as a useful member of society; of that political liberty which gives him full scope for a legitimate ambition, and for a patriotic activity in the interests of the commonwealth; of that religious liberty which permits

2. *Ibid*, 1 March 1878, p. 9; H. Adler, 'Can Jews be Patriots?', *Nineteenth Century*, April 1878, p. 643. This 'imperial' patriotism may not have mollified the Jews' critics.
3. The conjuncture of a pogrom in Odessa with the weakening of the Alliance Israelite Universelle as a result of the incorporation of Alsace, and with it a great portion of French Jewry, within Germany were the immediate stimuli for the new organisation. *JC*, 30 July 1871, p. 5; *ibid*, 7 August 1871, p. 11.
4. *Ibid*, 7 August 1871, p. 314.
5. *Ibid*, 30 July 1871, p. 9.
6. *Ibid*, 31 May 1878, p. 10.

a full development of his moral aptitude, and gives him the right to worship the God of his fathers after the manner and rites of his fathers.[7]

Similarly, Hermann Adler asserted in 1878 that when Jews approached the British government to mitigate the suffering of their co-religionists they were acting as true patriots.[8] But since the nature of patriotism and its practical political expression were hotly disputed, by adopting this political language English Jews made as many enemies as friends.

Jewish writers were forced by the range of the critique they faced to debate along a broad front. Goldwin Smith's essays, for instance, were widely noticed and criticised in the Anglo-Jewish press. Further, in two articles written for *Nineteenth Century*, Hermann Adler answered Smith and attempted to vindicate Judaism as a monotheistic religion with universal principles. Adler combined an uncompromising rejection of Christian dogma with an attempt to make Judaism conform to the temper of post-evangelical Christianity. In response to the developmental critique adopted by Goldwin Smith, Adler denied that Judaism was a religion of race. Endogamy was a device to preserve the religion, not the race; circumcision was not a tribal mark but obedience to a 'Divine behest'; and the Jews' reluctance to proselytise was an expression of their universalism – since Jews did not believe they possessed a monopoly of God's mercy converting the Gentiles was unnecessary.[9] But as well as answering these specific points, Adler set out, from the point of view of orthodox Judaism, to reconcile the particularist aspects of Judaism with universal principles. In doing so he also asserted that, far from being a relic of barbarism, Judaism was the originary progressive and universalising force in world history.

> The ritual ordinances of the Bible were . . . primarily intended for the Jewish race. But the sublime religious and moral principles which the book enunciates are applicable to the whole of mankind and have beyond a doubt become, by their having formed the foundation of Christianity and Islam, the great dynamic agent of modern civilisation.[10]

Likewise, the Balliol-educated Jewish theologian Claude Montefiore, though a religious reformer, claimed orthodox Judaism was now taught as a 'pure religious universalism'.[11] Both Montefiore and

7. Anglo-Jewish Association, *Seventh Annual Report* (London, 1878), p. 18.
8. Adler, 'Can Jews be Patriots?', p. 646.
9. H. Adler, 'Jews and Judaism: A Rejoinder', *Nineteenth Century*, July 1878, pp. 135–8; *idem*, 'Recent Phases of Judaeophobia', *Ninettenth Century*, December 1881, p. 814.
10. Adler, 'Jews and Judaism', pp. 139–40.
11. C. Montefiore, 'Is Judaism a Tribal Religion?', *Contemporary Review*, September 1882, p. 364.

Adler could agree that 'the great bond which unites Israel is not one of race but the common bond of religion'.[12]

These articles, written at the height of political controversy, drew on a longstanding debate. Throughout the 1860s and early 1870s writers in the Anglo-Jewish press skirmished with biblical critics and enthusiasts for the Hellenic inheritance who relegated the authority of the Hebrew Bible. These exchanges anticipated the lines of later debate; the integrity of Judaism was vindicated, anything which challenged its status as revealed truth was rejected, but aspects of the religion were adjusted in keeping with the demands of Christian critique. Gladstone's writings on the relation between Semitic revelation and Aryan mythology, for instance, were met with a firm contradiction in an editorial essay in the *Jewish Chronicle*.[13] Responses to biblical criticism, however, were more nuanced. Anything which undermined the authenticity of the Hebrew Bible 'as the production of external supernatural revelation' was spurned, but some Jewish writers accepted a developmental and historically informed interpretation of biblical teachings.[14] This allowed Judaism to conform to the changing emphases of Christian interpretation. After the appearance of the first volume of Colenso's work on the Pentateuch, Abraham Benisch published a series of articles in the *Jewish Chronicle* 'intended to quiet the minds of such of the author's co-religionists as had been unsettled by the Bishop's arguments'.[15] With regard to Colenso's evidences of composite authorship Benisch could be dismissive; so far as Jews were concerned, Moses' authorship was not crucial in determining the authenticity of the Pentateuch. What was vital was that the Bible now existed in the form passed on by Ezra and the last divinely inspired prophets.[16] Colenso's moral objections, however, were dealt with by incorporating the doctrine of development.

> In order to be able to judge of the ethical value of the Mosaic code, we must carefully distinguish between the broad and comprehensive moral principles enunciated by the Divine lawgiver, which formed a kind of ideal to

12. *Ibid*, p. 370; Adler, 'Recent Phases of Judaeophobia', p. 813; see also L. Wolf, 'A Jewish View of the Anti-Jewish Agitation', *Nineteenth Century*, February 1881, pp. 339, 354.
13. *JC*, 24 June 1870, p. 7; readers of the *Jewish Chronicle* were warned that any Jew who agreed with Max Muller's theory of pagan religion 'must be one that has no faith in the Bible': *ibid*, 1 April 1870, p. 12.
14. A. Benisch, *Judaism Surveyed* (London, 1874), p. 8.
15. Later published as a single volume, due to public demand, according to the author: A. Benisch, *Bishop Colenso's Objections to the Historical Character of the Pentateuch and the Book of Joshua* (London, 1863).
16. *Ibid*, pp. ix–x.

be aspired after, or rather the theory, and the actual enactments naturally bearing the stamp of the institutions of the period and the necessities of the moment and which constituted the practice.[17]

The legalism of the *Talmud* as well as the morality of the Hebrew Bible stood in need of defence in the face of incarnational theology. In 1867 Emanuel Deutsch published a lengthy essay on the subject in the *Quarterly Review* which was soon reprinted seven times.[18] For Deutsch the *Talmud* was a vital link between the Old Testament and the New. He found within it a 'faith of the heart' rather than 'the law' and of humanity rather than prohibition and vengefulness.[19] Judged historically, he claimed, the *Talmud's* 'rabbinical subtleties' stood out favourably. Its laws were 'humane in the extreme', its penal legislation 'almost refined', and its ethics the same as Christianity's.[20] It represented one further step in the moral education of mankind. Deutsch found that terms such as redemption, baptism, salvation, Son of Man, Son of God and Kingdom of Heaven were not invented by Christianity: 'they were household words of talmudical Judaism to which Christianity gave a higher and purer meaning' and a wider currency.[21] The *Jewish Chronicle* enthused that Deutsch had reconciled the old and new faiths, meaning Judaism and Christianity, and answered those who maligned the book of rabbinical wisdom.[22] The characteristic response to criticism of Judaism which derived from incarnational theology was to find similar values in the Jewish religion.

But in important respects these apologetics were unconvincing. It is very likely that there was a large gulf between these attempts to present Judaism to the Christian world and the religion practised by English Jews. This was the opinion of Abraham Benisch:

> The mass of the Hebrews so far as authentic history can go back, and the overwhelming majority to this day, have considered the Pentateuch and

17. *Ibid*, p. 138. Others were prepared to make fewer concessions to the theory of composition, but even they stressed the significance of 'the code of immutable ethics' found in the Bible above the political struggles of the ancient Israelites: *JC*, 14 January 1870, p. 11. The writer was A. Lowy, discussing Samuel Sharpe, *A History of the Hebrew Nation and its Literature* (London, 1869). Sharpe was a Unitarian and an Orientalist.
18. Deutsch was a Silesian Jew, born in 1829, who had come to England by 1855. A major Semitic scholar and Hebraist, from 1855 he worked as an assistant in the library at the British Museum: see B-2 Lask Abrahams, 'Emanuel Deutsch of "The Talmud" Fame', *TJHSE*, 1969–70, pp. 53–63.
19. E. Deutsch, 'The Talmud', *Quarterly Review*, October 1867, pp. 417–64, p. 438.
20. *Ibid*, pp. 437, 444–5.
21. *Ibid*, p. 438.
22. Lask Abrahams, 'Emanuel Deutsch', p. 57.

indeed the Hebrew Scripture in general, as inspired by the Deity; consequently as the production of an external supernatural revelation, and the former as a direct emanation from God, Moses having only performed the functions, as it were, of an amanuensis, simply recording the communications from on high vouchsafed to him.[23]

Benisch was driven to conclude that many aspects of Judaism were not suited to the present time and were antagonistic 'to established results of experience, science, or enlarged deepened theological and moral notions and refined feelings'.[24]

Moreover, despite claims that Judaism was an ethical and universal religion, there was a countervailing assertion that Jews were something more than just a religious minority; this apprehension was shared by many Jews as well as their critics. At the same time as theologians were repudiating the idea that Judaism was a religion of race, others were invoking the terminology of race to describe and legitimise Jewish traits – characteristic attitudes and patterns of behaviour – and to imply their origins were, at least in part, biological. Indeed, the Jews' practice of endogamy meant that the biological implications of 'race' were inescapable when the term was used with reference to them. Pride in Disraeli's achievements could be expressed in such terms. On the eve of the atrocities agitation, the *Jewish Chronicle* reflected: 'Benjamin Disraeli belongs to the Jewish people, *despite his baptismal certificate*. His talents, his virtues and shortcomings alike, are purely of the Jewish cast.'[25]

Jews tried to make the notion of 'race' work for them and draw the line where its influence ceased. In 1884 the journalist Lucien Wolf went so far as to assert that 'it is too little known that the Jews are as a race really superior physically, mentally and morally to the people among whom they dwell'. He estimated this superiority at between thirty and forty per cent.[26] In C.K. Salaman's apologia, first published in 1882, *Jews as They Are*, the writer was happy to find 'a remarkable buoyancy in the racial spirit' among Jews which enabled them 'to rise in the world'.[27] Less attractive aspects of the Jewish stereotype were consigned to human rather than Jewish nature: the purse-proud vulgarity of the *parvenu*, for example.[28] But, of course, Jews were unable to control the ways in which 'race' was appropri-

23. Benisch, *Judaism Surveyed*, pp. 7–8.
24. *Ibid*, p. 121.
25. *JC*, 15 August 1876, p. 312 (emphasis added).
26. L. Wolf, 'What is Judaism? A Question of Today', *Fortnightly Review*, August 1884, pp. 240–1.
27. C.K. Salaman, Jews as They Are (London, 1885 edn), p. 11.
28. *Ibid*, pp. 11, 16.

ated. Their critics saw Jews acknowledging and disavowing its operation just as it suited them.[29]

Jewish leaders and the Anglo-Jewish press intervened and tried to influence the ways in which Jews and the Jewish question entered political and intellectual debate. They also tried to establish rhetorical and practical expressions of their collective identity as Jews which did not contradict their obligations as Englishmen. These were not easy tasks. First, protestations of patriotism were more likely to enmesh Jews in controversy than liberate them from it. Second, the Judaism promoted by the theologians, which professed the ethical and universal content of Christianity within a Jewish framework, did not accord in many respects with the beliefs and practices of many English Jews. Third, the terminology of race was available to Jews and was used to describe and explain the ties between Jews and Jewish characteristics. But it was precisely the racial character of Judaism, hostile commentators argued, which meant that it never could be a universal religion and that prevented Jews from ever becoming true patriots.

English Jews and Russian pogroms

The anti-Jewish polemic and innuendo of the late 1870s provide a crucial and neglected bridge between the history of mid-Victorian Jewry and the later history of Jews in England. The pogroms of 1881–2 stimulated a dramatic increase in Jewish emigration from Russia. Historians have tended to treat the history of emancipation and its aftermath and the history of immigration and its consequences as discrete subjects.[30] Responses to the pogroms have been regarded exclusively in the light of the subsequent immigration. But this anticipates too much. For contemporaries, reactions to the pogroms were shaped by the memory and political legacy of the Bulgarian agitation and, for Jews particularly, by the wider debate on the Jewish question.

On 15 April 1881 three days of violence directed at Jews and their property broke out at Elizavetgrad. It quickly spread to other towns in south-western Russia such as Kiev, Kishinieff, Yalta and Odessa. These pogroms were concentrated in the Ukraine. Elsewhere, in the provinces of Lithuania and in White Russia in particular, the

29.　*The Truth*, 21 March 1878, p. 374.
30.　The one attempt to bridge the gap can be found in I. Finestein, *Post-Emancipation Jewry: the Anglo-Jewish Experience* (Oxford, 1980). See too T. Endelman, 'Native Jews and Foreign Jews in London 1870–1914', in D. Berger, ed., *The Legacy of Jewish Immigration: 1881 and its Impact* (New York, NY, 1983), p. 110.

authorities took measures to protect Jews. Scores of Jews were killed but the pogroms were chiefly characterised by looting and the destruction of property. An estimate placed before the United States Congress suggested that by the end of 1881 there had been outbreaks in 160 towns, leaving 20,000 Jews homeless and 100,000 reduced to poverty.[31]

The leaders of Anglo-Jewry responded to these events with a mixture of indignation and inactivity. Baron Henry de Worms, the Conservative MP for Greenwich and President of the AJA, raised the matter in the House of Commons.[32] In May a conjoint committee drawn from the AJA and JBD secured an interview with the foreign secretary, Lord Granville. Granville explained that the government would not interfere in Russia's internal affairs and would not make any official representations regarding the pogroms. The conjoint committee then considered whether to appeal to public opinion in the hope of influencing the Russian government; unanimously it decided not to hold a public meeting. Instead it indulged in some meagre fund-raising; just under £9,000 was raised by mid-August.

De Worms and others defended their passivity to the AJA, explaining that the question was 'difficult' and 'political'.[33] Wherein lay the difficulty and the politics? In view of the British government's position, it was suggested, a public meeting would exert no pressure either at home or in Russia. Some feared it might even injure the cause of Russian Jewry. But we should keep in mind that neither of these considerations had been removed in February 1882 when a great series of public meetings was staged. Sir Julian Goldsmid's advice, that a public meeting should not be held because of lack of unanimity in the country, was closer to the point.[34] For it was the public reception of the pogroms which, crucially, had changed in early 1882. This desire not to be seen as out of step with national sentiment and policy derived from issues of more general significance to Anglo-Jewry than the immediate problems of their Russian co-religionists. Throughout this crisis the tenor of the Anglo-Jewish response was determined largely by considerations regarding the

31. E. Tcherikower, ed., *The Early Jewish Labour Movement in the United States* (New York, NY, 1961), p. 19; J. Frankel, *Prophecy and Politics: Socialism, Nationalism and the Russian Jews* (Cambridge, 1981), p. 52; S. Baron, *The Russian Jews under Tsars and Soviets* (2nd edn, New York, NY, 1976), p. 45; I.M. Aronson, 'The Anti-Jewish Pogroms in Russian in 1881', in J. Klier and S. Lambroza eds., *Pogroms: Anti-Jewish Violence in Modern Russian History* (Cambridge, 1992), pp. 44–61.
32. *Hansard*, 3rd series, CCLXI, cols. 564–5, 16 May 1881.
33. University of Southampton, MS 137, A[nglo-]J[ewish] A[ssociation], council minute book, 22 May 1881; *ibid*, 24 May 1881.
34. *Ibid.*

state of English public opinion. It raised the problem of how far emancipated Jewry could press Jewish concerns in English politics.

Controversy over the Jewish question in British politics dragged on into the new decade and continued, literally, alongside news of events in Russia. *The Spectator*, for instance, suggested that the causes of the Jews' persecution in Russia were part of a wider Jewish problem.

> The Jews everywhere are foreigners, and in Europe, Asiatic foreigners, separated from the people by lines which though sometimes indefineable are ineffaceable. Moreover, the majority of them take no pains to efface them, but remain in their marriage laws, their ceremonial laws, their laws of diet, and, in Russia, their dress, separate and Asiatic.[35]

At the beginning of 1882 the *Daily News* acknowledged, 'there has been a tendency of late, even in this country, and far more in Germany, to speak disparagingly, not to say resentfully, of Jewish enterprise and Jewish success'.[36] Moreover, Jews continued to do battle with Goldwin Smith.[37] The shadow of the Jewish question inhibited the leaders of Anglo-Jewry as they faced the pogroms of 1881–2.

This much was recognised by the critics of the policy of inaction. David Schloss, at a conference called by the JBD and AJA in November 1881 to discuss the situation in Russia, complained:

> Where Jews are concerned we appear to be singularly reticent and hold off from exercising a privilege, which is admitted to be the most valuable birthright of all Englishmen, the right to meet in public and ventilate their grievances thereby creating a healthy public sentiment in favour of the particular object for which their sympathies have been enlisted.[38]

By the late autumn of 1881, as the situation in Russia deteriorated, there is evidence of rising dissatisfaction among English Jews at the passivity of their communal leaders, which Schloss reflected.

In southern Russia the summer was punctuated by more pogroms. Fund-raising for Russian Jewry in London was matched in Paris by the Alliance Israelite Universelle. The Alliance cautiously discussed the possibility of a limited and highly selective programme of emigration to the United States. In Russia, however, the emigration project became the subject of wild exaggeration. By the first week of November there were 10,000 Jews encamped at Brody – on the

35. *The Spectator*, 21 January 1882, p. 83.
36. *Daily News*, 17 January 1882, p. 5.
37. *JC*, 19 August 1881, p. 9; *Daily News*, 17 January 1882, p. 5.
38. *JC*, 25 November 1881, p. 4; see too *ibid*, 11 November 1881, p. 9.

Austrian border – hoping to escape to the United States.[39] It now became clear that the crisis of Russian Jewry was threatening to engulf Jews in the West. On 6 November the AJA and the JBD convened a conference to discuss what should be done. In fact, the conference gave rise only to the creation of yet another committee. Its fifteen members comprised two sets of five drawn from the AJA and JBD and five others who were not representatives of either body. These other five included the very elite of Anglo-Jewry: Lord Rothschild, B.L. Cohen and Nathan Adler. This new body determined that the problems before it were so sensitive that its proceedings would remain secret. The indecision with which the Anglo-Jewish leaders responded to events in 1881 created the conditions in which the initiative, briefly but crucially, was seized by their critics.

It was vital for those who wanted to divert communal policy to more vigorous and outspoken lines first to convert English public opinion. This would hand them the initiative in the communal arena. While the committee did nothing but deliberate *in camera*, news reached London that in mid-December the authorities in Warsaw permitted three days of attacks on the Jewish population. It was at this point that dissatisfaction among the second tier of communal activists turned to action. On 27 December 1881 the secretary of the AJA, Adolf Lowy, presented a report on the situation of the Jews in Russia to the organisation's executive committee. The AJA resolved to forward the report to the new Russian-Jewish Committee, advising that it should be published.[40] This was a clear indication that the tide was turning in favour of mobilising English public opinion. Four days later the AJA council presented the Russian-Jewish Committee with an ultimatum: some action on behalf of Russian Jews had to be taken and the grandees were given two weeks to provide a plan of action. If they failed to do so the AJA would withdraw from the Russian-Jewish Committee.[41]

Continuing violence in Russia and dissent at home induced even the Russian-Jewish Committee to act. It published a report on the persecution of Jews in Russia which it issued in pamphlet form and, in a considerable coup, placed in *The Times* on 11 and 13 January 1882. These revelations caused a sensation. Publications from *The Times* to the *Daily News*, from the *Daily Telegraph* to *The Spectator*, expressed outrage at the persecutions in Russia and indignation at the connivance of the local authorities. The AJA responded to the newly favourable state of opinion by proposing that 'immediate steps

39.   Frankel, *Prophecy and Politics*, pp. 58–9, 65; *JC*, 11 November 1881, p. 7.
40.   AJA, executive committee minute book, 27 December 1881.
41.   AJA, council minute book, 1 January 1882; *JC*, 6 January 1882, p. 5.

should be taken to arouse the sympathies of people of all denominations of all civilised countries in the cause of the oppressed Jews of Russia, and that for this purpose public meetings should be held to express indignation at the barbarous and inhuman treatment to which Jews were subjected'.[42] But the Russian-Jewish Committee remained cautious. It addressed a memorial to the Tsar, respectfully drawing his attention to the outrages against Russian Jews.[43]

In framing its resolution the AJA council would have known that steps had been taken by one of its members, Oswald Simon, finally to circumvent the Russian-Jewish Committee. On 13 January the *Jewish World* carried a letter from Simon in which he announced that he had approached leading Christians with the proposition that Christendom was on trial and that they were bound to denounce what had been committed in Russia in the name of Christianity. He had received favourable responses from the Archbishop of Canterbury, from Cardinal Manning and from the Dean of Westminster. He then challenged the authority of the Russian-Jewish Committee to represent Anglo-Jewry and to stand in the way of a public meeting: 'An important issue for our people is this. Fifteen gentlemen of our religion in the presence of their own report agreed that no public action should be taken. Is that the view of the Jews of England or only of their fifteen co-religionists?'[44]

On Monday 16 January *The Times* printed a letter from Lord Shaftesbury which called on the people of Great Britain and Ireland to protest against 'the unprecedented atrocities of every kind now perpetrated hourly on the Jewish race'.[45] The Bishop of Oxford added his voice the following day. On 21 January, thirty-eight prominent churchmen and intellectuals signed a letter to the Lord Mayor of London, J. Whittaker Ellis, requisitioning him to convene a public meeting at the Mansion House to voice public outrage at the persecution of Jews in Russia. The letter was notable for the broad range of opinion it represented, from Cardinal Manning to Lord Shaftesbury to Charles Darwin; it encompassed both Liberals and Conservatives, Anglicans, Roman Catholics and nonconformists.

The Anglo-Jewish radicals had won their public meeting by outflanking the notability on the most sensitive of questions: the state of English public opinion. First by pressing for publication of a report

42. AJA, council minute book, 15 January 1882.
43. *JC*, 20 January 1882, p. 6; *ibid*, 27 January 1882, pp. 10–11. By this time, however, even leading figures on the Russian-Jewish Committee, such as Arthur Cohen, President of the JBD, and Samuel Montagu had come to the view that the memorial was a necessary prelude to any public meeting.
44. *Jewish World*, 12 January 1882, p. 3.
45. *The Times*, 16 January 1882, p. 8.

on the condition of Jews in Russia, and second by soliciting support from the foremost Christian clergymen, those who favoured an active policy of protest placed the cautious notability in a position in which any further opposition to a public campaign would bring them into conflict with that most precious thing – English public opinion.

Russia via Bulgaria

The Mansion House meeting was held on 1 February, and with reason the Lord Mayor alluded to the unity of Christian creeds and political parties in the memorial which had called for the meeting.[46] This was not an isolated occasion. It was followed by large meetings in at least thirty-six towns, presided over by the local Lord Mayor or Lord Provost. To a considerable extent, therefore, the protests were removed from the arena of party politics. They were instated as moments of civic unity in which men and women united to express common values irrespective of their political and religious differences. It was typical that the *Sunderland Herald and Daily Post* described the local protest as 'a towns meeting in the best sense of the word'.[47]

But political meanings did obtrude despite the consensual language of protest. The Bulgarian atrocities and agitation provided the point of reference through which events in Russia and the British reaction to them were perceived and interpreted. The *Daily News* welcomed plans for the Mansion House meeting because since the Bulgarian atrocities the cruelty of the pogroms were unparalleled. Not only had houses been burned to the ground but infants had been murdered and women dishonoured.[48] A.V. Dicey responded enthusiastically to the Mansion House meeting. He called on all those who had denounced the Bulgarian atrocities to speak again or else lay themselves open to the charge of hypocrisy.[49] Whereas the Bulgarian agitation and its political legacy in Britain had inhibited a more activist response from Anglo-Jewry in 1881, it was comparison to these same massacres that provided the frame of reference for public outrage in 1882.

The divisive potential of the parallel with Bulgaria was brought to the surface as discussion moved to what, if anything, the practical

46.   *JC*, supplement, 3 February 1882, p. 1.
47.   *Sunderland Herald and Daily Post*, 7 February 1882, p. 2; *Manchester Guardian*, 4 February 1882, p. 9.
48.   *Daily News*, 17 January 1882, p. 5.
49.   *The Spectator*, 28 January 1882, p. 115.

consequences of the protests should be. In contrast to the situation in 1876, the Liberals now formed the government and were unwilling to sour relations with Russia – a friendly power – on account of the way the Russian populace treated its Jews. The government and the Liberal press claimed, therefore, that a strict parallel between 1876 and 1882 did not exist. In the case of Bulgaria, intervention would have been justified by the fact that Turkey was defended and guaranteed by Britain and had given 'solemn promises' regarding the treatment of its Christian subjects. Gladstone argued that the well-being of the Sultan's Christian subjects had become 'a European responsibility' following the Treaty of Paris of 1856. There was no treaty guaranteeing good government to the Tsar's Jewish subjects and the British government had no right to interfere. Gladstone professed to believe that the Emperor and his government 'regard these outrages with the same feelings as we contemplate them ourselves.'[50] In the circumstances, informal representations might influence the Russian government whereas official censure from another state would only antagonise those who might otherwise be sympathetic.[51]

The organisers of the public meetings deferred to the government's sensibilities; their purpose was to express indignation not to induce the government to act. The Conservative press and some MPs, though not the party leadership, were less restrained. Gleefully, they contrasted Gladstone's eloquence in 1876 and his eagerness then to intervene in the internal affairs of another state with his present refusal to pass judgement on the Russian government.[52] This was revenge for 1876; evidently, Conservatives then had been wise to doubt whether Russians had moral qualities superior to the Turks.[53]

These divisions were replicated within Anglo-Jewry. A meeting of the Manchester branch of the AJA at the beginning of February, convened to consider what to do in the face of events in Russia, witnessed a public row over the Bulgarian parallel. Baron de Worms disavowed that the question was party political but went on to

50. *Pall Mall Gazette*, 18 January 1882; A. Ramm, ed., *The Political Correspondence of Mr Gladstone and Lord Granville 1876–86* (Oxford, 1962), p. 340; *Hansard*, 3rd series, CCLXVII, cols. 38, 46, 49, 3 March 1882.
51. *Ibid*, cols. 42–3. It may be that personal criticism of Gladstone was particularly unjust. He wrote to Granville asking if he might subscribe to the fund established at the Mansion House meeting for the relief of Russian Jews with the understanding that the gesture was not political but purely charitable. However, the foreign secretary advised against this: A. Ramm, ed., *The Political Correspondence of Mr Gladstone and Lord Granville*, p. 338.
52. See for example *Daily Telegraph*, 18 January 1882, pp. 4–5; *ibid*, 27 January 1882, p. 4; *Hansard*, 3rd series, CCLXVII, cols. 31–2, 68, 3 March 1882.
53. *Sunderland Herald and Daily Post*, 12 January 1882, p. 3.

recount a partisan history of the atrocities agitation: 'What they wanted was the same amount of public opinion in England for the oppressed Jews of Russia as was elicited five years ago for the Bulgarians. The only distinction between the two cases was that then they were Bulgarians and now they were Jews. A further distinction was that Turkey was a weak power and Russia a strong one.[54] However, the next speaker from the platform, the Reverend H.D. Marks, the minister at South Manchester Congregation, defended the Prime Minister and expressed his confidence in men such as Gladstone, Granville and Bright, who had 'proved themselves friends of the Jews in the past'. Unfortunately, Marks was unable to conclude his speech since de Worms threatened to walk out if he did so.[55] This was not an isolated incident. When de Worms placed a motion before the House of Commons which called on the government to make representations to the Russian government he was opposed by two leading Jewish Liberals: Arthur Cohen, President of the JBD, and Serjeant Simon, a member of the executive council of the AJA.[56] Subsequently, Serjeant Simon resigned from the AJA when its council passed a vote of thanks to de Worms for bringing his motion to the House of Commons.[57]

The terms of denunciation in 1882 were similar to those with which the Turks had been excoriated: the pogroms were deplored by 'Englishmen and Christians', 'in the name of God and in the name of humanity'.[58] As in 1876 persecution was condemned as un-Christian and inhumane with no distinction made between the two values. The mayor of Southampton, at a town meeting at the Guildhall, claimed 'it was not a question of creeds or politics but one of common humanity. It was a question that appealed to them as Christian men and women.'[59] In Manchester the protest was presented as the voice of 'a civilised and Christian people'.[60] At Sunderland the Liberal Member of Parliament, Alderman Storey, supported the protest 'in the name of God and in the name of humanity'.[61] The English nation, with its particular and close relationship with liberty, assumed a unique position from which to condemn the persecution of the Jews. At the Mansion House

54. *Manchester Guardian*, 3 February 1882, p. 6.
55. *Ibid.*
56. Neither was de Worms supported by Nathan de Rothschild, a Conservative, and the President of the Russian-Jewish Committee.
57. AJA, Council minute book, 5 March 1882.
58. *Sunderland Herald and Daily Post*, 7 February 1882, p. 3.
59. *Southampton Times*, 11 February 1882, p. 3.
60. *Manchester Guardian*, 8 February 1882, p. 9.
61. *Sunderland Herald and Daily Post*, 7 February 1882, p. 3.

Shaftesbury affirmed to loud cheers that 'if there is one thing an Englishman loves better than another it is freedom'.[62]

But the principles called into service to condemn the persecution of the Jews were, at the same time, ambivalent in relation to Judaism. The pogroms were condemned in the name of Christianity, humanity and England. But it was this same characterisation of Christianity, as both universal and particularly English, which over the previous five years had been used to highlight the deficiencies of Judaism. In this view, Christianity was able to speak for humanity in a way that Judaism never could. The Jewish religion could be diminished at the same time as Jews were defended. Thus the ambitions of conversionists were represented at the Mansion House by Shaftesbury himself who, as we have seen, was a leading figure in the London Society for the Promotion of Christianity among Jews. This two-sided aspect to the denunciation of the pogroms was also expressed by Gladstone in the House of Commons in March 1882. His criticism of the pogroms was allied to an assertion of the Christian character of Parliament and a reiteration of the claim that Christianity had surpassed all preceding theological and ethical systems.

> I may be permitted to add, what I think we all must feel, that if we are in this place an assembly almost uniformly professing Christianity, and if we as Christians believe, as we do believe, that it was part of the office and effect of Christianity to establish a new and a far higher standard of humanity, then we must also feel that those deeds, so far as they have been done by Christians, are more guilty, and not less guilty, than if they had been done by persons not professing that religion.[63]

Once again, the view taken of the Jewish question depended on the form it took rather than on a categorical doctrine regarding Jews. In this case, abhorrence of the Jews' ill-treatment overrode but lay alongside a critical opinion of Judaism and a view of Jews as members of a nation represented by an essentially Christian Parliament.

Here we find one illustration of a more general phenomenon, namely that in mid-Victorian England attitudes towards Jews emerged from discussions and debates in which Jews were not the central category but into which they were interpolated. Above all, I have argued that the Jewish issue arose in political argument as one facet of a debate between contending visions of that nation. Since

62. Indeed, a proprietorial relation to freedom could lead to some serious distortions of history. At the same meeting, James Bryce claimed that Englishmen were bound to express a judgement on the horrors in Russia 'because it is England which was the first to admit the Jews to the privileges of full political and civil equality', *JC*, supplement, 3 February 1882, p. 1.
63. *Hansard*, 3rd series, CCLXVII, col. 47, 3 March 1882.

conceptions of the nation changed over time so too did controversy over the Jews.

Discussion and controversy over the Jews utilised longstanding stereotypical images of the Jew; they also drew on more recent developments such as those, for example, in biblical criticism and anthropology. However, none of these influences determined the view of the Jews anyone would take at any particular moment. It is because of the discontinuities in attitudes towards the Jews that attempts to categorise individuals, discourses or institutions as anti-Semitic or tolerant, or to fix the degree of anti-Semitism or tolerance they displayed, prove to be inert. What was at issue in most of the debates we have discussed was not so much whether a person or a position was anti-Semitic but the extent to which Jews, at any particular moment, could be contained within the national community and, if so, upon what terms.

Whigs, radicals and nonconformists not only promoted the rights of rational, propertied individuals to exercise the vote, to sit in Parliament regardless of their particular religious beliefs; they also promoted a particular view of English national identity. If, indeed, liberalism and Jewish emancipation were concerned not only with the rights of individuals but also with an image and account of the national community to which the Jews were being admitted, then much else has to be revised. For it is the supposed absence in England of any positive community, producing religious, cultural or racial standards, to which the Jews had to conform, which has underpinned assessments of the history of anti-Semitism and of Jewish acculturation in England. But as we have seen, ideologies of the nation and a theological critique of Judaism pressured Jews to reform their religious practices and constrain their political activity.

In 1881 the demands of patriotism inhibited the Anglo-Jewish response to the pogroms. In part this was because a policy of protest would bring Jews into conflict with the government's policy. But still more significant was the desire to defer to the state of public opinion and not to press Jewish interests upon it. Even in 1882, once the protest movement was well under way, the AJA instructed its members in the provinces that 'in all instances' indignation meetings 'should be convened by Christians, and that Jewish speakers should confine themselves to proposing and seconding votes of thanks to the respective chairmen'.[64]

Nevertheless, the practical consequences of deference to English public opinion were not predictable. Jews were in a position to mobilise their position and connections within metropolitan society

64. AJA, executive committee minute book, 24 February 1882.

to influence public opinion, if they chose to do so. In these circumstances, deference to public opinion did not inhibit but created conditions which favoured political activity on behalf of Jewish interests. Thus at the turn of 1881–2, communal conflict between the cautious elite and a more activist second rank was fought and won on the ground of English public opinion.

In the long term, however, the pogroms would exacerbate the problems in Jewish emancipation and mercilessly expose the contradictions in Jewish apologetics. In 1882, writing in the *Contemporary Review*, Claude Montefiore, responded to the question 'Is Judaism a tribal religion?' Although a Reform Jew at this time, Montefiore agreed that orthodox Judaism was, in a sense, a missionary faith, diffusing by example its doctrine of the unity of God. Far from being an anachronism, Judaism was the mainspring of human progress. Montefiore conceded that in Jewish scriptures and rabbinical texts it was possible to discover 'tribal tendencies', but in Judaism as it was now taught the reader would discover 'a pure religious universalism'. Fixing the terms of debate still further, Montefiore explained that in discussing the Jewish religion, he would confine himself 'to the religion of educated Jews, in the civilised countries at the present time'.[65] It was a misfortune for English Jews that just as their leaders and spokesmen were presenting themselves as superpatriots and representatives of a modern, universal faith, the first large wave of Jewish immigration from eastern Europe should have arrived in London. For these new Jews were widely perceived to be uneducated and uncivilised, and to have been deeply marked by a country whose temper was medieval and whose sympathies were bounded by the ghettos in which they had been raised.

65. C. Montefiore, 'Is Judaism a Tribal Religion?', pp. 361–82.

PART 2

Immigrants and Workers, 1880–1914

Introduction

After 1880, debate on the problematic integration of Jews within the nation was supplemented by commentary on the impact of Jewish immigrants within English society. This reflected the greatly increased number of Jewish immigrants settling in Britain. This 'alien invasion', as it was termed in the English vernacular, was, in fact, one offshoot of a movement of more than 2 million Jews out of Russia, Austria and Roumania between 1880–1914. Most emigrants travelled to the United States but between 120,000 and 150,000 settled in Britain.[1] But the changing debate on the Jews also reflected the growing importance of social problems within public debate. Increasingly, political argument disclosed a new concern over housing, working conditions and poverty.

It was as workers and industrial competitors that Jewish immigrants drew the attention of some of the foremost late Victorian and Edwardian social investigators: Beatrice Potter, Charles Booth, Hubert Llewellyn Smith and R.H. Tawney among them. One conclusion drawn by these and by a host of other observers was that Jewish workers conformed to a particular type and that they did so because they were Jews. This is how Potter described the Jew in London: 'As a figure of our many sided metropolis he is unmoved by those great gusts of passion which lead to drunkenness and crime; whilst on the other hand he pursues the main purpose of existence undistracted by the humours and aspirations arising from the unsatisfied emotions of our less disciplined natures.'[2]

According to Potter, the extreme degree to which Judaism was centred on this world rather than the next, as well as the talents of an

---

1. H. Pollins, *Economic History of the Jews in England* (London, 1982), p. 132.
2. C. Booth, *Life and Labour of the People of London*, 1st series, vol. iii (London, 1902), p. 190. See too D. Englander, 'Booth's Jews: The Presentation of Jews and Judaism in "Life and Labour of the People of London"', *Victorian Studies*, Summer 1984, pp. 555–8.

intellect trained by generations of Talmudic study, meant that Jews were characterised by the extreme instrumentality of their social behaviour. They lacked pride and any definite standard of life – morally and materially Jewish immigrants were able to live at a level Englishmen could not. It is interesting to note how Potter recycles the Christian critique of Talmudism; this tradition still deforms the Jews' inner life but now, that life is conceived in social not religious terms. Thus armed, Jews took advantage of low barriers to entry as employers in the workshop trades of East London and behaved as the incarnation of Ricardo's 'economic man'. On the one hand 'love of profit' was 'the strongest impelling motive of the Jewish race', on the other, as workers they possessed 'neither the desire nor the capacity for trade combination'.[3]

This stereotype was central to the ways in which Jewish immigrants were presented in public debate; it was propagated with different moral and political baggage by their friends and their enemies. Charles Russell, a sympathetic observer writing from Toynbee Hall, commented on 'the single eye with which the Jew will always strive after what is profitable'.[4] W.H. Wilkins, a hostile witness and a pioneer propagandist against immigration, claimed that 'they [Jewish immigrants] appear to have only one dominant passion, the love of gain'.[5] But the same image, though presented more sympathetically, was reproduced by Jews and immigrants themselves. Mark Moses, a prominent master tailor in the East End of London, attributed the profits made by immigrants in the unpromising vest trade 'to the usual perseverance of our race'.[6] Jewish trade unionists, seeking to explain the disorganisation of the immigrant workforce, frequently ascribed their difficulties to the Jews' individualist cast of mind. One of them complained, 'the Jewish worker was not like his English brother brought up in the atmosphere of a trade union . . . he was not in a real sense a proletarian, blessed with a fertile and inventive mind he continually contemplated becoming a master.'[7]

As this last quotation indicates, the prevailing image of the Jewish immigrant had a counterpart – a characterisation of the English working man. This provided the yardstick of normal development from which the Jews deviated. It is present, for example, in Hubert

3. B. Potter, 'East London Labour', *Nineteenth Century*, August 1888, p. 167.
4. Less delicately he also commented on the 'the sleuth eye with which the Jew will always strive after what is profitable': C. Russell and H.S. Lewis, *The Jew in London* (London, 1900), pp. 5, 51.
5. W.H. Wilkins, *The Alien Invasion* (London, 1892), pp. 66–7; *idem*, 'The Immigration of Destitute Foreigners', *National Review*, September 1890, p. 123.
6. GLRO, JBD, B2/1/4, replies of Mr Moses to questions upon alien immigration.
7. *JC*, 9 January 1903, p. 25.

Llewellyn Smith's investigation of the effects of immigration, published in 1894.

> This double life of the Jew, the concentration of half his thoughts on material gain and the other half on his race, its history and its literature, must be understood in order to grasp his place in the industrial world. He is thus enabled to survive and find an interest in life under conditions which to an English workman would be intolerable, while the continual study of the rabbinical law, in the opinion of those who are entitled to speak with greatest authority on such a subject, has been no mean instrument in sharpening those faculties which make him so formidable a competitor in industry. The English skilled workman often finds in his trade union, with its ideal of the amelioration of the conditions of labour, the satisfaction for a great part of his social even religious instincts. With the foreign Jew, the two sides of life are kept more apart – in industry he is a purely economic competitor, while his 'communistic' feelings run in the direction of race patriotism rather than trade organisation.[8]

Jews, then, were seen as economic individualists whose loyalties were to other Jews rather than to members of the same class. In this they were contrasted with English workers whose natures were not determined by the rules of political economy and whose loyalties, it was said, were informed by 'class feeling'.[9]

Many historians have drawn on this opposition. Lloyd Gartner, the pre-eminent historian of Jewish immigrants in England, has claimed that 'the immigrant community's economy was created by and in its turn helped to create a type known as the "Jewish worker"'. This figure bears a notable resemblance to the one found in so many contemporary accounts. He did not, Gartner tells us, 'regard himself as one endowed with a fixed station in life', and 'was convinced he could rise to the top'.[10] It is as if within every Jewish tailor there was

8. *Report on the Volume and Effects of Recent Immigration from Eastern Europe*, PP 1894, LXVIII, p. 42.
9. See for example C.H. de Leppington, 'Side Lights of the Sweating Commission', *Westminster Review*, March 1891, p. 510. 'In reading the evidence given by the working men who appeared before the committee [the House of Lords Select Committee on Sweating], we are struck with the tone of class feeling which prevails throughout it. The speakers are anxious enough to improve the condition of themselves, and their fellows; not however by facilitating the passage of status of employee to the higher position of an independent worker, but by raising the entire wage earning class to a higher level of comfort by means which would tend, at the same time, to intensify the line of demarcation which cuts them off from the rest of society.'
10. L. Gartner, *The Jewish Immigrant in England, 1870–1914* (London, 1973 edn), pp. 66, 100; B. Kosmin, 'Exclusion and Opportunity: Traditions of Work among British Jews', in S. Wallman ed., *Ethnicity at Work* (London, 1979).

a Rothschild bursting to get out. This has now become a minor orthodoxy, inscribed in surveys and text books; Dudley Baines, for example, tells us the immigrants 'all attempted to become proprietors ("sweaters") and were willing to forgo journeymen's incomes to do so'.[11] These assessments draw strength from the long-term social trajectory of Anglo-Jewry. Since 1945 the Jewish working class has shrunk to become a disproportionately small percentage of the Jewish working population.[12] This striking phenomenon lends plausibility to the comments found in so many of the late nineteenth-century and early twentieth-century sources and repeated by later historians. It tempts us to see a great continuity in Anglo-Jewish social history and to regard the period before 1914 in terms of a tendency to upward mobility which achieved fuller expression fifty years on.

Yet there are good reasons for scepticism. First, no one has produced any evidence for widespread and exceptional immigrant social mobility for the period between 1880–1914. What we have been offered is a mixture of assertion and inference. Second, we can note the teleological bias of the upward mobility thesis. The immigrant past is seen as a headlong rush towards the Anglo-Jewish present. This runs the risk of confusing the immigrants' aims with their grandchildren's achievements and, in doing so, of presenting a misleading picture of both. Finally, the extent to which the image of the Jewish immigrant as an individualist archetype retains traces of a Christian critique of Judaism and theories of racial type, may give us cause to wonder whether an idea which utilises so much discarded knowledge is not fit for reappraisal.

Indeed, in recent years the portrayal of Jewish immigrants as so many individualists has been challenged by a second view. This seeks to assimilate the history of immigrant workers to the prevailing image of the English working class. It does so by highlighting the history of trade unionism among them or by finding a class culture in their routines of daily life. According to Bill Williams, in Manchester in the 1880s 'Jewish workers identified themselves with the mass of English workers seeking better conditions.' Writing about Leeds, Joseph Buckman discerns 'the substantial progress of Jewish workers

11. D. Baines, 'The Labour Supply and the Labour Market, 1860–1914', in R. Floud and D. McCloskey, eds., *The Economic History of Britain since 1700*, vol. ii (Cambridge, 1981), p. 163; see too E.H. Hunt, *British Labour History* (London, 1981), p. 182.

12. S.J. Prais and M. Schmool, 'The Social Class Structure of Anglo-Jewry, 1961', *Jewish Journal of Sociology*, June 1975, pp. 5–15; S. Waterman and B. Kosmin, *British Jewry in the Eighties: A Statistical and Geographical Study* (London, 1986), pp. 44–5.

towards a strong working-class instinct and specific working-class action', which is focused on trade union growth.[13] This rediscovery of the Jewish labour movement recovers a lost history and redresses a skewed historiography.[14] But, as will be seen, it misses the mark when it places trade unionism and class conflict at the centre of the associational and ideological life of the Jewish immigrants.

We have been presented, then, with two contradictory images of the Jewish worker. Yet, notably, both develop from a view of working-class history which remains focused on the advancing strength of organised labour and the independence of working-class culture. Many historians regard the period between 1875–1914 as one in which the English working class was 're-formed'. In part they see this to have been underpinned by structural changes in the economy which led to the emergence of a more homogeneous proletariat; they find it expressed in the growing number of workers organised industrially and in the growing strength of the Labour Party; and in part, too, they locate it in a particular and independent working-class culture.[15]

In one version of the past, Jewish immigrants measure up to the yardstick provided by an increasingly organised and culturally enclosed English working class, in another they do not. The representation of Jewish immigrants as so many 'Ricardian men' segregates within the ghetto of Jewish history the behaviour of a potentially disruptive group which is said to be have been determined by its own racial, religious or ethnic causality. Jewish historians too have been complicit in this division of labour which emphasises the particularity of Jewish history. The revisionists have merely turned matters on

---

13. J. White, *Rothschild Buildings: Life in an East End Tenement Block, 1887–1920* (London, 1980); B. Williams, 'The Beginning of Jewish Trade Unionism in Manchester, 1889–91', in K. Lunn, ed., *Hosts, Immigrants and Minorities: Historical Responses to Newcomers in British Society, 1870–1914* (Folkestone, 1980), pp. 263–307; J. Buckman, 'Alien Working Class Response: The Leeds Jewish Tailors, 1880–1914, in *ibid*, pp. 222–262; *idem, Immigrants and the Class Struggle* (Manchester, 1983); A. Kershen, 'Trade Unionism amongst the Jewish Tailoring Workers of London and Leeds, 1872–1915', in D. Cesarani, ed., *The Making of Modern Anglo-Jewry* (Oxford, 1990), pp. 34–53. Most of these historians do acknowledge the fragility of their subject; an exception, however, is Buckman, from whose work all qualifications have been purged.
14. In this context special mention must be made of the pioneering work of W.J. Fishman, especially his *East End Jewish Radicals, 1875–1914* (London, 1975).
15. G. Stedman Jones, 'Working-Class Culture and Working-Class Politics in London', *Journal of Social History*, Summer 1974, pp. 460–508; E.J. Hobsbawm, *Worlds of Labour* (London, 1984), chapters 10–11; R. McKibbin, 'Why was there no Marxism in Britain?', *English Historical Review*, April 1984, pp. 297–331; N. Kirk, ' "Traditional" Working-Class Culture and "the Rise of Labour" ', *Social History*, May 1991, pp. 203–16.

their head and have presented the history of Jewish immigrants so that it conforms to the expectations of a model of proper working-class development.

The account which follows does not lie somewhere between these two lines of departure; rather, it starts out from a different place. For it is not only Jewish immigrants but a great many other groups and facets of working-class culture and politics which have been marginalised in the conventional view of the late Victorian and Edwardian working class. A preliminary inventory includes the unor-ganised, the penny capitalists, and those for whom national, reli-gious or ethnic loyalties were more than a peripheral presence. One aim of this second part, then, is to investigate and conceptualise the economic and labour history of Jewish immigrants anew. The inter-dependence of interpretations of the immigrant and English work-ing classes, and the inadequacies of both, invest this enquiry with implications which extend beyond the particular case at hand. At the very least, the history of Jewish immigrant workers can draw atten-tion to the large sections of the native working class who also escape the limitations of historical orthodoxy. Finally, this account of Jewish immigrants and the Jewish working class will prepare the way for a reconsideration of the history of Jewish integration in England after 1880.

Chapter 6

Emigration and the Jewish Working Class

The causes of emigration

Jewish migration to London and the growth of a Jewish working class were closely related. Migration was, in large part, a response to proletarianisation or its threat and, ironically, in London the Jewish working class grew to comprise a far greater portion of the Jewish working population than had ever been the case in eastern Europe. Although many historians approach migration as a prelude to upward social mobility, the pioneering generation of East European scholars such as Elias Tcherikower and Jacob Lestchinsky did not do so.[1] The insights to be gained from their perspective have not yet been exhausted.

The pogroms of 1881–2 mark a major discontinuity in the history of Jewish emigration. The number of Russian Jews entering the United States was three times higher in 1882 than it had been in 1881, and between then and 1914 the trend was upwards. Apart from the immediate consequences of the pogroms, the indulgence shown to rioters by the authorities in many towns, and the imposition of the Temporary Regulations of May 1882, which aimed to expel Jews from the countryside, loosened the ties of sentiment to Russia among the Jewish population. Among the intellegentsia, these events led to a turn away from assimilationist prescriptions for the Jewish future in Russia and, briefly, fermented visions of a mass exodus.[2] Some of the emigrants to England claimed they had left Russia to lead an existence free from persecution. Solomon Rosenberg told the House of Lords Select Committee on the Sweating

1. J. Lestchinsky, *Di Onhoybn fun der Emigratsie bay Yidn in 19-tn Yorhundert* (Berlin, 1929); E. Tcherikower, *Di Geshikhte fun der Yidisher Arbayter Bavegung in di Faraynikte Shtatn*, 2 vols. (New York, NY, 1943–5): see especially vol. i, chaper 13.
2. J. Frankel, *Prophecy and Politics: Socialism, Nationalism and the Russian Jews, 1862–1917* (Cambridge, 1981), pp. 49–132.

System, 'I left Russia and came to England because here Jews and Gentiles have no distinction made, they can live as brothers together.' A tailors' presser, Solomon Franks, declared he had no wish to return home, even though he now worked 17–18 hours each day, whereas in Russia his working day had lasted only 12–13 hours, because in London he had his freedom.[3] The sense of alienation from their homeland felt by Russian Jewish emigrants is reflected in the small proportion among them who returned home.[4]

Nevertheless, pogroms were not an everyday occurrence – the next outbreak was in 1903. It was also the case that migration southwards within the Pale of Settlement continued despite the fact that it was a movement away from an area in which relations between Jews and Christians were relatively untroubled by pogroms towards one situated at the centre of every anti-Jewish outbreak.[5] Except over short periods the rhythm of emigration was independent of anti-Jewish violence or regulations. Years of particularly high immigration – 1882, 1891–2, 1903–6 – did coincide with new government measures or popular violence directed against Jews but in general emigration had other causes. For most of the nineteenth century Jews lived in small towns which acted as the commercial and manufacturing centres for the surrounding peasantry and lesser nobility. In the last three decades of the century the Jewish population in Russia confronted a combination of forces – demographic growth, the beginnings of state-managed industrialisation, and government restrictions – which undermined their customary economic activities. In this respect, Jewish emigration was one response to the loss of economic independence.

The Jewish population in Russia grew from between 1 to 1.5 million at the beginning of the nineteenth century to just over 5 million by its end. Between 1880–1914 the population continued to grow slowly despite the emigration of more than 2 million Jews.[6] In 1897 almost 94 per cent of these Jews were contained within the Pale of Settlement. This area comprised 15 western and southern provinces and the Kingdom of Poland. Whether or not Russian agiculture was in a state of crisis in the late nineteenth century is a point of debate.[7] But what is clear is that the development of the

3. *Select Committee on the Sweating System*, PP 1888, XX, qq. 1,000, 3,489–91.
4. S. Joseph, *Jewish Immigration to the United States from 1881–1910* (New York, NY, 1914), tables XXXVIII, XLV, pp. 179, 183.
5. M. Mishkinsky, 'Regional Factors in the Formation of the Jewish Labour Movement in Tsarist Russia', *YIVO Annual of Jewish Social Science*, 1969, p. 48.
6. J. Silber, 'Some Demographic Characteristics of the Jewish Population in Russia at the End of Nineteenth Century', *Jewish Social Studies*, Fall 1980, pp. 269–80.
7. J.Y. Simms, 'The Crisis in Russian Agriculture at the End of the Nineteenth Century: A Different View', *Slavic Review*, September 1977, pp. 377–98;

agrarian economy was too sluggish to support the increasing number of Jews who depended on it. Following the emancipation of the serfs in 1861, peasant living standards were inhibited by rising rents and taxes, state procurement of crops for export and falling grain prices. These misfortunes inevitably rebounded on the Jewish traders whose livelihood depended on the peasants' surplus.[8] In 1897 it was still the case that one half of Jewish merchants in the Pale dealt in agricultural products and that 90 per cent of all grain dealers were Jews.[9] The same forces restricted opportunities for others, such as rural artisans and middle men dealing at regional fairs, whose markets were in the countryside. Development as well as stagnation restricted petty commerce. The extension of the railway network, though it increased the fortunes of some financiers in the Russian Jewish elite, disrupted the *shtetl* economy. Railway development came in two spurts, between 1866–75 and 1893–1905. Railways integrated national and regional markets, breaking into the local markets served by Jews and displacing Jews who had worked as carriers and carters.[10] They also brought the world beyond Russia within closer reach of the Jews: they brought new knowledge and took away people.[11]

Overcrowding in the field of petty commerce led to a shift towards manufacturing occupations. Lestchinsky estimated that in 1825 the working population of Russian Jewry included 30 per cent who were traders, a further 30 per cent who were inn-keepers, farm tenants and leaseholders, and just 18 per cent who worked as artisans.[12] Some historians have suggested that these figures underestimate the

E. Wilbur, 'Was Russian Peasant Agriculture really that Impoverished?', *Journal of Economic History*, March 1983, pp. 137–148.

8. A. Gerschenkron, 'Agrarian Policies and Industrialization in Russia, 1861–1917', in H.J. Habbakuk and M. Postan, eds., *The Cambridge Economic History of Europe*, vol. vi (Cambridge, 1965), pp. 765–778; C. Trebilcock, *The Industrialization of the Continental Powers, 1780–1914* (London, 1981), pp. 213–14, 247–9.

9. I.M. Rubinow, 'The Economic Condition of the Jews in Russia', USA House Documents, *Labor Bureau Bulletin*, September 1907, p. 556.

10. H. Abramovitch, 'Rural Jewish Occupations in Lithuania', *YIVO Annual for Jewish Social Science*, 1947–8, pp. 205–21; Trebilcock, *The Industrialization of the Continental Powers*, pp. 247–9; Rubinow, 'The Economic Condition of the Jews in Russia', pp. 555–6, 559–60; A. Kahan, 'The Impact of Industrialization in Tsarist Russia on the Socioeconomic Conditions of the Jewish Population', in R. Weiss, ed., *Essays in Jewish Economic and Social History* (Chicago, Ill., 1986), p. 10; J. Metzer, 'Railroad Development and Market Integration: The Case of Tsarist Russia', *Journal of Economic History*, September 1974, pp. 529–49.

11. S. Zipperstein, 'Haskalah, Cultural Change, and Nineteenth Century Russian Jewry', *Journal of Jewish Studies*, Autumn 1983, pp. 205–6.

12. J. Lestchinsky, 'The Economic and Social Development of the Jewish People', in J. Finkelstein, ed., *The Jewish People, Past and Present*, vol. i (New York, NY, 1946), p. 375.

proportion of Jewish artisans but the trend over the century is not in question. The most reliable figures, those for the Russian census of 1897, are shown below.

Table 1   Jews in gainful occupations in the Pale of Settlement in 1897[13]

Occupation	Number	Per cent
Agricultural pursuits	38,538	2.9
Professional service	67,238	5.1
Personal service	228,192	17.1
Manufacturing and mechanical pursuits	504,844	37.9
Transportation	44,177	3.3
Commerce	448,514	33.7

The shift towards manufacturing occupations did not occur with equal force over the entire Pale. It was most marked in Lithuania and White Russia where manufacturing accounted for 44.2 per cent and 42.2 per cent of those in gainful occupations and it had progressed the least in south Russia where the same category amounted to just 34.7 per cent.[14] The proportion employed in commerce in the north-west was correspondingly low and was significantly higher in southern Russia. Nevertheless, it was in Lithuania, White Russia and Poland that Jews most dominated the commerce of the region.

Table 2   The concentration of Jews in commerce in different areas of the Pale of Settlement in 1897[15]

Region	Percentage of gainfully employed Jews in commerce	Jews as a percentage of the total employed in commerce
Lithuania	25.9	88.2
White Russia	29.2	89.3
Southern Russia	37.0	54.4
South-west Russia	38.9	76.0
Poland	33.7	71.9

13. Rubinow, 'The Economic Condition of the Jews in Russia', p. 502. Rubinow adjusted the original figures to make them compatible with the United States census returns. Here the figures have been changed back from figures given in *ibid*, p. 556. Rubinow's alteration had the effect of reducing the figure for those involved in commerce.
14. *Ibid*, p. 502.
15. *Ibid*, pp. 554–5.

This pattern suggests that Jews were being driven into manufacturing occupations because they were no longer able to sustain themselves and their families through commerce once that sector had become saturated.

Typically, Jews involved in manufacturing produced finished goods for immediate consumption: the production of clothing and footwear together accounted for just under one half of all Jews in manfacturing in 1897.[16] This concentration meant that Jews did not participate directly in those areas of the economy experiencing rapid growth – railways, mineral extraction, iron and steel production – while the internal market for manufactured goods grew only slowly. By the 1890s Jewish production was characterised by advancing proletarianisation and declining independence. In the 1880s and 1890s the size of workshops increased. It became more difficult for journeymen to establish themselves as independent masters, particularly as under-employment and downward pressure on wages made saving more difficult.[17] A survey made in 1898 for the Jewish Colonisation Society calculated that one half of the 501,000 Jewish artisans in the Pale of Settlement were wage earners.[18] Where other employments were most saturated a significant minority of Jews became factory workers. In 1897, in the north-west, Jews accounted for 54 per cent of all factory workers, whereas they accounted for just 11 per cent and 6.2 per cent of factory workers in the south-western and southern provinces of the Pale. By 1907 there were between 100–150,000 Jewish factory workers in Russia.[19] The independence of many master artisans also declined. The ejection of Jews from villages left them more dependent on intermediaries to connect them with markets, while low returns due to intense competition made them dependent on the same figures for materials and machinery. In Vitebsk, by the beginning of the twentieth century, 'the tailors work[ed] mainly for dealers in ready-made clothing, a trade condition that approaches the system of sub-contracting

16. Kahan, 'The Impact of industrialization on the Jews in Tsarist Russia', table A5, pp. 52–3.

17. E. Mendelsohn, *Class Struggles in the Pale: the Formative Years of the Jewish Workers Movement in Tsarist Russia* (Cambridge, 1970), pp. 9–10; Kahan, 'The Impact of Industrialization on the Jews in Tsarist Russia', p. 26.

18. Rubinow, 'The Economic Condition of Jews in Russia', p. 523. At the same time as workers became entrenched in their subordinate positions there was also a tendency towards the increased sub-division of labour within trades: see for example *Letter from the Secretary of the Treasury Transmitting a Report of the Commissioners of Immigration upon the Causes which Incite Immigration to the United States*, 52nd Congress, 1st session, House of Representatives executive document 235 (Washington, 1892), part 1, p. 75.

19. Rubinow, 'The Economic Condition of Jews in Russia', p. 542.

which is so familiar to the student of economic conditions in New York City'.[20]

Legislation compounded the effects of agrarian stagnation and industrial development. The Temporary Regulations of May 1882, the government's response to the pogroms of 1881–2, aimed at evacuating all Jews from rural areas within the 15 western districts of Russia. They marked the beginning of a period in which the effect of government measures was to press the Jewish population into large urban centres within the Pale.[21] But even though the 1882 Regulations did not extend to Russian Poland, here the process of urbanisation was more rapid than anywhere else in the Pale, excepting the southern portion. Government action did not initiate change but compounded a movement already in process due to demographic and economic pressures.

The consequences for the *shtetl* of legal restrictions and demographic growth at a rate beyond the expansion of economic opportunities were seen in 1891 by United States Commissioners of Immigration travelling in the Pale. They found the 'townlet' of Samokvalovich, outside of Minsk: 'without manufacturing or labor employing industries, [it] presents in itself no adequate means of support for one half of the permanent inhabitants'. At the same time, commerce was stunted by regulation.

> The inhabitants are not permitted to do any business outside of the circumscribed limits of the townlet, and if found selling simply fruit or milk on the road outside, their stock is seized and confiscated, and yet in this townlet, 18 versts from Minsk, are tailors, stonemasons, bricklayers, and other artisans driven from their homes under the decrees.[22]

20. *Ibid*, pp. 523, 525–6.
21. In 1887 the passage of Jews between villages was restricted, and the inheritance of property bequeathed by a Jew settled in another village was prohibited. In 1897 a major source of Jewish livelihood in rural areas – inn-keeping – was further restricted. Over the same period it became increasingly difficult for those Jewish artisans and merchants who were privileged to live outside of the Pale, or who were living there illegally, to continue to do so. Jewish artisans in the interior found that their licences were not renewed and that those without licences were less likely to be tolerated. In 1891 about 2,000 Jews were expelled from St Petersburg and about 20,000 from Moscow when the residence rights of Jewish artisans were revoked and merchants were ejected from the city if they did not fulfil the qualifications for residence. In these conditions, Jewish businesses which were allowed to remain were unable to obtain credit and many were thus forced into bancruptcy: S. Dubnow, *History of the Jews in Russia and Poland from the Earliest Times until the Present Day*, vol. ii (Philadelphia, Pa, 1918), pp. 341–2, 399–413; *ibid* vol. iii (Philadelphia, Pa, 1920), pp. 22–3.
22. *Letter from the Secretary of the Treasury*, p. 72.

Enforced displacements added thousands to the labour markets of towns within the Pale and fuelled emigration. Economic conditions were depressed, for example, by the expulsions from Moscow and St Petersburg in 1891. In Minsk the United States Commissioners found hundreds of unemployed Jews congregated in the town's main square.

> Willing and able to work, they are unable to obtain it; forbidden to work outside the city, forbidden to trade in the country, unable to leave the precincts where they now are, excluded from governmental work, it is no wonder they wish to fly somewhere where they can breathe and can have an equal chance in the struggle for existence. The only thing which prevents them from going *en masse* to other countries is their poverty.[23]

An apothecary told the commissioners that 'many of those who have been expelled from the interior come here and overcrowd the labour market, compelling numbers already here to leave for Africa, Australia, Palestine, Argentine, and America – most of them to America'.[24]

Emigration was not the only response to these circumstances. At the same time as 2 million Jews left Russia there was a massive redistribution of the Jewish population within the Pale: from *shtetl* to city and from Lithuania and White Russia to Poland and New Russia. The southward movement had commenced in the first half of the nineteenth century but gathered pace in the last decades. Between 1881–97 the Jewish population of the north-west increased by just 14 per cent whereas that of south Russia did so by 61 per cent, and that of Poland by 17 per cent between 1890 and 1897 alone.[25] The level of wages in the southern provinces were so high as to 'reach a level practically unknown in the northwest', commented the American investigator I.M. Rubinow.[26]

Networks of information and prospective support influenced the direction in which individuals and groups chose to migrate; whether to move west, beyond Russia, or to migrate south within it. One emigrant described the stimulus to emigration caused by the arrival in Podambitz of a letter from England containing money: 'in that small town as soon as a letter comes in the morning, in the evening everybody all over the place knows what letter has come and how

23. *Ibid*, p. 67.
24. *Ibid*, pp. 67, 84.
25. Lestchinsky, *Di Onhoybn fun der Emigratsie bay Yidn*, p. 6; Rubinow, 'The Economic Condition of the Jews in Russia', pp. 495, 535.
26. *Ibid*, p. 530.

much money – everything'.[27] One key influence on the sort of information passed was the trade cycle. Kuznets suggests that Jewish immigration to the United States, like the movement of other migrant groups, was sensitive to fluctuations in business cycles there. In the case of Britain no accurate immigration figures exist to test a parallel proposition but the Deputy-Comptroller of the Commercial, Labour and Statistical Department of the Board of Trade, H. Llewellyn Smith, believed that immigration responded strongly to the state of trade: 'not only the absolute state of the labour market here, but the relative state of the United States and this country'.[28]

But migration was more than the sum of influences repelling Jews from eastern Europe and attracting them westwards. Migration was also a business. Its possibilities were seized by shipping entrepreneurs and their agents. There was strenuous competition to carry the human traffic streaming out of Russia, and ticket agents ensured that a price war continued even when the companies arrived at an agreement. The British vice-consul at Libau reported in 1893 that 'a regular trade in the forwarding of emigrants has been established – each firm vieing with each other to see who will forward cheapest'. Jews converged on the port from all over Russia as a result of advertising in the interior.[29] Others crossed the border and embarked ships bound for London at Hamburg, Bremen or Rotterdam. The conditions in which they travelled were described by Aaron Gorelick, who sailed from Hamburg in 1903: 'It was a great, black dirty trough. They put us in the bowels of the ship – as dark as Egypt – once our eyes became accustomed to the darkness we saw great dormitories for sleeping, without separate places for men and women. The air became suffocating, the stench was even worse than in prison.'[30]

The most lucrative and competitive trade was to the United States. The transatlantic fare was £2 cheaper from England than from continental ports such as Hamburg and Rotterdam and, conse-

27. *Royal Commission on Alien Immigration*, [henceforth *RCAI*], PP 1903, IX, qq. 3,361–3.
28. S. Kuznets, 'Immigration of Russian Jews to the United States: Background and Structure', *Perspectives in American History*, 1975, p. 45, *RCAI*, q. 170.
29. PRO, FO 400/16, C.J. Hill to H.G. Wagstaff, 23 July 1893. The steamers from Libau sailed with cargo as well as passengers: 'the tween decks fitted up with passenger accommodation of the most primitive description'. In 1895 Hill attributed the rise in the number of emigrants over the previous year to 'the increased and more regular facilities for emigration being better known in the interior': *ibid*, C.J. Hill to H.G. Wagstaff, 10 January 1895.
30. A. Gorelick, *Shturmedike Yorn* (New York, NY, 1946), p. 125.

quently, a large traffic of transmigrants travelled through Britain.[31] Ticket agents and money changers in London served the needs and profited from East European Jews en route to the United States. They also provided a range of commercial services for the Jewish East End. One passage broker was not only a money changer but also ran the Post Office in the Whitechapel High Street.[32] The principal bank in the Jewish East End sent remittances to the value of 1 million roubles (£100,000) to Russia and Poland each year. A portion of this was sent to support family members still in Eastern Europe but the bank was also one centre for the business of migration. An early twentieth-century investigator reported, 'it transacts every kind of business connected with banking, shipping, emigration and immigration. It has agents in every important town of Russia and in all provinces of the empire', as well as in Bremen, Hamburg and Rotterdam.[33] Migration was embraced and enabled by profit-seeking networks which ranged from shipping magnates such as Sir Donald Currie to the dock-side money changers, passage brokers and lodging housekeepers.

Economics not only created the channels through which migrants travelled: in most years it shaped the circumstances which led them to leave their homes. Before 1905, the years of greatest Jewish immigration to Britain, the majority of Jewish emigrants were from the most stagnant part of the economy in the Pale of Settlement – the north-west – in which increasing numbers of Jews were turning to manufacturing occupations because they could no longer secure a livelihood from their former commercial pursuits.[34] If, as seems likely, internal and external migration were alternative responses to proletarianisation or its threat, ways of seeking to hang on to economic independence, we shall see that the latter option – emigration – was by no means successful for those who settled in London.

The shape of an immigrant population

Our guide to the level of Jewish immigration must be the numbers of Russians and Russian Poles recorded in the censuses for England

31. N.V. Geldshtayn, *Di Yidishe Virtshaft in London* (Vilna, 1907), pp. 2–3. On the transmigrant trade see *RCAI*, q. 1,431, 16,286; GLRO, JBD, B2/1/3, alien immigration, memorandum, November 1898.
32. *RCAI*, qq. 1,425–6; PRO, H0 45/100063/B2840A/74, German, Russian and Austrian Emigrants from Rotterdam to London, 23 November 1894.
33. Count E. Armfelt, 'Russia in East London', in G. Sims, ed., *Living London*, vol. i (London, 1902), p. 27.
34. Rubinow, 'The Economic Condition of Jews in Russia', p. 492.

and Wales. These figures are far more reliable than the immigration returns compiled by the Board of Trade.[35] The census never counted Jews but the immigrants appear instead under their country of origin. In the cases of Russians and Russian Poles this distinction is of little importance as Jews comprised almost all the immigrants under these headings.[36] But there are greater problems with the immigration of Austrians, since the proportion of non-Jewish immigrants from that country was larger.[37] The figures used here will be for Russians and Russian Poles and, therefore, represent a modest estimate of the growth of the Jewish immigrant population. There are two other ways in which these figures underestimate the number of Jewish immigrants to London. First, transmigrants left only a trace on the census and are included only insofar as they were caught within the snapshot of each enumeration. Yet the population of transmigrants was large, and added both numbers and instability to the Jewish population. According to Geldshtayn, 15 per cent of all Jewish emigrants to the United States went through London.[38] Second, those who intended to remain in England were, in several thousands of cases, unable to do so. In London alone, between 1880 and 1914 the Jewish Board of Guardians repatriated over 50,000 of those who applied to them for poor relief.[39] The number of East European Jews who did settle in London in this period is, perhaps, a little more than half of the number who tried to do so.

Jewish immigrants settled in significant numbers in Manchester, Leeds, Liverpool, Birmingham and Glasgow but London did not

35. The Board of Trade was unable to distinguish between immigrants and transmigrants before 1906. No Jewish communal institution was sufficiently comprehensive in its reach to provide figures that could be used for this purpose: L. Gartner, 'Notes on the Statistics of Jewish Immigration to England', *Jewish Social Studies*, April 1960, pp. 97–102.

36. The most significant example is the Lithuanian miners who settled in Lanarkshire: see K. Lunn, 'Reactions to Lithuanian and Polish Immigrants in the Lanarkshire Coalfield', in *idem*, ed., *Hosts, Immigrants and Minorities* (Folkestone, 1980), pp. 308–42.

37. It is possible to say, however, that a smaller proportion of Jewish immigrants were from Austria than in the case of the United States. In England and Wales, Austrians amounted to 11.9 per cent of all immigrants from Russia, Russian Poland and Austria enumerated in 1911, whereas in the United States, Austrian Jews comprised 23.1 per cent of all Jewish immigrants between 1881–90, and 21.3 per cent between 1891–1900 and 15.7 per cent between 1901–10. These figures are taken from the *Census of England and Wales, 1911*, PP 1913, LXVIII, table 5, pp. 206–7; Joseph, *Jewish Immigration to the United States*, table 8, p. 162.

38. Geldshtayn, *Di Yidishe Virtshaft in London*, p. 2. Those who entered the country but died before an enumeration escaped in a similar way.

39. This is discussed in greater detail in Part 3 of the book.

Table 3 Russians and Russian Poles enumerated in England and Wales and in London, 1871–1911[40]

Year	Russians and Russian Poles in England and Wales	Russians and Russian Poles in London	
		Number	Per cent of total
1871	9,569	5,294	55.3
1881	14,468	8,709	60.2
1891	45,074	26,742	59.3
1901	82,844	53,537	64.6
1911	103,244	63,105	61.1

merely attract the largest number of immigrants, it attracted over 60 per cent of them.

As was the case with Jewish immigration to the United States, the flow to Britain increased with time. But there were also differences between the two cases. Most obviously, the Aliens Act of 1905 was designed to restrict immigration and reversed the rising trend. Immigration to Britian was in decline when the largest number of Jews were leaving Russia. But even before the Act was passed, Jewish immigration to Britain was rising less dramatically than that to the United States.[41] Qualitative as well as quantitative differences arose from the Aliens Act. The occupational, cultural and political background of the emigrants changed over time. Jews leaving Russia after 1900 were more likely to have had experience of manufacturing occupations, and to have been touched by new political movements such as socialism and zionism and by the emergence of an intelligentsia writing in Yiddish and Hebrew. Jewish immigrants to Britain were less touched by these currents of change in Eastern Europe.

Who were the immigrants? Women comprised a growing minority among them. A large imbalance between men and women in 1871

40. Compiled from *Census of England and Wales, 1871*, PP 1873, LXXI, summary table xxiii, p. li; *ibid*, division 1, table 15, pp. 25–6; *Census of England and Wales, 1881*, PP 1883, LXXX, summary table 12, p. xxviii; *ibid*, division 1, table 13a, pp. 23–5; *Census of England and Wales, 1891*, PP 1893–4, CVI, summary table 9, p. xxxii; *ibid*, division 1, table 10, pp. 19–21; *Census of England and Wales, 1901*, PP 1904, CVIII, p. 142; *ibid*, County of London, table 37, pp. 157–8; *Census of England and Wales, 1911*, PP 1913, LXVIII, vol. ix, table 3, p. 114; *ibid*, table 5, pp. 206–7.

41. Taking the period 1881–1900 for the United States, Jewish immigration divided 32.5 per cent between 1881–90 and 67.4 per cent between 1891–1900: Joseph, *Jewish Immigration*, table xxix, p. 173. In England and Wales, the census returns for Russians and Russian Poles rose by 43.9 per cent between 1881–90 and 56 per cent between 1891–1901.

*Table 4   Russian and Russian Polish females within the total Russian
and Russian Polish population in London*[42]

Year	Females	Percentage of total	Female percentage of total increase
1881	3,671	42.2	
			39.5
1891	11,969	44.8	
			46.4
1901	24,408	45.6	
			57.1
1911	32,509	48.0	

was transformed into virtual numerical equality by 1911. These changes are set out in table 4.

We learn a little about these women from an investigation carried out by Clara Collett for the Board of Trade. She traced 92 women who landed at the Port of London in May 1892. From Collett's report it appears that few Jewish women migrated independently or joined other women.[43] When it did not occur in connection with the movement of their husbands, the emigration of Jewish women was closely tied to the nuclear family, and in 75 per cent of these cases to the male members of it. The rising proportion of women shown in the table reflects the numbers joining husbands or other male relatives who had already migrated.[44]

42.   These figures have been taken from the *Census of England and Wales, 1871*, division 1, table 15, pp. 25–6; *Census of England and Wales, 1881*, division 1, table 13a, pp. 23–5; *Census of England and Wales, 1891*, division 1, table 10, pp. 19–21; *Census of England and Wales, 1901*, PP 1902, CXX, table 37, pp. 157–8; *Census of England and Wales, 1911*, table 5, pp. 206–7.

43.   *Report on the Volume and Effects of Recent Immigration from Eastern Europe into the United Kingdom*, PP 1894, LXVIII, pp. 99–102; also *ibid*, appendix XII, pp. 196–200. 38 of the women were either with their husbands when they entered the country or else came with the intention of joining them. Of the remainder, of those for whom information was found, all but 7 joined relatives or friends, who were male in most cases; 12 joined their brothers, 6 their fathers, 6 their sons, 3 went to other relatives or friends, 7 joined their sisters, and 4 went to their daughters. Of the 7 women who arrived alone and had no one to contact, 3 were German and possibly were not Jewish.

44.   It is consistent with this that the percentage of Russian and Russian Polish women in London between 15 and 45 increased from 66.3 per cent to 71.4 per cent between 1871 and 1901: S. Rosenbaum, 'A Contribution to the Study of the Vital and Other Statistics of the Jews', *Journal of the Royal Statistical Society*, September 1905, p. 535. But the leap in the percentage of women entering the country between 1901–11 must also be attributed to the Aliens Act which prohibited the immigration of anyone unable to demonstrate that they could support themselves or be provided for 'decently'. This not only reduced the

As we might expect in view of the large proportion of adult women, the proportion of children was also high. In 1901, in England and Wales as a whole, for every 1,000 men there were 82 under the age of 15, and the figure for women was 121; among Russians and Russian Poles the male figure was 138 and the female 158.[45] The tendency of entire families to migrate was a feature of Jewish immigration which marked it off from many other migrations composed more largely of single, male wage earners: workers who, in many cases, intended to return to their country of origin and frequently managed to do so.[46] The rate of return among Jewish migrants to the United States was particularly low: 8 per cent between 1908–10. Among non-Jewish Lithuanians and Poles the rate of return was higher – 14 per cent and 30 per cent in these same years – and the proportion of women among them far lower than among Jewish immigrants – 29.4 per cent and 30.5 per cent of the whole.[47] Although rate-of-return figures are not available in the case of Britain, when the American and British evidence is taken together we can suggest that Jewish immigration to London was generally intended to be a move away from Eastern Europe once and for all.

All but a few Jewish immigrants arrived in Britain with scant financial resources. 22 per cent of the Russian, Roumanian and Galician immigrants who arrived at the port of London between 1894 and 1903 claimed to be penniless. A further 15 per cent produced less than 10s per adult, and the average figure was 26s per adult.[48] There were exceptions. The Superintendent of Immigration to the United States reported in 1892 that 'the immigrants from

total number of immigrants but it also increased the proportion of dependants – women and children – among those who did enter the country.

45. *Ibid.*
46. On the non-Jewish Poles going to the United States and returning, see E. Morawaska, 'Labour Migrations of Poles in the Atlantic World Economy, 1880–1914', *Comparative Studies in Society and History*, April 1989, pp. 237–72. We should not ignore the incidence of wife desertion in this period, the connections between Jewish migrations and international prostitution, nor the possibility that migration placed family cohesion under great strain. On wife desertion, see *Select Committee on emigration and immigration*, PP 1888, XI, qq. 3, 714–15; on Jewish prostitutes see E.J. Bristow, *Prostitution and Prejudice: The Jewish Fight against White Slavery, 1870–1939* (Oxford, 1982).
47. Joseph, *Jewish Immigration to the United States*, tables XXXVIII, XLV, pp. 179, 183. J.D. Sarna, 'The Myth of no Return: Jewish Return Migration to Eastern Europe, 1881–1914,' *American Jewish History*, December 1981, pp. 256–68, argues that the figures for the period after 1908 cannot be extrapolated backwards but he does not offer any convincing evidence to suggest a higher figure is appropriate.
48. Calculated from *RCAI*, appendix, tables LXII, LXIII, LXIIIa, pp. 76–8. These figures refer to arrivals from the ports of Hamburg, Bremen and Rotterdam.

Russia have the widest variations in financial condition of any people who come to our country'.[49] In 1891, United States Commissioners for Immigration came across a Jewish sheet and railroad iron merchant in Moscow who the authorities were forcing out of the city and who was in the process of selling up and migrating to England. This man had property worth 200,000 roubles and made profits of 1,000 roubles each month. He was able to salvage only a small portion of his wealth; nevertheless, he arrived in London with 16,400 roubles.[50] There were several other less spectacular cases. In 1892 a customs officer reported that a number of the immigrants arrived with sums of £30 or more.[51] But the typical situation of a new arrival was conveyed by a Jewish immigrant tailor in 1888. He observed that 'in fact everyone who comes over here comes rather poor, a man who has two or three pounds of course is a poor man, it will not last him very long'.[52]

In 1903 Georg Halpern put forward the view that 'the Jewish worker has only in England become a wage earner. He may have belonged in Russia to the lowest stratum of the unemployed proletariat or of artisans and small traders – a wage earner he was not.'[53] A number of historians have echoed this characterisation, particularly as a description of Jewish emigration before 1900.[54] The male immigrants of this period are seen as former traders, pedlars, dealers and under-employed day labourers – the *luftmenshn* who had improvised a precarious existence in the interstices of economic life. For the period after 1900 a different image has been presented by historians who base their findings on the occupations returned to United States immigration officials by Jewish immigrants between 1899 and 1914. According to these figures, 64 per cent of Jews reporting a gainful occupation were skilled workers, 21 per cent had been labourers or servants and just 5.5 per cent had been involved in commerce.[55] At first sight these returns suggest a large discrepancy with the occupational distribution of Russian Jewry revealed by the census of 1897 in which just 37.9 per cent of the occupied Jewish

49. *Annual Report of the Superintendent of Immigration to the Secretary for the Treasury* (Washington DC, 1892), p. 26.
50. *Letter from the Secretary of the Treasury*, pp. 44–5.
51. *Report on Recent Immigration*, p. 11.
52. *Select Committee on Emigration and Immigration*, q. 2,993.
53. Cited in I. Hourwich, 'The Jewish Labourer in London', *Journal of Political Economy*, December 1904, pp. 94–5.
54. J. Lestchinsky, 'Di Yidishe Emigratsie in di Faraynikte Shtatn', in E. Tcherikower, *Di Geshikhte fun der Yidisher Arbayter Bavegung*, vol. i, pp. 37–40; M. Rischin, *The Promised City: New York's Jews, 1870–1914* (Cambridge, Mass., 1977 edn), pp. 58–9.
55. Kuznets, 'Immigration of Russian Jews to the United States', pp. 104–5.

population were found in manufacturing and mechanical pursuits and 26.8 per cent in commerce. Accordingly, Simon Kuznets has described Jewish emigration from Russia as highly selective and heavily biased towards those Jews engaged in occupations who were able to transfer skills to the United States. Whereas artisans were able to do this, he suggests, those engaged in petty commerce were not. Kuznets argues that this made a vital contribution to the social mobility of the next generation.[56] Some historians of Jewish immigration to Britain also have supported the view that the emigrants were chiefly artisans, but have done so on the basis of more flimsy evidence.[57]

But the accuracy of the United States immigration statistics is questionable. Arcadius Kahan pointed out that inquiries conducted after entry to the United States 'reveal that the share of those gainfully employed in commerce prior to their arrival in the United States varied between 20–30 per cent of the total employed'. He suggests that many immigrants on arrival lied because they feared being turned away; men engaged in commerce represented themselves as labourers, and women without an occupation inflated the numbers recorded as domestic servants.[58] English data, taken from the Poor Jews' Temporary Shelter in London, lends powerful support to this sceptical view of the official returns in the United States. The shelter was located in Whitechapel and acted as a house of first call for between 1,000 and 5,000 immigrants each year between its foundation in 1885 and 1904. The information on inmates contained in the shelter's annual reports provides valuable data on the occupations of emigrant Jews.[59] The shelter records suggest that in the 1880s about 35 per cent of all adult male immigrants had previously derived their livelihood through trading or as *luftmenshn* and that this proportion fell to about 25 per cent by the early twentieth century. Among those immigrants who had been occupied in manufacturing in Eastern Europe the shelter records between 1895–6 and

56. *Ibid*, pp. 104–13.
57. J. Buckman, *Immigrants and the Class Struggle* (Manchester, 1983), pp. 3–4; H. Pollins, *Economic History of the Jews in England* (London, 1982), pp. 135–6; J. White, *Rothschild Buildings: Life in an East End Tenement Block, 1887–1920* (London, 1980), pp. 251–2.
58. A. Kahan, 'Economic Opportunities for Some Pilgrims' Progress', in R. Weiss, ed., *Essays in Jewish Economic and Social History* (Chicago, 1986), p. 236. See too J. Perlmann, *Ethnic Differences: Schooling and Social Structure among the Irish, Italians, Jews and Blacks in an American City, 1880–1935* (Cambridge, 1988), pp. 289–90.
59. On this see my doctoral thesis, 'Immigrants and Workers, Englishmen and Jews: Jewish Immigration to the East End of London 1880–1906' (University of Cambridge, 1986).

1907–8 reveal that the greatest concentrations were among garment makers, boot and shoe workers and carpenters, who accounted for 22.7 per cent, 10.8 per cent and 7.9 per cent respectively.[60] We can draw three conclusions from this material. First, the figures confirm that over time an increasing proportion of Jewish immigrants came from a manufacturing background. Second, they also suggest that the contrast between the immigrants who left Russia before and after 1900 has been overstated.[61] Third, and most significant, far from indicating a migrating population that was highly selective in its occupational profile these figures are broadly in line with the proportion revealed in the Russian census of 1897. The shelter figures lend strong support to Kahan's suggestion that the US returns are unreliable. The propensity to social mobility which Kuznets reads into these figures must be set aside.

Rather than social mobility, settlement in London led to a loss of economic independence for Jewish emigrants; for some it confirmed their position as wage earners, for others it was the occasion of their proletarianisation. As a first step to establishing this point table 5 presents the occupational distribution of Russians and Russian Poles in East London in 1891 and in London as a whole for 1901. Jewish immigrants found employment mostly in the consumer trades of the Jewish East End. The concentration and distribution of occupations changed little over the decade. There was some slackening of the immigrants' intense involvement in the clothing trades. Among male workers this was accounted for by the decline of the boot and shoe trade in London and by the growing significance of cabinet making within the immigrant colony. Among women's employments there was an increase in the number working in cigar and cigarette factories.

Of those Russians and Russian Poles who were gainfully occupied in 1891, 81 per cent were involved in manufacturing, mechanical or labouring trades, and in 1901 the figure was 82 per cent. What proportion of these were likely to have been wage earners at any one moment? In the absence of a comprehensive survey of workplaces the answer given here is bound to be an approximation, but it will

60. L. Gartner, *The Jewish Immigrant in England 1870–1914* (London, 1973 edn), pp. 57–8. The percentages given here are not the same as Gartner's because, on the basis of his own figures, those for carpenters and boot and shoe makers are inaccurate.

61. But insofar as the character of those emigrating did change then it is clear that this affected immigration to England far less than that to the United States. Not only did the Aliens Act greatly slow the influx after 1905, but even taking the period up to this point a greater proportion of the immigration to England took place, as we have seen, in the 1880s.

Table 5   Occupational distribution of Russians and Russian Poles in (East) London in 1891 and 1901[62]

Occupation	Percentage of occupied males		Percentage of occupied females		Percentage of total occupied	
	1891	1901	1891	1901	1891	1901
Boot and shoe makers and slipper makers	16	13	2	2	13	11
Tailors, tailoresses, mantle makers and dressmakers	42	42	59	54	45	44
Cap makers	3	3	3	4	3	3
Furriers	3	1	5	3	3	2
Other clothing workers	1	—	3	5	1	1
Cabinet makers	6	11	—	—	5	9
Other manufacturing, labouring and mechanical occupations	12	11	4	9	11	13
Trading and commerical occupations	16	17	10	9	15	15
Domestic servants and waiters	—	1	14	13	3	3
Total (rounded)	100	100	100	100	100	100

allow us to assess in broad terms the impact of migration on the occupational status of those who undertook the journey.

Most Jewish workers in the East End were employed in small workshops. In 1889 Beatrice Potter found that of the 901 Jewish tailoring workshops she visited in her investigations for Charles Booth, 76 per cent employed fewer than 10 people, 22.3 per cent

62. *Report on Recent Immigration*, appendix IV, pp. 148–54; *Census of 1901*, County of London, table 376, pp. 162–9. The percentages for 1891 have been calculated from a table composed by H. Llewellyn Smith and were compiled by him from the census returns, in the course of his investigation into the effects of immigration. It is for this year alone that there exists an occupational breakdown of Russians and Russian Poles living in East London. Indeed, 1901 is the only other year in the period for which the printed census returns provide data on the occupations of different groups of foreigners and which does so for units smaller than the entirety of England and Wales; for that year the information for the County of London is available. Since the East End accounted for about eighty per cent of all Russians and Russian Poles in London, the percentages for the county can act as a surrogate, in the absence of information for the East End itself, so long as small changes are not allowed an undue emphasis. For the sake of comparability, wherever possible, Llewellyn Smith's treatment of the census categories for 1891 has been followed.

employed between 10 and 25, and under 2 per cent employed more than 25 hands.[63] The most comprehensive survey of workplaces was produced by the house-to-house registration of workshops conducted by Medical Officers of Health under the Factory Act of 1901. D.L. Thomas, the Stepney Medical Officer of Health, informed the Royal Commission on Alien Immigration that in Stepney there were 1,778 workshops which employed 15,317 Jews and 5,307 Christians. These figures yield an average of 11.6 workers per workshop. Under the Act a workshop was defined as a workplace in which more than two workers were employed and in which no mechanical power was used. Few Jews were employed as 'homeworkers' as the term was understood by the Act and so few would have escaped the survey in this way. However, by 1900 there were a number of large boot and shoe and tailoring factories using mechanical power and therefore excluded from the survey. While this would have led to an underestimate of the number of Jewish workers per workshop, the fact that the survey excluded Bethnal Green where there was the largest concentration of Jewish cabinet makers had the opposite effect. In cabinet making Ernest Aves found that 4 to 8 workers were employed in a typical workshop.[64]

If, then, approximately 80 per cent of occupied Jewish immigrants were engaged in manufacturing, mechanical or labouring occupations and roughly 11 per cent of these were employers, we can calculate that 9 per cent of the working immigrant population were employers in these areas and 71 per cent were wage earners. By contrast, the proportion of Jews engaged in mechanical and manufacturing trades and in transportation in the Russian empire in 1897 amounted to just 41 per cent of the Jewish working population. Despite the rough and ready character of the calculation for London, and notwithstanding the problematic nature of comparing census returns from two different countries, the transformation of

---

63. Potter, 'East London Labour', *Nineteenth Century*, August 1888, p. 167. The next comprehensive estimate for the tailoring trade came from Mark Moses, a leading master tailor and political figure in the Jewish East End. In the late 1890s he placed the number of Jewish tailoring workers accurately at 10,000 and suggested that they worked for 1,000 master tailors: L. Soloweitschik, *Un Prolétariat Méconnu* (Brussels, 1895), p. 36. This figure is confirmed by information taken from a survey of 29 Jewish tailoring workshops in the early 1890s which found an average of 9.7 workers employed in each workshop. The same study found an average of 11.5 workers employed on the premises of 16 Jewish boot and shoe manufacturers and chamber masters. However, among outworkers in the same trade, less than 4 workers were found in each shop: *Report on Recent Immigration*, appendices XIV, IX, pp. 171–82, 203–6.
64. C. Booth, *Life and Labour of the People of London*, 1st series, vol. iv (London, 1902), pp. 172–5; *RCAI*, qq. 5,803–5,816.

the social condition of East European Jews after migration which is indicated by the figures is so immense that it must stand as one of the overarching determinants of immigrant life in the East End of London.

Both nineteenth-century commentators and subsequent historians have been dazzled by the entrepreneurial ambition and aptitude of those East European Jews who settled in Britain. But these images should not obscure the centrality of proletarianisation to the history of Jews in Eastern Europe *and* the countries to which they emigrated between 1880–1914. Many emigrants were artisans, journeymen and casually employed day labourers; others became wage earners for the first time in London. In London the working class grew to encompass a far greater portion of the Russian Jewish population than it did in Russia. Emigration extended the loss of economic independence among Jews.

Chapter 7

The Impact of Immigration

The dimensions of 'Jew-town'

Many social investigators and observers commented on the impact made by Jewish immigration on the streets of East London. In 1902 when Charles Booth reflected on the changes in Whitechapel and St George's in the East since he had begun his social investigations in 1887 it was the expansion of the Jewish colony which dominated his impressions. 'The whole district has been affected by the increase of the Jewish population,' he observed. 'It has been like the slow rising of a flood, street after street is occupied. Family follows family.'[1] A year later the statistician Simon Rosenbaum estimated that the Jewish population – immigrant and native-born – had reached between forty-five and fifty per cent of the total in the two districts. 'No wonder Whitechapel has not inaptly been called Jew-town,' he commented.[2] When George Duckworth, another social investigator, toured the streets of Whitechapel, Mile End and St George's he too experienced the commonplace sensation that he was walking in a foreign town. He observed the generally well-dressed, well-fed children, the immigrant costers in their fur caps and high boots, women in wigs (these were worn by pious women who shaved their heads) and shawls, and, in Spitalfields and the western part of Mile End New Town, the unusually close proximity of the Jewish poor to the well-to-do. According to Duckworth, the Jewish East End even possessed its particular detritus: the waste of the street markets and workshops, fish heads, orange peel, bread, vegetables and paper.[3]

These sights, sounds and smells, exotic or repulsive to the British social explorer, may have been more reassuring to the succession of

1. C. Booth, *Life and Labour of the People of London*, 3rd series, vol. ii (London, 1902), pp. 1–2.
2. *JC*, 5 June 1903, p. 13.
3. London School of Economics, Booth Collection, B351, George Duckworth's police notes, pp. 35, 49.

immigrants from Eastern Europe. But the impression they received was the same: of a corner of Eastern Europe transplanted to London. When the Russian Jewish scholar Jacob Lestchinsky reflected on why the immigrants felt at home in Whitechapel he decided that 'first, it was just as crowded and dirty as in the Pale'; there were 'the same small poor stores . . . the same dark and dirty workshops. The same worn out, hungry, pallid faces wander in the streets. . . . Yiddish is the language through which the immigrant lives.'[4] Likewise, when Sholem Aleichem's fictional creation Mottel Paysi arrived in London he rejoiced to find that the food and the goods in the shops were familiar. It was 'even just as muddy as at home. And it smells as bad. Sometimes even worse. We were delighted with Whitechapel.'[5]

The familiarity was circumscribed, however. It was in relation to the enormity and strangeness of London that the Jewish quarter appeared to lie 'as a single island in a wide sea . . . a small world which lives and breathes alone'.[6] Lestchinsky for one was keenly aware of this. His pamphlet *Der Yidisher Arbayter in London* begins by enumerarating the bridges, streets, railway stations, squares and gardens of the capital, creating an impression of the city's unique scale.[7] London was immense. In 1881 it held 4.8 million inhabitants and by 1910 this figure had risen to 7.3 million. At the earlier date only two other European cities held more than 1 million – Paris and Berlin – and the larger of these, Paris, contained just 2.3 million inhabitants.

What was the demographic impact of Jewish immigration on the East End of London? Since their resettlement there had been a concentration of Jews in the City of London. In 1850 two-thirds of London's Jews – that is to say, 12,000 to 13,000 people – remained in the eastern City wards or in the area between Houndsditch and Old Castle Street, and in the Goodman's Fields area extending south to Wellclose Square. This Jewish colony grew rapidly during the three decades before the onset of mass immigration from Eastern Europe.[8] By 1882 its numbers had risen to just over 30,000, in part as a result of immigration from Holland, Germany and Eastern Europe. Nevertheless, the effect of immigration after 1882 was dramatic: by

4. J. Lestchinsky, *Der Yidisher Arbayter in London* (Vilna, 1907), p. 7.
5. Sholom Aleichem, *Adventures of Mottel the Cantor's Son*, translated by T. Kahana (London, 1958), p. 199.
6. N. Geldshteyn, *Di Yidisher Virtshaft in London* (Vilna, 1907), p. 1; see too L. Soloweitschik, *Un Prolétariat Méconnu* (Brussels, 1895), pp. 30–1.
7. Lestchinsky, *Der Yidisher Arbayter in London*, p. 3.
8. V.D. Lipman, *Social History of the Jews in England, 1850–1950* (London, 1954), pp. 26–8.

the end of the decade the Jewish population of the East End had doubled.[9]

By 1871 the concentration of East European Jews in the districts just to the east of the City of London was well established. In that year 78 per cent of all Russians and Russian Poles in London were enumerated in the City of London, Whitechapel, St George's in the East and Mile End Old Town. Higher rates of immigration only served to make this bias more intense, and in 1881 the same districts accounted for 82 per cent of the Russians and Russian Poles in the capital.[10] At the same time, the immigrant colony began to expand more deeply into the East End. The Jewish East End did not have fixed geographical boundaries. After 1881 the settlement spread from its traditional centre in the area between the eastern extremities of the City and Commercial Street. Immigration pushed Jews southwards into the northern part of St George's in the East, westwards through Spitalfields, beyond Commercial Street and into Mile End New Town. Spitalfields remained a district dominated by established immigrants and English Jews, whereas Mile End New Town contained a concentration of immigrants that was half as large again. Jewish settlement spread south of the Whitechapel Road too, through the western district of Mile End Old Town, to reach the more established Anglo-Jewish population around Stepney Green. From the mid-1890s, the immigrants pressed northwards into Bethnal Green.[11] Moreover, throughout these decades there was also a movement of Jews across London to Hackney and to Soho. In 1911, over 2,000 Russians and Russian Poles were enumerated in both of these districts.[12] But this did not diminish the significance of an expanding Jewish East End. In 1911, 83 per cent of London's Russian and Russian Polish population remained in Stepney and Bethnal Green.[13]

But these units are too broad to reflect the different local concentrations of immigrants. In the case of Bethnal Green the incursion of Jewish immigrants was contained within the south-western corner of

9. *Select Committee on Emigration and Immigration*, PP 1889, X, appendix 6, p. 93.
10. Calculated from the *Census of England and Wales, 1871*, PP 1873, LXXII, division 1, table 15, pp. 25–6; *Census of England and Wales, 1881*, PP 1883, LXXX, division 1, table 13, pp. 23–5.
11. *Report on the Volume and Effects of Recent Immigration from Eastern Europe*, PP 1894, LXVIII, appendix 1, pp. 138–9; *Royal Commission an Alien Immigration*, PP 1903, IX, qq. 6,576, 17,246, 17,255–6; Lipman, *Social History*, pp. 95–6; see too the map reproduced here, from C. Russell and H. Lewis, *The Jew in London* (London, 1900).
12. On Jewish immigrants in Soho see A. Sherwell, *Life in West London: A Study and a Contrast* (London, 1897).
13. *Census of England and Wales, 1911*, PP 1913, LXXVIII, vol. ix, p. xix.

JEWISH EAST LONDON

SCALE

This Map shows by Colour the proportion
of the Jewish population to other residents of East
London, street by street, in 1899.

EXPLANATION OF COLOURING.

Proportion of Jews coloured.

95% to 100%.

75% and less than 95%.

50% and less than 75%.

25% and less than 50%.

5% and less than 25%.

Less than 5% of Jews.

NOTE.—In all streets coloured blue the Jews have a majority of the
inhabitants; in blue coloured red, the Gentiles predominate.

Table 6   *The total number of Russians and Russian Poles in districts of*
Stepney and their percentage of the population in those districts,
1871–1901[14]

	1871		1881		1891		1901	
Whitechapel	2,912	4%	5,293	8%	13,538	18%	20,882	27%
St George's in the East	238	1%	566	1%	4,973	11%	11,827	24%
Stepney	24	—	30	—	78	—	915	1%
Mile End Old Town	261	—	893	1%	3,440	3%	10,088	9%

the borough. Something of the pattern of immigrant settlement in
Stepney is shown in table 6 above. But even at this level the figures
conceal wide variations within the four districts. We have records of
these differences for 1891 only. In that year, all but 7 of the Russians
and Russian Poles in St George's in the East lived in the north of the
borough where they comprised 13 per cent of the population. Likewise, all but 216 of the Russian and Russian Polish population of
Mile End Old Town lived in its western portion, where they accounted for 8 per cent of the population.[15]

The demographic effect of social and cultural change was heightened by the tendency of the native-born population to move away
from the area. Although the total population in Stepney grew from
274,446 to 298,600 between 1871 and 1901, the number of British
subjects in the borough fell by 16,126; a decline from 95 per cent to
82 per cent of the borough's population. In Bethnal Green the
proportion of British subjects fell from 99 per cent in 1881 to 94 per
cent in 1911.[16] The high birth rates and low death rates among the
immigrant population made the impact of immigration still more
intense. In 1901, 48 per cent of the population in England and
Wales were between the ages of 15 and 45; in the case of Russian and
Russian Polish immigrants the percentage was 75 per cent for males
and 71 per cent for females.[17] In table 7 we can see the effect on the

14. Compiled from *Select Committee on Emigration and Immigration*, PP 1888, XI,
     appendix 8, pp. 256–62; *Report on Recent Immigration*, appendix 1, pp. 138–9;
     RCAI, table XXXV, q. 10,911; *JC*, 5 June 1903, p. 13.
15. *Report on Recent Immigration*, appendix 1, pp. 138–9.
16. *Census of England and Wales, 1911*, PP 1914, LXXXI, summary tables, table 14,
     pp. 64–5; *ibid*, PP 1913, LXXVIII, table 3, pp. 136–146; *RCAI*, table xxxv,
     q. 10,911.
17. Rosenbaum, 'A Contribution to the Study of the Vital and Other Statistics of
     the Jews of the United Kingdom,' *Journal of the Royal Statistical Society*, Septem-
     ber 1905, p. 535.

Table 7   Birth rate per 1,000 living in Whitechapel, St George's in the East, Southwark and London [18]

	1886–90	*1891–5*	*1896–1900*
Whitechapel	35.7	40.7	39.2
Comparative figure	100	114	110
St George's in the East	39.9	41.4	43.3
Comparative figure	100	104	109
Southwark	35.5	35.1	29.8
Comparative figure	100	96	93
London	32.2	30.9	29.8
Comparative figure	100	96	93

immigrant birth rate by noting the tendency of the birth rate in Whitechapel and St George's in the East and comparing it with another working-class district, Southwark.

The Jewish population also enjoyed a low rate of infant mortality.[19] In 1901 S.F. Murphy, the London County Council Medical Officer of Health, carried out a survey of the dilapidated Backchurch Lane area of St George's in the East. The streets contained 1,296 inhabitants of whom 1,258 were working-class and nearly all were Jews. Among them the death rate per 1,000 children between the ages of 0–5 was 58.5; within St George's in the East as a whole the figure was 90.9.[20] Indeed, whereas infant mortality in London as a whole rose by 5 per cent between 1886–90 and 1896–1900, in Whitechapel over the same period it fell by 15 per cent.[21] The effects of a high birth rate and low infant mortality were such that in 1905 Rosenbaum calculated that the Jewish population of Stepney was growing by 6.7 per cent per annum and that only 3.7 per cent of this was due to immigration.[22] The proportion of young adults and children in the Jewish East End was very high. Rosenbaum estimated that in 1901, among 119,770 Jews in the East End, 69,490 were under 20 years old.[23] The demographic impact of Jewish immigration far exceeded the number of immigrants.

18. *RCAI*, appendix, table LXXIV, p. 89; see the evidence of the Whitechapel Medical Officer of Health, *ibid*, qq. 4,557–9.
19. Some of the causes of low infant mortality are discussed in L. Marks, ' "Dear Old Mother Levy's": The Jewish Maternity and Sick Room Helps Society 1895–1939', *Social History of Medicine*, April 1990, pp. 61–88.
20. GLRO, LCC, Housing of the Working Classes Committee, presented papers, case 65, Backchurch Lane (St George's in the East) area, report by S.F. Murphy, 27 March 1901.
21. *RCAI*, appendix, table LXXIV, p. 89.
22. Rosenbaum, 'A Contribution', p. 554.
23. *Ibid*, p. 540; on this see also J. White, *Rothschild Buildings: Life in an East End Tenement Block* (London, 1980), p. 145.

The effects of immigration, a high birth rate and low infant mortality were estimated in 1889 by Llewellyn Smith, who judged that 'there are at least 60,000 Jews in the East End of London', of whom he reckoned one half were foreign-born.[24] The next serious estimates of the Jewish population's size were not made until the early twentieth century. Between 1901–5, five different assessments were made which variously placed the Jewish population of the capital at between 104,000 and 150,000. The most sophisticated of these was made by Rosenbaum and presented in a paper in 1905 to the Royal Statistical Society. He placed the Jewish population of London at 144,000, of which, he suggested, 120,000 lived in Stepney.[25]

Jewish immigrants and the housing market

Apart from employment, the immigrants had one fundamental need – housing. But throughout this period the East End was synonymous with bad housing conditions. In 1908 a Board of Trade report coolly noted 'the density of population usually reaches its maximum just beyond the city wall. This is the oldest and most crowded portion of London in which rents are highest and accommodation worst.'

> The houses contain usually six or more rooms, and are generally either two or three stories in height, sometimes having in addition a basement or half-basement. The architectural variations are considerable, the houses being erected at different periods. In some streets the plain fronts of houses rise direct from the pavement without forecourt or front garden.[26]

24. *Select Committee on Emigration and Immigration*, PP 1889, X, appendix 6, p. 93.
25. Rosenbaum, 'A Contribution', pp. 540–1. Rosenbaum calculated the total Jewish population for the borough by establishing the ratio of all marriages of Jews in the City, Bethnal Green, Whitechapel and St George's in the East to the marriage rate of natives of Russia and Poland. As the total number of Russians and Russian Poles was known from the census, the ratio of marriages could be used to estimate the total number of Jews. Clearly, this estimate contains many possible sources of error. The higher percentage of immigrants of marriageable age, and the social and geographical mobility of English-born Jews who may have resided in the East End but married elsewhere, meant that the figures possibly underestimate the number of English-born Jews. But considerations the other way are the exclusion of Austrian Jews from the reckoning and the probable under-registration of immigrant marriages. On the dimensions and impact of immigration see C. Holmes, *John Bull's Island: Immigration and British Society, 1871–1971* (London, 1988).
26. *Report of an Enquiry by the Board of Trade into Working Class Rents, Housing and Retail Prices together with the Standard Rates of Wages Prevailing in Certain Occupations in the Principal Industrial Towns of the United Kingdom*, PP 1908, CVII, p. 5.

At the rear were back yards, 15 to 40 feet long, which could be used to accommodate a workshop. The houses themselves were always shared, each family occupying one to three rooms.[27]

The difficulty Jewish immigrants faced, and which they aggravated, was that at the same time as they were adding to the population in the East End the amount of residential property there was in decline.[28] The growth of the population in Stepney between 1881–1901 was anomalous. Only Southwark and Bethnal Green of the other boroughs in the inner circle of London experienced population growth in these decades; and in the 1890s even their populations stagnated while Stepney's increased by 4.7 per cent. Of course, it was in Stepney that Jewish immigration provided a source of growth which did not arise elsewhere.[29] The same period was one of rapidly advancing rents in London. Between 1880 and 1900 rents rose by between 10 per cent and 12 per cent over the capital as a whole but in the eastern boroughs the increase was 25 per cent. Stepney was most severely affected: here rents increased by an average of 25 per cent in the 1890s alone.[30] This cannot be attributed to increased numbers alone but immigration was undoubtedly one contributory factor.

The gradual depopulation of the central districts was caused by the expansion of the financial and commercial functions of the City of London, the development of railways and the decline of established industries.[31] The side-effects of commercial development were demolitions, overcrowding, increased rents and a slow drift to the suburbs. In 1900 a London County Council report explained that the increase in land values caused by industrial and commercial development meant that builders found it 'unprofitable to pay the commercial value of land in such districts for the purpose of building working-class dwellings thereon'.[32]

Jewish settlement in the East End, against the trend of depopulation, was encouraged by its proximity to the docks, the momentum created by the earlier settlement of *landslayt* and family members,

27. *Ibid.*
28. On the depopulation of central districts of London and the impact of Jewish immigration see A. Wohl, *The Eternal Slum: Housing and Social Policy in Victorian London* (London, 1977), pp. 303–8.
29. *Census of England and Wales, 1911*, PP 1914–16, LXXXI, Summary tables, table 15, pp. 64–5. For a definition of the inner circle see G. Stedman Jones, *Outcast London* (Oxford, 1971), p. 141.
30. A. Offer, *Property and Politics, 1870–1914* (Cambridge, 1981), p. 268; Stedman Jones, *Outcast London*, p. 325.
31. *Ibid*, pp. 152–5.
32. C.J. Stewart, *The Housing Question in London* (London, 1900), p. 63.

and the existence of Jewish institutions in the locality. All these factors, however, were underpinned by the existence of low-skilled employment opportunities in the workship trades; opportunities which required both workers and masters to live in the East End because of the irregularity of demand and working hours.[33] The activity of Jewish immigrants in these trades not only led to an increased demand for housing in the East End: it also resulted in more properties being used for production as well as residence. This pushed up rents still further. Some observers believed that, had it not been for the higher rents paid by Jewish immigrants, even more land in the East End would have been cleared for commercial uses.[34]

The successful landlord in a working-class district attended to a number of hazards: arrears, moonlight flits, vacant properties and the attentions of the sanitary and factory inspectorates. The detailed work and knowledge this required meant that the market for working-class housing included a plethora of small capitalists. Jewish landlords were well placed to perform successfully as rentiers among the Jewish and immigrant population of the East End. But, fundamentally, the immigrant landlord was no different from any other metropolitan rentier entrepreneur working on a small scale.[35] Among vulnerable immigrants, however, the Jewish East End allowed rich pickings. As table 8 indicates, immigrant landlords were more likely to raise rents than native ones, and immigrant tenants were more likely to suffer from this. Religious scruples or ethnic solidarities were rhetorical weapons used to reprimand landlords rather than considerations which tempered the tough economics of the housing market. Harry Lewis related that one of his friends had 'asked a land-lord how he came to oppress one of his tenants, a very poor man and a Jew like himself. "When I go to synagogue," came the reply, "I am a Jew, when I come for my rent, I am a *goy*".'[36]

---

33. *Report on Recent Immigration*, pp. 36–7.
34. *RCAI*, q. 15,762.
35. As Avner Offer has described the situation, 'urban property was held for the most part by a multitude of small and medium-scale owners. This house owning multitude (between, say one seventh and one tenth of all households) let out their properties at rack rent or occupied their own shops, dwellings, sweatshops and factories': Offer, *Property and Politics*, p. 119. On the difficulties landlords faced, see too M. Daunton, *House and Home in the Victorian City: Working Class Housing, 1850–1914* (London, 1983), p. 130.
36. Russell and Lewis, *The Jew in London*, p. 174. However, on the use of communal power as a stick to beat landlords, see J. White, 'Jewish Landlords, Jewish Tenants', in A. Newman, ed., *The Jewish East End, 1840–1939* (London, 1981), pp. 210–11.

Table 8   The number of landlords and of tenants of a certain number of houses visited in the borough of Stepney between 1890 and 1902 with the number and percentages of cases where rents were raised by British and alien landlords respectively[37]

		Number of houses visited	Cases where rent was raised	Percentage of the total
Total figures		608	484	80
Nationality of landlords	British	231	153	66
	Alien	374	329	88
Nationality of tenants	British	206	155	75
	Alien	402	329	82

Writing from Toynbee Hall in 1900, Charles Russell observed that 'a good deal of house property has lately been changing hands, and has been bought up purely as an investment by the shrewder and wealthier among the foreigners themselves . . . such investments are extremely profitable'.[38] A survey of houses in Whitechapel, St George's in the East, Mile End Old Town and Bethnal Green, made haphazardly between 1890 and 1902, revealed that 58 per cent of the properties had 'alien' landlords.[39] Jewish or immigrant land-lordism was a well established form of investment by the 1890s and was not created by the rent inflation of that decade. This can be seen in table 9 by looking at the density of immigrant rentier activity in different parts of the East End alongside the proportion of houses in the district which had changed hands. In Whitechapel (1–3) there was clearly an established practice of immigrant landlordism but during the 1890s there was a movement of immigrant land-lords into areas which hitherto had been the preserve of native rentiers.

Some observers claimed that the conditions of the 1890s brought into existence a new speculative house owner. This figure bought properties and gave tenants notice to pay higher rent or leave. In either event, on the basis of increased rents the property was re-sold at a profit, at which point the cycle could begin again.[40] Another type

37. *RCAI*, appendix, table XLVI, p. 50. These figures must be treated cautiously, for increased rents were often linked to the addition of new space in the form of a workshop, as will be seen, although an effort was made to exclude properties where alterations had been made: see *ibid*, q. 11,521.
38. Russell and Lewis, *The Jew in London*, p. 17.
39. *RCAI*, appendix, tables XXXVIII, XXXIX, XL, XLI, pp. 45–8.
40. *Ibid*, q. 6,579; *JC*, 8 April 1898, p. 9.

Table 9   Percentage of houses surveyed between 1890 and 1902 rented by alien landlords, and the percentage of houses which had changed hands since 1896[41]

District	Percentage of alien landlords	Percentage of houses which had changed hands since 1896
1. Christchurch Spitalfields	53	7
2. Mile End New Town	45	15
3. Whitechapel (parish)	71	19
4. Mile End Old Town	68	33
5. Bethnal Green	25	30
6. St George's in the East	68	36

of investor redeveloped as well as leased properties. H.H. Gordon, a Stepney borough councillor and a Jewish communal worker, observed that 'this work is very largely in the hands of Jewish builders like Davis Brothers'.[42]

After 1890, where wholesale demolition did not occur, there was a tendency to build workshops on to existing houses, either as extensions at the rear or as additional stories above. As early as 1893 a LCC report had noted that the addition of 'purpose-built' workshops was well under way to the north and south of the Whitechapel Road.[43] The effect on rents, as well as some features of immigrant property investment, can be illustrated by the case of Albert Square. The square, which was located half a mile west of Stepney station, was made up of 'good houses' with back gardens. The estate was bought in January 1899 by Morris Cohen, a successful manufacturer of ladies' mantles. Cohen had arrived in England in 1877 and began work as a tailor; by 1902 he employed 180 hands. He presents an example of the degree of upward social mobility achieved by some immigrants, particularly early ones, the level of wealth they could accumulate and the importance of property as an outlet for its investment. When Cohen bought the properties in Albert Square the houses yielded an average rent of £35 per year. Within two years this figure had been raised

41.   *RCAI, ibid.*
42.   *RCAI,* q. 17,723.
43.   LCC, Public Health and Housing Committee, presented papers, E32, report of the Medical Officer of Health submitting a report by Dr Hamer, 4 May 1893; On cabinet makers' workshops in Bethnal Green erected by a Jewish entrepreneur, see R. Samuel, *East End Underworld: Chapters in the Life of Arthur Harding* (London, 1981), p. 96; also Booth Collection, B351, George Duckworth's police notes, p. 151.

to £65, but the new rents were not being paid on the same amount of space, as workshops had been added at the rear of the houses.[44]

Houses were, in many cases, left by landlords in a state of ill repair. In 1894 the LCC's investigation into the sanitary condition of Whitechapel found that 58 per cent of the properties had defects. The figure given by the JBG was roughly the same, 66 per cent. In Mile End Old Town the Board discovered faults in 61 per cent of properties.[45] In the medium term the tendency of conditions could be regressive, and improved only as a result of demolition and displacement. The Bell Lane area of Whitechapel had been the subject of investigation since 1877 when the Metropolitan Board of Works had first considered it for a clearance scheme. In 1889 the area was found still to consist of 'dilapidated accommodation', which suffered from want of ventilation, with closet accommodation 'as bad as it could be' and many cottages fit to be condemned.[46] In 1893 the area was found to be deteriorating. In 1896 there was still no sign of improvement.

> In nearly all of the houses evidence was found of the existence of dilapidated roofs, slack pipes and gutterings, broken ceilings and floors, dirty rooms, damp walls, defective brick work, uncovered domestic cisterns. In a few instances the faulty state of the drains had led to a stopped condition of the yard drain inlets and water closets.[47]

But damp and insanitary conditions such as these were favourable if compared to the worst dwellings in the Jewish East End, such as the notorious Booth Street Buildings.[48]

---

44. *RCAI*, qq. 11,525, 11,531, 11,535.
45. In Mile End Old Town there was a discrepancy between the Council's findings and those of the JBG. Here the LCC found that 32 per cent of houses had defects. The difference can be accounted for by the broader scope of the LCC survey. This would have included all parts of Mile End, which was the most affluent of the East End districts. The JBG would have been concerned only with the area of Jewish settlement in the western part of the district. Certainly, the JBG blamed landlord neglect: LCC Public Health and Housing Committee, presented papers, E65, report of the Medical Officer of Health on the sanitary condition of Whitechapel, 15 October 1894; *ibid.*, E64, report of the Medical Officer of Health on the sanitary condition of Mile End Old Town, 7 June 1894.
46. LCC, Public Health and Housing Committee, presented papers, A20, report of the sub-committee on the Bell Lane improvement scheme, 29 July 1889.
47. *Ibid*, report on the present position in the Bell Lane, Sandys Row, Whitechapel area, 6 December 1893; *ibid*, report by Dr Young on the Bell Lane, Whitechapel, area, 28 January 1896.
48. Booth Collection, B351, George Duckworth's police notes, p. 151; *RCAI*, qq. 4,880, 5,540; White, *Rothschild Buildings*, pp. 63–4.

Apart from the physical inadequacy of properties, the inevitable consequence of immigration and rising rents was overcrowding. Typically, overcrowding was worst among unskilled workers who had the misfortune to arrive in the country with their families. The general point was made in a report of 1894 which also gave two pathetic instances.

> Some of the most extreme instances of overcrowding were met with in the case of Russians or Russian Poles who had not long been in the country, thus at No. 3 New Court, Hanbury Street, a man, his wife, and seven children were found occupying a single room of 800 cubic feet capacity, again two rooms in Plough-Street Buildings were it was admitted occupied by a man and wife and their family consisting of a grown son and his wife and three children, two grown up daughters and a second son.[49]

Between 1891 and 1901 overcrowding decreased in every London borough except Stepney where its advance followed the uneven spread of the immigrant population in that decade. St George's in the East suffered an increase in its population living in overcrowded conditions of 6.9 per cent, Whitechapel of 2.3 per cent, and Mile End Old Town of 1.8 per cent. In contrast in Shadwell, Ratcliffe and Limehouse, where immigrant settlement was negligible, overcrowding decreased by almost 1 per cent.[50]

The incidence of overcrowding was determined by the relation of wages to rents.[51] High rents and low earnings produced overcrowding simply because it was necessary to cram as many people as possible into the space rented. The variability of rents, of wage rates and of the size of households makes it difficult to generalise on the burden that rents placed on wage earners. In 1887 a survey of working-class rents and wages in some London districts included St George's in the East and distinguished between the responses of English and foreign workers. There were 378 foreign tailors included in the survey, all but 10 of whom lived in St George's in the East.[52] Of these, 290 claimed they were the sole wage earners in their

---

49. LCC, Public Health and Housing Committee, presented papers, E65, report of the Medical Officer of Health on the sanitary condition of Whitechapel, 15 October 1894.
50. *RCAI*, appendix, table LIV, p. 61.
51. The *Report of Her Majesty's Commissioners Inquiring into the Housing of the Working Classes* acknowledged that the relation of wages to rents determined the level of overcrowding: PP 1884–5, XXX, p. 16.
52. *Tabulation of the Statements made by Men Living in Certain Selected Districts of London in March 1887*, PP, 1887, LXXI, pp. ix, 36–7. We can assume almost all were East European Jews: see *Census of England and Wales, 1891*, PP 1893–4, CVI division 1, table 10, p. 20.

families. These tailors reported average earnings of 20s 2d when in work. Their average rent was 6s 7d, just under one-third of their average weekly earnings. But unemployment or the need to find space for a large family often meant that rent accounted for a larger share of earnings. When the survey was carried out, in March 1887, 248 said they had been out of work for 8 weeks or more since the end of the previous October, 148 for more than 12 weeks.[53] Only 48 said they had regular employment. Moreover, in 190 of the 378 cases the respondent was the father of 3 or more children. The weekly rent of a single room in the Jewish East End in the mid-1880s was 3–4s. As table 10 indicates, the marginal cost of additional rooms was less, but given the prevailing level of earnings, a family's attempt to inhabit more than one room would be difficult in the slack season. The problem could be resolved either by moving into a single room or by sub-letting space; either way by increased overcrowding.

Over the last decade of our period, conditions in the housing market swung back in the tenants' favour. In Stepney, rents declined by 10 per cent between 1905–10 and, in the west of the borough, the area where Jewish settlement was most dense, the figure was 15 per cent.[55] In part this was because the population of Stepney declined by 6.3 per cent in the decade 1901–11: in part because the Aliens Act drastically diminished the influx from Eastern Europe. But living standards as well as numbers of people were significant. Over the same period, the number of vacant houses in Stepney increased: from 1,093 in 1904 to a peak of 2,944 in 1908.[56] The years between

Table 10   Rooms let and rent paid by foreign tailors in London in March 1887[54]

Space	No. of cases	Rents paid	No. of cases
Part of a room	10	Less than 3s	34
1 room	90	3s to less than 4s	57
2 rooms	106	4s to less than 6s	92
3 or more rooms	171	6s to less than 8s	78
		More than 8s	116

53. *Tabulation of the Statements Made by Men*, pp. 36–7.
54. *Ibid.*
55. *Report of an Enquiry by the Board of Trade into Working Class Rents and Retail Prices together with the Standard Rates of Wages in Certain Occupations in the Principal Towns of the United Kingdom*, PP 1913, LXVI, pp. 6–7. In the western portion of Bethnal Green, rents fell by 12 per cent.
56. *JC*, 11 August 1911, p. 22. In 1910 there were still 2,529 empties in Stepney.

1896–1914 are acknowledged to have been a time in which working-class real wages stagnated or declined, and the coincidence of falling rents and a growing number of 'empties' in Stepney are consistent with this picture.[57] Between 1901–11 the average number of persons in each inhabited house rose slightly.[58] Rents fell but pressure on living standards may have meant that many families continued to overcrowd their accommodation rather than take advantage of the growing number of vacant rooms.

The housing market and social relations

Social relations in the housing market did not resolve into a straightforward opposition between landlord and tenant. The offer of accommodation, which was so useful to new arrivals, generated chains of petty rentiers. Sometimes these operated through connections established before emigration.[59] Single male 'greeners' gathered together to share rooms and beds, and their needs dovetailed with the attempts of established immigrants to supplement their income by letting space to new arrivals.

Rent inflation and scarcity generated ambiguous social relations. Depending on the framework within which they were construed, these could be seen to exhibit either mutual assistance or exploitation as, for example, established immigrants offered accommodation to new arrivals. A Jewish trade unionist wrote to the *Jewish Chronicle* to complain that rackrenting landlords were only one part of the rents problem and that 'the behaviour of the tenants to the sub-tenants is simply atrocious'.[60] But this complaint contrasts with instances of mutual satisfaction. Thomas Eyges recalled how a chance meeting resulted in an opportunity to get an introduction to both an employer and a place to live. 'He also offered to share his bed with Mot [Eyges]. This reduced Samuel's rent from two shillings to eighteen pence – a shilling and a half – a week. The housekeeper also gained a shilling in rent, receiving a shilling from two persons instead of two shillings from one, and everybody was happy.'[61] Immigrants used tactics such as this to cope with the financial strain of young children. One man with a wife and six children rented two

---

57. I. Gazely, 'The Cost of Living for Urban Workers in Late Victorian and Edwardian Britain', *Economic History Review*, May 1989, pp. 207–17.
58. From 9.49 to 9.59: *Census of England and Wales, 1911*, PP 1912–13, CXIII, table 5, p. 340.
59. *Report Inquiring into the Housing of the Working Classes*, q. 4,989.
60. *JC*, 25 November 1898, pp. 9–10.
61. T. Eyges, *Beyond the Horizon* (Boston, Mass., 1944), p. 60.

rooms at a rent of 5s 6d. One room was sublet to two single men at 2s each, while he and his family crammed themselves into a single room. They did, however, pay only 1s 6d rent from out of their own pockets.[62]

Key-money offered tenants another way to recoup income at a time of rapid rent inflation. As early as the 1870s key-money had been regarded 'as a sort of tenant right' in parts of the Jewish East End.[63] It was a sum paid either to a landlord or to an outgoing tenant. Generally, if paid to the landlord it was a bribe so that he should turn out the existing tenant, if to the tenant it was to ensure that the payer would be the first to apply for possession of vacant property. In fact, it was this latter form of key-money which was by far the most common in the Jewish East End. Tenants not landlords were the chief beneficiaries. In a survey of 686 occupancies made between 1890 and 1902, key-money had been paid in 347 cases, and in 261 of these it was received by the outgoing tenant. Moreover, the amounts paid to tenants were higher than those to landlords: the former received £11 15s on average and the latter an average payment of just under £8. In all but 30 cases the sums were paid by immigrants.[64] As the practices of sub-letting and of exchanging key-money illustrate, in the housing market Jewish immigrants generated contractual arrangements which combined assistance and profit.

These patterns can be seen in their full significance in the context of conflict and competition between the immigrant and native populations. Jewish immigration contributed to increased competition for scarce accommodation. But competition was not only a matter of aggregate demand; it took shape through the ways in which individual and collective agency affected the market. Immigrant tenants, for example, used key-money to win advantages over the native population. Rent inflation affected both immigrants and natives but whereas English households, in many cases, refused to pay and moved away from the area, immigrants did pay. In Whitechapel changes of ownership and increased rents of up to 100 per cent led to the replacement of Englishmen by foreigners as tenants.[65] In places such as Albert Square where workshop space was added prior to rent increases the effect was generally the same because the English tenants had no use for the additional workshop space.[66]

62. *RCAI*, qq. 3,422–3, 3,515.
63. *Ibid*, q. 18,162.
64. *Ibid*, appendix, tables XLVII, XLVIII, p. 51.
65. *Ibid*, q. 17,247; *JC*, 8 April 1898, p. 9.
66. *RCAI*, q. 11,735, 19,045.

Another factor which assisted immigrants at the expense of the native population was the clearance of courts and alleys with their lodging houses, inhabited by native and Irish casual workers, and the erection of tenement blocks or model dwellings in their place. The former inhabitants could not afford the rents in the new dwellings but this was not the case with Jewish immigrants.[67] Llewellyn Smith outlined this process as it developed in the 1880s in Whitechapel, east and west of Commercial Street. In this area demolitions were carried out under the Cross Act, which reduced the population from 9,209 to 8,511 between 1883–4. Since the immigrant influx of 1881 there had been an increase of Jews in the area but until the clearances they were contained on the City side of Commercial Street. The effect of the clearances was to allow immigrants to move across this line into Fashion Street, Old Montague Street and the surrounding offshoots.[68] The same process was repeated at the end of the century at the northern limit of the Jewish quarter. There the Boundary Street estate was built on the site of clearances carried out between 1890 and 1900. By 1903, 27 per cent of the new tenements were occupied by Jewish immigrants.[69]

In 1900 Harry Lewis was able to give an impressive list of fifteen streets described by Booth as inhabited by the 'vicious and semi-criminal' which had become 'Jewish and respectable'.[70] Several of the Anglican clergy in Spitalfields welcomed the immigrants as allies in the struggle against crime and vice in the rookeries of their parish. 'No Gentile with any thread of respectability comes here,' complained a clergyman at Christ Church, and he saw the only hope for the area to be 'the ousting of Gentiles by Jews'.[71] However, the dirt, the overcrowding, the inflated rents, the desecration of the Christian Sunday and the strangeness of the immigrants weighed heavily, even for a measured observer such as Charles Booth.

> No Gentile could live in the same house with these poor foreign Jews and even as neighbours they are unpleasant; and since people of this race, though sometimes quarrelsome amongst themselves, are gregarious and sociable, each small street or group of houses tend to become entirely Jewish. The crowding that results is very great, and the dirt reported as indescribable. House and land values rise, however.[72]

---

67. On wages, see below, pp. 205–9.
68. Booth, *Life and Labour*, 1st series, vol. iii, pp. 78–9, 103.
69. LCC, *Minutes of Proceedings*, report of the Housing of the Working Classes Committee, 17 March 1903.
70. Russell and Lewis, *The Jew in London*, p. 176.
71. Booth Collection, A39, Whitechapel and St George's in the East, pp. 1–3.
72. Booth, *Life and Labour*, 3rd series, vol. ii, pp. 1–2.

This argument would have found widespread assent among those who felt driven out on account of the offence the immigrants caused to norms of English respectability. One resident complained to the LCC that 'Plumbers Row . . . is worse than the Black Hole of Calcutta. It is a wonder that fever does not break out in the neighbourhood (which I'm certain will not be very long) owing [to] the horrible smells from the foreign Jews who now inhabit nine–tenths of the street.'[73] One English tenant wrote to his landlord as follows:

> No doubt you will be surprised to hear that I am thinking of giving up the house, but the neighbourhood is so bad now it is crowded with the foreigners that I shall try and get further away. My wife has been to look at some new houses to-day at East Ham. . . . We made up our minds to go in a hurry, or the wife should have told you on Monday, but our own people are leaving the street and I cannot stand the foreigners.[74]

On occasion, rent increases demanded by Jewish landlords were greeted by an outbreak of window-breaking. Elsewhere there was resistance to the spread of Jewish settlement, and at particular points a similar tactic of resistance established boundaries to it. The south ward of St George's in the East remained largely free of Jewish immigrants. One witness before the Royal Commission on Alien Immigration explained, 'they will not have them there. . . . They smash the windows and the doors in when the aliens get there and they soon clear out.'[75] Other boundaries were less permanent. In the late 1890s an observer reported from a part of Stepney beyond the eastern limit of settlement that 'Jews bought up cheap houses but they dare not put in any Jewish tenants just yet, they would have too hot a time. They will wait until they have got the whole street.'[76] Children learnt to regard parts of the East End as unsafe or only to be crossed in groups.[77] But territorial claims were not absolute. Inspector Reid of Leman Street police station observed, 'there is a mixture of English and Jews in some streets but friction and quarrels [are] the inevitable result. The repulsion felt of one for the other is mutual.'[78]

The owners and managers of some estates also resisted the arrival of 'aliens'.[79] One instance was on the Chapman estate in St George's

73. LCC, Public Health and Housing Committee, presented papers, A12, 3 July 1890.
74. *RCAI*, q. 17,247.
75. *Ibid*, q. 2,122–3.
76. Booth Collection, B350, George Duckworth's police notes, p. 151.
77. Conway Hall, London History Workshop, Jerry White transcripts, 7.3, pp. 1, 3–4.
78. Booth Collection, B351, George Duckworth's police notes, p. 49.
79. *RCAI*, q. 4,117–463, 4,523–4.

in the East, owned by the Earl of Winterton and managed by Walter Belcher who was also a borough councillor. Winterton made it a rule that houses would only be let to natives or to Jews born on the estate, and Belcher tried to use the state or his own physical force to evict those immigrants he found living in overcrowded conditions. Since tenants sub-let their accommodation these rules could not be enforced thoroughly. At the same time, however, weekly tenants could be ejected at will. Immigrants were necessarily vulnerable to the prejudices and predilections of native landlords.

These boycotts, even if they were not successful, served to reinforce the nexus of profit and mutual assistance within the Jewish colony. They made it more difficult for immigrants to escape such relations and, by confirming an image of a hostile Gentile world surrounding the Jewish colony, they reinforced the importance of those relations. The housing market was one context in which the ties and divisions of nationality and religion inflected the experience of proletarianisation. Although immigration greatly accelerated the formation of a Jewish working class, the social relations of the Jewish East End did not resolve into a single opposition between capitalists and rentiers on one side, workers and tenants on the other.

Chapter 8

The Structure of Industry in the Jewish East End

Sweating and modernity

If we are to reach an historical understanding of the behaviour of Jewish immigrants – rather than one based on *a priori* assumptions about the propensities of Jews or proletarians – we have to reconstruct the structure and dynamic of the local economy. We need to understand the ways in which the industrial context produced not only goods but also a range of possibilities and constraints in which individuals acted, and a set of social relations in which they were placed. Once we have mapped these we shall be better placed to reach an historical understanding of the sorts of choices the immigrants made.

The consumer trades of the East End were the principal source of employment for Jews. A multitude of small workshops were the environment in which a class of Jewish wage earners was created. Through their work, moreover, Jewish immigrants impinged on the lives of the native-born: as producers of cheap goods, as competitors in the labour market and as trade unionists. But if the centrality of the workshop trades to the history of immigrant Jews is not in question, their significance for a wider economic and social history remains to be established. The trades have generally entered accounts as one facet of the problem of 'sweating'. 'Sweating', by the late nineteenth century, is generally seen to have constituted an anomalous form of small-scale production, engaged in a doomed struggle for survival as factory production advanced.[1] If this were so

---

1. J.H. Treble, *Urban Poverty in Britain, 1830–1914* (London, 1979), pp. 29–35; R. Davidson, *Whitehall and the Labour Problem in Late-Victorian and Edwardian Britain* (Beckenham, 1985), p. 50. Duncan Bythell has argued that 'the essential point is that within a given industry there was no necessary antithesis between outwork and factory systems'. But he also claims that by the end of the century outwork was in decline: D. Bythell, *The Sweated Trades: Outwork in Nineteenth Century Britain* (London, 1978), pp. 15, 199.

then the history of workers in these trades would be of little relevance to any broader consideration of working-class history. Indeed, it will be argued here that the characterisation of Jewish immigrants as restless individualists was closely connected to the view of late nineteenth-century observers that the East End workshop trades were remnants of a former system of manufacture struggling to survive in the face of factory production. The explanatory force this stereotype had for so many social investigators and commentators followed from their view that 'sweating' was an industrial anachronism.

In the mid-1880s the term 'sweating' customarily referred to the practice of sub-contracting. In this way, the evils of low wages and excessive hours could be blamed on a single figure – the middle man. John Burnett's report to the Board of Trade on the sweating system in the East End of London identified the sweater as a middle man who merely contracted for work supplying neither capital nor labour but extracting profits. The sweater took advantage of an overstocked labour market to which, Burnett argued, Jewish immigration greatly contributed.[2] Likewise George Keir, who represented the Amalgamated Society of Tailors, explained to the Royal Commission on Labour that 'the sub-contractor is a sweater'. By paying low wages he was able to make a profit as a middle man. 'The essence of the sweating system is merely one man living off another man's work to begin with.'[3] This critique of 'sweating' followed from an acceptance that capitalism was a system to which both capital and labour contributed and from which each deserved its fair reward.[4] What distinguished the middle man was that he contributed nothing. 'Sweating' was capitalism deformed by the presence of the middle man who was brought into existence by cost-cutting competition among producers and an abundance of cheap labour.[5] Some established employers who found their markets under attack by firms who drove down wages could, therefore, join with trade unionists in condemning the 'sweater'. This was particularly the case in the boot and shoe trade. One manufacturer told the House of Lords Select Committee on the Sweating System that he 'would define sweating as the distribution of work by a middle man at a reduction on the wages paid by the manufacturer'.[6]

2.   *Report to the Board of Trade on the Sweating System at the East End of London*, PP 1887, LXXXIX, p. 4.
3.   *Royal Commission on Labour*, PP 1892, XXXVI, qq. 14,617–18.
4.   E. Biagini, 'British Trade Unions and Popular Political Economy, 1860–80', *Historical Journal*, December 1987, pp. 811–40.
5.   *Hansard*, 3rd series, CXLV, cols. 291–4, 6 June 1890; *Report to the Board of Trade on the Sweating System*, pp. 5–6, 18.
6.   *Select Committee on the Sweating System*, PP 1888, XX, q. 10,048; see too q. 4,213.

This analysis of the problem was swiftly challenged. In response to Burnett's report, Beatrice Potter and David Schloss were quick to show that low wages, long hours and insanitary conditions could be found where work was not sub-contracted and, conversely, that not all sub-contracted work was carried out under such conditions. They pointed out, moreover, that 'sub-contracting' was the normal state of affairs in most industries and amounted simply to the separation of production from distribution. Not only did the middle man not play the economic role Burnett had claimed for him but, empirically, both writers debunked the notion of the bloated idle 'sweater': most masters worked hard and made do with small margins of profit.[7] This view was also accepted by the House of Lords Select Committee which, in 1890, concluded that the term 'sweating' could not be given a precise meaning but that it was characterised by three evils: long hours, low wages and insanitary conditions.[8]

The view that sweating was synonymous with sub-contracting and the middle man was replaced by an analysis of the problem as partly a reflection of the character of the men and women engaged in it, and partly a consequence of the failure to establish factory production. The reformers' attention passed to the capacity of trade unions or the state to regulate the conditions of labour and to the character of the labour itself. On the one hand, these emphases led Potter and Schloss to call for the extension of the Factory Acts to domestic workshops.[9] But, at the same time, Potter and Schloss considered 'the human material upon which the system or method [of sweating] works'.[10] Potter described 'the indefinitely low standard of life peculiar to Jews and to women. . . . In this readiness and freedom among a certain class of producers to do any work at any price, under any conditions we find the kernel of the sweating system.'[11] Sweating was, to this extent, the result of the pliability of Jews and women, and of the absence among them of the qualities which

7. D. Schloss, 'The Sweating System', *Fortnightly Review*, December 1887, pp. 835–56; B. Potter, 'The Sweating System', *The Charity Organisation Review*, January 1888, pp. 12–16; B. Potter, 'East London Labour', *Nineteenth Century*, August 1888, pp. 173–4.

8. *Select Committee on the Sweating System*, PP 1890, XVII, p. xlii.

9. Schloss, 'The Sweating System', pp. 835–56; *idem*, 'The Sweating System', *Charity Organisation Review*, January 1888, pp. 1–12; B. Webb, *My Apprenticeship* (Cambridge, 1979 edn), p. 335, in which Webb quotes from her article, 'The Lords and the Sweating System', *Nineteenth Century*, June 1890. (Beatrice Potter became Beatrice Webb on her marriage to Sidney Webb in 1892)

10. B. Potter, 'The Sweating System', p. 15; see too Schloss, 'The Sweating System', p. 853.

11. Potter, 'East London Labour', pp. 181–2.

distinguished English working men. 'The necessity of the widow or the greed of the Jew' left them vulnerable in the context of the small or domestic workshop.[12] Through this emphasis on the character of the workers, Potter's analysis of sweating and her portrait of the Jewish immigrant as *homo economicus* reinforced each other.

> Hence a Jew may begin in Backchurch Lane, but he may end in Bayswater. On the other hand, the prices at which work is taken are constantly reduced by a race of workers who have neither the desire nor the capacity for trade combination, and who are endowed with a standard of life that admits of an almost indefinite amount of work in the worst possible conditions. Long and irregular hours, periods of strain and periods of idleness, scanty nourishment, dirt and overcrowding, casual charity – all the conditions which ruin the Anglo-Saxon and Irish inhabitant of the East End seem to leave unhurt the moral and physical fibre of the Jew; and untroubled by conflicting ideals, the manifold desires, the complicated necessities of our social life, the children of Israel resist the temptations of the city and pursue with untiring zeal and undivided aim the reward granted by the Old Dispensation to those who are faithful to the law: 'Length of days and riches and honour'.[13]

The association of sweating with non-factory production and with women's work became more firm in the early twentieth century. The report of the 1908 Select Committee on the subject concluded that sweating was a problem affecting 'mainly women who worked in their homes'.[14] It found wages paid far below the minimum necessary for adequate clothing, food and accommodation. Moreover, this state of affairs was bound to continue for as long as there was competition between homeworkers and well-equipped factories making the same article.[15] In this phase of discussion, therefore, the phenomenon of sweating was feminised and the factory was seen to be not only the solution to the problem but also to offer a higher standard of industrial evolution. According to Sidney Webb, 'the state of London slop-clothing and low-grade furniture trades in 1902 is, in fact, closely parallel to that of the Lancashire cotton trade in 1802'.[16] He elaborated upon this theme in his paper on 'The Economics of the Minimum Wage', given at the Guildhall conference in 1906 organised by the National Anti-Sweating League. Home work

12. Potter, 'The Lords and the Sweating System', cited in Webb, *My Apprenticeship*, p. 337.
13. Potter, 'East London Labour', pp. 176–7.
14. *Select Committee on Home Work*, PP 1908, VIII, p. iii.
15. *Ibid*, pp. iii, vi.
16. S. Webb, 'Introduction', in B.L. Hutchins and A. Harrison, *A History of Factory Legislation* (London, 1903), pp. ix–x.

was a degenerate and parasitic type of production, Webb argued. It was degenerate because it allowed the 'old-fashioned or incompetent employer' to thrive by employing cheap labour. It was parasitic because the earnings of those receiving wages below subsistence were subsidised by poor relief paid out of the rates or by wage earners employed in other industries. A minimum wage, he argued, would remove the subsidy received by this lower industrial type.[17]

This analysis produced an anomaly, namely the Jewish sectors of the workshop trades, tailoring above all. For here one found a workforce composed largely of adult men in which, it was acknowledged, wages were not below subsistence and, in some cases, were relatively high. As R.H. Tawney admitted in 1915, the continued existence of workshops alongside the factory had 'puzzled inquirers for a generation'. His answer to this conundrum was both economic and what he termed 'racial'. The Jewish workshop held its own, he suggested, as a result of its concentration on one branch of the trade but also because of the 'extreme degree of application' on the part of workers within it.[18] Barbara Drake, whose research into the tailoring trade was carried out at the London School of Economics under Sidney Webb's supervision, placed still greater emphasis on the character of the Jew as the clue to the thriving state of workshop production.

> The patient endurance and nervous apprehension of the Jew are qualities weak to resist industrial pressure which his facile and indefatigable industry are quick to evade. The Jew is the despair of the trade union official. . . . But in the pliability of the Jew is strength as well as weakness, and the Jewish branch of the trade has shown a vigorous growth in recent years.[19]

For J.A. Hobson too the contribution made by Jewish immigrants to the problem of sweating was not only a matter of their effect on the labour market: there was also the Jews' lack of social morality, his flexible standard of life and his 'superior calculating intellect' which made him such a 'terrible competitor'.[20] It was these qualities, Hobson claimed, which allowed outwork to thrive: 'the foreign Jews are engaged in producing articles of commerce which but for their

17. National Anti-Sweating League, *Report of a Conference on a Minimum Wage* (London, 1907), pp. 20–30.
18. R.H. Tawney, *Minimum Wage Rates in the Tailoring Industry under the Trade Boards Act of 1909* (London, 1915), pp. 16–17.
19. B. Drake, 'The West End Tailoring Trade', in A. Freeman and S. Webb, eds., *The Seasonal Trades* (London, 1912), p. 77.
20. J.A. Hobson, *Problems of Poverty* (London, 1891), p. 61.

presence would be produced by native workers under better industrial conditions'.[21]

The explanatory force of the image of the Jewish worker as 'economic man' was derived in large measure from its apparent capacity to explain the anomaly of a thriving sector of workshop production employing adult *male* labour. Here I shall present a different view: one which suggests the workshop trades of the Jewish East End were an integral part of industrial expansion in the late nineteenth century.

*

In recent years, historians have come to appreciate the varied forms of capitalist development in Britain. Vast increases in production, organised by capitalist enterprises, and destined for both international and national markets, did not always coincide with the appearance of centralised and capital-intensive forms of production.[22] Such a model of economic modernity does indeed correspond to the development of the cotton industry, of engineering and of coal mining in this period. More widely, however, industrial concentration remained patchy, even at the turn of the century. In 1898–9 the average workshop employed just 29.26 male employees.[23] The industrial economy in Britain was typified by the small scale of its plant. Above all, this was the case in London, where in 1914, 97 per cent of firms employed fewer than 100 people.[24] Patterns of demand, labour markets and technologies which allowed and encouraged the development of sub-contracting and outwork, were recurrent features of nineteenth-century economic history and have been renewed to the present day.[25] The consumer trades of the Jewish East End present

21. *Ibid*, p. 63; see too B.L. Hutchins, 'Home Work and Sweating: The Causes and the Remedies', in S. Alexander, ed., *Women's Fabian Tracts* (London, 1988), p. 41.
22. R. Samuel, 'The Workshop of the World: Steam Power and Hand Technology in Mid-Victorian Britain', *History Workshop Journal*, Spring 1977, pp. 6–72; C. Sabel and J. Zeitlin, 'Historical Alternatives to Mass Production: Politics, Markets and Technology in Nineteenth Century Industrialization', *Past and Present*, August 1985, pp. 133–76.
23. Cited in R. McKibbin, 'Why was there no Marxism in Britain?', p. 6 in *idem, The Ideologies of Class* (Oxford, 1990), p. 6.
24. A.L. Bowley, 'The Survival of Small Firms', *Economica*, May 1921, 113–15.
25. Bythell, *The Sweated Trades, passim*; R. Price, *Masters, Unions and Men: Work Control in Building and the Rise of Labour* (Cambridge, 1980), pp. 173–8; H. Gospel, 'The Development of Management Organisation in Industrial Relations', in K. Thurley and S. Wood, eds., *Industrial Relations and Management Strategy* (Cambridge, 1981), pp. 94–7; A. Phizacklea, *Unpacking the Fashion Industry* (London, 1990), pp. 13, 16, 75–6.

one example of the fragmentation of production and contractual arrangements within the context of dramatically increased output. In this light, the responses of Jewish immigrants to industrial fragmentation assume a far greater relevance to any general view of the working class in the period than they have been allowed.

London and the 'home counties' were at the centre of Victorian economic growth. Second to the service sector, the consumer trades such as furniture and clothing contributed significantly to the region's progress.[26] This advance can be seen in the expanding markets at home and abroad. The value of exports in clothing and apparel rose from £3.7 million in 1881 to £5.1 million in 1901 and £8.6 million in 1914.[27] Demand for new clothing also rose steadily, fuelled by rising real wages between 1873–96, expanding white-collar employment and the great significance of apparel in the symbolic language of respectability. Asa Briggs has estimated that in 1845 a working man spent about 6 per cent of his income on clothing, and by the turn of the century this figure had doubled.[28] Multiple store retailers cultivated the mass market. In 1880 there were 21 multiple-shop firms with 500 branches selling footwear; by 1910 the numbers involved had risen to 70 firms with 3,544 branches. In men's clothing the period of expansion came after 1890. By 1900 there were 22 firms with 500 branches, and by 1910 this figure had almost doubled.[29] But demand for clothing was due not only to rising real incomes but to falling prices for garments as well. In 1911 one analyst compared the market for tailored garments then with its state in the 1870s and '80s.

> About 40 years ago the English working classes were not dressed as they are now. Especially is this the case with women's apparel. Thirty years ago, working women and even middle-class women were dressed quite differ-

26. C. Lee, 'Regional Growth and Structural Change in Victorian Britain', *Economic History Review*, August 1981, p. 449.
27. Tawney, *Minimum Wage Rates*, p. 2; *Report on the Volume and Effects of Recent Immigration from Eastern Europe*, PP 1894, LXVII, appendices XI, XVI, pp. 156–9, 208–11; *Royal Commission on Alien Immigration*, PP 1903, IX, appendices, XX, XXI, XXII, pp. 28–30. On the significance of boot and shoe exports from the East End see *ibid*, 19,300; on the tailoring trade to South Africa, known as the 'kaffir trade', see Tawney, *Minimum Wage Rates*, pp. 6, 18–19. On the exports from the East End furniture trade see for example London School of Economics, Booth Collection, A6, interviews with cabinet makers, p. 76.
28. A. Briggs, *Friends of the People* (London, 1956), p. 128, cited in W. Hamish Fraser, *The Coming of the Mass Market* (London, 1981), p. 58.
29. *Ibid*, pp. 58–65, 115–19; J.B. Jefferys, *Retail Trading in Britain, 1850–1950* (Cambridge, 1954), pp. 256, 356–8; B. Supple, 'Income and Demand, 1860–1914', in R. Floud and D. McCloskey eds., *The Economic History of Britain since 1700*, vol. ii (Cambridge, 1981), pp. 125, 137–8.

ently. The tailor-made costume and jacket, quite unknown to them. Only rich ladies, who could afford to pay 12 and 16 guineas for a costume, wore them. Forty years ago a working man did not go to work in a tweed or worsted suit; he did not wear the latest style of overcoat. Now he can get a nice suit *to order* for 30s. Thirty years ago, one could not get any suit to order for less than £2 10s or £3. A woman can now be dressed to look like a duchess for 30s.[30]

Historians have acknowledged that production in the Jewish East End was a response to the growth of new demand.[31] Nevertheless, the form of production in the East End workshop has generally been regarded as an archaic competitor with the more capital-intensive factory and bound to give way before its inexorable advance.[32] More recently, however, James Schmiechen has argued for the modernity of home work or workshop production and has emphasised the significance of technological innovation in these trades. The development of the sewing machine, its adaptation to the boot and shoe trade as well as tailoring, and other small-scale technological innovations such as those in boot finishing, he argues, represented the advent of economic modernity in the London clothing trades. Subdivision, he writes, was 'a natural outgrowth of machine production'.[33] To a degree, this can be borne out. The introduction of the spokeshave allowed boot finishing to be divided into two parts:

30. GLRO, JBD, B2/1/9, questions on aliens and labour placed before a labour specialist, February 1911.
31. P. Hall, *The Industries of London* (London, 1962), p. 64; C. Wilson, 'Economy and Society in Late Victorian Britain', *Economic History Review*, August 1965, pp. 189–92.
32. See for example Treble, *Urban Poverty*, pp. 29–35; Davidson, *Whitehall and the Labour Problem*, p. 50. A view which acknowledged the new markets supplied by the workshop trades is compatible with one which sees that form of production as 'parasitic' and backward. See the comments of Sidney Webb, 'Preface', Hutchins and Harrison, *A History of Factory Legislation*, pp. ix–xiii.
33. J. Schmiechen, *Sweated Industries and Sweated Labour; the London Clothing Trades 1860–1914* (Beckenham, 1984), p. 28. Another argument has concentrated on the conditions that were said to characterise 'sweating': low wages, above all. Jennifer Morris has pointed out that low wages for women's work in tailoring were a feature of factory production in Leeds as well as home work in London. This comparison between London and Leeds highlights the persistence of low pay for women even within large units of production, but since the focus is on conditions of work, the question of whether the decentralisation of production, in homes and workshops, was archaic is left unanswered: J. Morris, 'The Characteristics of Sweating: The Late Nineteenth Century London and Leeds Tailoring Trade', in A.W. John, ed., *Unequal Opportunities: Women's Employment in England, 1800–1918* (London, 1986), pp. 95–121. Also J. Morris, 'The Sweated Trades, Women Workers and the Trades Boards Act of 1909: An Exercise in Social Control' (London School of Economics PhD, 1982).

knifing and finishing.[34] In tailoring, the sewing machine led to the sub-division of tasks as machinists began to specialise in parts of the garment and as a hierarchy developed between more and less competent workers. But even here the extent of sub-division was also related to the quality of the garment being made and the level of wages, not to the development of technology alone. Thus in making bespoke coats, the calibration of tasks was inhibited by the quality of work required. In the case of the cheapest slop work it did not pay a master to employ the additional male workers. It was in the manufacture of medium-quality, ready-to-wear coats that it was possible to divide work among up to four grades of machinist who, in descending order of competence, specialised in cuffs and pockets, the body of the coat, the lining and the sleeve linings.[35]

However, among boot and shoe lasters, for example, sub-division bore a different relation to technological innovation: it was a substitute for it.[36] As one master tailor explained, the sub-division of pressing, by using less-skilled labour where possible, was a device to cut wage costs rather than the result of technological development.

> Good class coats require to go through the pressers' hands four times. In the first process the whole of the cloth is pressed in order to get a proper surface and take off the gloss; the second time the seams are pressed after being worked by the machine; the third process was when the lining has been put in; and there was the pressing off of the completed garment. The under-presser performed the first three operations, and the presser-off, the final process, the one being able to keep pace with the other three.[37]

Cabinet makers' workshops also adopted a team system of sorts, which was not related to technological change. Ernest Aves observed that here 'specialisation is almost uniformly found, not in the making of parts, but in the making and working on one or a very few, out of a large variety of articles'.[38]

Although it is likely that sub-divisional team systems were introduced in order to keep up with the faster production generated by machinery at other points in the production process, it is also true that the plentiful supply of labour could inhibit the introduction of power-driven machinery. In the boot trade the processes of lasting

34. *Select Committee on the Sweating System*, PP 1888, XX, qq. 808–27.
35. Potter, 'East London Labour', p. 172; S.P. Dobbs, *The Clothing Workers of Great Britain* (London, 1928), pp. 20–22.
36. C. Booth, *Life and Labour of the People of London* (London, 1902), 1st series, vol. iv, pp. 96–7; *RCAI*, q. 19,323.
37. London School of Economics, Booth Collection, A19, interviews with tailors, p. 56.
38. Booth, *Life and Labour*, 1st series, vol. iv, p. 216.

and finishing provide two such examples. The *Shoe and Leather Record* found that machinery had not been introduced even where work had been taken inside the factory. In 1901 it reported, 'human labour is forthcoming at a price which renders the most modern machinery too costly for employment'.[39]

An emphasis on technological innovation as a criterion of economic modernity is not conclusive in these trades. But the choice of the criterion itself adopts an excessively formal and undynamic view of the place of outwork in the late nineteenth-century economy. Ultimately, the case for regarding outwork as an integral part of development in these industries rests on the symbiotic development of factory and workshop production.[40] In cabinet making, workshops in Spitalfields and Bethnal Green depended on more highly capitalised units in the same neighbourhood. In saw mills the timber was cut to the necessary dimensions by piece masters operating a power-driven band saw; here too timber was brought by workshop masters to be turned or fretted. In tailoring there was a similar relationship, but in this case it was with the warehouses or merchant clothiers who cut the cloth before it was distributed.[41] In the boot and shoe trade, the boot passed in and out of the factory as it was being made: machining, lasting and finishing were sent outdoors while other tasks – clicking and rough stuff cutting – were performed in the factory. At the very lowest end of the market, uppers were imported from Germany ready-made or brought in from factories in the provinces.[42]

Even after processes were mechanised or taken within the factory, seasonal fluctuations meant that outwork did not disappear. 'Whatever the machinery cannot do, when they have more than the machinery can do, they have put up bills in the windows, "outdoor finishers" or "outdoor lasters wanted",' an immigrant boot finisher observed in 1903.[43] By 1911 the introduction of machinery had brought lasting indoors but upper machining and finishing continued to be given to outworkers.[44] In cabinet making large employers sub-contracted to lesser ones to the extent that this was recognised as

39. *Shoe and Leather Record*, 11 January 1901, p. 89.
40. On the inter-war period see J. Gillespie, 'Economic and Political Change in the East End of London in the 1920s' (University of Cambridge PhD thesis, 1985), Chapters 4, 5.
41. Booth, *Life and Labour*, 1st series, vol. iv. p. 165; Hall, *The Industries of London*, p. 54.
42. *Report on Recent Immigration*, pp. 74–6, 86–90; Booth, *Life and Labour*, 1st series, vol. iv, pp. 80–124.
43. *RCAI*, qq. 3,726.
44. JBD, B2/1/9, questions on aliens and labour placed before a labour specialist, February 1911.

one method through which workmen could become small masters.[45] In ready-made tailoring too it was commonplace for a firm to divide production between factories and sub-contracting workshops. In the busy season large and regular orders would be sent to provincial factories and the residue to sub-contracting workshops in the East End. Moreover, in boot and shoe making and some branches of tailoring, production was divided between factory and workshop according to the different qualities of goods that were produced in each location.[46]

Irregular demand, caused by seasonality and changes in fashion, was an obstacle to the development of factory production independent of an outwork sector, particularly since the technology used could be operated equally well in either location. In ladies' tailoring, where changes in fashion were more frequent than in the men's trade, short production runs were endemic. Outwork disposed of the burden of idle space and capital in the slack seasons, and it allowed for a flexible response to changes in taste. In view of the costs of rental and building in central London these were major considerations.[47] The existence of a pool of labour and the glut of potential suppliers, the workshop masters, were further incentives to reduce labour costs through outwork and left little incentive to invest in more advanced technology where this did exist. Insofar as the same work could be performed in both contexts, competition did exist between factory and workshop locations. But this competition was not absolute, and to conceive of it as a struggle between advanced and backward forms of production is an abstraction.[48] In practice, within the capital, workshop and factory production not

45. *JC*, 1 February 1901, p. 29.
46. In mantle making it was the domestic market which Jewish workshops supplied; cheaper export work was sent to non-Jewish women working in their homes or in factories. In the boot and shoe trade the cheapest orders were subcontracted: *JC*, 19 June 1895, p. 14; Booth Collection, B110, tailors and bootmakers, p. 79; *Report on Recent Immigration*, pp. 112–13, 127. In the boot and shoe trade, factories bought in the lowest-quality goods from sub-contractors: see *RCAI*, qq. 19,447–80.
47. GLRO, LCC, Special Committee on Contracts, presented papers, 12 December 1890, p. 41. The manager of a uniform clothing factory explained, 'we give a certain amount out because we have not sufficient space to do it all inside': *Report on Recent Immigration*, pp. 112–14; *RCAI*, q. 19,655; *Select Committee on the Sweating System*, PP 1888, XX, q. 3,288.
48. The only exception being the competition between London and provincial centres of production in the boot and shoe industry. But even in this case, in 1914 London remained the third-largest centre of production: Board of Trade, *Handbook on London Trades* (London, 1914). But provincial centres had their own ancillary outwork sections. On boot and shoe production in Leicestershire villages, see Bythell, *The Sweated Trades*, pp. 114–15.

only competed for some of the same work with similar technologies but also developed in symbiosis. Outwork was integrated within a larger system of modern capitalist production. The pattern in the East End was not unique. Small-scale production was typical of most sectors of the British economy at the turn of the century. The workshop trades were part of a dual industrial structure which, Piore has argued, has been reproduced in the advanced economies through the twentieth century.[49] The history of work and the behaviour and beliefs of workers in trades such as these must be taken into account alongside those in industries in which the tendency was to larger and more capital-intensive units.

A stereotype of Jewish immigrants was employed by early twentieth-century social scientists to paper over the cracks in a flawed theory of industrial development. In their view, 'sweated' workshops housed an archaic system of production that could survive only by paying wages below subsistence level. The vigorous Jewish sectors in many of these trades, employing male labour, created a problem for their analysis. This conundrum was resolved by recycling an image of the peculiar racial or cultural characteristics of the Jew. But there is no reason for late twentieth-century historians to reproduce this line of reasoning. We need to develop a different understanding of the economic and labour history of Jewish immigrants.

The consequences of competition and the sexual division of labour

Apart from the small scale of the workplace, the constraints and possibilities of economic life in the workshop trades were structured by two conditions: the competitive character of their markets at every level and the sexual division of labour at the workplace. I shall deal with competition first.

The East End trades were characterised by extreme competition and irregular demand. Even the wholesalers, retailers and factors who sub-contracted a portion of their orders to Jewish workshop masters were vulnerable both to their competitors and to the tyranny of the consumer. This was most evident in the market for cheap bespoke clothing. In 1912 *Men's Wear* described the effects on manufacturers of the policies of retailers and wholesale houses.

> They have encouraged the public to expect a measure suit to be ready in a few hours from the time of ordering; or, if a man is measured one evening, they inform him that the suit will be waiting for him in the morning. With so much cut-throat competition prevailing, especially

49. M. Piore, *Birds of Passage: Migrant Labour and Industrial Societies* (Cambridge, 1979), pp. 35–43.

among the multiple shop concerns, the individual retailer has to keep his end up as best he can. If he is not willing to accept an order for a suit at a few hours notice, the nearest branch of the multiple shop concern will willingly promise to perform the task, and the master tailor stands the risk of losing his trade if he fails to fulfill his part of the contract.[50]

Among retailers at home and abroad there was a growing tendency to 'buy small and buy often' as they sought to carry smaller, more manageable debts. One effect was that wholesalers and manufacturers found it more difficult to organise continuous production, to invest in capital and to offer continuity of employment.[51] The burdens of competition and uneven demand were passed from wholesalers to sub-contractors and from sub-contractors to their workforces. This dynamic was at the heart of social relations in the workshop trades.

Workshop production had its disadvantages. Contractors saved on rent, capital and supervision but they lost direct control over the quality of work and the promptness of delivery. In the boot and shoe trade, contractors were faced with the problem of coordinating production as work was returned and then sent out again for different processes. In tailoring, wholesalers had to supply both cloth and design, whereas if an order was sent to a provincial factory neither were required.[52] But the drawbacks to outwork were diminished by the numbers of sub-contractors prepared to undercut one another in the struggle for work. Manufacturers, wholesalers and retailers, who were pressed by competition at their own level of the industry and by the public's 'craze for cheapness', strove to pass these burdens on to the sub-contracting masters.

Small masters proliferated as the sub-division of labour and technological improvements reduced the threshold of skill needed to become an employer. Particularly was this so in boot finishing where the introduction of the spokeshave made 'knifing' an easier process and a speedier one: one knifer, the employer, was now able to prepare work for three or four finishers, while his wife 'socked' the work.[53] The trade became a refuge for unskilled immigrants. In tailoring there is some evidence to suggest that employers were capable workers, necessarily so in the bespoke branch of the trade. But in the slop trade, where soap and muscle replaced the needle, this was not the case; here 'green' masters crowded into the lowest

50. *Men's Wear*, 19 December 1912, p. 83; see too *Select Committee on the Sweating System*, PP 1888, XX, q. 9,396.
51. *Tailor and Cutter*, 31 May 1906, p. 431.
52. Potter, 'East London Labour', p. 163.
53. Booth, *Life and Labour*, 1st series, vol. iv, pp. 103–11.

branches of the trade. Throughout the industry the small amount of capital required to establish a small front-room or attic workshop (though not one in a purpose-built, sanitary and less overcrowded workshop) left the trade open to a constant infusion of new petty employers.[54]

The multitude of sub-contracting outdoor finishers and lasters in the boot and shoe trade meant that, in the words of one trade unionist, 'the manufacturers are rising from day to day'.[55] Factors took advantage of the situation and depressed prices.[56] They occupied warehouses, bought in samples from a manufacturer and then engaged smaller firms to imitate the shoes at lower prices. If they had spare capital they were able to buy stock cheaply in the slack season and gave 'any price for it that they can get'. These aggressive tactics pushed larger manufacturers into using 'sweated' labour.[57] Whereas manufacturers and factors had once had to maintain stocks and to some extent had distributed production throughout the year, by the mid-1880s seasonality was unchecked. Contractors could rely on their orders being speedily completed at any time of year.[58] Simultaneously, piece rates were falling, by up to 30–40 per cent between 1884 and 1888. This was due to the introduction of new, cheaper lines of boot as well as the growing number of outworking sub-contractors. The two developments were connected. Manufacturers found it unprofitable to produce the cheapest lines in factories but, since rates for outworkers were 1s per dozen lower, if they sub-contracted parts of the labour process even these lines could be made to pay.[59]

54. Potter, 'East London Labour', pp. 173, 176; Booth Collection, A19, interviews with tailors, pp. 58, 66, 75; *Report of the Chief Inspector of Factories and Workshops for the Year 1894*, PP 1895, XIX, pp. 56–7.
55. *Select Committee on the Sweating System*, PP 1888 XX, q. 916.
56. Factors employed travellers for the domestic trade and issued circulars to the colonies. They performed the same role as merchants in ladies' tailoring, making good the inability of small manufacturers to provide a wide range of shoes. But these middle men emerged also because small manufacturers could ill afford to extend credit to retailers, whereas factors were able to offer manufacturers immediate payment. The separation of production and distribution became more common in the ladies' tailoring as well. Here too the range of styles required by any retailer could not be satisfied by a single wholesale manufacturer. A tier of merchants emerged who bought in the goods of ten or twelve manufacturers and who sent out travellers: *Select Committee on the Sweating System*, PP 1888, XXI, qq. 12,203–4.
57. *Select Committee on the Sweating System*, PP 1888, XXI, q. 11,538–9; *Report on Recent Immigration*, p. 80; *RCAI*, qq. 11,353, 12,209.
58. *Ibid*, q. 781.
59. *Ibid*, qq. 756, 771, 3,811–20; *Report on Recent Immigration*, p. 83. Prices paid for outwork continued to decline: *RCAI*, 3,629, 3,782–4.

Not surprisingly the profits of sub-contracting finishers were low. It was customary here for the sub-contractor to take one half of the piece rate price and for the remainder to be divided among his employees.[60] During this period of declining piece rates masters stood to lose more than their workmen, just as they would gain more if prices rose. David Schloss gives two examples of masters who employed three journeymen and who took out relatively high-priced work: one made a net profit of £3 per week, the other £1 13s 5d. In both cases the profit included remuneration for the finisher's wife's labour in socking, packing and other tasks.[61]

In ready-made tailoring there were price reductions in the 1880s.[62] In 1888 Mark Moses, who ran one of the largest workshops in the stock trade – he employed 40 workers – and had regular work, claimed that prices had declined by between 15–20 per cent in recent years. Others claimed that there were still more drastic reduction.[63] In the bespoke trade the situation was less clear-cut. In 1888 one Jewish tailor claimed that although prices had undergone a long-term decline since 1870 they had risen in recent years. But a constant level of prices could be deceptive. In 1912 the secretary of the Jewish Master Tailor's Federation complained that 'if in the past an "Ulster" was paid for at a given rate, the next season it was called an "overcoat" and paid for at "overcoat" prices, meaning a reduction in the price for making of 10 per cent to 20 per cent'.[64] In 1906, in the face of a strike timed at the height of the summer season, merchant tailors and warehousemen, to enable masters to settle, increased the prices they paid by 12½ per cent. But rates quickly returned to their former level, forced down by contractors 'playing one master off against another, and beating them down'.[65]

Masters who undercut their competitors found themselves in a vicious circle of small profits, generating a desperate need for work which could be satisfied only by under-bidding. One sub-contractor

60. *Select Committee on the Sweating System*, PP 1888, XX, q. 769.
61. Booth, *Life and Labour*, 1st series, vol. iv, pp. 108–11.
62. In the early part of the decade the less fortunate masters working in the wholesale trade went to a middle man, who contracted for the work with a large clothier and then parcelled it out to the workshops. By the end of the decade, however, this system was virtually extinct. Its decline was a sign of the falling prices in the ready-to-wear trade which left no margin for the middle man: *Report of the Chief Inspector of Factories and Workshops for the year ending 31 October 1880*, PP 1881, XXIII, p. 19.
63. Booth Collection, A19, interviews with tailors, p. 89. See too *ibid*, pp. 73–4, 80, 92, 94.
64. *Men's Wear*, 19 October 1912, p. 80.
65. *Ibid*.

who had a reliable supply of orders compared his circumstances to those of a new workshop master: 'His [the newcomer's] only chance of getting into a shop was by taking the work cheaper than the master who had done it. This he did not mind so long as he got the introduction. He would be able to do it cheaper than the man who had a workshop's expenses to pay but the difference would usually go to the shopkeeper.'[66] Manufacturers incurred risks when contracting work to low-quality tailors or to others who gave themselves too little time to complete the order satisfactorily. They insured against shoddy work and late delivery by enforcing fines for bad workmanship and withholding payment for an order until the entire batch was returned to their satisfaction.[67]

Nevertheless, some sub-contractors in tailoring were able to make large profits relative to the trade as a whole, particularly if they were able to keep a sizeable workforce occupied with regular orders. Although even the most advantaged employers could rely on no more than nine months' work in the year, when in work they could make roughly £5 per day.[68] The wealthier employers lived in prestigious streets such as Great Prescott Street, Albert Square and Arbour Square. One visitor to a tailor in Great Prescott Street noted that the occupier, Mr J. Smith, 'evidently makes something by his business for his parlour was over-loaded with expensive furniture and in the back-room I saw some carved oak dining room chairs much superior to the usual East End types'.[69] But most masters were not so well placed. In 1890 the factory inspectorate gave an impression of the gradations of income and status among employers in the Jewish East End.

66. Booth Collection, A19, interviews with tailors, p. 76. In the wholesale trade 'a sort of mock auction' took place at the clothiers' premises during which sub-contractors attempted to underbid one another: *Select Committee on the Sweating System*, PP 1888, XX, q. 198.
67. *Ibid*, qq. 8,664, 8,679, 8,680. On fines in the boot and shoe trade see *ibid*, qq. 1,271–3; A. Sherwell, *Life in West London* (London, 1892), p. 98; *JC*, 21 April, p. 27. Contractors might also demand security against the disruption of a strike or theft by the workshop master: *Report of the Chief Inspector of Factories and Workshops for the year ending 31 October 1885*, PP 1886, XIV, p. 16. On the same practice in the boot and shoe trade see the *Select Committee on the Sweating System*, PP 1888, XX, q. 704. Thus, when strikes were called without notice the complaints from masters were bitter. See for example *JC*, 10 August 1906, p. 36.
68. Booth Collection, A19, interviews with tailors, pp. 54–5, 76, 129; *Report of the Chief Inspector of Factories and Workshops for the year ending 31 October 1887*, PP 1888, XXVI, p. 95. *Report on Recent Immigration*, pp. 142–3. This figure took account of wages and 'general expenses' but not of rent.
69. Booth Collection, A19, interviews with tailors, p. 72.

In two streets the largest employers dwell, having capacious workshops built in rear of dwelling house, rent £80, taxes £25. In the next two best streets in order of position, the rent is £50 and £18 taxes. Here the workshops are in the dwelling houses; then we come to the numerous small masters who for a six-roomed house pay weekly 21s inclusive with workshops in the house. These men let off a portion to lodgers, and when trade is brisk they overcrowd the little workshops to any extent, and lastly we come to the employers in filthy places, very old houses, filled with foreigners, stairs narrow and dark, and workshops on the top floor, it is in such places that we find causes for all the evils of insanitation.[70]

The variations of income and skill among masters and, above all, the fierce competition between them, bred conflict and division. There were attempts among the Jewish master tailors to combine and protect their interests collectively against contractors and trade unions.[71] The most stable of these organisations – the Jewish Master Tailors Federation – was formed in 1906. Its longevity was due to the growth of government legislation – the introduction of workmens' compensation, trades boards and national insurance – which established issues on which master tailors needed to represent their views collectively and which did not divide their interests. There were also attempts to combine against the merchant tailors and warehousemen. Workshop masters complained they were given too little time to complete orders, and the threats of fines and non-payment meant that work was carried on late into the night. Pressure was most severe in those workshops in which sub-contractors took out 'specials' – rush orders given out on an evening to be returned complete the next morning. But these only made more irregular a working week in these trades in which Sunday and Monday were slow days and the hours increased to a crescendo of activity before the Sabbath.[72] In response, workshop masters adopted the rhetoric of anti-sweating. In 1896 the Temporary Committee of Jewish Master Tailors issued this plea.

> Brothers – How long shall we compete with each other and look with fierce eyes upon each other, think ill of each other, and accuse each other of

70. *Report of the Chief Inspector of Factories and Workshops for the year ending 31 October 1890*, PP 1890–1, XIX, p. 12.
71. See for example *JC*, 8 July 1895, p. 14.
72. In the boot and shoe trade, manufacturers and factors demanded the immediate return of the shoe even in slack periods. *Report of the Chief Inspector of Factories and Workshops for the year ending 31 October 1880*, PP 1881, XXIII, p. 18; *Report of the Chief Inspector of Factories and Workshops for the year 1905*, PP 1906, XV, pp. 50–1; *RCAI*, qq. 3,581, 3,446; *Life and Labour*, 1st series, vol. iv, p. 202; Booth Collection, A19, interviews with tailors, p. 58.

ruining the tailoring trade? How long shall we submit to the employers sucking our blood?

Consider what a bad position we are in today. Our trade gets worse every day. Brothers, how long shall we allow people to call us 'sweaters' and hate us?

Here in England, in this free country, when Sabbath comes, how dark are our homes. How unhappy are our wives and children, because we cannot enjoy ourselves with our Holy Sabbath!

Why is it? Because we are oppressed by the large clothing firms who send us work ('specials' they call them) when Sabbath approaches, and we are compelled to work on the Sabbath to finish the work or get discharged?[73]

But masters' organisations were generally short-lived, called together to face a strike or an ominous revival of trade unionism and dissolved soon after the immediate threat subsided.[74] Strikes, particularly those led by socialists or anarchists, could elicit a powerful collective response from the small employers but this was quickly diluted after any settlement. Employers who tried to uphold strike agreements were unable to do so as their competitors broke away to steal an advantage. Although historians have drawn attention to the disputes and divisions within immigrant trade unions, these were if anything even more marked among masters' organisations.[75] More generally, there was a conflict of interest between established subcontracting employers and the newcomers who undercut prices in the trades. In a dispute in the cap-making trade this led a number of larger employers to support a strike fund when the union was in conflict with the lowest paying workshop master.[76]

Nowhere was the competition between workshop masters more evident than in the flood of accusations sent to the factory inspectorate informing against neighbours and rivals who failed to obey factory and workshop legislation. In 1888 the inspectorate commented that 'there is no class of operatives to be found who so readily give information to the detriment of their neighbours (and, indeed, they admit this themselves) as the Jewish tailors'.[77] The complaints came

73. From *The Master Tailor and Cutters Gazette*, August 1896, p. 151. See too *Select Committee on the Sweating System*, PP 1888, XX, 8662–4; *JC*, 31 March 1911, p. 39; *Men's Wear*, 19 October 1912, p. 80.
74. On the organisational apathy among Jewish workshop masters execpt during strikes see *JC*, 23 October 1896, p. 18.
75. *AF*, 13 September 1889, p. 1; *ibid*, 4 April 1890, p. 2; see also *JC*, 22 June 1906, p. 47. For complaints by the secretary of the Master Tailors Improvement Organisation that some members had made arrangements to work during a strike, see *ibid*, 23 October 1896, p. 18.
76. *Ibid*, 9 August 1895, p. 10.
77. *Report of the Chief Inspector of Factories and Workshops for the year ending 31 October 1887*, PP 1888, XXVI, p. 47.

from the law-abiding and the law-breaking alike. One inspector observed that 'very frequently the man who commits the most offences under the Factory Acts is most willing to tell you about somebody else'.[78] Moreover, at all grades of work both in boot and shoe making and in tailoring there was widespread bribery and tipping of cutters and foremen in the struggle to attain orders.[79] Relations between masters were more often characterised by unbridled competition than by any group consciousness derived from their economic position.

So far I have analysed the conditions in these trades which followed from the nature of consumer demand and from competition at different levels. But there was another determining condition shaping the strategies of workshop masters, namely the sexual division of labour. As many commentators noted, in Jewish workshops adult men were employed on tasks that were performed elsewhere, in factories or in homes, by female workers who commanded lower rates of pay. Women were employed in Jewish tailoring workshops, and in a large workplace might have amounted to half the workforce, but with few exceptions they were confined to buttonhole sewing, felling and working as 'general hands'; machining, pressing and basting were tasks reserved for men.[80] In tailoring, wages accounted for between two-thirds and three-quarters of total costs.[81] Employers could endeavour to reduce their wage bill by dividing the labour process, employing cheaper hands where appropriate and, of course, by trying to keep individual wages as low as possible. But the wages of the men could never be reduced to the levels paid to female homeworkers and factory hands. Jewish workshops therefore survived or, in some cases, thrived on low profit margins on each order. The inevitable corollary was that a greater number of orders had to be completed for the workshop to survive profitably. The imperative of speed determined the demands sub-contractors made on their workforce. Speed was also crucial to the profitability of a Jewish workshop because orders were spread unevenly through the week

78. *Report of the Chief Inspector of Factories and Workshops for the Year 1902*, PP 1903, XII p. 1; *RCAI*, q. 1,756.
79. On this practice among tailors see Booth Collection, A19, p. 59; *Select Committee on the Sweating System*, PP 1888, XX, qq. 4,103–4, 4,139; *Report of the Chief Inspector of Factories and Workshop for the year 1894*, PP 1895, XIX, pp. 48–9. For the same in the boot and shoe trade see *Select Committee on the Sweating System*, PP 1888, XX, qq. 869–73, 3,435–6.
80. Booth Collection, A19, interviews with tailors.
81. R. Wechsler, 'The Jewish Garment Trade in East London, 1875–1914' (Columbia PhD dissertation, 1979), p. 138. The proportion was probably larger among outworkers in the boot trade. Booth, *Life and Labour*, 1st series, vol. iv, pp. 108–9.

and through the year. This generated great pressure to complete as many orders as possible whenever they were to be had.[82] Jewish workshops were notorious for the intensity and ceaselessness of work within them.

But the ability to turn a profit from a particular order did not depend on the pace of the individual worker only. The ability of the workshop owner to organise continuous production was crucial. In the tailoring trade the sub-contractor had to ensure that a garment passed from one part of the labour process to the next without interruption. A bottleneck at any point could convert profit into loss, an employer back to a mere hand. Sub-contractors manipulated different numbers and combinations of workers with the aim of securing continuous production: one overlooked and arranged the work himself, a second set the pace himself by working as a machinist, a third employed his daughter to prepare the work and write the accounts, a fourth employed a master tailor to work as a manager and a fifth dispensed with an under-presser and employed three competent pressers; the extra wages did not bother him since he believed he could turn out more coats: 'he preferred to have all good men, so the work could go straight on'.[83] Far from inhabiting an archaic sector, Jewish workshop entrepreneurs were innovators.

When historians observe that the Jewish sector of these trades were characterised by the division of labour this indicates only part of the reason for their success. The division of labour without its coordination was a recipe for disaster. This was particularly the case because so much of the labour being divided was male and had to be remunerated at a level of wages determined, in part, by gendered norms. Instead of analysing the real entrepreneurial skills required in the workshop trades historians have mystified those qualities. We have been left with the impression that the division of labour, when combined with a particular Jewish will to upward mobility and a bit of luck, was a prescription for success. But this does not help us to understand why some workshops survived or prospered and others failed. Failures can, of course, be ascribed to seasonal fluctuations, to the severity of competition and to individual misfortune. These were considerable hazards but at least it can now be seen that there was also a structural challenge which each sub-contractor faced. We should acknowledge the abilities of those who did succeed and what may have been the failings of many others who were unable to sustain their status as small employers.

82. Booth Collection, A19, interviews with tailors, pp. 60, 75–6.
83. *Ibid*, 58, 66, 73–4, 80. This is why, as Beatrice Potter commented, in the Jewish tailoring workshops of the East End there was no clear fit between the size of workshop and the quality of work undertaken.

Wages and conditions

Intense competition and the sexual division of labour also structured the labour market and determined conditions of work. For
most of this period there was a chronic over-supply of labour, except
among the most able machinists and pressers.[84] The sub-division of
labour in tailoring and the team systems in cabinet making, boot
lasting and finishing rendered most workers easily replaceable.
Seasonality made matters worse. These conditions were exacerbated
by unrestricted immigration before 1906. But the beneficial effect of
the Aliens Act on the labour market was offset by the exceptionally
large number of young adults in the Jewish East End, children of
earlier immigrants, entering the labour market. The unemployed
wandered in the street labour markets of the East End: one at the
end of Goulston Street, the other at the junction of Commercial
Road. One Jewish trade unionist observed, competition for work was
'comparable with the system that existed among the dockers at the
dock gates before their great strike'.[85]

John Burnett discovered an 'infinite variety of wage rates' in the
course of his investigation of the sweating system in 1886.[86] The
weakness of trade unions, the discontinuity of employment between
seasons, the varied divisions of labour and, in some branches of
tailoring, the shifts of fashion which led to the re-negotiation of
piece rates from order to order, account for this lack of unformity.
Not only were there considerable differences between the rates paid
to machinists, for example, within the same workshop and between
workshops, the rate for a task varied according to the branch of the
trade as well.[87] Despite this 'infinite variety' we can draw a rough and
ready picture of rates of pay in the trade. Indeed, it is notable that
the range of rates remained largely stable throughout our period.

In 1908 the President of the Master Tailor's Improvement Association, Abraham Levi, assured the House of Commons Select Committee on Home Work that a first machinist could earn between 7s 6d
and 8s per day, a first presser between 7s and 7s 6d and a first tailor
between 6s and 6s 6d. These rates were confirmed by a less partial
observer three years later.[88] Among the lower grades of male worker,

84. On the scarcity of skilled workers during the busy season see *Ibid*, p. 76; Potter,
    'East London Labour', p. 177; *RCAI*, q. 18,983.
85. *Select Committee on the Sweating System*, PP 1888, XX, q. 3,714; *RCAI*, q. 14,111.
86. *Report to the Board of Trade on the Sweating System*, p. 7.
87. Booth Collection, A19, interviews with tailors, gives several examples of varia-
    tions between workshops. On different rates between stock and order sections
    see *Report on Recent Immigration*, p. 109.
88. *Select Committee on Home Work*, qq. 1,179–1,181; JBD, B2/1/9, questions on
    aliens and labour placed before a labour specialist, February 1911.

Levi reported that a second machinist would earn between 4s 6d and 6s 6d, a second presser 5s and a second tailor between 4s and 4s 6d. This is a range of rates very similar to those reported by Clara Collett in 1892 and consistent with the findings of Burnett in 1886.[89]

The incidence of unemployment and under-employment mean that daily wage rates are a poor guide to earnings. Beatrice Potter estimated that 'it would be fair to state the average work per week throughout the year as four to four and half days in the shops of large contractors and for the most competent and skilled hands throughout the trade; three days for medium shops and average labour; and two and a half days and under for the great majority of permanently unskilled or imperfectly trained workers'.[90] As mantle making and bespoke work became more important, seasonality grew more severe. In 1911 one commentator wrote:

> The Jewish tailor works on an average no more than six or seven months out of the twelve months. Often he has to be in the workshop for three days to make one and a half days. . . . when he works at full steam, his average earnings for the year are from 25s to 30s per week, for best tailors, and from 18s to 20s for second class tailors.[91]

A guide to the significance of these figures is that Booth's poverty line lay at a weekly income of 18–21s per week.

But earnings varied widely within trades. A Board of Trade survey made in March 1887 reveals that 56.8 per cent of foreign tailors in St George's in the East usually earned less than 21s per week when they were in work; at the other end of the scale, however, 26 per cent received over 30s. These distinctions were enlarged by the incidence of unemployment: 56.7 per cent of these tailors, most likely the least able and lowest-paid, had been out of work for 12 or more weeks between the end of October 1886 and March 1887.[92] Immigrant occupations in the boot and shoe trade were poorly paid. The survey found foreign boot and shoe workers earned less than tailors – 61.3 per cent of them earned less than 21s per week – but they were more likely to be in work – 35.3 per cent had been out of work for 12 weeks or more. Of all the principal trades, there is least information on

---

89. *Select Committee on the Sweating System,* PP 1888, XXI, appendix H, pp. 584–9; *Report on Recent Immigration,* p. 108.
90. Potter, 'East London Labour', p. 172.
91. JBD, B2/1/9, questions on aliens and labour placed before a labour specialist, February 1911.
92. *Tabulation of the Statements Made by Men Living in Certain Selected Districts of London in March 1887,* PP 1887, LXXI, pp. 36–7.

wage rates and earnings in cabinet making and, indeed, the little
that there is, is contradictory. Estimates of the highest weekly wage
an immigrant cabinet maker might earn varied from £1 10s to £1 16s
to £2 5s, for a working week of up to 60 hours. The impression of
Booth's investigator Ernest Aves, nevertheless, was that cabinet making was one of the better-paid immigrant occupations.[93]

In general, work in the immigrant trades was remunerated both
poorly and variably. It is probable that earnings rose in the Jewish
East End in this period, in part because of changes in the balance of
the local trades: boot and shoe making and the least well-paid
branches of tailoring declined in importance and cabinet making
and bespoke tailoring grew.[94] It is probable too that there were gains
in the higher grades of tailoring, and these can be attributed to the
shift in the balance of work undertaken in Jewish workshops after
1900 and to the effect of the Aliens Act of 1905. The rise of bespoke
work in the Jewish East End placed a premium on skilled labour and
the Aliens Act, masters complained, had created a shortage of labour
during the season.[95] Nevertheless, a large portion of the Jewish
colony continued to live in poverty, and most within it inhabited an
economy of debt – accumulated in the slack time and paid off in the
season.[96] Above all, there was wide diversity of experience among
Jewish immigrants. Differences between them depended on the
amount of time they had been in the country, their strength, speed
and competence, the way they were affected by under-employment
and seasonality, their age and the number of their dependants.
Inevitably, these considerations militated against any spontaneous
unity among them.

Employers made great demands on the stamina of their workers.
A report to the Jewish Board of Deputies in 1911 observed that 'the
chief characteristic of the Jewish tailor as well as of every other Jewish
worker, is the "intensity" of his work'.[97] Observers who had witnessed
or experienced a range of industrial conditions also emphasised the
driving pace in the immigrant workshops. In 1881 the factory inspectorate reported that 'one is much struck with the never ceasing
industry of these men [in a Jewish tailors' workshop] they speak to us
while working; it is impossible to get an uninterrupted conversation
with them . . .'. Seven years later the inspectors reported that the

93. Booth, *Life and Labour*, 1st series, vol. iv, pp. 199–200.
94. See above, p. 163; see below, pp. 210–11.
95. *JC*, 31 March 1911, p. 39.
96. *JC*, 3 November 1905, p. 28; *ibid*, 26 November 1909, p. 28.
97. JBD B2/1/9, questions on aliens and labour placed before a labour specialist,
    February 1911.

intensity of the work in the workshops was unequalled among other classes of worker.[98] Labour was long as well as hard. The chronic violations of the Factory Acts testify to the many hours worked in Jewish workshops.[99]

As we have seen, the high proportion of male workers meant that there was pressure to complete an order speedily, to clear the way to undertake another. One employer explained, 'long hours were necessary as the men wanted such high wages'.[100] To maintain profits in the face of diminishing prices and relatively inflexible male wages, employers demanded harder work, longer hours and unpaid overtime. Many workers were paid by a task rate – a piece rate set by the day. In these circumstances, rather than reduce wages rates employers increased the amount of output demanded in a day.[101] In 1912 a letter from 'a Jewish worker' reflected on these conditions.

> The wages of the Jewish worker are, generally taken, not so terrible, and in comparison with many English workers the Jewish worker is well paid. The trouble is he pays for his wages with inhumanly long hours. And piece work makes for long hours. The abolition of piece work and the introduction of a fixed working-day is the first step to the creation of normal working conditions for Jewish workers.[102]

These conditions were not restricted to the tailoring trade. The organising secretary of the National Amalgamated Furnishing Trades Association reported that among alien workshops in his trade 'the general condition of the workmen with regard to chivvying the men and supervision, and policing the men, are very bad indeed'.[103] The hours worked in boot and shoe finishing were notoriously long: in the busy season a week comprising five days of 17 to 18 hours' work, and one day of 12 to 13 hours was quite usual. One finisher remembered his experiences in the 1880s and that 'when it came to the seventh day, instead of enjoying myself, I simply

98. *Report of the Chief Inspector of Factories and Workshops for the Year ending 31 October 1880*, PP 1881, XXIII, p. 19; *Report of the Chief Inspector of Factories and Workshops for the Year ending 31 October 1887*, PP 1888, XXVI, p. 94.
99. *Report of the Chief Inspector of Factories and Workshops for the Year 1894*, PP 1895, XIX, pp. 46–7; *Report of the Chief Inspector of Factories and Workshops for the Year 1900*, PP 1901, X, p. 191; *Report of the Chief Inspector of Factories and Workshops for the Year 1901*, PP 1902, XII, p. 34; *Report of the Chief Inspector of Factories and Workshops for the Year 1905*, PP 1906, XV, p. 50.
100. Booth Collection, A19, interviews with tailors, p. 128.
101. On unpaid overtime see *ibid*, p. 53. One machinist explained, 'the plan was to work the machinist on day work during the busy season, and on piece work in the slack time': *ibid*, p. 105.
102. *AF*, 6 September 1912, p. 9.
103. *RCAI*, q. 13,887.

had to lay and rest my bones'.[104] In a poorly-paid trade such as boot making intense effort was needed to earn a sufficient wage. An owner of a Jewish boot factory denied that piece rates were low; he argued that good earnings depended on concentration, speed and dexterity on the part of the operative: 'it all depends on the workman getting through his work quickly'.[105]

The iniquities and burdens of piece work should not be stressed indiscriminately, however, and for some workers piece work and the imperative of speed signalled an opportunity. Although middle-class observers and some trade unionists were concerned that piece workers who 'sweated themselves' would become prematurely exhausted, many immigrant workers preferred a system which rewarded speed and dexterity. When the Alliance Cabinet Makers declared its intention of abolishing piece rates from the cabinet-making trade, immigrant workers broke away from the union to form the Independent Cabinet Makers Association in defence of piece work. In tailoring, groups of privileged workers acquired a stake in piece rates while their under-workers remained on fixed day rates.[106] The effect of piece work was to create further divisions within the Jewish workforce.

One factory inspector claimed, 'whatever is taken from the tailor is restored to him by the system of fleecing the people who work for him . . .'.[107] This image may exaggerate the extent to which small employers were able to cast off their burdens but it does capture the central dynamic of the workshop trades. It was not a dynamic, however, that created a natural unity of interests among workers.

Jewish immigrants and English journeymen

Competition in the labour market and speed in the workshop also created the conditions in which Jewish immigrants and English artisans came into conflict. Historians have taken an optimistic view of the economic impact of Jewish immigration on English labour. They have discounted complaints made by English workmen that immigrants were reducing wage rates and taking their jobs. In this light, contemporary accusations have appeared merely to apportion

104. Booth, *Life and Labour*, 1st series, vol. iv, p. 104; *RCAI*, q. 3,616.
105. *Ibid*, q. 19,302. The same applied to outworkers in the trade: Booth, *Life and Labour*, 1st series, vol. iv, p. 105.
106. LCC, Special Committee on Contracts, presented papers, 12 December 1890, p. 36; *Select Committee on Home Work*, q. 1,179, p. 54.
107. *Report of the Chief Inspector of Factories and Workshops for the Year 1894*, PP 1895, XIX, p. 48.

blame to a conspicuous and vulnerable target.[108] In fact, conflicts were not imagin-ary, and proved an important element in the labour history of the immigrant quarter.

In the case of tailoring, it has been suggested that Jewish workers were confined to production for the ready-to-wear market.[109] If this was correct then they did not impinge to any great extent on the bespoke trade – the province of the English journeyman – in which coats were made right through by a single male craftsman with the help of one or more female assistants. In fact, as early as the 1880s Jewish workshops in the East End were receiving bespoke orders, as Beatrice Potter observed. Her remark that the native and immigrant sectors of the trade occupied 'separate compartments' was meant to refer to methods of production and labour markets only. The boundary between the markets supplied from each compartment was contested, she noted, and shifting to the advantage of the immigrant sector: 'The whole of the "bespoke" for retail shops might be executed by English journeymen tailors. As it is only a certain and, I fear, decreasing proportion of orders are made under the old system.'[110] Her prediction was accurate. The growing competence of immigrant workers attracted greater quantities of bespoke work to their workshops. Lower costs drove the process on. The incursions were widely noticed over the next two decades. Booth observed that 'some of the first class firms have a regular supply of garments made by the Jew sweaters, as in the busy time they cannot get West End tailors to work at the price they have reduced them to'.[111] In 1915 R.H. Tawney reported that the quality of the garments made in the workshops of some Jewish master tailors was hard to distinguish from the quality of those produced by English journeymen. As a result, the latter were restricted to the highest class of bespoke work.[112] The growing market for bespoke clothing may have meant there was no reduction in demand for the work of English skilled tailors but undoubtedly immigrants competed with them and allowed the merchant tailors to depress prices.[113]

---

108. L. Gartner, *The Jewish Immigrant in England, 1870–1914* (London, 1973 edn), p. 82; B. Gainer, *The Alien Invasion: The Origins of the Aliens Act of 1905* (London, 1972), pp. 23–6; J. Garrard, *The English and Immigration, 1880–1910* (London, 1971), pp. 50–1.
109. Gainer, *The Alien Invasion*, p. 24.
110. Potter, 'East London Labour', pp. 164–5.
111. Booth, *Life and Labour*, 1st series, vol. iv, p. 148.
112. Tawney, *Minimum Wage Rates*, pp. 5, 9.
113. Writing in 1894, Llewellyn Smith suggested there was a second type of competition, namely the substitution of immigrant-made ready to wear garments for bespoke. This may have been how the trade looked in the 1880s and 1890s but it is doubtful whether the ready-to-wear trade did expand at the

Competition between male labour in Jewish workshops and English and Irish female labour engaged in factory and home work contributed a second dimension to competition in the labour market. Jewish tailoring workers made coats. This was the best paid branch of the trade. In manufacturing the cheapest coats, destined for export, immigrant men came into competition with English and Irish women.[114] The threat from cheap female labour led Jewish workshops to concentrate on clothing for which particular skill was needed or which it was difficult to adapt to factory production.[115] Inevitably this pushed immigrant production towards the bespoke sector and thus to compete with English male artisans.

In the boot and shoe trade there was a measure of interdependence between immigrant and English workers, as the former were involved in lasting and finishing and the latter were employed in other departments such as clicking and rough-stuff cutting. But there was a transparent state of competition with some native workers in those tasks which immigrants did perform. This was seen by Llewellyn Smith, who made a special study of the effects of immigration on the trade.[116] In both lasting and finishing, tasks were subdivided so that the level of skill was reduced and this lower class of work was opened to cheap immigrant labour.[117]

The view held by English artisans of the work performed by immigrants was shaped not only by competition in the labour market but also by their conception of skill.[118] In the tailoring trade, as we have seen, labour competition was indirect insofar as it arose through competition between two systems of production. Journeymen disdained the sub-divisional system and tended not to work on it. They expressed contempt for the products which came out of Jewish workshops and the methods used in them. James Macdonald, secre-

expense of the bespoke in anything other than the short term. Indeed, the growth of bespoke production on the sub-divisional system suggests that there was some competition between ready-to-wear and bespoke branches within the Jewish East End. In 1911 the secretary of the Jewish Master Tailors Federation complained that the rise of the cheap made-to-measure suit had supplanted a great deal of the stock trade: *RCAI*, q. 22,663; *JC*, 31 March 1911, p. 39; see too *ibid*, 26 November 1909, p. 28.

114. *RCAI*, q. 20,271; JBD, B2/1/4, replies of Mr M. Moses to questions upon alien immigration.
115. Tawney, *Minimum Wage Rates*, p. 19.
116. *Report on Recent Immigration*, p. 71.
117. Booth, *Life and Labour*, 1st series, vol. iv, pp. 97–8, 102–4. But competition was not only a matter of price: as in tailoring, immigrants were more reliable and more willing to work on Mondays and Tuesdays than their British counterparts. *Select Committee on the Sweating System*, PP 1888, XXI, qq. 11,342, 12,220.
118. P. Joyce, 'The Historical Meanings of Work: An Introduction', in *idem*, ed., *The Historical Meanings of Work* (Cambridge, 1991), pp. 21–2.

tary of the West London branch of the AST, told a committee of the LCC, 'you would not employ them [Jewish immigrants]. You would not employ a bricklayer to lay down gas pipes, and why should you employ an unskilled worker to make a coat?'[119] Likewise, according to Edward Madden of the East End branch of the same trade union the foreigners were 'not really tailors.'[120] In the 1880s and 1890s a similar estimate of immigrant workmanship was common even among men and women who were more sympathetic to their impact upon tailoring.[121] But as Jewish workmen occupied ever higher branches of the trade, the complaint was heard less often.[122] Middle-class observers such as Clara Collett noted the extreme reluctance of English tailors to work with labour divided as it was in Jewish workshops. She regarded this as obstinacy in the face of industrial progress.[123] A partner in a factory which manufactured uniforms explained, 'we employ foreigners simply because they have no traditions and are willing to submit to organisation on the principle of sub-division'.[124]

Nevertheless, it was not mere obstinacy or a dogmatic belief in the superiority of the hand-made garment which inhibited AST members from embracing machine work. The extensive use of the sewing machine and an elaborate sub-division of labour not only evaded the particular skills of the English artisan; these techniques also led to a loss of control at the workplace. As Michael Daly – the organising secretary of the AST – pointed out, the introduction of machine work was 'accompanied by a considerable amount of rushing and hurry that does not characterise the higher section of our trade'.[125] The freedom to work at their own pace was important to the organised English tailors. In 1891 the AST had won an improved log which, though it determined wages by hourly piece rates, reckoned

---

119. LCC, Special Committee on Contracts, presented papers, 12 December 1890, p. 15.
120. *Select Committee on the Sweating System*, PP 1888, XX, q. 7,938.
121. 'There is no fit – there can be no fit – in a coat made by the machine and by sub-divided and unskilled labour.' Potter, 'East London Labour', p. 162.
122. Likewise, in finishing and lasting in the boot and shoe trade it was among the immigrants that team systems were introduced. Llewellyn Smith reported, 'the foreign Jew . . . is thought (not without some reason) to have no feeling for the dignity of his trade'. For cabinet making see *Royal Commission on Labour*, q. 19,951.
123. *Report on Recent Immigration*, pp. 132–3; see too *RCAI*, qq. 19,664, 19,772.
124. LCC, Special Committee on Contracts, presented papers, 12 December 1890, p. 32.
125. *Select Committee on Home Work*, PP 1907, VI, q. 3,508.

by the amount of work the slowest tailor would produce; a competent tailor would take thirty minutes to produce one hour's work.[126] Moreover, at the end of the nineteenth century, members of the AST still claimed the right 'to be off on the spree', to regulate their own hours – something they were able to do as very few worked on the clothiers' premises – and not to touch work below a certain quality. In contrast, Jewish tailors were found 'more obliging', prepared to work through the night on 'specials', and willing to take stock work to tide them over the slack time.[127] It was not cheapness and the immigrants' advancing abilities alone which account for their encroachments into the bespoke trade. In 1911 Barbara Drake commented:

> In the rush of the summer season it is the firm best able to cope with 'specials' which does the best trade. So long as the 'cut' is smart, rapid delivery counts for us much as, or more than, good workmanship, and an ever-ready alacrity to meet the most exacting demands of the most exacting customer is among the most valuable qualifications of the West End tailor.[128]

In the eyes of English journeymen the immigrants were unskilled. The Jewish tailor was not trained to perform the range of tasks his English counterpart believed a genuine craftsman should have been able to carry out. But this estimate was not reproduced among the immigrants themselves. Far from being an undifferentiated mass of unskilled labourers, perhaps 40 per cent had worked as tailors, boot and shoe makers or cabinet makers in Eastern Europe. But, above all, the nature of work in the immigrant workshops created a different measure of skill. The speed of work, which the English tailors feared and despised, was a crucial yardstick of competence in the Jewish workshops.[129] In East End tailoring workshops there was not the same value placed on control of the pace of work as among native artisans. Workers who refused to come in early were ragged as clerks – men who thought they were members of the 'leisure class'.[130]

It was women's work, performed in factories or the home, that was stigmatised as unskilled by Jewish workers and workshop masters alike. Both groups attempted to discredit women as economic com-

126. *The Times*, 6 May 1912, p. 6.
127. *Tailor and Cutter*, June 1906, p. 321.
128. Drake, 'The West End Tailoring Trade', p. 85.
129. J. Dyche, 'The Jewish Immigrant', *Contemporary Review*, March 1899, p. 386.
130. Booth Collection, A19, interviews with tailors, p. 141.

petitors in a similar fashion to the way in which English artisans disparaged immigrant labour.[131] But in addition they presented the work done in Jewish workshops as a legitimate sphere of masculine skill even though machine stitching was customarily regarded as women's work.[132]

The workshop trades were characterised by industrial fragmentation and extreme competition. This much was seen by some of the most eminent late nineteenth- and early twentieth-century social investigators. The account of the trades given here owes a great deal to their researches. But I have also argued that their accounts, which have influenced successive historians, combined a partial theory of industrial development with a racial characterisation of the Jew; indeed, the two elements were mutually reinforcing. Here I have dispensed with these tools of analysis, maintaining the emphasis on competition at every level of these trades but revising the way we understand the consequences of the sexual division of labour within them. The upshot is the revelation not of a Jewish type but of pandemic economic warfare. Retailers were in conflict with wholesalers, manufacturers with sub-contractors, sub-contractors with each other and with their workers, immigrants with English artisans on one side and with English and Irish women on the other, workers paid by time with workers paid by the piece. How, then, did immigrants respond in the face of these cross-cutting interests?

131. (J. Finn), *A Voice from the Aliens: About the Anti-Alien Resolution of the Cardiff Trade Union Congress* (London, 1895); JBD, B2/1/4, replies of Mr Moses to questions upon alien immigration.
132. Board of Trade, *Handbook on London Trades*, p. 12 assumes that the development of the sub-divisional system in Jewish workshops will lead to an increase in female employment; p. 6: upper machining in the boot and shoe trade was done by women and girls except in the Jewish East End.

Chapter 9

Organised Labour

Coalitions of workers

The emergence of the Jewish working class in the 1880s coincided with an expansion of the labour movement and with the appearance of socialism as a current within it. From the last quarter of the nineteenth century, trade unionism in Britain was extending to groups of hitherto unorganised workers, including Jewish immigrants. At the same time as trade unionists urged immigrants to organise in their interest as tailors, cabinet makers, boot finishers and so on within capitalism, socialist and anarchist revolutionaries called on them to act in the interests of the entire working class against their capitalist exploiters. These developments have attracted the interest of several historians. In this way the growth of labour history and of 'history from below' has been reflected in the historiography of Jewish immigration. Attention has shifted from the institutions and leaders of Anglo-Jewry to the organisations and activists who claimed to represent the interests of Jewish workers. This has also involved a reinterpretation of immigrant history. Some optimists now present the history of the immigrant labour movement as a story of hard-won success, and the immigrants themselves are no longer seen as economic individualists, striving for entry into the ranks of the middle classes, but as members of the working class and conscious of their interests as such.

But the immigrant labour movement is both more and less remarkable than the revisionists allow: less so because in this period its practical achievements, in combatting employers and building secure institutions, were negligible. But the development of the labour movement is more remarkable than has been acknowledged because of the complexity of economic and social relations in the workshop trades. As we have seen, these did not resolve into a single opposition between workers and employers. There was potential for conflict to develop around several axes. We should not assume that when trade unionists and socialists presented the interests of Jewish workers in direct and necessary opposition to the interests of their employers we find here a reflection of the state of social relations. The speeches and writings of labour activists must be seen as efforts to persuade and not, in a simple sense, as mirrors on society. When workers did ally against their employers, this was not an inevitable outcome but one that was crafted by careful planning or the motivating force of ideology.[1] We can illustrate this argument by examining three of the great strikes of Jewish workers in London: the tailors' strikes of 1889 and 1912 and the boot and shoe workers' strike of 1890.

*

In 1889–90 the growth of unionisation in Britain extended to the Jewish East End. On 26 August 1889 a meeting of Jewish tailoring workers issued a manifesto calling for a general strike in the trade. Their main demands were for a twelve-hour working day that would include breaks of an hour for lunch and a half hour for tea, and for overtime to be restricted and paid. This was the immediate origin of the first general strike of Jewish immigrants in London.[2] The number of strikers remains uncertain but it ran into thousands. According to the *Tailor and Cutter* there were two thousand tailors involved at the beginning of September and ten thousand just before the settlement at the end of the month.[3] The strike brought together trade unionists and revolutionaries, immigrants and English workers, strikers and shopkeepers.

Conventionally, these years are seen to mark a watershed in labour history: they are characterised by a surge of trade union membership and strike activity which mobilised workers previously outside the labour movement, even if, in most cases, the unskilled soon fell away.[4] But among Jewish immigrants in London the strikes of 1889–90 had a still greater significance, irrespective of their achievements.

1. A. Reid, 'Politics and Economics in the Formation of the British Working Class', *Social History*, October 1978, pp. 347–61.
2. There was a general strike among Jewish tailors in Leeds in 1888: J. Buckman, *Immigrants and the Class Struggle* (Manchester, 1983), pp. 72–80.
3. *Tailor and Cutter*, 26 September 1889, p. 352; *ibid*, 5 September 1889, p. 333. William Fishman suggests that by mid-September six thousand tailors had quit work: W. J. Fishman, *East End Jewish Radicals* (London, 1975), p. 171.
4. E. Hunt, *British Labour History, 1815–1914* (London, 1981), p. 301; E.J. Hobsbawm, 'The New Unionism Reconsidered', in W.J. Mommsen and H.-G. Husung eds., *The Development of Trade Unionism in Britain and Germany, 1880–1914* (London, 1985), p. 19.

They were among the first in any country in which large numbers of Jewish workers took part. They did not signify merely the broadening of a pre-existing trade union movement, they constituted its birth. They announced the emergence of a new force in modern Jewish history.[5]

A feature of the Jewish labour movement from Lithuania to London to New York was the encounter between Russian Jewish revolutionaries and the emergent Jewish working class. The growth of the Jewish working class offered the revolutionaries an opportunity to transfer the ideals of Russian populism – of a revolutionary intelligentsia 'going to the people' – to the Jewish context. In the 1880s and early 1890s London was the central location of this encounter.[6] In 1884 Jewish radicals established the International Workers Educational Club – it became known simply as the Berners Street Club – and the same year they issued *Der Poylishe Yidel* – the first Yiddish newspaper professing radical politics to appear anywhere in the world. The original alliance of Jewish radicals soon divided, and the more doctrinaire, socialist newspaper, *Der Arbayter Fraynd*, was published for the first time in July 1885.

Whereas in the Pale of Settlement in the 1880s, Jewish socialists strove to create a worker intelligentsia rather than a mass labour movement, in London they were forced to take a different path.[7] Speakers at the meeting which announced the general strike of Jewish tailoring workers included both William Wess, a stalwart of the Berners Street Club, and Konstantin Gallop, editor of *Der Arbayter Fraynd*.[8] In the beginning, however, the socialists were at best ambiguous in their attitudes towards trade unions; fortified by Lassalle's appropriation of Ricardo's 'iron law of wages' as well East European habits of organisation, they dismissed the efficacy of trade unionism.[9] Nevertheless, the density of the working class within

5. In the perspective of a Jewish past, new unionism resembled more its European than its British variant. By this it is meant that only in Britain did the upsurge of trade unionism in the late 1880s and early 1890s occur where there already existed a significant force of trade unionists: *ibid*, pp. 13–14.
6. J. Frankel, *Prophecy and Politics: Socialism, Nationalism and the Russian Jews, 1862–1917* (Cambridge, 1981), chapter 2; W.J. Fishman, *East End Jewish Radicals*, chapter 5.
7. E. Mendelsohn, *Class Struggle in the Pale: the Formative Years of the Jewish Workers Movement in Tsarist Russia* (Cambridge, 1970), chapter 2.
8. *AF*, 30 August 1889, p. 2. Indeed, the origins of the strike also owed something to the influence of English trade unionists and socialists such as Charles Mowbray and David Nicoll. Nicoll, editor of *Commonweal*, addressed the Jewish tailors on 26 August.
9. See the report of a discussion at the International Workingmen's Education Club on the proper attitude to strikes: *AF*, 1 June 1888, p. 4. Compare the editorial in *ibid*, 13 January 1888, p. 1, which is dismissive of workers striving for higher wages, with the editorial in *ibid*, 4 May 1888, p. 1.

the Jewish population in London, the legal freedoms which trade unions enjoyed and, crucially, the growth of the English labour movement forced Jewish revolutionaries into a closer involvement with trade unionism. By 1889 the revolutionaries had not entirely abandoned their sceptical assessment of strikes but they now regarded trade unions as institutions which could propel workers towards an understanding of the exploitative nature of capitalist society, and of the benefit for workers of unity and organisation.[10]

The *Jewish World* described the tailors' strike as 'a contagion spread from the docks'.[11] The excitement and example in the East End of the theatrical and successful dock strike that summer does help account for the way three discrete tailoring disputes were transformed into a general strike in the trade. Beyond its origins, the strike allowed socialists and trade unionists to build friendly connections between Jewish immigrants and English workers. Parades of Jewish workers met up with processions and rallies of English socialists and strikers from other trades.[12] The strike committee quickly received organisational and financial support from the AST in London. The West London branch gave £10 to the strike fund and sent two delegates to join the strike committee. The union's executive council in Manchester gave £25.[13] In view of the overlap, even in 1889, between the classes of garment made by journeymen in the West End of London and by immigrants working under the subdivisional system in the East End, the AST's assistance could be given from a position of enlightened self-interest. James Macdonald, one of the West End delegates, told a meeting in London that 'if the regular tailors could raise the condition of the sweated workers, they would be raising their own'.[14] From this connection with the English union, from the parades and rallies which publicly identified Jewish immigrants with the cause of 'labour', and from the new determination of Jewish workers to stand out against 'sweating', a fragile spirit of unity developed. It crossed, even if it did not erase, differences of nationality, religion and skill.[15] At a meeting held at the close of the dispute, Lewis Lyons, the most prominent trade union leader among the Jewish tailors, was proud to proclaim that 'the Jewish tailors had been used against the English mechanic to reduce the value of his labour, but they refused to be so used any longer'. Macdonald, a member of the SDF, responded enthusiastically in the terms of the

10.   *Ibid*, 6 September 1889, p. 1.
11.   *Ibid*, 30 August 1889, p. 2; *Jewish World*, 6 September 1889, p. 5.
12.   *AF*, 13 September 1889, p. 1; *ibid*, 4 October 1889, p. 3.
13.   *Ibid*, 6 September 1889, p. 3; *ibid*, 20 September 1889, p. 3.
14.   *Tailor and Cutter*, 12 September 1889, p. 337.
15.   *Ibid*, 3 October 1889, p. 363; *AF*, 4 October 1889, p. 3.

new unionism: 'He said that he was bound to admit that the trades unions of the country had not done their duty to those like the Jewish tailors, who were outside the influence of the unions. It was recognised now that Jewish tailors were striking a blow at a great grievance, and they would find that 'labour' would support them.'[16]

The prominence of atheists and socialists within the strike committee, preaching godlessness and class conflict, challenged the possibility of a Jewish community as well as slender margins of profit. The prominence on the masters' side of leading communal figures within the Jewish East End such as Mark Moses only intensified this aspect of the conflict. The tailors' strike brought into question the authority of masters in the locality as well as in the workplace. The conflict was not restricted to picket lines and closed meetings. The tailors took their fight to the streets of the East End and beyond. Parades and open-air rallies were held almost daily. At first their function was to move from workshop to workshop, exhorting tailors still at work to leave their places. The parades were also used successfully to mobilise public support and to collect money; the strikers' position was fortified by a credit arrangement with some local shopkeepers.[17] Beyond this, however, the parades may have had a symbolic meaning, as the tailoring workers announced their arrival as a collective presence in the Jewish East End.

In an attempt to reassert the masters' authority, the Master Tailors Improvement Association refused to recognise the strike committee or to sign an agreement with it. Instead, the MTIA invited workers to return to work and to accept its word that the strikers' demands would be upheld. The strike comittee would thus have been marginalised. At the same time, the MTIA proposed that when the workers returned they should be employed by the hour. The strikers hoped that a shorter working day would reduce the irregularity of the working week. The employers' proposal, by contrast, threatened to introduce terms of employment still more precarious by turning sections of the workforce into casual workers. As William Wess, the secretary of the strike committee, explained, hourly work would counteract any attempt to enforce a regular working day.[18] It was the political conflict between the MTIA and the anarchists and socialists on the strike committee, and the question of work by the hour, not the original list of strike demands, that was at issue after the first two weeks of the strike.[19]

16. *JC*, 4 October 1889, p. 8.
17. *AF*, 13 September 1889, p. 1; *ibid*, 27 September 1889, p. 2.
18. *East London Observer*, 21 September 1889, p. 5.
19. *AF*, 20 September 1889, p. 3; *Tailor and Cutter*, 19 September 1889, p. 348.

By mid-September the conflict had reached an impasse. Increasing numbers of tailors were on strike and refused to return to work under a new system of payment, and relations between the strike committee and the masters' association had broken down. It was at this point that both Lord Rothschild and Samuel Montagu, independently and competitively, offered themselves as mediators. There is no clearer indication of the danger perceived by the Anglo-Jewish notability at the emergence of the Jewish labour movement than the concerned and amenable messages written and telegraphed to Wess by Montagu, Rothschild, their secretaries and agents.[20]

Montagu's mediation was successful in two senses: he brought the strike to an end, and he did so on his own, having ensnared Rothschild in a cumbersome arbitration process from which he quickly withdrew, thus enabling himself to act independently.[21] Montagu had a record of support for trade unionism among unorganised workers and for a shorter working day. As the Liberal MP for Whitechapel and as the patron of East End Jewish institutions, he was uniquely well-placed to bring pressure on the masters to give way. The *Jewish World* reported, 'the interposition of Mr Montagu was largely directed to persuading the masters to accept the socialists as the legitimate representatives of the men'.[22] On 6 October the tailors returned to work: their demands had been acceded to, their committee had been recognised and hourly payment was not introduced. In return, the strike committee undertook not to raise the question of wages for a year.[23]

Victory was illusory. Wholesalers and merchant clothiers refused to raise their prices following the 1889 settlement and as a result workshop masters were compelled to depress wages to accommodate fewer hours or to ignore the limit on the working day.[24] Accordingly, the agreement was never brought into force on a wide scale. From the outset there were complaints that it was being broken.[25] In the following two summers there were unsuccessful, demoralising campaigns to enforce the terms won in 1889. In 1890 a strike was declared against workshop masters by one of the two Jewish tailoring

20.   Warwick University, Modern Records Centre, A.R. Rollin Collection, MSS 240, Samuel Montagu to William Wess, 28 September 1889; *ibid*, Samuel Garcia Asher to William Wess, 30 September 1889.
21.   *AF*, 4 October 1889, p. 3.
22.   *Jewish World*, 11 October 1889, p. 3. On Montagu's wider role in the Jewish East End see below, Part 3.
23.   *AF*, 4 October 1889, p. 3; *ibid*, 11 October 1889, p. 6.
24.   *People's Press*, 10 May 1890, p. 12; *ibid*, 17 May 1890, p. 8.
25.   *JC*, 25 October 1889, p. 16; *ibid*, 8 November 1889, p. 12.

unions then in the East End. It was rapidly transformed into a short-lived alliance with the masters which aimed to force higher prices from the wholesale warehouses and retail clothiers. But, on both sides, the individuals promoting this tactic were defeated.[26] The following year a strike was called, inspired by the opposite strategy: its aim was to abolish the middle men and secure direct employment. After three weeks it was over. Its impact on the trade had been negligible. The *Tailor and Cutter* reported, 'in spite of picketing and similar actions by strikers there was not at any time a serious interruption of business, the principal employers finding no difficulty in getting work done'. Its impact on the union was more substantial: it was left with a debt of £800.[27]

The tailors' strike of 1889 was notable for the degree of unity established between immigrants and English workers, trade unionists and revolutionaries, the strikers and the shopkeepers of the East End. In the face of the failures which followed, the coalition which came together in August and September 1889 fragmented. The editor of *Der Arbayter Fraynd*, Saul Yanofsky, and the leading Jewish trade unionist, Lewis Lyons, became locked in a bitter feud.[28] The question of whether to ally with or to abolish the sub-contractor created divisions. The complexity of social relations could not be evaded. Some workers did not see their interests as opposed to those of the sub-contractors, or did so only in a qualified way. There was also growing antagonism between anarchists and social democrats. Their war spilled out of their clubs and newspapers to disrupt trade unions.[29] Above all, relations deteriorated between the Jewish and English tailoring unions to the extent that the latter abandoned the immigrants in their strike in 1891.[30]

The history of unionisation among immigrants in the boot and shoe trade in these years, as in the tailoring trade, was characterised by a precarious unity and formal success which dissolved into failure and fragmentation. In this case, because of the direct competition

26. The Tailors and Pressers Union called the strike, the Machinists Union opposed it: *People's Press*, 10 May 1890, p. 12; *ibid*, 17 May 1890, pp. 8–9; *ibid*, 24 May 1890, p. 8; *ibid*, 14 June 1890, p. 5; *ibid*, 25 June 1890, pp. 13–14; *The Times*, 6 May 1890, p. 11; *ibid*, 8 May 1890, p. 12.

27. *Tailor and Cutter*, 4 June 1891, p. 218; *ibid*, 11 June 1891, p. 222; *ibid*, 25 June 1891, p. 242; *The Times*, 1 June 1891, p. 6; *ibid*, 30 June 1891, p. 11.

28. S. Yanofsky, *Ershte Yorn fun Yidishen Frayhaytlekhn Sotzializm* (New York, NY, 1948), pp. 151–5.

29. B. Ruderman related these clashes in a series of articles in the New York newspaper *Di Fraye Arbayter Shtime*, September 1924–September 1925; see also Fishman, *East End Jewish Radicals*, pp. 191–201.

30. J. Schmiechen, *Sweated Industries and Sweated Labour: the London Clothing Trades, 1860–1914* (London, 1984), p. 110.

posed by Jewish immigrants, the coalition of immigrant and native workers was consciously manufactured by the English union. At the beginning of April 1890, the Jewish finishers and lasters, along with 10,000 English workers, went on strike. They demanded indoor work – an end to sub-contracting.[31] The strike ended quickly. On 16 April the employers' association agreed to provide workshops, and the union accepted arbitration in all disputes which did not involve wage reductions. The two parties agreed also to draw up a statement of prices for all work outside the first- and of second-class sectors of the trade.[32]

English workers hoped that indoor work and a third-class statement would bring the immigrants under trade union control and prevent them from undercutting native labour. Accordingly, planning for the strike took close account of the immigrants' interests. To enable Jewish immigrants to adapt to the conditions of indoor work, the London metropolitan branch of the National Union of Boot and Shoe Operatives proposed that manufacturers should allow their Jewish employees to work on Sunday (assuming that Jews would not work on their own sabbath) and also that, to take account of immigrant work practices, where necessary finishing should be divided into two processes – knifing and finishing.[33] In early April *Der Arbayter Fraynd* claimed that the strike was removing barriers between Jews and Christians, foreigners and Englishmen.[34] The sentiment was matched by leaders of the English union. At its general conference one of them enthused that 'now Jew and Gentile are working together, before they were working in enmity'. The *People's Press* emphasised that without the help of the Jewish workers the strike could not have succeeded.[35] In both the strike of tailors in 1889 and that of boot and shoe workers in 1890, English trade unions provided allies without whom immigrant workers would not have won their victories.

Even in victory, however, there was disunity. Throughout the boot

31. They refused to concede the introduction of a system of arbitration: A. Fox, *A History of the National Union of Boot and Shoe Operatives, 1874–1957* (Oxford, 1958), pp. 110–15.
32. Sectors for which statements already existed: see *ibid*, pp. 115–16; For a further interpretation of these events in the context of the London trade as a whole and on tensions within the English union see G. Thorn, 'The Politics of Trade Unionism in a Sweated Industry; Boot and Shoe Makers in Late Nineteenth Century London' (Warwick University PhD, 1983), chapter 6.
33. National Union of Boot and Shoe Operatives, *Monthly Report*, January 1890, p. 6.
34. *AF*, 2 May 1890, p. 2.
35. National Union of Boot and Shoe Operatives, *Monthly Report*, p. 9; *People's Press*, 26 April 1890, p. 10.

and shoe workers' strike the union had directed that those out-workers employed by manufacturers who had undertaken to provide direct employment should return to work under old conditions until new workshops were ready. The final settlement maintained this arrangement. But these concessions were opposed by a section of Jewish strikers. For them the strike had been undertaken to destroy outwork: 'No more double sweating,' was one of the slogans of the strike.[36] The dramatic hopes invested in it were expressed at its end by the public *hesped* (funeral oration) for the sweating system delivered by the socialist and atheist Benjamin Feigenbaum. Indoor work would bring more regular employment and also higher wages as the profits of the middle man were removed. These expectations were joined to a belief that manufacturers would never build work-shops unless they were forced to do so by the complete cessation of outwork.[37] The strike ended in confusion as a number of workers did not accept it was over.[38]

Very quickly, the Jewish boot and shoe unions, which had been incorporated within the National Union of Boot and Shoe Opera-tives in the course of strike, were reporting difficulties and failures in their attempts to enforce the settlement. Outwork had not ceased. Manufacturers outside the employers' trade association continued to sub-contract work, and some knifers and finishers remained will-ing to deal with them.[39] In August 1890 a mass meeting of the Inter-national Boot and Shoe Finishers Union was invited to condemn manufacturers who gave outdoor work and, above all, the workers and sweaters who accepted it. The resolution was passed but not before some of the men protested that they were forced to under-take outwork because it was impossible to find places indoors.[40] In the slack time of summer 1891, when unemployment in the trade was severe, manufacturers took advantage of the glutted labour market to cut costs and to reintroduce sub-contracting more extensively.[41]

The lock-out of November 1891 was the climax to the continued confusion and conflict which surrounded the 1890 agreement in

36. *AF*, 4 April, p. 2; *ibid*, 25 April 1890, p. 2; *ibid*, 2 May 1890, p. 2.
37. *Ibid*, 18 April 1890, p. 6.
38. *Ibid*, 25 April 1890, p. 2; *ibid*, 2 May 1890, p. 6; Jewish malcontents joined with a militant section of English workers, who also challenged the authority of the union leadership. On the wider ramifications of this revolt see Fox, *A History of the National Union of Boot and Shoe Operatives*, pp. 116–17; Thorn, 'The Politics of Trade Unionism', pp. 214–16, 226–9.
39. National Union of Boot and Shoe Operatives, *Monthly Report*, July 1890, p. 9; *ibid*, October 1890, p. 5; *AF*, 29 August 1890, p. 3.
40. *Ibid*, 29 August, 1890, p. 3.
41. National Union of Boot and Shoe Operatives, *Monthly Report*, July 1891, pp. 8–9; *ibid*, August 1891, pp. 2, 9; *AF*, 21 August 1891, p. 3.

the English as well as the immigrant sections of the trade. The ineffectiveness of the 1890 agreement led disgruntled workers to challenge the arbitration process. The result was a series of unofficial strikes. Manufacturers had hoped that arbitration would reduce the number of strikes, not act as a spur to them. They responded with a counter-attack against the trade union radicals whom the union was unable to control. This policy culminated in the lock-out. It was speedily concluded with a victory for the manufacturers and a reassertion of control by the union leadership. The national union agreed to police the arbitration process and to expel members who struck against its judgements.[42] In the East End manufacturers followed their victory with a more widespread and concerted reintroduction of outdoor work. By the turn of the century, older boot and shoe workers regarded the period between 1890 and 1892 as a golden age of regular hours and higher wages.[43] East End manufacturers broke away from the employers' association and hence from the arbitration process, they increased the amount of work sub-contracted so as to produce cheap lines, paid below the agreed general statement, and demanded that workers leave the union.[44]

As it became clear that a section of the boot and shoe trade continued to thrive beyond the bounds of the 1890 settlement, strains grew within the coalition of immigrant and native workers built in spring 1890.[45] Even during the strike, relations had not been entirely harmonious. There was a report that English workers were refusing to work alongside Jews where 'indoor' work had been introduced. Subsequently, immigrant workers claimed that their willingness to take outwork was due to ill-treatment by English workers inside the factories.[46] In December 1890, resentment at the immigrants once again became evident when the London metropolitan branch of the National Union of Boot and Shoe Operatives blamed 'imported foreign paupers' for price reductions which the introduction of a uniform statement had been intended to prevent.[47] At this stage friction had not been translated into a demand for immigration restriction; more conventional trade union demands remained

42. Fox, *A History of the National Union of Boot and Shoe Operatives*, pp. 116–17; Thorn, 'The Politics of Trade Unionism', pp. 264–74.
43. *Royal Commission on Alien Immigration*, PP 1903, IX, q. 3,624.
44. *Ibid*, qq. 3,627, 3,776, 19,533.
45. For an estimate of the dimensions of this sector see *Report on the Volume and Effects of Recent Immigration from Eastern Europe*, PP 1894, LXVIII, p. 87.
46. *People's Press*, 19 April 1890, p. 8; *RCAI*, q. 20, 511.
47. National Union of Boot and Shoe Operatives, *Monthly Report*, December 1890, pp. 10–11.

the policy. In August 1891, however, after further months of frustration and disappointment, a deputation from the London metropolitan branch waited on East End MPs at the House of Commons to urge them to support the exclusion of pauper aliens.[48] The demand for immigration restriction did not contradict the fundamental goals of the 1890 strike. It was an attempt to gain a measure of control over the metropolitan labour market by other means: by excluding the immigrants instead of organising them.

Jewish trade union branches within the National Union of Boot and Shoe Operatives were reduced to uninfluential, small combinations of workers. But within them political divisions became increasingly pronounced. First, there was conflict over the influence of anarchists in the branches.[49] Second, although cooperation with the English union remained a shibboleth among the organised immigrants, the question of who represented the English workers – the union leadership or its socialist critics – was a matter for debate.[50] In the boot and shoe trade, as in tailoring, the alliance of immigrant and native workers, trade unionists and political radicals that marked the initial surge of organisation and success was unable to withstand the strains of failure.

Nationally, the organisation of less skilled workers between 1889 and 1891 produced little which was not won back by the employers' offensive which followed. Above all this was the case where unions did not receive recognition from employers.[51] In the highly competitive circumstances of the East End workshop trades this was never a likely outcome. Not only was labour too plentiful and the competition between employers too intense, but wages constituted too large a portion of costs and large workloads an integral part of profitability. There was no leeway in which a deal with organised labour might have seemed an attractive option to small masters. But even though the new unionism in the Jewish East End did not establish improved rates of pay or conditions, and failed to give rise to stable trade unions, it did establish precedents and memories, forms of organisation and resistance, among groups of workers which had previously existed beyond the ranks of organised labour. In the context of the Jewish East End it provided a new axis for politics and for associational life: one which, despite failures and defeats, was not

48. *Ibid*, August 1891, p. 10.
49. *AF*, 28 December 1891, p. 6.
50. But it is notable that both sides claimed their position was one of unity with the 'Christian' workers. For some these were represented by the union leadership, for others by the rebels: *Der Veker*, 13 January 1893, p. 4; *ibid*, 27 January 1893, P. 3; *AF*, 6 November 1891, p. 6.
51. Hobsbawm, 'The "New Unionism" Reconsidered', pp. 18–19.

eradicated and into which, from time to time, new life was forced so as to present a challenge to both local employers and communal leaders. In this way, industrial relations and politics in the Jewish East End would never be the same again: the trade and the class had been established as axes of organisation, association and agitation. But it is important for us to see that they did so on the basis of fragile coalitions of different material and ideological interests which cut across the solidarities of trade and class.

Dimensions of defeat

The defeats suffered in 1890–1 were never overcome before 1914. In 1910 one activist in the tailoring trade, Arthur Hillman, reflected on the state of the labour movement. He found

> On one side the comical pursuit of 'building' and 'creating' new organi-
> sations every Monday and Thursday always with fresh-baked programmes,
> always with heaven-praised and quickly buried 'leaders', with fresh in-
> spiration and rapid disappointments; and on the other side, the brutal
> sweating-system, the large number of bloody struggles almost without any
> success; the worst working conditions, the long hours, the terrible insani-
> tary conditions – and that's not to speak of unpaid work and the constant
> uncertainty of existence.[52]

In a more detached manner, in 1904 Isaac Hourwich observed that 'the Jewish worker can be brought together by a strike or a lock-out, but after the specific object of organising has been accomplished they lack the cohesive power needed to hold them permanently together'.[53]

Each trade union offensive was followed by a counter-attack by workshop masters in which agreements were questioned, gains challenged and the union dragged into a series of debilitating petty disputes during which membership fell away and, frequently, the leadership splintered acrimoniously. The dynamics of this process are well illustrated by the brief and meteor-like history of the International Boot and Shoe Workers Union. The union was formed in 1900 and was an initiative of immigrant workers independent of the English union. It grew rapidly and by the beginning of 1901 it had enrolled 1,200 members.[54] Intense competition in the workshop

52.   *Der Yidisher Trayd Yunionist*, 14 July 1910, p. 3.
53.   I. Hourwich, 'The Jewish Worker', *Journal of Political Economy*, December 1904, p. 94.
54.   *Shoe and Leather Record*, 11 January 1901, p. 89.

trades made employers unwilling to recognise trade unions, and seasonality allowed them to turn this into deed.[55]

The boot and shoe workers' strike of 1901 erupted when an employer dismissed two men. The union declared a strike against his factory, and the manufacturers in turn responded with a lock-out and presented a document for the men to sign and thereby dissociate themselves from the union.[56] It was only after the lock-out was under way that the union formulated demands for increased piece rates. The strike concluded with a victory for the union. The cases of the two dismissed men were sent to arbitration with the understanding that they would be reinstated if either was shown to have been punished for joining the union. The manufacturers withdrew their document and agreed to give preference to union men when hiring. Provisional increases in piece rates were agreed which, it was said, were worth between 3s and 4s per week.[57] But this outcome signalled another false dawn. In November 1902 the *Jewish Chronicle* reported that the union had collapsed.[58] Just four months after the strike the same newspaper printed a cogent analysis of the pressures pulling the union apart, which it rightly saw as typical of the immigrant labour movement as a whole.

> Almost all Jewish trade unions in the past have undergone similar crises brought about by similar causes. External aggression in the shape of petty lock-outs, and strikes fostered by some employers, in sheer alarm at the union's influence in the workshop; disputes that cannot always be ended favourably to the union men, entail a great deal of arduous toil on the responsible officials, and denude the funds. Thus the external aggression is the main cause of internal strife and disagreement, and of impatient individuals gradually leaving the fold. This disheartening feature is bound to react upon the rank and file, and also on the energy and hope of the officials who are compelled to remain as Gideon's faithful three hundred fighting the bitter struggle to the end.[59]

In fact, our period concludes, in 1912, with a lengthy and victorious strike by Jewish ladies' tailors in the East End of London. This has allowed some historians to present an optimistic view of Jewish trade unionism. The 1912 victory has been seen as the culmination of earlier struggles and as the foundation for future success.[60] But

55. *JC*, 20 December 1901, p. 30.
56. *Shoe and Leather Record*, 11 January 1901, p. 89.
57. *Ibid*, 18 January 1901, p. 132; *ibid*, 25 January 1901, p. 215; *ibid*, 15 February 1901, p. 385.
58. *JC*, 21 November 1902, p. 34.
59. *JC*, 10 May 1901, p. 20.
60. Fishman, *East End Jewish Radicals*, p. 299.

this perspective is misleading. As the comments of Hillman and Hourwich suggest, there was little continuity of labour organisation in the trades of the Jewish East End. On the eve of the 1912 strike, *Der Arbayter Fraynd* observed that there were 12 or 13 unions in the tailoring trade which accounted for only 1,000 workers; any strike, it concluded, would have to reach the unorganised majority.[61] The strike of 1912 was not the culmination of a continuous process of organisation but a response to a particular conjuncture: the strike called by workers in the West End trade, a broad advance of unionisation in this year, along with an extension and intensification of organised industrial conflict, and the rising prestige of anarchists in the Jewish East End. Indeed, to a large extent, 1912 reproduced conditions similar to those which had characterised the first burst of Jewish trade unionism in 1889–90.

The success of the 1912 strike was qualified in ways which have not been recognised by its historians. In the ladies' trade, after six weeks, workers returned to their places having secured trade union workshops, a working day limited from eight in the morning to eight at night, a 10 per cent increase in wages and the abolition of dual systems of payment (that is, piece rate and time rate) in the same branch of work.[62] As *Der Arbayter Fraynd* acknowledged, the question of whether the workers could maintain the agreement and regulate conditions by adhering to the union was more important than the formal victory.[63] But a glance ahead will show that the strike did not provide a foundation for strong trade unionism. Notwithstanding the highly favourable circumstances produced by the war, in 1918 only 3,000 workers were members of the London Ladies Tailors Union and the number of organised workers in the trade declined once again during the 1920s. Between the wars ten per cent was the largest portion of the workforce that the United Ladies Tailors and Tailoresses Union claimed to control.[64]

In the men's trade the strike of 1912 had little impact. It was concluded with improved terms for the workers after just three weeks but here, more than in the ladies' trade, victory was formal only.[65] Even *Der Arbayter Fraynd* conceded that support for the strike

---

61. *AF*, 10 May 1912, p. 1. *Men's Wear* reported that the strike had been called by 6 trade unions with a combined membership of 2,000–2,500 workers: 10 May 1912, p. 215.
62. *Ibid*, 21 June 1912, p. 1.
63. *Ibid.*
64. J. Bush, *Behind the Lines: East London Labour 1914–1919* (London, 1984), p. 135. On the 1920s see Gillespie, 'Economic and Political Change in the East End of London in the 1920s' (University of Cambridge PhD, 1984), pp. 307–10.
65. *Men's Wear*, 1 June 1912, p. 272.

was not strong in the men's trade and it attributed this to the effects on the work force of a severe slack period. But it may also have been because most of the West End strikers, whose action had precipitated conflict in the East End trade, were ladies' tailors.[66] Few workers were affected by the agreement between the East London Gentleman Tailors Trade Union and the Jewish Master Tailors Association.[67] The state of trade unionism was also left unchanged. In November of the same year just 2,000 of 10–12,000 workers in the trade were organised and the number of members in good standing was still fewer. That autumn a great deal of the energy of the two main unions, the AST and the Independent Tailors, Pressers, Machiners, Plain Machiners and Under Pressers, was taken up in feuding and mutual competition.[68]

The heroic narratives which have been written around the history of Jewish trade unionism in England are misleading. But these accounts form part of a wider trend in historical research, which has been to focus upon the history of the organised working class and, generally, upon its advance. There is a point to this. In the periods 1871–3, 1889–92 and 1911–13 there were three substantial surges of trade union membership; the latter two reached into the ranks of less skilled workers previously outside the labour movement.[69] From the mid-nineteenth century until the end of the First World War the trend in trade union membership was upward, and this period also witnessed the emergence of independent labour politics. But there are problems with looking at the history of labour in this perspective.[70] The long view is a partial one. As Eric Hobsbawm has pointed out, before trade unions were institutionalised their growth was necessarily discontinuous.[71] The years 1888–92 did mark a leap forward for trade unionism: the number of organised workers rose from 0.75 million to 1.6 million. But the following decade was one of slow advance. Between 1910–12, when union membership grew from 2.5 million to 3.4 million, the increase was as great as it had been between 1892–1909. Over the period as a whole, despite

66. *AF*, 31 May 1912, p. 1; see too *Men's Wear*, 25 May 1912, pp. 242–4.
67. For the terms see *ibid*, 1 June 1912, p. 272.
68. *AF*, 4 October 1912, p. 10; *ibid*, 11 October 1912, p. 10; *ibid*, 25 October 1912, p. 9; *ibid*, 22 November 1912, p. 9.
69. S. Pollard, 'The New Unionism in Britain: Its Economic Background', in W.J. Mommsen and H.G. Husung, eds., *The Development of Trade Unionism*, pp. 32–52.
70. See *ibid*, pp. 40–1 for a statement of the long view. For a more pessimistic view see J. Hinton, 'The Rise of a Mass Labour Movement; Growth and Limits', in C.J. Wrigley, ed., *A History of British Industrial Relations* (Brighton, 1982), pp. 20–46.
71. Hobsbawm, ' "New Unionism" Reconsidered', p. 15.

the upward trend, it is the discontinuities and absences of trade unionism which remain typical. In 1901 just 25 per cent of the male workforce were in trade unions.[72] Female workers, of course, were barely touched by trade unionism. The history of trade unionism in this period has to be seen in this two-sided way: it was a form of association that was making important advances but, at the same time, membership was restricted to a minority of workers. There is a great need, therefore, for historians to examine and take account of the behaviour and attitudes of the unorganised, as well as the erratic progress of the organised, workforce.[73] This is what I shall do in the next chapter.

72. B. Mitchell and P. Deane, *Abstract of British Historical Statistics* (Cambridge, 1971), p. 68; H. Clegg, A. Fox and A. Thompson, *A History of British Trade Unionism*, vol. i (Oxford, 1964), p. 467.
73. For a similar point see J. Benson, *The Working Class in Britain 1850–1939* (Harlow, 1989), p. 2.

Chapter 10

Unorganised Labour

Neither organisation nor apathy

The weakness of the labour movement was not only a negation of unity. When coalitions disintegrated they did not pull apart into a void but in specific directions. The ways workers strove to safeguard their standard of life and to improve their conditions of work, the collectivities they entered, the social identities they adopted were more than obstacles in the way of unity: they help reveal the pattern of social relations, identification and aspiration in the Jewish East End.

The weakness of trade unions did not mean there was a general absence of conflict in the trades of the Jewish East End. Without the force of effective trade unions to gather them, conflicts over wages and conditions were diffused through the workshops of the district in a multiplicity of fissiparous and informal disputes. To a degree, workers called on the state to mitigate their organisational weakness. First, they could apply to the magistrates' court to recover wages which had been promised but not paid.[1] Second, complaints to the factory inspectorate could help workers improve the conditions at the workplace or exact revenge on employers.[2] More significantly, workshop conflicts were chronic in trades such as mantle making, where payment was by the piece and in which the significance of fashion caused frequent changes in the specifications of work produced.[3] Informal bargaining over remuneration extended even into the factories. Hebbert and Co. was one factory firm which specialised

1. *Royal Commission on Alien Immigration*, PP 1903, IX, qq. 12,840, 12,883, 12,887.
2. *Report of the Chief Inspector of Factories and Workshops for the year ending 31 October 1890*, PP 1890–1, XIX, p. 10. Indeed, trade unions as well as individuals used this agency: *AF*, 11–18 January 1889, p. 2.
3. *JC*, 4 April 1902, p. 25.

in government contracts. In 1890 William King, a partner in the firm, explained its system of bargaining and tendering.

> Whenever it is possible . . . we select the best workers and put it before them in the different divisions. They are called together and invited to give their price for the separate divisions in the form of a combination. They will say, 'we will not do it for less than that price' and they will give that price to me, and the total price is used as a basis for tender.[4]

Workers attended mass meetings to announce their opposition to 'sweating'. Indeed, the mass meeting rather than the workshop remained the basis of recruitment to trade unions until the twentieth century.[5] Inevitably, these meetings were attended by many workers who were not union members. Their presence indicates a constituency of opinion and feeling which must be taken into account even though it lay beyond formal trade union membership. Some of the largest and most enthusiastic meetings took place in the midst of the winter slack period.[6] There may have been a pragmatic aspect to this since it was out of the busy season that workers had time enough to attend. But these were occasions when workers, whose bargaining position was severely constrained and who complied with the demands of the market to gain as much as possible in the busy seasons, nevertheless protested collectively against 'the sweating system'.

We can further highlight the complexity of the attitudes and behaviour of immigrant workers by looking at the place of trade union affiliation within the experience of individual members. Union membership was very unstable: not only did gross numbers fluctuate but there was also a high turnover among members. Between 1903–8 the total membership of the Independent Cabinet Makers Union varied by a factor of more than six.

Table 11   Total Membership of the Independent Cabinet Makers Union between 1903 and 1908[7]

Year	1903	1904	1905	1906	1907	1908
Members	334	120	186	760	680	270

4. GLRO, LCC, Special Committee on Contracts, presented papers, 12 December 1890; p. 37. This system could be manipulated by the firm to bring the cost-cutting competition between workshop masters to bear directly upon the workers. King explained that he 'sometimes put it before them that the competition will be excessively keen, and that they must think the matter out thoroughly': *ibid*, p. 43.
5. *JC*, 9 August 1901, p. 22.
6. *Ibid*, 18 January 1901, p. 22; *ibid*, 9 December 1904, p. 37.
7. *Der Yidisher Trayd Yunionist*, 1 June 1910, p. 6.

Der Yidisher Trayd Yunionist, which published the figures, added that they were typical of Jewish trade unions. Equally significant was that in 1904, 466 members were admitted to the union and 460 erased; the following year the respective figures were 123 and 337.[8] Similarly, between 1895 and 1896 over 3,000 East End Jewish tailors were members of a trade union but at any one time only 1,000 were enrolled.[9]

Trade unionism was just one strategy among many through which immigrants strove to improve their situation. It was not, moreover, markedly successful in this period. Failure and need turned even committed trade unionists and socialists towards other strategies. Joseph Finn, a former secretary of the Mantle Makers Union, observed that 'the masters of today have been workmen yesterday and even strong and devout members of the union'.[10] Samuel Osipov was a social democrat who led the upper machinists in a strike in 1905. After a period of three months, during which it became clear that the strike was heading for defeat, Osipov wrote to his brother in America asking him to send a ticket for a passage.[11] It was not only petty entrepreneurship and emigration which were attractions. Thomas Eyges, a boot finisher and a supporter of *Der Arbayter Fraynd,* found a position as a life insurance agent. He did so on account of failing health and also so that he would be able to devote more time to the anarchist newspaper.[12]

Individual examples such as these, in conjunction with the evidence of a large flow in and out of trade unions, indicate the plurality of positions, the differing degrees of antagonism and complicity, taken by workers at different moments. The historical choices which immigrant workers faced were not, apart from exceptional moments, between opposition to the sweating system and acceptance of it, or between organisation and apathy. The implications of this observation operate in two directions: just as it prompts a re-examination of any totalising ascription of class consciousness to even a minority of workers in the trades, it does so equally for other totalising descriptions, above all those concerning the immigrants' famed 'individualism'. Indeed, an historiographical emphasis on the origins of Jewish individualism has led historians to ignore other, equally pervasive, patterns that cut across identifications of class and trade. The processes of workshop bargaining, the use of the courts

8. *JC,* 12 May 1905, p. 37.
9. *Ibid.* The most dramatic turnover in membership came during and in the aftermath of strikes in these trades.
10. *RCAI,* q. 20,2271.
11. S. Osipov, *Mayn Lebn: Deringerungen un Iberlebungen fun a Yidishn Sotsialistn* (Boston, Mass., 1954), p. 144.
12. T. Eyges, *Beyond the Horizon* (Boston, Mass., 1944), pp. 97–8.

and the factory inspectorate, movement in and out of trade unions, as well as strategies of petty enterprise, indicate the complex character of the immigrant workers' responses to their situation. These forms of action indicate the need to explore strategies beyond trade unionism pursued by Jewish immigrant workers and to examine the social relations and attitudes they reveal.

'The antagonistic interests of the workers themselves'

One line of division was between new immigrants and others who had been in the country for a longer period. If Jewish immigrants were a threat to native workers, still more did they compete with each other. In part this was because of the effects of immigration on the labour market. As one trade unionist observed, 'the first effect of alien immigration upon wages is a reduction of the wages of the alien immigrants already here. As a new arrival he hardly ever competes with native labour direct.'[13] This was felt with particular force in boot finishing, the most common occupation for an unskilled immigrant. In 1888, Solomon Rosenberg, a trade unionist, complained of the effects of 'greeners' on the trade.

> There are a number of boot finishers in existence now, 5,000 or 6,000, and those are only greeners; they have been here only five or six months, they do not know whether work in London was better some years ago; they do not know whether work in London is worse now; as they come over from foreign parts they think that London was always in the same circumstances as it is at the present time. Therefore those greeners do not belong to the society; they say that they can do without the society. If they can earn 3s or 2s 6d a day they are satisfied.[14]

From this viewpoint the newcomers' vulnerability and ignorance was compounded by the fact that many of them were single men and consequently were in a position to save 1–2s from a wage of only 10–12s per week.[15]

The undercutting and unorganised greeners also presented a threat because they appeared to confirm the prevailing image of alien immigration in the eyes of English workers. This was felt particularly by immigrant trade unionists and socialists for whom the good opinion of their English counterparts was of great political importance.[16] Hostility to immigration among English workers could

13. *RCAI*, q. 12,209.
14. *Select Committee on the Sweating System*, PP 1888, XX, q. 933.
15. Eyges, *Beyond the Horizon*, p. 62.
16. *Der Veker*, 27 January 1893, p. 1.

be a stimulus to activity.[17] After the turn of the century, this became a matter of increasing urgency for Jewish trade unionists for whom unionisation and above all amalgamation with English unions seemed to be the answer to the anti-alien agitation.[18]

Trade unionism stimulated by this goal engendered an inclusive attitude towards organisation and membership. But just as the failures of organisation led many English trade unionists to adopt an anti-alien position so too it had the same effect on some immigrant trade unionists. The International Tailors, machinists and pressers Trade Union had a policy that 'no apprentices, greeners or others are allowed to be taken on to be taught either machining, pressing or basting, unless bound for a fixed term not less than four years, irrespective of age and sex'.[19] This was a hopelessly unrealistic attempt to regulate entry into the labour market and passage through it. More successful, for a period, was the agreement in 1890 to introduce indoor work and an agreed statement in the boot and shoe trade. Llewellyn Smith described its effect upon a new arrival.

> He is shut out by the barrier of the standard wage. The only capacity in which 'greeners' could enter the workshop would be as learners, like boys, and this door has now been closed by the action of the union soon after the new agreement. Since then its members declined to teach the trade to any immigrants who have not already practised one branch of it in their native country. The result is that 'greeners' can no longer learn the trade or find a place in workshops over which the union has any control.[20]

On occasion, meetings of immigrant workers passed resolutions which recommended measures of immigration restriction. In 1888 the Jewish Journeyman Bootfinishers Union resolved 'that the greeners should be kept away from London or from the trade entirely'. The secretary of the union reflected, 'I am very sorry (because I am a foreigner also) that I should speak out against my own brothers.'[21] A similar current of anti-immigration feeling can be found among Jewish workers at the turn of the century. Lewis Lyons informed the Royal Commission on Alien Immigration that 'those who have been here a number of years resent the growing influx'.[22]

---

17. London School of Economics, Booth Collection, B81, notes on furniture trades, p. 41.
18. *JC*, 18 April 1902, p. 28; *ibid*, 24 July 1903, p. 26.
19. LCC, Special Committee on Contracts, presented papers, International Tailors, Machinists and Pressers Union statement of prices for all workhands in the coat trade, 1891.
20. *Report on the Volume and Effects of Recent Immigration from Eastern Europe*, PP 1894, LXVIII, p. 78; *RCAI*, q. 3,795.
21. *Select Committee on the Sweating System*, q. 940.
22. *RCAI*, qq. 14,065–6.

The ambiguity of some immigrant trade union responses to the anti-immigration movement led by the British Brothers League is indicated by a banner which read 'British Brothers and Jewish Workers United.'[23] Writing in *Der Arbayter Fraynd*, I. Kaplan pointed out the type of foreign Jew who, 'when he sees new arrivals, points at them with his finger and mutters between his teeth, "why are they here? Why didn't they stay at home? How can we be rid of them?"'[24] Attempts to legislate against free immigration were largely opposed by East End Jews. But opposition to what was widely perceived to be anti-Semitic legislation should not be confused with an unequivocal response to immigration itself. On the contrary, the problem of continuing immigration reveals some of the contradictory currents within the alien workforce and further highlights the diverse axes of collective action which coexisted and competed among them.

The division of labour within workshops and the different systems of remuneration also generated conflicts. These were most fully elaborated in the tailoring trade. Joseph Finn, secretary of the Mantle Makers Union between 1893 and 1895, argued that some of the greatest obstacles in the way of successful trade unionism were 'the antagonistic interests of the workers themselves'. Finn described two sorts of relation: sectional antagonisms between different groups of workers, and hierarchical relations produced by internal sub-contracting. There was friction as workers engaged on different tasks, and dependent on each other in the labour process, were remunerated on different systems – time rate and piece rate. It was in the interests of machinists and pressers, who were paid by the piece, to work fast, whereas basters, who prepared the work and were generally paid on time rates, had no such incentive. Other divisions were created by the practice of senior machinists and pressers hiring their own assistants.[25] But at the same time as it hindered the formation and stability of unions which encompassed all branches of the tailoring trade, the divisions of labour stimulated the formation of unions which pursued the grievances and interests of particular groups of workers.

Sectional conflicts surfaced even at moments of apparent unity. One counterpart to the organisation of men's tailors as a body in the strike of 1889 was the emergence of separate unions of pressers and machinists.[26] These societies became a force during the conflict. They shared and disputed its leadership with the strike committee

---

23. *JC*, 17 October 1902, p. 26; see too *ibid*, 23 January 1903, p. 28.
24. *AF*, 3 April 1903, p. 1.
25. *RCAI*, q. 20,271.
26. *AF*, 6 September 1889, p. 3; *ibid*, 13 September 1889, p. 1.

and they became acknowledged forces to the extent that separate meetings of machinists on the one side and of pressers and tailors on the other were held to vote on the terms offered by the masters' association. Mark Moses, a leading master tailor, complained that workers were continually forming themselves into quasi-independent branches, 'each of which presumes to act on its own authority'.[27]

In the boot and shoe trade conflict between master finishers and their workmen was converted into a sectional conflict once work was taken indoors. The distinction between the two groups was based on a difference of competence: between those who could 'knife' and those who could not. One problem was created by the need to re-negotiate the division of payment between knifers and finishers, since the knifers – the former sub-contractors – no longer had to look for work and provide a workroom, gas and materials.[28] The knifers' and finishers' societies remained distinct branches within the National Union of Boot and Shoe Operatives and relations between them were poor.[29]

It was in tailoring that internal sub-contracting and the conflicts connected with it developed most clearly. It emerged from and supplemented distinctions of skill within the workshop and differences between established immigrants and 'greeners'.[30] A stratum of under-workers also existed in cabinet making. In furniture-making factories some workers took the position of 'piece masters': workers who were paid at piece rates and who themselves paid underworkers at time rates.[31] As these examples indicate, internal sub-contracting developed around piece rate systems. In tailoring it was most prevalent in mantle making and uniform tailoring. Even where less skilled workers were employed directly by the workshop master, different systems of payment and the hierarchy of workplace authority created conditions for conflict within the workforce: overworkers were responsible for quality and were paid by the piece, whereas underworkers were remunerated at time rates.[32]

As early as 1887 some men can be found employing their own

---

27. *Tailor and Cutter*, 5 September 1889, p. 337; *ibid*, 26 September 1889, p. 356; *AF*, 20 September 1889, p. 3.
28. In the workshops the knifer/master had taken half the price and the remainder had been divided between his finishers. Indoors, this 1 : 1 ratio between the two departments became 7 : 17 or $3^1/_2$d : $8^1/_2$d of each shilling: *Report on Recent Immigration*, p. 78.
29. *AF*, 21 November 1890, p. 6; *ibid*, 16 May 1890, p. 2; *ibid*, 13 February 1891, pp. 2–3; *ibid*, 17 April 1891, p. 6.
30. *JC*, 5 August 1904, p. 23. See too S. Solomon, *Deringerungen fun der Yidisher Arbayter Bavegung* (New York, NY, 1952), pp. 111–13.
31. Booth Collection, A6, p. 153; *RCAI*, q. 14,018.
32. *Select Committee on Home Work*, PP 1908, VIII, qq. 1,179–80.

assistants in first-class ladies' tailoring but the practice had not emerged in the men's trade at this date.[33] By 1893, however, writing in *Der Veker*, M. Shire claimed that many workers had acquired a stake in 'sweating'. He blamed the failure of the tailors' strike of 1891 on the refusal of the principal workers to stop work.[34] Finn, too, believed that the dual system of payment 'was responsible for all the jealousy and ill-feeling that prevented tailors from uniting in one large body'.[35] Nine years later Arthur Hillman made the point still more vehemently, arguing that it applied to the boot and shoe trade, cabinet making, baking and cap-making trades, as well as tailoring.

> There is no confidence between one worker and another, and the constant plague of sub-contracting brings out a perpetual opposition of under-worker to over-worker. It is no more the question of master and worker, but how to fight a general evil, the perpetual struggle among the workers themselves. It is no longer the master who mistreats a worker but another worker. It is no longer the foreman who is a force in the workshop but the largest bundle and the lowest price, the earliest and the latest workers. It is no longer the master who sacks his 'men' but the worker who provides him with 'new hands'. Now in some cases they even fix the price, the labour and the time. There is a constant struggle and competition between the workers themselves.[36]

At times these tensions took an institutional form. Between 1900–6 there were attempts by under-workers and their allies within the revolutionary groups to organise against this system. In January 1902 the International Mantle Makers Union was formed. Its emergence highlights the way some trade unions had become vehicles for maintaining their members' status and workplace privileges against recent immigrants and less skilled workers. The *Jewish Chronicle* pointed out that the new union did not comprise a splinter from the well-established Ladies' Tailors and Mantle Makers Union: 'The great majority [of its members] had never been organised before, and the old society had not employed any means to reach these people. Indeed its system of high entrance fees and sundry objections usually raised against newcomers repelled rather than attracted them.'[37] Entry to the new union was free and the subscription required was just 2d per week. By contrast, the established union

33. I draw this conclusion from the material in the Booth Collection, A19, interviews with tailors.
34. *Der Veker*, 24 February 1893, p. 3; *ibid*, 21 March 1893, p. 3.
35. *JC*, 12 April 1901, p. 27.
36. *Der Yidisher Trayd Yunionist*, 14 July 1910, p. 4.
37. *JC*, 31 January 1902, p. 27.

demanded a slightly higher subscription and an entrance fee of 5s. Indeed, the stability of the Mantle Makers Union over this period can be attributed to the extent to which it catered to the needs of a relatively privileged stratum of workers in the trade. Members of the International Union attempted to dislodge members of the rival organisation from their favoured position and undercut their wage rates within the workshop.[38]

Two other unions were established at this time, both of which had as their principal aim that 'no worker should be employed by a second': these were the Under Presser, Plain Machiner and Plain Hands Union and the International Anti-Sub-Contracting Union.[39] More significantly, in 1905 and 1906, after all the unions in men's tailoring had, briefly, become absorbed within the AST, the grievances of under-workers continued to come forward. In one dispute in January 1906 the strikers demanded that 'all work hands shall be equally treated in the matter of work to be done and shall be amenable to the masters' sole instructions'.[40] The under-workers were one important element in the movement of popular militancy which culminated in the strike of tailors in 1906. As well as a ten-and-a-half-hour day, the strike committee's initial demands were for wages to be fixed by the week and to be negotiated directly between worker and employer.[41]

Workers and masters

The workshop trades generated common as well as conflicting interests between masters and men. The prices given by wholesalers and retailers largely determined the hours and wages of the sub-contractor and his employees. One response to this situation among the organised workers was to demand indoor work. They hoped that after the abolition of the small master and, with him, the profits of the middle man, trade unions would be able to bargain more successfully for higher wages. But a second and recurrent response was to ally with employers against contractors. It was this which bound the alliances of workers and small masters that did arise.

Once sub-contracting was accepted as a given condition, the economics of the workshop trades produced common interests between

38. *Ibid*, 23 May 1902, p. 27.
39. YIVO, New York, English Territorial Collection, Zionist Materials, membership card of S. Kopelovitch; *JC*, 29 April 1904, p. 30.
40. *Ibid*, 26 January 1906, p. 29.
41. *Men's Wear*, 16 June 1906, p. 427.

workers and their employers. These were clearly recognised in the
report of the factory inspectorate for 1887. The remarks deal with
tailoring but apply equally to the other sub-contracted and seasonal
trades: 'The spasmodic nature of trade spurs each on to complete
the assigned task within the time assigned by the taker-in, so that the
chances of getting another batch of work may be improved. To a
small sweater this is very important as it equally affects his workers,
therefore a necessitous co-operation is forced on them all.'[42] Any
strike in the busy period, at moments of maximum leverage for the
workers, had to be weighed against the workers' dependence on
these months for earnings.[43] The cooperation this brought is
revealed in the constant and common battle of masters and workers
against the curtailment of female labour by force of law. The factory
inspectors reported: 'It is comparatively easy to distinguish between
the half-hearted support an overworked milliner girl will give her
employer when the latter orders her to 'tell the gentlemen what time
you leave' and the energetic manner in which the Jewish tailoress
urges her wish to work on a Saturday night.'[44] The ingenious devices
used by master and workers to evade detection operated through a
degree of complicity on the part of the male and female workers.
Inspectors were refused entry while female workers were hidden in
bedrooms, kitchens and water-closets.[45] The popular opposition to
the inspectors is indicated by an incident when, having left a workshop after a night visit, they 'were met by a crowd of about eighty
people laughing and making fun of them'.[46]

Relations between employers and workers could incorporate
friendship and sympathy as well as conflict and contempt. A.
Rosebury, a Jewish trade unionist in the tailoring trade, observed
that, 'owing to the small workshops and to the fact that the master
frequently took part in the actual work, employers and employed
were on intimate terms, very often on terms of equality, and were
very often warm friends'.[47] M. Shire described the predicament of

42.   *Report of the Chief Inspector of Factories and Workshops for the Year ending 31 October
      1887*, PP 1888, XXVI, p. 94.
43.   *Der Veker*, 17 February 1893, p. 3 claims that slipper makers did not demand
      higher wages in the busy season, in the hope of getting work during the slack.
44.   *Report of the Chief Inspector of Factories and Workshops for the Year ending 31 October
      1887*, PP 1888, XXVI, p. 94; see too *Report of the Chief Inspector of Factories and
      Workshops for the Year 1900*, PP 1901, X, p. 191.
45.   *Report of the Chief Inspector of Factories and Workshops for the Year 1894*, PP 1895,
      XIX, pp. 46–7.
46.   *Ibid*, p. 46. D.L. Thomas, the Medical Officer of Health for Stepney, reported
      that inspection was a hopeless affair on account of neighbourhood opposition.
      After one house had been visited by the inspector, 'everybody in the street
      knows what his object is and they answer accordingly': *RCAI*, q. 7,214.
47.   *JC*, 9 January 1903, p. 25; also see *RCAI*, q. 20,271.

the small master in pathetic terms and indicated what in his view were the social and political consequences of this.

> What is a sweating master? A poor soul who was earlier sweated and thought that he would better himself if he became a master. But he made a great miscalculation and he did not improve his situation. He is forced to compete with other sweaters and the price for a making a coat falls so far that he is forced to increase the workers' hours and reduce their wages. And still he is forced to work much longer and harder than his workers. (This is a fact which everbody knows! We will not speak about the exceptions now.) This manner of sweating others and himself makes it wholly impossible for the workers to organise and fight. Workers organise and fight out of hatred for their exploiter. But here there is no hatred, and if it is present it is mixed with feelings of pity.[48]

Accounts such as these must be treated carefully. Shire was making a controversial reformist argument in a debate among Jewish socialists in the East End, and his comments must be read in this light. He argued that it was impossible to pursue the class struggle under existing conditions, and advocated state regulation of the trade. The observations of Shire, Rosebury and others were designed to support the view that only in the factory could class-consciousness develop. Similarly, remarks by Beatrice Potter and Charles Booth and others on the amicability of social relations within the immigrant workshop must be read in the light of their intention to deflate the image of a bloated, idle sweater.[49] Complaints of bad language and ill-treatment at the hands of employers, theft by workers at the workplace and occasional violence between masters and workers suggest that close work relations exacerbated antagonism as much as they could diminish it.[50]

In the case of new arrivals, however, relations between master and worker had a particular quality: benevolence and the exploitation of 'greener' labour went hand in hand. We have seen how this sort of relationship proliferated in the housing market. Immigrants who arrived in London without any appropriate skill were particularly vulnerable. One furrier described how 'masters . . . go to the market . . . and pick out foreigners that have just come over, that have practically no knowledge of the trade, and they take them into

48. *Der Veker*, 24 February 1893, p. 3. For a similar attitude expressed towards masters in slipper making see *Der Veker*, 20 January 1893, p. 3.
49. C. Booth, *Life and Labour of the People of London*, 1st series, vol. iv (London, 1902), pp. 338–9; B. Potter, 'East London Labour', *Nineteenth Century*, August 1888, p. 173; H. Lewis and C. Russell, *The Jew in London* (London, 1900), pp. 192–3.
50. J. White, *Rothschild Buildings: Life in an East End Tenement Block 1887–1920* (London, 1980) p. 253.

their place and they promise to give them some work. Of course men as a rule are very glad to get some shelter, and they employ them all week.'[51] Such arrangements were not restricted to the fur trade. A man who had formerly been a landlord in Russia arrived in England penniless in 1879. He pawned his suit for 10s which he paid to 'a sweater' who undertook to teach him the work of a machinist. For the first four weeks the 'greener' was paid nothing and subsisted on a diet of bread and herring.[52] In general, entrants to the tailoring trade were likely to have arrived with some appropriate experience. It was the boot and shoe trade, and 'finishing' above all, that was the resort of the least skilled.[53] Here too newcomers had to pay a premium to work under a 'knifer'.[54] This was recognised as one of the costs integral to emigration; some arrivals fully expected to pay it and to live on charity or the generosity of friends for a time, in other cases it was deducted from wages.[55]

The new immigrants' need for work and shelter coincided with the use to which unskilled labour could be put in these trades. Employers were able to present their actions in terms which emphasised the practice of mutual aid between Jewish immigrants rather than the exploitation of cheap labour. In 1899, Mark Moses defended the East End sub-contractors' use of greener labour in terms of the obligations held by relatives and friends to poor and ignorant dependants.

> I believe there are a good many Jewish alien immigrants who arrive here without money and without the knowledge of a trade. But in those cases they are taken care of for a time by their relatives and friends and taught to work at some branch of a trade, so that, in the course of a few weeks they, with the perseverance which characterises them, learn sufficient to earn a little money, and as a rule become capable workmen.[56]

There was much in these formulations which stemmed from the need felt by the small employers of the East End to remove the opprobrium heaped on them as 'sweaters', particularly by those who sought public recognition and communal prestige.[57] Nevertheless,

51. *Select Committee on the Sweating System*, q. 5,280.
52. *Ibid*, q. 2,832.
53. *Ibid*, q. 3,291.
54. *Ibid*, qq. 668–71.
55. *Ibid*, qq. 3,575–9, 3,583, 19,783; *Report of the Chief Inspector of Factories and Workshops for the Year ending 31 October 1880*, PP 1881, XXIII, p. 17; *RCAI*, q. 3,416.
56. GLRO JBD, B2/1/4, replies of Mr M. Moses to questions upon alien immigration.
57. *JC*, 9 May 1884, p. 6.

the ties of religion and nationality, and the connections between kin and *landsmen,* may also have had a meaning for those who took the weaker part in these relations. One witness before the House of Lords Select Committee on Sweating mentioned that 'only this morning before I came out I had a poor Jew who kissed my hand when I promised him some work for next week'.[58] This gesture did not, of course, preclude the possibility of a more independent posture towards wealth and authority at other moments. But it does indicate at least a qualified understanding of economic relations in terms of mutuality or benevolence. These could be reinforced by ties of kinship. As some immigrants established themselves as employers they would send to Eastern Europe for relatives to come and work for them.[59] In one large workshop where between thirty-five and forty were employed, the majority were relations or *landsmen* of the employer. The consequence was that the workshop continued to operate during a dispute in the trade; only four workmen joined the strikers.[60]

To what extent did these currents, drawing masters and men together, take an institutional form? Attempts to form alliances between employers and workers occurred in two ways. In some cases the interests invoked were solely economic and the programme one of extracting better prices from contractors.[61] At times, however, sabbath observance or zionism added a religious or political imperative. Both issues proposed a vision of Jewish unity, one through religion, the other through nationhood, which might elide or contain the conflicting interests within an alliance of masters and men. In 1900–1901 the Jewish National Tailors, Machinists and Pressers Union sought to ally trade unionists, the orthodox Jewish clergy of the East End, the master tailors, Anglo-Jewish communal leaders and English socialists to secure sabbath observance and a ten-and-a-half-hour working day, as well as the elimination of piece work and street labour markets.[62] *Der Yidisher Ekspres,* a newspaper which represented orthodox, zionist, opinion supported the union: 'When all machinists, tailors and pressers become members of the union, when it grows large, it will be possible to keep the sabbath properly. Jews in

---

58. *Select Committee on the Sweating System,* q. 5,241.
59. *Ibid,* q. 3,504.
60. *Ibid,* qq. 3,477, 3,481, 3,541.
61. For example, the alliance between the Tailors Improvement Society and the International Tailors, Machinists and Pressers Union, reported in the *Jewish World,* 23 April 1897, pp. 10–11; also the joint action by employers and journeymen in the strike in the boot and shoe trade in April 1890.
62. *JC,* 5 January 1900, p. 22; *ibid,* 12 January 1900, p. 17; *ibid,* 18 January 1901, p. 22; *Reynolds News,* 20 January 1901, p. 1.

London should have a day of rest as God has commanded and as our people has always had.'[63] Presented in these terms, workers' demands did not offer a challenge to the possibility of Jewish communal life but were seen to be a condition of its realisation.

In the 1890s Anglo-Jewish communal leaders attempted to act as midwives to projects of cooperation between masters and workers. Following the defeat of new unionism there was a series of attempts to promote sabbath observance in the trades. These were sponsored by a group of pious Jews within the East End and by Anglo-Jewish notables such as the Chief Rabbi, Samuel Montagu, and F.D. Mocatta.[64] Sabbath observance provided an issue through which the clergy were able to address industrial questions and express concern for the welfare of workers. This sort of intervention was seen to be an urgent need following the influence of atheists and revolutionaries revealed during the 1889 tailors' strike.[65] These initiatives elicited a positive response from a minority of workers. They attended meetings of the Sabbath Observance League and took the opportunity to relate the difficulties they encountered in keeping the sabbath.[66] In 1897 the Chief Rabbi and Samuel Montagu issued a circular to contractors in the tailoring trade on the question of sabbath observance which, they claimed, was written in response to an approach by 'a large body of our Jewish working men'.[67]

But the perception of elite figures within Anglo-Jewry as potential allies in the struggle to improve industrial conditions was not restricted to the orthodox. In December 1891, following their defeat in a lock-out the previous month, the organised boot finishers revolted against anarchist influence in the union and turned towards the patronage of Anglo-Jewry and of Samuel Montagu in particular. At a meeting held at Toynbee Hall, the secretary accused the anarchists of breaking up unions. Another speaker unfavourably compared the financial support received from the anarchists with that given by the 'capitalists'.[68] The appeal to Montagu was expressed in language which expressed the imperatives of Jewish solidarity and obligation. When Saul Yanofsky, the editor of *Der Arbayter Fraynd*, spoke vehemently against the decision to invite Montagu he was told the aim of the meeting was to gather all 'Jewish patriots' in order to

63. *Der Yidisher Ekspres*, 13 July 1900, p. 6.
64. University College London, Gaster papers, *Shomre Shabat* to M. Gaster, 7 February 1891; *ibid*, *Shomre Shabat* to M. Gaster, 2 June 1891; *Jewish World*, 6 May 1892, p. 6; Booth Collection, B197, religious influences (Jews), p. 21.
65. *JC*, 1 November 1889, p. 15.
66. *Jewish World*, 6 May 1892, p. 6.
67. Booth Collection, B197, religious influences (Jews), p. 21.
68. *AF*, 25 December 1891, p. 6.

show 'their brothers' who was responsible for the sweating system.[69]

None of these alliances between masters and workers achieved even the passing success attained by trade unions. If tensions at the workplace undercut fellow-feeling between pressers and basters, machinists and under-machinists, still more was this the case between employers and workers. In 1890 an alliance between the Tailors Improvement Association and the Pressers Union fell apart within a week when the employers refused to introduce a shorter working day before receiving an increase in prices from the contractors.[70] Attempts to ally employers and workers consistently precipitated divisions in both parties and foundered upon them. Sabbatarianism and zionism inevitably divided workers and masters internally on ideological grounds, even as the issues were intended to overcome economic conflicts between workers and masters.

Independence and Individualism

Having examined conditions in the workshop trades and many of the workers' responses to them, we are now in a position to see petty enterprise in the context of the other choices Jewish immigrants were able to make in the local economy. In a modest way upward mobility was almost inevitable as immigrants acquired skills and found new positions. One employer described the situation in tailoring.

> A young fellow will serve nine months as an apprentice and then he will seek a situation, if a presser, as an under presser. He will stop a little while, until he thinks he can do the presser's work, possibly helping the presser when he is busy. He will then get a place as a first hand, if he cannot do the work he will be discharged, but he will be gaining experience. This would apply to pressers, machinists and basters.[71]

Similar mobility was achieved in other trades. The wages of one boot finisher after three months were 2s per week but rose to 35s; another who earned 8s after six months in the trade was eventually able to earn between 18s and 22s per week.[72] It is little wonder, then, that Beatrice Potter wrote of the Jewish immigrants: 'as a mass they shift upwards'.[73] The transition to becoming a small master followed

69. *Ibid*, 1 January 1892, pp. 2–3.
70. *People's Press*, 24 May 1890, p. 8; *ibid*, 14 June 1890, p. 5; *ibid*, 21 June 1890, p. 13.
71. Booth Collection, A19, interviews with tailors, pp. 68–9.
72. *RCAI*, q. 3,616; *Select Committee on the Sweating System*, q. 911.
73. In Booth, *Life and Labour*, 1st series, vol. iii, p. 186.

these other upwardly mobile steps a worker took earlier in his career. Moreover, many masters were forced to resume positions as
waged labourers.[74] Nevertheless, in some respects to work on one's
own account was an important departure: it meant providing at
least some of the means of production, it involved risk and
management in procuring and executing contracts, and it placed
the former 'hand' in a new position of authority within the
workshop.

In the workshop trades, the multiplication of small units, developing in symbiosis with factory production and an expanding market,
provided opportunities for workers to move into the ranks of the
petty employers. This process was propelled by the ease with which
the small amounts of necessary capital could be found. A factory
inspector noted that 'the facilities offered for the hire of sewing
machines and other necessary tools are so numerous that a workman
starting without any capital becomes a master in the space of a week
or two'.[75] One master tailor informed Booth's investigator that 'he
thought a man could start if he had £1 in his pocket. He could get
his table and machine on the "hire system" '. Another pointed to the
importance of loan offices as a reason for the continuing emergence
of small masters: in the boot and shoe trade Jewish manufacturers
were helped by the supply of leather on credit from merchants.[76]
There were also less formal methods of collecting funds. The House
of Lords Select Committee on Sweating was told that 'there are those
who get a start by going to friends, or by assistance of the Jews who
are very liberal in their assistance of these people'.[77] This function
was also undertaken by *landsmanshaftn*. Above all, there was a large
supply of small capital sums, in the form of loans, passed into the
East End of London by the JBG. Between 1880 and 1906, £183,013
were distributed in the form of 34,346 loans: an average of about
£5 7s.[78] The onset of mass Jewish immigration coincided with a
reorganisation and decisive expansion in the work of the loan committee. The committee enjoyed access to substantial trust funds
separate from the general income and disbursements of the Board.[79]
The entrepreneurial activities of Jewish immigrants were in many

74. *RCAI*, q. 20,271.
75. *Report of the Chief Inspector of Factories and Workshops for the Year 1894*, PP 1895,
    XIX, pp. 56–7.
76. Booth Collection, A19, interviews with tailors, pp. 62, 76; *RCAI*, qq. 1,862,
    1,985–90.
77. *Select Committee on the Sweating System*, q. 5,222.
78. Calculated from V.D. Lipman, *A Century of Social Service 1859–1959: The Jewish
    Board of Guardians* (London, 1959), table 1, pp. 278–83.
79. *Ibid*, pp. 60, 106.

respects an effect of their access to small capital and the use to which this could be put in the East End trades.

The most detailed studies of Jewish social mobility have dealt with Russian Jewish emigrants who settled in the United States. In these cases historians have been helped by detailed census data that is not available for Britain. Russian Jews in the United States showed very different occupational profiles in different urban and economic contexts. In New York in 1905, 54 per cent of Russian Jewish household heads were employed as manual workers.[80] By contrast, in 1915 in Providence, Rhode Island, the equivalent figure was just 23 per cent.[81] The key differences between Rhode Island and New York lay in the opportunities afforded by the industrial and commercial structures of the two cities. In New York the garment industry provided employment and, indeed, was dominated by Jewish employers and workers. In Providence a different set of opportunities were available to Jewish immigrants. Not only did the garment industry not provide many jobs: Joel Perlmann suggests that it may have been easier in the economy of a small town for Jewish immigrants to make a living as pedlars or to set up as retailers on a small scale.[82] The composition of Jewish immigration to the two cities did not differ in ways that can explain these differences, and the same applies to London where the working class comprised 71 per cent of the immigrant population – a considerably larger portion than was the case in New York. The evidence from the United States, then, supports an interpretation which places great weight on the occupational structure and opportunities in the local economy in determining the economic experience of Jewish immigrants.

It is possible to find impressive examples of upward mobility among the immigrants in London: the few who became large employers or who had profits substantial enough to invest in the inflated property market of the East End.[83] More rarely too we can find affirmations from within the immigrant colony that this was seen as a goal to be pursued consciously. Soon after Aaron Gorelik arrived in London his cousin, who had been settled for some time, told him, 'this is a land of work, and in England one works, you put a shilling with another shilling and with a few pounds in the bank

80. T. Kessner, *The Golden Door: Italian and Jewish Immigrant Mobility in New York City, 1880–1915* (New York, NY, 1977), p. 60.
81. J. Perlmann, *Ethnic Differences: Schooling and Social Structure among the Irish, Italians, Jews and Blacks in an American City, 1880–1935* (Cambridge, 1988), p. 133.
82. *Ibid*, pp. 138–9.
83. See above, pp. 174–7.

you are another person'.[84] He presented emigration as a process of individual transformation to be achieved through upward mobility. But an explanation which assumes that entrepreneurs were formed from a pursuit of upward mobility is liable to confuse motives and destinations. The evidence reveals more nuanced motives and more complex attitudes. In many cases the move to become an employer or small trader was a response to adversity. Llewellyn Smith reported that in some cases tailors turned to street trading in the face of unemployment.[85] Similarly, in 1902 a boot and shoe worker told the Royal Commission on Alien Immigration, 'during the slack time there is a lot of people go out hawking with barrows in the street; I have done it for a nice few slack times because I could not get money in another way'.[86] In the furniture trade, workers established themselves as masters and hawked goods around the Curtain Road dealers when they became unemployed.[87]

Of course, for whatever reasons Jewish immigrants entered petty enterprise, their behaviour towards their employees was greatly determined by their new position in the chain between contractor and sub-contractor, master and worker, worker and under-worker. But this is not the same as assuming that they entered that position with those intentions, as John Dyche, a Jewish immigrant trade unionist, observed.

> He does not intend to become a sweater. Oh no! He simply intends to work for himself, so that his head, his will, his self shall not belong to a master. But he soon becomes convinced that he cannot execute his orders in time by himself; that in order to keep out of the 'sweater's prison', or the pawn-shop, he must employ one or two hands. He gradually loses his trade union principles, his conscientious scruples against being a sweater, and lo! our irreconcileable enemy of the 'Jewish sweater' has loomed into a full fledged employer, often of a worse type than the one he has for years been engaged in denouncing.[88]

One of the main attractions of self-employment was that it presented an opportunity to minimise the effects of seasonality. David Schloss pointed out that some of the masters in the 'sew-round' branch of the shoe trade earned less than their employees but they gained 'an increased chance of continuous employment'.[89] It is this which makes more comprehensible the reasons why employers per-

84.   A. Gorelik, *Shturemdike Yorn* (New York, NY, 1946) p. 114.
85.   *Report on Recent Immigration*, p. 42.
86.   *RCAI*, q. 3,534; see too *ibid*, qq. 3,869, 8,731.
87.   Booth, *Life and Labour*, 1st series, vol. iv, p. 177.
88.   J. Dyche, 'The Jewish Immigrant', *Contemporary Review*, March 1899, p. 388.
89.   *Ibid*, pp. 121–2.

sisted and why others aspired to join their ranks, despite complaints
such as the following from a Jewish sub-contractor in Greenfield
Street: 'He said the men were better off than the masters. Often he
woke up in the morning and tried to think about what work he
should have until it made his head ache. And then sometimes at the
end of the week he would not have sufficient money with which to
pay the men and would have to leave a few shillings over until next
week.'[90] But it was workers' experience of irregular and short payment and their vulnerability to the market which might render an
employers' insecurity preferable to their own.

Because the reasons that led to petty enterprise were pragmatic,
not culturally determined, in extreme circumstances such as those
which confronted the boot-finishing masters many small employers
were led to reconsider their position. Not least of the problems with
accounts that present an essentially individualistic Jewish worker is
that they leave little space to accommodate the actions of the boot-
finishing masters who, during the strike of 1890, came out alongside
their workers, demanded indoor work and thus, effectively, led their
own proletarianisation. In the face of the deterioration and extreme
insecurity of 'finishing', the advantages attached to being a sub-
contractor had shrunk to the extent that the majority wanted to
relinquish them. For a period, moreover, *Der Arbayter Fraynd* was
received by a large section of the members of the masters' boot-
finishing society as a newspaper which defended their interests.[91]
The case of boot finishing was unusual. Profits and conditions in it
were worse than in the tailoring and furniture trades. It was also
distinguished from the other trades insofar as those within it did not
assemble or produce a complete article but performed one function
in the production process. These circumstances may have made it
easier for masters to identify their cause with that of the working
class.

Although a demand for proletarianisation was not repeated
among employers in other trades, the boot finishers expressed an
extreme rather than an anomalous attitude. Among another group
of petty entrepreneurs, costermongers, there was also a robust
current of collective organisation. The Whitechapel and Spitalfields
Costermongers Union was established in 1894 and by the turn of the
century it had between 400 and 500 members. The need to deal with
potentially antagonistic interests and forces such as the ratepayers,
local government, the police and shopkeepers was the reason for
combination. The union identified itself with other trade unions

90. Booth Collection, A19, interviews with tailors, p. 81.
91. *AF*, 25 January 1889, p. 7.

and, because it included a large proportion of English Jews as well as foreigners, it became a force in Liberal and nascent independent labour politics in Whitechapel.[92]

Trade unionism was presented frequently as a force for independence, self-respect and education, in contrast to the economic and spiritual slavery of the sweated worker.[93] A similar self-conception was promoted by a manifesto from a workers' cooperative in the 'fancy shoe and slipper trade'. The members urged their fellow workers to 'endeavour to become their own masters and enjoy equal rights and the full fruits of their labour'.[94] Cooperatives were regularly formed and with equal regularity failed financially in the Jewish East End.[95] Their appeal too suggests that forms of collectivism and entrepreneurship were less complete opposites than alternative forms of independence. John Dyche's explanation of the decision of a trade union activist to become a petty employer lends further support.

> One can often see a trade union official or one of the rank and file, who has been for many years engaged in denouncing the 'Jewish sweater', all of a sudden become an employer. If you should ask for an explanation of his inconsistency, he will tell you that he can no longer stand the tyranny of his employer; that life has become a burden to him; that he is not a 'donkey'.[96]

Petty enterprise thus emerges as one path among a range of responses to proletarianisation within the Jewish East End. The turn of the finishing sub-contractors to trade unionism was a change of means rather than of ends. It is in this context rather than as the expression of an ethnically determined individualism that the multiplicity of small masters and traders should be seen. Some workers, with their access to small sums of capital, and the utility of such sums in the Jewish East End, were able to resist poverty, insecurity and proletarianisation by striving after a precarious upward mobility; or at least they attempted to do so. The contrast drawn by so many contemporaries and historians between the behaviour of Jewish immigrants and the English working class begins to look weak. Immigrants, when they took up positions as sub-contractors, were responding to the structure of opportunities in the local economy, not to an ethnically specific desire for upward social mobility. It

92. *RCAI*, qq. 19,883, 19,934–77; *JC*, 6 September 1901, p. 21.
93. *JC*, 14 December 1906, p. 42; *Der Yidisher Trayd Yunionist*, 1 June 1910, pp. 2–3.
94. *JC*, 8 February 1901, p. 30.
95. *Ibid*, 5 July 1907, p. 33.
96. Dyche, 'The Jewish Immigrant', p. 388.

stemmed from their predicament as workers rather than from their identity as Jews.

How Jewish were the Jews?

Was there, then, no aspect of the immigrants' activity in the work-shop trades that can be identified as Jewish? Conversely, how much can their history tell us about the working class more widely? Were Jews really just like everyone else? Of course, at one level the answer to this last question self-evidently is 'no'. Regardless of its structure, the quality of the immigrants' social and economic life was Jewish. There was an identifiable Jewish sector of the economy in which landlords and tenants, workers and employers were Jewish. 'The ghetto' appeared to be 'a fragment of Poland torn off and dropped haphazard into the heart of Britain'.[97] Yiddish as well as English was the medium for its transactions and conflicts. Even when social conflict was presented in class terms by Jewish revolutionaries, propagandists were well aware that they faced the problem of evangelising among *Jewish* workers.[98]

Beyond this level of generality, the Jewish context influenced the social trajectory of Jewish immigrants in a number of specific ways. First, their entry to the labour market was mediated by contacts between Jews and immigrants which fostered the continuing con-centration of Jews in a few trades. These networks were one example of the localised labour markets in London.[99] The immigrants' exclu-sion from these other labour networks discouraged them from work-ing in broader sectors of the metropolitan economy. Labouring jobs in the docks or in the building trades, for example, depended on pub contacts and Irish connections; Jewish immigrants were not welcome there.[100] Second, as we have seen, Jews had access to small but significant sums of capital in ways that the general population did not. The JBG was the conduit for these loans. Moreover, Jewish philanthropy was an obstacle to downward mobility. The JBG, the body chiefly responsible for poor relief among Jews, did not have

97. S. Gelberg, 'Jewish London', in G. Sims, ed., *Living London*, vol. ii (London, 1902), p. 29.
98. On this see below, pp. 329–35.
99. E.J. Hobsbawm, 'The Nineteenth-Century London Labour Market', in *idem*, *Worlds of Labour*, (London, 1984), pp. 131–51.
100. On the building trade see Price, *Masters, Unions and Men: Work Control in Building and the Rise of Labour, 1830–1914* (Cambridge, 1980), pp. 174–5; on dock work see G. Stedman Jones, *Outcast London* (Oxford, 1971), pp. 114–23.

recourse to the workhouse. It was forced to offer outdoor relief, saving Jews from the worst social marginalisation to which the English working class was prey. At the same time, the JBG had a method more effective than the workhouse for removing the poorest elements from society: 50,000 of those least able to support themselves – those from whom an immigrant 'under-class' might have been recruited – were repatriated to Eastern Europe.[101]

Jewish children in the East End of London were more likely to attend school than their non-Jewish counterparts. The high value Jews placed on education is a commonplace and, particularly in the context of American Jewish history, a number of historians have argued that this was a cause of upward social mobility.[102] Of course, any consequences that this had were more likely to become evident among English-born Jews than among immigrants. In Whitechapel and St George's in the East it is possible to distinguish between schools whose rolls were composed entirely of Jewish children and other schools whose intake was predominantly non-Jewish, and compare the rates of school attendance among their respective pupils.[103]

Table 12   Percentage of Average Attendance to Average Roll at Schools in Whitechapel and St George's in the East between 1905–6 and 1907–8[104]

Area and type of school	Average attendance as a percentage of the average roll
London	88.3
Whitechapel	91.9
Whitechapel Jewish	94.1
Whitechapel non-Jewish	87.0
St George's in the East	89.4
St George's in the East Jewish	94.9
St George's in the East non-Jewish	87.5

101. This is discussed in detail below, pp. 302–4.
102. N. Glazer, 'Social Characteristics of American Jews', *American Jewish Yearbook* (1955), pp. 3–41; J. Perlmann, *Ethnic Differences*, especially pp. 122–62. For a contrary view see J. Steinberg, *The Ethnic Myth: Race, Ethnicity, and Class in America* (New York, NY, 1981), chapters 3, 5.
103. This meant that the schools observed Jewish holidays. At the turn of the century, there were seven such schools in Whitechapel, three in St George's in the East; The Jewish schools were of two sorts: denominational schools, such as the Jews' Free School, and board schools, provided by the state but 'run on Jewish lines'. Jewish children, however, did comprise minorities in some board schools not 'run on Jewish lines' and in some Christian denominational schools: *RCAI*, qq. 10,281–4.
104. *London Statistics*, 1905–6, pp. 277–8, 281–3; *ibid*, 1906–7, pp. 263, 267, 270–1; *ibid*, 1907–8, pp. 300, 304–5, 306–7.

Attendance at Jewish schools was not only above that at predominantly non-Jewish schools in the East End: it was higher than the average rate for the capital as a whole. But the difference between the rates was low – just 7.1 per cent in Whitechapel and 7.4 per cent in St George's in the East. Moreover, the number of East End Jews who went on to secondary education was small: just over 1,000 between 1893 and 1914.[105] It may be that the basic literacy and numeracy that Jewish children acquired provided a further guarantee against downward social mobility. Nevertheless, it is not self-evident that the type of education provided at elementary schools or the difference between the rates of Jewish and non-Jewish attendance can acount for much of the upward mobility experienced by young immigrants who went to school in England or by their English-born children.[106] Certainly, it is for those who want to argue that this causal connection did exist, to suggest how it operated.

Finally, we should consider whether the immigrants' occupational background influenced their performance in the British economy. Experience in the clothing trades and in petty commerce in Eastern Europe did equip many Jewish immigrants with important skills: an understanding of how to contrive a livelihood from narrow margins of profit and the ability to use a needle. Beyond this, we can point to the fact that for Jewish immigrants proletarianisation in the late nineteenth century remained a process; it was not an accomplished fact. Typically, workers have resisted proletarianisation, and this is what immigrants who took up petty enterprise were doing. It would be possible, then to translate the distinction between Jewish individualists and English workers into a contrast between a group actively resisting proletarianisation and one that had been conquered by the disciplines of industrial capitalism.[107]

But this distinction has only limited validity and serves to reinscribe a stereotyped and misleading image of the English working class. Recent research on the history of work has done much to undermine an interpretation we once had of an English working class that was becoming increasingly homogeneous in the last

105. I. Osborne, 'Achievers of the Ghetto', in A. Newman, ed., *The Jewish East End, 1840–1939* (London, 1981), p. 166.
106. The most sophisticated study of the relationship between educational achievement and social mobility among immigrants and blacks in the United States, Perlmann's *Ethnic Differences*, is notably cautious on the impact of elementary schooling: see p. 40. Of course the period after 1945 in Britain, which witnessed an expansion both in educational opportunities and white-collar employment, presented the possibility of far closer links between educational achievement and social mobility.
107. For a contemporary view arguing this point, see Dyche, 'The Jewish Immigrant', pp. 387–8.

quarter of the nineteenth century. In fact, the social relations and strategies in which Jewish immigrants were engaged were variations upon others diffused among workers more widely. There is plenty of evidence to suggest that the practice of sub-contracting and sub-employment within the workshops of the Jewish East End was just one example within an extensive patchwork of two-tier systems. In his 1892 study of *Industrial Remuneration,* David Schloss found internal sub-contracting to be 'practically ubiquitous' in British industry.[108] By the 1890s, it was 'virtually universal' in bricklaying and plastering in London and was a significant presence in all other branches of the building trade.[109] In the pottery industry in the early twentieth century, 'in every department skilled workers negotiated a piece-rate for a task with the owner or manager and then employed a team', often female.[110] Other industries in which sub-contracting was extensively used were civil engineering, mining, iron and steel making, and engineering. Where there was not full-blown sub-contracting there were often 'helper' systems, in which the managerial functions of the superior worker were more restricted.[111] In shipbuilding the boiler makers had up to eight 'helpers' under their direction, who were paid on time rates while the superior workers enjoyed piece rates. A similar situation had developed in cotton spinning where the 'minders' were assisted by 'piecers'.[112]

If we turn from systems of sub-employment to full-scale petty enterprise, John Benson has estimated that between 1890 and 1914 40 per cent of working-class families engaged in some sort of self-employment or penny capitalist enterprise and, perhaps, 10 per cent – chiefly middle-aged men with some savings moved full time

108. D. Schloss, *Methods of Industrial Remuneration* (London, 1892), p. 120. The variety of forms of employment has led Patrick Joyce to observe that 'very many nineteenth-century workers can only be called "proletarian" with very great qualification': see P. Joyce, 'Labour, Capital and Compromise: A Response to Richard Price', *Social History,* January 1984, pp. 67–76.

109. Price, *Masters, Unions and Men,* pp. 174–5.

110. R. Whipp, 'Work and Social Consciousness: The British Potters in the Early Twentieth Century,' *Past and Present,* May 1988, pp. 137–9.

111. W. Garside and H. Gospel, 'Employers and Managers; their Organisational Structure and Changing Industrial Strategies', in C. Wrigley, ed., *A History of British Industrial Relations, 1875–1914* (Brighton, 1982), pp. 101–2.

112. K. McClelland and A. Reid, 'Wood, Iron and Steel', in R. Harrison and J. Zeitlin, eds., *Divisions of Labour: Skilled Workers and Technological Change in Nineteenth Century England* (Brighton, 1985), p. 165; W. Lazonick, 'Industrial Relations and Technical Change; the Case of the Self-Acting Mule', *Cambridge Journal of Economics,* September 1979, p. 247.

into penny capitalism. Its varied incidence was determined by the nature of opportunities in the local economy.[113]

Indeed, if we glance at the case of the English tailoring trade we can notice that structurally the position of Jewish sub-contractors was the same as that of the members of the English craft union, the AST. Both were petty entrepreneurs who contracted to produce garments, which they did with the assistance of waged employees. English tailors in the West End of London received orders from merchant and retail tailors which they manufactured in 'sittings' – that is, in workrooms hired by them. Jewish master tailors took the work away to the East End where Jewish men as well as Jewish and non-Jewish women were employed. In the journeymen's 'sitting', labour was not sub-divided to the degree it was in the Jewish workshop; nevertheless, the idea that the English tailors made the garment right through was a myth: anything from two to six female workers were employed as assistants by the artisan entrepreneur.[114]

On examination, the contrast between individualist immigrants and labourist English journeyman is gravely weakened. Nevertheless, this contrast was drawn by English journeymen. It might be suggested that in doing so, English tailors evaded the implications of their own entrepreneurial activity. The practices for which they stigmatised Jewish immigrants, in fact, were also present among themselves. It is interesting to speculate whether it was the fact that his employees were female which enabled the English journeyman to set aside his own entrepreneurial activity and, at the same time, to condemn his Jewish competitors. Not the least of what was objectionable about the Jewish sector of the trade may have been that it upset the normal sexual division of labour in which subordinate workers had been exclusively female. As we shall see, one charge brought against the immigrants by English workers was that they were 'unmanly'.

When English trade unionists contemplated social relations in the Jewish East End, like the social investigators, invariably they employed a particular image of the Jewish immigrants as individualists. In doing so, they confirmed an equally partial image of English labour. But the history of Jewish immigrants resists reduction to either a class or ethnic stereotype. Sectionalism and class conflict, collectivism and individualism, mutuality and rivalry, worker militancy and cooperation with employers, were all present

113. J. Benson, *The Working Class in Britain, 1850–1939* (London, 1989), p. 29; see too *idem, The Penny Copitalists* (Dublin, 1983).
114. London School of Economics, Webb Trade Union Collection, A14, tailors, pp. 213–14; *Men's Wear*, 4 May 1911, p. 158; *ibid*, May 1912, p. 208.

among Jewish workers. Amidst these cross-cutting potentialities, the collective interests and identities within which Jewish immigrants and Jewish workers enlisted cannot be analysed as reflections of their experience in society. That experience was too variegated, too diffuse to be captured by any single vision of collective interest and identity. The consequences of competition at every level, and the sexual division of labour, generated a plurality of axes of conflict and cooperation as workers struggled to achieve greater economic security. Interests and identities emerged as social actors made choices in specific situations between the options offered by revolutionary groups, trade unions, warehouses and shopkeepers hungry for new sub-contractors, and the Anglo-Jewish elite. The terms through which each of these groups presented social relations and collective identities signalled efforts to persuade and to marshal a constituency. Rather than subscribe to one or other of these contemporary arguments as historical truth, these chapters have aimed to uncover the conditions which they claimed to describe and which they were intended to ameliorate, to survey the circumstances in which they were available to Jewish immigrants and workers, to probe the meanings they had for them, and to analyse the structural and contingent forces which shaped the contest between them.

It will be clear that the analysis of Jewish immigrants proposed here draws strength from much of the recent work in labour and social history which has given us a new and more complex view of the English working class; indeed, it would have been impossible without this work. But in at least one significant respect the argument here departs from and goes beyond it. The focus of revisionism in labour history has been on the minority of organised workers and the ways in which they have used trade unions to protect sectional goals at the workplace.[115] A return to the institutional history of organised workers has undermined idealised views of the unity and anti-capitalist instincts of manual workers. But there is loss as well as gain as a once generously conceived, if flawed, history of the working class becomes the history of industrial relations. It has meant that the scope of study has narrowed as our understanding has advanced. Far from being marginal, the history of Jewish immigrants should remind us of the unorganised majority of workers. It affords us a well-documented view of these workers, and allows us to see them as historical subjects, and not simply as a group awaiting to enter

115. J. Zeitlin, 'From Labour History to the History of Industrial Relations', *Economic History Review*, May 1987, pp. 159–84; R. Price, *Labour in British Society* (London, 1986).

history when they join trade unions or they receive the attention of the philanthropists or the state.

Nevertheless, this view of the Jewish immigrant workforce leaves an important question unanswered. The idea that Jewish immigrants were becoming integrated within the labour movement, and the leading role in trade unions and strikes taken by anarchists and socialists, did at least present an account of immigrant politics in the pre-war period. In contrast, the shrunken stature of the Jewish labour movement which has been presented here cannot encompass the history of politics in the Jewish East End. It leaves open the question of what that history was. But more generally the development of popular politics in Britain also stands in need of some rethinking. Many historians have argued that popular politics in Britain before the First World War was driven by the rise of class alignments. Both the advance of the Labour Party and the continuing popularity of the Liberal Party have been explained in these terms.[116] But, as some scholars have pointed out, the continuing diversity of working-class experience at the workplace and in labour markets undermines these interpretations of popular politics, which are predicated on a growing homogeneity of labour.[117] One aim of the final section of this book, then, will be to attempt to determine what, in the absence of a vibrant labour movement, was the shape of politics in the Jewish East End and, in doing so, to see whether this can contribute to a new understanding of the dynamic of popular politics more widely.

116. See for example P.F. Clarke, *Lancashire and the New Liberalism* (Cambridge, 1971); R. McKibbin, *The Evolution of the Labour Party, 1910–24* (Oxford, 1974).
117. G. Stedman Jones, 'Why is the Labour Party in a Mess?', in *idem, Languages of Class* (Cambridge, 1983); D. Tanner, *Political Change and the Labour Party, 1900–14* (Cambridge, 1990); A. Reid and E. Biaggini, 'Currents of Radicalism, 1850–1914', in *idem*, eds., *Currents of Radicalism: Popular Radicalism, Organised Labour and Party Politics in Britain, 1850–1914* (Cambridge, 1991).

PART 3

The State, the Nation and the Jews, 1880–1914

Introduction

The following chapters develop further the history of Jewish integration and acculturation. They examine the relation of Jews to the state and to the idea of the nation in the new conditions provided by an unprecedented flow of Jewish immigration. They also focus on the cultural and political conflicts between institutions which Jewish immigrants created for themselves and those created by Anglo-Jewish organisations with the aim of educating the immigrants into the ways of English society. However, these chapters also take up the questions left unanswered at the end of part two. They explore the history of associational and political life in the Jewish East End as it developed in the absence of an institutionally significant labour movement. The separate concerns of the first two parts thus come together in this the third part of the book.

In addition, this part also presents some significant causal links. Above all, the final chapter attempts to demonstrate that there is a connection between the ways in which Jews figured in political argument before immigration and the ways in which the problem of immigration was dealt with by politicians and governments after 1880. Secondly, it argues that the actions of governments and politicans acting under the influence of these continuities shaped the development of politics and acculturation in the Jewish East End.

The state in Eastern Europe had a bearing on Jews which was completely different from that the British state had on its Jews. Whereas British Jews enjoyed civil and political equality, Jewish immigrants came from empires where they had lived under a wide range of disabilities. In Russia more than 1,400 statutes and regulations restricted their rights of settlement, barred them from university and public employment and prevented them from owning land. Jewish self-government in Russia, although eroded by the centralising state, continued to have a force it did not possess in Britain. The *kehila* continued to administer conscription and special levies imposed on the Jews.[1]

Jewish religion and culture in Eastern Europe were equally distant from Anglo-Jewish norms. Until the last decades of the nineteenth century, the prestige of religious learning and rabbinical culture was unchallenged. In Mir, Telz, Slobodka and elsewhere in Lithuania, there were Talmudical academies of great distinction. The great Hasidic courts were in White Russia, Ukraine and Poland. The vast mass of East European Jews, even when distant from rabbinical culture, spoke a language – Yiddish – that was quite different from the one used by their Gentile neighbours. In England, the culture of religious orthodoxy that the immigrants brought with them defied the norms of Jewish religious life and self-definition.

By the 1880s the *haskalah* – the Jewish enlightenment – had made inroads in Eastern Europe. Particularly in the cities, a Russified Jewish leadership had emerged. These luminaries criticised what they conceived to be the backwardness and insularity of Jewish life. But as this modernising current developed after 1880 it took socialist and nationalist directions.[2] To most English Jews, these modernising ideologies were as threatening as the religious orthodoxy against which they were in revolt. The development of zionist, socialist and anarchist movements challenged the framework of Jewish integration in English politics and society.

But it was not only the impact of immigration which gave new shape to the Jewish problem in this period. There was also a shift in the content of English political argument – namely, the re-emergence of the social question. This led to the examination of the Jewish minority in new ways. After 1885 the content of political debate extended beyond its former preoccupation with property, religion and the pale of the constitution, to include a greater a concern for the defenceless needy and regulation of the 'unfit'. Most notably, this was evident in the programme of social legislation introduced by the Liberal government elected to power in 1906. The measures then introduced included minimum wages in specified trades (tailoring among them), old age pensions, and state-supported schemes of insurance against ill-health and unemployment. But the Conservative Party was also permeated by demands for social reform, expressed most forcefully by Joseph Chamberlain and his supporters.[3]

1. S. Dubnow, *History of the Jews in Russia*, vol. i (Philadelphic, PA., 1916), p. 60.
2. This account follows S. Zipperstein, 'Haskalah, Cultural Change and Nineteenth-Century Russian Jewry', *Journal of Jewish Studies*, Fall 1983, pp. 191–207.
3. P. Clarke, *Liberals and Social Democrats* (Cambridge, 1978); B. Semmel, *Imperialism and Social Reform* (London, 1960); E.H.H. Green, 'Radical Conservatism and

There was an intellectual and ideological dimension to the slow growth of collectivism. State building was connected to nation building: new visions of the national community were used to express and prescribe a new relation between state and society. The problem of poverty was linked by 'new Liberals' to the idea of citizenship and by Conservatives to the nation's imperial role. The changing terms of electoral politics gave urgency to these ideas. After the franchise reforms of 1867 and 1884, and the redistribution of constituencies in 1885, the working classes were not only the objects of policy: to an unprecedented extent, they were active subjects within the political contest. As a result, they were addressed as part of the nation more insistently than ever before. Political parties still dominated by holders of landed, rentier and industrial wealth tried to broaden their appeal.[4] New Liberal conceptions of citizenship and the Conservative project of building a race capable of sustaining and defending the empire were, in part, attempts to integrate the enfranchised working classes in the political system.

The concept of citizenship proposed a more positive role for the state than had previously been allowed within the liberal tradition. The function of the state was now, as L.T. Hobhouse expressed it, 'to take care that the economic conditions are such that the normal man who is not defective in mind or body or will can by useful labour feed, house and clothe himself and his family'.[5] But this new degree of state provision also made demands on its beneficiaries. The social rights enjoyed by individuals were defined by their contribution to 'the common good'.[6] This raised the problem of what the status was to be of those deemed 'defective in mind or body or will': those who could not or would not meet their obligations to the well-being of society. In other words, there might be limits to how 'common' the 'common good' would be. If this was so, then the question would arise of whether it extended to include Jewish immigrants – would the state protect or reject them?[7]

the Electoral Genesis of Tariff Reform', *Historical Journal*, September 1985, pp. 667–92.

4. On the social composition of the Liberal Party in Parliament see G.R. Searle, 'The Edwardian Liberal Party and Business', *English Historical Review*, January 1983, pp. 28–60; on the Conservatives and the mass electorate see M. Pugh, *The Tories and the People, 1880–1935* (Oxford, 1985).

5. S. Collini, *Liberalism and Sociology: Political Argument in England 1880–1914* (Cambridge, 1979), p. 137.

6. *Ibid*, p. 125. See too M. Richter, *The Politics of Conscience: T.H. Green and his Age* (London, 1964), p. 344 and M. Bentley's piquant observations in *The Climax of Liberal Politics: British Liberalism in Theory and Practice, 1868–1918* (London, 1987), pp. 74–82.

7. As Geoffrey Alderman has commented, 'as the Welfare State began to be

Elements of the Conservative Party proposed a different sort of community: the empire. The jingo enthusiasm first encountered in 1878 revived and flared again in 1900. The Conservative Party's triumph in the 'khaki' election that year appeared to confirm that the patriotism of empire offered the party a way to appeal to the mass electorate. Radical Conservatives offered material benefits to both the middle classes and the masses through a programme of tariffs and social reform, wrapped in a rhetoric of imperial patriotism.[8] This strand of Conservatism developed most fully after 1902, once Salisbury's cautious leadership was no longer in place. In this context too, the question would arise whether there could be a place for Jewish immigrants within an imperial and protectionist vision of the nation. If cheap foreign goods were to be shut out, what should be done about cheap foreign labour?

Radical Conservatism and new Liberalism were only two of the ideological currents in British politics. However, both gained in strength after 1900. Their growing prominence once again raised the question of how and whether Jewish immigrants were to be integrated in English society. Necessarily, Jewish politics developed in relation to the new pressures and novel opportunities they created.

*

Before discussing these new developments, it will be important to acknowledge some of the continuities in the politics of Jewish integration. In general, after 1880 the issue of Jewish immigration overshadowed criticism of the Jews' want of 'patriotism'. But this was not always the case, and the political attack encountered in the late 1870s recurred: most notably, during the Boer War and the Marconi scandal.

At the turn of the century, the Jewish problem was once again central to the arguments propounded by Liberal opponents of Conservative, imperial policy. In this case the issue concerned relations between the British government and the Republic of the Transvaal. On 12 October 1899 these descended to a state of war. The osten-

shaped in the years preceding the Great War, a "Jewish dimension" in British government and politics was bound to arise'. G. Alderman, *The Jewish Community in British Politics* (Oxford, 1983), p. 87. See too *idem, London Jewry and London Politics 1889–1986* (London, 1989), pp. 27–53. On this problem in other areas of social policy see D. Garland, *Punishment and Welfare: A History of Penal Strategies* (Aldershot, 1985).

8. Green, 'Radical Conservatism: The Electoral Genesis of Tariff Reform', pp. 667–92.

sible issue was the Transvaal government's refusal to grant political rights to 'Uitlanders' – settlers who had been attracted to the Rand by the discovery there of gold in 1886. The war was a shambles. Only in the spring of 1900 did it turn in Britain's favour, though the Afrikaners' guerilla tactics embarassed the War Office for a further two years.

The best-known analysis of the war as a fight for Jewish interests was made by J.A. Hobson in a series of articles written in the *Manchester Guardian* in the autumn of 1899, published in 1900 as *The War in South Africa: Its Causes and Effects*, and in an article titled 'Capitalism and Imperialism in South Africa' which appeared in the *Contemporary Review* in January of the same year. Hobson conceded, 'it is difficult to state the truth about our doings in South Africa without seeming to appeal to the ignominious passion of the Judenhetze'.[9] The war, he argued, was being fought, under the cloak of patriotism, in the interests of financiers among whom 'the foreign Jew must be taken as the leading type'.[10] Specifically, through their control of the press in the Cape and in England, Rand mining magnates, mostly Jews, had conspired to exploit 'the stupid Jingoism of the British public'.[11] Their aim was to use public policy for private gain: above all, they wanted access to a larger supply of labour, if necessary by coercion, and so 'our international capitalists are expanders of the British empire'.[12]

The war divided the Liberal Party. It was opposed by Liberals who placed themselves in a tradition of foreign policy which they traced back to Cobden and Bright, as well as by more innovative Liberals such as Hobhouse, in whose view imperialism had eclipsed the cause of social reform.[13] It was also opposed by all but one of the six Labour MPs, by the Social Democratic Federation, the Independent Labour Party and by much of the Trade Union Congress and the Labour Representation Committee. The arguments brought by these opponents of the war bore a great similarity to Hobson's.[14]

---

9. J.A. Hobson, *The War in South Africa: Its Causes and Effects* (London, 1900), p. 189.
10. *Ibid.*
11. *Ibid*, p. 217.
12. *Ibid*, pp. 232–3; see too C. Holmes, 'J.A. Hobson and the Jews', in *idem*, ed., *Immigrants and Minorities in British Society* (London, 1978), pp. 137–42.
13. P. Clarke, *Liberals and Social Democrats* (Cambridge, 1981), p. 67.
14. B. Porter, *Critics of Empire: British Radical Attitudes to Colonialism in Africa, 1895–1914* (London, 1968), pp. 124–30. The anti-Jewish aspects of the movement are discussed in C. Hirschfield, 'The British Left and the "Jewish Conspiracy": A Case Study of Modern Anti-Semitism', *Jewish Social Studies*, Spring 1981, pp. 95–112; C. Holmes, *Anti-Semitism in British Society 1876–1939* (London, 1979), pp. 66–80.

John Burns argued in the House of Commons in February 1900, 'Wherever we go in this matter we see the same thing. Wherever we examine there is the financial Jew operating, directing, inspiring the agencies that have led to this war'.[15] According to John Morley, 'a ring of financiers . . . mostly Jewish, are really responsible for the war'.[16]

This critique of the Jews was dissimilar to the one encountered in the late 1870s insofar as now the Jews' financial interests were central. It now offered one way of understanding the evident interplay between finance and politics in British expansion overseas, most notably in Egypt and South Africa.[17] But the continuities with earlier arguments are equally significant. The critique was driven by the same oppositions between disinterestedness and corruption, patriotism and the self-seeking influence of the Jews. In *The Psychology of Jingoism* published in 1901, Hobson argued that 'the businessmen who mostly direct modern politics require a screen, they find it in the interests of the country, patriotism. Behind this screen they work seeking private gain under the name and pretext of the commonwealth'.[18] Opposition to national policy in wartime invited accusations of disloyalty. The noisy calls to imperial patriotism were countered by the claim that the war was not being fought for British interests, let alone patriotic ones. The British army had become, in Burns' colourful phrase, 'the jannissary of the Jews'.[19]

The pro-Boers were led to question the health of political life in Britain. Their analysis of the war's origins, and the apparent public enthusiasm for the war, threw into question the relation between the press and public opinion. For Liberals, the manipulation of the mass electorate was a matter for the gravest alarm, as had been the case in 1878. As the war turned in Britain's favour, the jingo crowds forced the pro-Boers to hold private meetings or to admit the public by ticket only. In these circumstances critics became worried for their constitutional freedoms. F.W. Hirst, Gilbert Murray and J.L. Hammond feared that 'possibilities are brought near to us which may involve in vital danger even a commonwealth so massively stable

15. *Hansard*, 4th series, LXXVIII, cols. 795–6, 6 February 1900.
16. J. Galbraith, 'The Pamphlet Campaign of the Boer War', *Journal of Modern History*, June 1952, p. 119.
17. S. Marks, 'Scrambling for Africa', *Journal of African History*, 1982, vol. 1, pp. 97–113; P. Cain and A. Hopkins, 'Gentlemanly Capitalism and British Expansion Overseas II: New Imperialism, 1850–1945', *Economic History Review*, February 1987, pp. 1–26.
18. Quoted in Clarke, *Liberals and Social Democrats*, p. 94.
19. *Hansard*, 4th series, LXXVIII 6 February 1900, col. 795; see too H.M. Hyndman's speech to a 6,000 strong rally at Trafalgar Square published in *Justice*, 15 July 1899, p. 6.

as our own'.[20] Likewise, the threat to representative government was central to Hobson's concerns in 1899–1901. He concluded his essay in the *Contemporary Review* with a quotation from Sir Thomas More: 'Everywhere do I perceive a certain conspiracy of rich men seeking their private advantage under the name and pretext of Commonwealth'.[21] Once again the attack on the Jews was tied to a defence of the constitution.

This discourse was not exclusively the property of the left of British politics. In the face of Liberal collectivism, one Conservative response was to accuse ministers of milking the public purse for personal gain. Their most celebrated opportunity to do so was provided by the Marconi scandal of 1912–13, which centred on accusations of insider stock trading.[22] Of the four ministers at the centre of the scandal two were Jews: Rufus Isaacs and Herbert Samuel, respectively Attorney-General and Postmaster-General. (The other two ministers were Lloyd George, the Chancellor of the Exchequer and the Liberal Chief Whip, the Master of Elibank.) Recent research has made clear, however, that belief in ministerial speculators was not widely diffused: the Conservative leadership distanced itself from charges of corruption and the overt Jew-baiting of Leo Maxse's *New Witness*. In doing so it assisted the four ministers to refute the charges against them.[23]

The significance of the Marconi scandal has been overstated. In order to understand the character of Jewish integration in Edwardian England we have to turn away from the travails of the Jewish monied and political elite. The collision between collectivism and Jewish immigration generated problems which both touched the Jewish population more widely and reveal more of the nature of political culture and government in Britain in the early twentieth century.

20. F.W. Hirst, G. Murray and J.L. Hammond, *Liberalism and the Empire* (London, 1900), p. xvi.
21. J.A. Hobson, 'Capitalism and Imperialism in South Africa', *Contemporary Review*, January 1900, p. 17.
22. On corruption in general see G.R. Searle, *Corruption in British Politics, 1895–1930* (Oxford, 1987).
23. B.B. Gilbert, 'David Lloyd George and the Great Marconi Scandal', *Historical Research*, October 1989, pp. 295–318; K. Lunn, 'The Marconi Scandal and Related Aspects of British Anti-Semitism, 1911–14' (University of Sheffield PhD, 1978), pp. 107–9; Searle, *Corruption*, pp. 2–3, 188–90.

Chapter 11

Immigration, Social Policy and Politics

Jewish immigration and social policy

In the 1880s, the East End of London was the territory which most inspired fear of revolution and concern for the problems of 'pauperism' and 'poverty'. At the turn of the century, the health and efficiency of the people at the heart of the empire became one focus for premonitions of imperial decline in the face of international competition. The question of immigration erupted in both these areas of public debate. As it did so 'Jews' and 'aliens' became associated less with constitutional politics and more with debates on social policy.

Following the repeal in 1826 of wartime legislation, the ports of Britain were open to all comers without restriction. But in April 1886 the first public meeting to call for a new measure of statutory restriction was held in the East End. 1,500 people gathered to hear Lord Brabazon, Arnold White and local MPs speak on the subject.[1] In the following decade the immigration question was driven by a mixture of apprehension and fear among the propertied classes in the face of the outcast masses. Some trade unionists also opposed immigration in the face of the failures of new unionism among the immigrant labour force. Accordingly, Jewish immigrants and their impact on the surrounding English-born population provided one focus for investigations into public health, poverty and sweated labour in London. As J.A. Hobson pointed out in 1891, the prospects for an Aliens Act depended 'in large measure upon the success of other schemes for treating the over-supply of low-skilled labour'.[2]

---

1. B. Gainer, *The Alien Invasion: The Origins of the 1905 Aliens Act* (London, 1972), pp. 60–1.
2. J.A. Hobson, *Problems of Poverty* (London, 1891), p. 126.

Hobson's view that the debate on Jewish immigration was located within a wider discussion of poverty has not been developed. Instead, the main aim of historians has been to convict or absolve the individuals or movements opposed to Jewish immigration from charges of anti-Semitism and prejudice.[3] The terms of analyis have been drawn not from the opponents of immigration but from their antagonists. This approach is limited. We have learned little of the intellectual currents, cultural symbols and political visions which made opposition to immigration meaningful for those people who took this position. Yet, at the very least, our recognition that the policy of immigration restriction arose in the context of the discussion of pauperism and poverty in the capital does suggest that we should take greater account of its intellectual rationale. When we do this we shall see that the hostility and opposition aroused by Jewish immigrants was more than an episode in the history of xenophobia or anti-Semitism. It was part of an attempt to redefine the role of the state and the idea of the nation.

The unemployment and riots which marked London winters in the mid-1880s stimulated several palliatives or remedies. One of these was the proposal to restrict 'pauper foreign immigration'.[4] Fears that immigrants were flooding the capital's labour market were frequently connected to other interpretations and solutions which regarded the social crisis in terms of gross numbers. Restrictionists as diverse as Arnold White and J.A. Hobson presented their arguments as corollaries to schemes for emigration or to concern with the effects of rural depopulation on the cities. John Burnett, the labour correspondent to the Board of Trade, commented that immigration was 'rendering useless the sacrifice of thousands of our own emigrants who go or are sent abroad'.[5]

Advocates of immigration restriction rarely believed that measure alone would be a panacea. Alexander Baumann, the Conservative MP for Peckham between 1886–92, was a moderate enthusiast for state intervention to control sweated labour. Stricter regulation of

3. See for example J.A. Garrard, *The English and Immigration 1880–1910* (London, 1971); Gainer, *The Alien Invasion*; Holmes, *Anti-Semitism in British Society 1876–1939*; an interesting exception is A. Lee, 'Aspects of the Working-Class Response to the Jews in Britain 1880–1994', in K. Lunn, ed., *Hosts, Immigrants and Minorities: Historical Responses to Newcomers in British Society, 1870–1914* (Folkestone, 1980), pp. 107–33.

4. On responses in general see G. Stedman Jones, *Outcast London* (Oxford, 1971), Part III; J. Harris, *Unemployment and Politics: A Study in English Social Policy* (Oxford, 1972), Part III.

5. *Report to the Board of Trade on the Sweating System in the East End of London*, PP 1887, LXXXIX, p. 18; Hobson, *Problems of Poverty*, p. 57; A. White, 'The Invasion of Foreign Paupers', *Nineteenth Century*, March 1888, p. 414.

workshop and domestic production, he hoped, would force outwork into factories by raising overheads. He entertained an Arcadian vision of factories being established in 'pure country air'. At the same time, Baumann advocated immigration restriction, and did so in a way which also saw the problem as one of numbers: 'It is not the slightest use opening the lock-gates at one end unless we are prepared to shut them at the other. It is no good drawing the trade away from London by stricter laws, unles we keep out the tide of immigration from Europe'.[6] This argument became stronger if the overall demographic change could be tied to the experience of particular trades. In 1887 John Burnett argued that although immigration was not the cause of sweating in the East End of London, without its effects 'there would be no demand for an inquiry upon the subject'.[7]

Within three years the House of Lords Select Committee on Sweating had come to the conclusion that there was no such thing as a 'sweating system' but a collection of symptoms – low wages, long hours, overcrowded conditions – the root cause of which lay in an overstocked labour market to which immigrants did not greatly contribute.[8] The proposals and legislation which arose from this formula concentrated on the symptoms and did not seek to act on the labour market. This was the case with the Factory Act of 1891 which extended sanitary inspection to every workshop except domestic workshops, and required every employer to keep a list of the persons employed in or out of the workshops. More radical solutions went no further in attacking the root causes of sweating. Writers such as Beatrice Potter and David Schloss left to one side the intractable problems of the labour market. They believed that state regulation could render workshop production unprofitable and that factory conditions themselves would produce trade unionism and decent wages and conditions.[9]

What distinguished advocates of immigration restriction at this time, whether Liberals such as Hobson, Tory democrats such as the Earl of Dunraven, or trade unionists such as Charles Freak, was their

6. A.A. Baumann, 'Possible Remedies for the Sweating System', *National Review*, November 1888, pp. 296, 298. For the views of Schloss on 'sweating' and on the solution of pushing outwork into factory production see D. Schloss, 'The Sweating System', *Fortnightly Review*, December 1887, pp. 8–11.
7. *Report to the Board of Trade on the Sweating System*, p. 4.
8. *Select Committee on the Sweating System*, PP 1890, XVII, p. cxxv.
9. B. Webb, *My Apprenticeship* (Cambridge, 1979 edn), pp. 335–7. On the Factory Acts see B.L. Hutchins and A. Harrison, *A History of Factory Legislation* (London, 1903), pp. 216–18. Indeed, Hutchins and Harrison, writing in 1903, asserted that factory legislation represented 'the reasoned effort of the best sense of the community' to mitigate the effects of 'a constant supply of cheap labour', to which it was acknowledged the 'immigration of destitute aliens' did contribute: *ibid*, p. 218.

insistence on the labour market as a cause of 'sweating' and the need for policy to be directed towards it.[10] However much they overestimated the effects of immigration, their position addressed a major inconsistency between the analyses and prescriptions of their rivals. They sought to make an intervention in the labour market in one of the few ways available: one which did not involve an unacceptable degree of state intervention in relations of employment.[11] Further, in their insistence that immigrants did compete with native workers these restrictionists were undoubtedly correct.

All agreed, however, that wherever English workmen and Jewish immigrants came into competition the Jewish workman had the advantage over the Englishman on account of his 'lower standard of comfort'. Even Stephen Fox, who had rushed into print to combat Arnold White's restrictionist prescriptions, conceded that 'it is undoubtedly true that the foreigner will take less wages than a native worker, and, owing to his low standard of existence can maintain himself on what would mean starvation to an Englishman'.[12] These opinions reproduced existing stereotypes of the Jew. But they gained explanatory force from the way in which they also drew on and in turn supported the concept of 'urban degeneration'. The proponents of this theory, which pervaded debate in the late 1880s, argued that London life produced a lower physique and a diminished capacity for work in successive generations. Llewellyn Smith claimed that provincial migrants dominated the skilled trades and better-paid unskilled occupations in the capital on account of their rude health.[13] The Jewish immigrant was portrayed as the mirror image of the sturdy countryman: a figure who had adapted so well to the demands of urban life that he was inevitably the victor when thrown into competition with the London-born. Booth characterised the situation of the East End worker in this way:

> He is met and vanquished by the Jews fresh from Poland or Russia, accustomed to a lower standard of life, and above all of food, than would be possible for a native of these Islands; less skilled and perhaps less strong,

10. Hobson, *Problems of Poverty*, pp. 89–91; Earl of Dunraven, 'The Invasion of Destitute Aliens', *Nineteenth Century*, June 1892, pp. 990–4; S. Jeyes, 'Pauper Foreign Immigration', *Fortnightly Review*, July 1891, pp. 18–19. On the attitudes of trade unionists in the boot and shoe industry, see earlier, Chapter eight.

11. Hobson's survey of the alternative policies liste of the following: co-operative production, an eight-hour day, public workshops, state contracts on uncommercial terms, factory legislation and trade unionism. Hobson, *Problems of Poverty*, Chapter six.

12. S. Fox, 'The Invasion of Foreign Paupers', *Contemporary Review*, June 1888, p. 859. See too D. Schloss, 'The Jew as Workman', *Nineteenth Century*, January 1891, p. 102.

13. Stedman Jones, *Outcast London*, chapter six.

but in his way more fit, pliant, adaptable, adroit . . . or he is pushed on one side by the physical strength of the man whose life has hitherto been spent among green fields.[14]

The policy of immigration restriction held a respectable place in the debate on social policy in the late 1880s; it was not the preserve of isolated cranks and political zealots.

By 1887 public interest in immigration had developed to the extent that the JBG's annual report observed that the year had been 'rife almost to overflowing with writings and speeches on the subject'.[15] Even when it did not advocate restriction this attention frequently took an unfavourable view of immigration. The Select Committee of the House of Commons which investigated the subject in 1888–9 found that 'there is general agreement that pauper immigration is an evil, and should be checked'.[16] Its members shrunk from advocating legislation 'because of the difficulty of carrying such a measure into effect' and not on grounds of policy. However, the Select Committee advocated inaction in the short term only: 'They contemplate the possibility of such legislation becoming necessary in the future, in view of the crowded condition of our great towns, the extreme pressure for existence among the poorer part of the population and the tendency of destitute foreigners to reduce still lower the social and material condition of our poor.'[17]

This passage was inserted in the face of opposition from three of the Liberal members of the Committee: Charles Bradlaugh, W.R. Cremer and Samuel Montagu. Their opposition should not be misinterpreted, however. Elsewhere, Montagu argued that statutory action was unnecessary, not because immigration was a boon or harmless but because 'leading Jews' had already taken action to regulate it.[18]

This was not an isolated instance of agreement on the effects of immigration between the advocates and opponents of an Aliens Act. In 1894 Lord Salisbury introduced an Aliens Bill into the House of Lords. A part of his case was based on the danger that Britain's hospitality would be abused to plan anarchist terror across Europe. But another part consisted of a predictable recapitulation of the

14. C. Booth, *Life and Labour of the People of London*, 1st series, vol. iv, p. 340. See too E. Clerke, 'The Dock Labourers' Strike', *Dublin Review*, October 1889, pp. 390–1.

15. J[ewish] B[oard of] G[uardians], *29th Annual Report* (London, 1888), p. 15.

16. *Select Committee on Emigration and Immigration*, PP 1889, X, p. x.

17. *Ibid.*

18. University of Southampton, Samuel Montagu's scrapbooks, AJ/1, *Jewish World*, 22 April 1886; see too *Eastern Post*, 8 June 1892, p. 6; also *East London Advertiser*, 13 July 1895, p. 5.

restrictionist case. Immigrants, he said, were able to undercut English workers because they possessed a lower standard of life, they dragged down the price of unskilled labour and added to the burdens of the ratepayers. In reply, Rosebery dismissed Salisbury's terrorist nightmare but continued, 'with regard to what he said about the exclusion of destitute aliens I am not prepared to offer much objection'.[19] This consensus extended to the government. In the spring of 1892 there was a scare that the unusually large migration of Jews from the Russian empire which had taken place in the previous two years would be repeated. This led the government to consider introducing a bill to restrict immigration. The flood never arrived but the fears it had stimulated within the civil serivce were based upon the same arguments as those put forward by the propagandists for statutory restriction.[20]

At the turn of the century, when the issue of immigration once again acquired great urgency, there was a similar breadth of agreement. From the late 1890s it was the effects of the immigrants' presence in the housing market which attracted most comment.[21] The report of the Royal Commission on Alien Immigration contained the principal elements of the restrictionist's argument on this point: 'the 38,312 Aliens who have arrived in the borough [of Stepney] since 1881 have had to be provided with house accommodation, and have of necessity taken great share in causing the regrettable condition of the district in respect to overcrowding'.[22] The consequences of overcrowding were found in low standards of health, cleanliness, decency and morality. Above all, the high levels of overcrowding which the immigrants tolerated enabled them to pay higher rents, offer key-money and drive out the English population.[23] This view of the housing problem was propounded by restrictionists at all levels of political debate: by Alderman Silver before Stepney Borough Council and by Akers Douglas as Home Secretary before the House of Commons.[24]

As in earlier years, there was wide agreement that immigration was a menace. The Royal Commission recommended legislation to ex-

19. *Hansard*, 4th series, XXVI, cols. 1,047–55, 6 July 1894.
20. PRO, HO 45/10063/B2840A/35, copy of despatch from Lord Salisbury to Sir R. Morier, 29 March 1892; HO 45/10063/B2840A/36, emigration of destitute Jews from Russia, 8 April 1892.
21. See for example GLRO, JBD, B2/1/1, 'The Immigration of Pauper Aliens: Correspondence between the Parliamentary Committee on Alien Immigration and the Prime Minister'.
22. *Royal Commission on Alien Immigration*, PP 1903, IX, p. 23.
23. *Ibid*, p. 25.
24. *East London Observer*, 9 March 1901, p. 6; *Hansard*, 4th series, CXXXIII, col. 1,145, 25 April 1904.

clude classes of alien, including those unable to show they were capable of supporting themselves and their families.[25] One commissioner, Sir Kenelm Digby, an under-secretary at the Home Office, submitted a memorandum which dissented from the majority conclusion, and he was supported by another commissioner, Lord Rothschild. Their point of disagreement, however, was not over whether immigration was desirable but over the best way to mitigate its effects.

> It is no doubt desirable that we should have among us as few as possible of the class of immigrants who are sought to be excluded, and that the overcrowding which prevails to a great extent in the East End of London in connection with alien immigration should be abated. But I cannot agree with some of the proposed remedies for such evils as are stated to exist. I believe that legislation carrying out the recommendations would be impracticable, and would fail to accomplish the object aimed at.[26]

Opponents of statutory restriction advocated fiercer enforcement of the by-laws on overcrowding amd sanitation, arguing that if they were 'steadily and systematically enforced people would find their own accommodation'.[27] But this remedy for the housing problem was discredited in many eyes and, from the perspective of the present, was misguided. By the late nineteenth century it was widely understood that the working classes were kept within overcrowded districts by their need to live close to their place of work. Among Medical Officers of Health this realisation had led to disenchantment with enforcing disciplinary legislation against overcrowded and insanitary conditions. John Foot, the officer for Bethnal Green, went so far as to call the laws on sanitation and overcrowding 'a dishousing machinery'. He argued, 'what is wanted is much more house accommodation at the lowest possible cost . . . instead of which we have an increased population both home and alien'.[28] In other words, at times the anti-alien case contained within it a perception that the combined disciplines of the law and the market were an insufficient response to overcrowding and poor sanitation in working-class housing. William Beveridge, at this time a worker at Toynbee Hall, while opposing the Aliens Bill, acknowledged that existing legislation attacked the symptoms of overcrowding only. He responded weakly, 'admitting the criticism, can one in these days hope to do anything better?'[29] The comfortable assessment of many

25. *RCAI*, pp. 40–3.
26. *Ibid*, pp. 45–52.
27. *Ibid*, qq. 4,102–3.
28. *Ibid*, q. 6,602. For a contrary view see the evidence of Drs S.F. Murphy and J. Loane, *ibid*, qq. 5,111–17, 4,584–5.
29. W.H.B. [everidge], 'The Aliens Bill', *Toynbee Record*, May 1904, p. 118.

historians that the opponents of an Aliens Act possessed a monopoly of wisdom in this argument will not bear close examination.

In this second phase of debate, immigration restriction was advocated by enthusiasts of empire and others drawn to the modish pursuit of 'efficiency'.[30] The poor stature and physical condition of recruits to the army during the Boer War produced an urgent concern for the health of the nation and fear of 'deterioration' among the working classes. In this light, the annual immigration of thousands of Russian Jews, who were represented as physically enfeebled, without marketable trades and willing to work for a pittance, became an issue of grave concern. Writing in *Nineteenth Century and After*, H. Hamilton Fyffe detailed his alarm at the influx of aliens 'who teach us nothing, who bring no wealth or spending power into the country . . . . Is it not clear that this continual inflow already hampers us in the great fight we have to wage against ignorance and inefficiency with all their hateful brood, and that its hampering effect must increase in a more and more rapid ratio so long as we let it go on?'[31] The influx of these aliens could only advance the decay of national intelligence and physique.

The language of efficiency and empire was not restricted to the periodical literature. It was spoken by platform orators in the East End and by the Home Secretary and Prime Minister in Parliament.[32] Restrictionists thus aligned their cause with other reforms inspired by the need to adjust to a world in which Britain's industrial, commercial and naval pre-eminence was increasingly open to question. It was characteristic that the practice of allowing unlimited immigration was compared unfavourably with the restrictive laws enforced by Britain's competitors, Germany and the United States.[33] The opponents of restrictive legislation were portrayed as sentimentalists, attached to outdated shibboleths and at odds with new realities.[34] The

30. G.R. Searle, *The Quest for National Efficiency: A Study of British Politics and Thought* (Oxford, 1971).

31. H.H. Fyffe, 'The Alien and the Empire', *Nineteenth Century and After*, pp. 415–19. See too 'Foreign Undesirables', *Blackwood's Magazine*, February 1901; 'The Alien Immigrant', *ibid*, January 1903, p. 141.

32. *Eastern Post*, 1 March 1902, p. 6; also the evidence of James William Johnson, chairman of the executive committee of the British Brothers League, before the *RCAI*, q. 8,558. For the Home Secretary, Akers Douglas, see *Hansard*, 4th series, CXXIII, col. 989, 29 March 1904, and for Balfour, *ibid*, CXLV, cols. 797–8, 2 May 1905.

33. 'The Alien Immigrant', *Blackwood's Magazine*, pp. 137, 141.

34. For instance, William Evans Gordon contrasted efficiency in the form of an Act to restrict immigration to the sentimentalism of those who upheld an absolute right of asylum from which the burden fell upon 'the poorest and most helpless of our population': *Hansard*, 4th series, CXXXIII, 1,083, 25 April 1904.

campaigns for fair trade and immigration restriction were similar in their appeals to unsentimentality and to the need to place the nation's interests first. Indeed, tariff reformers tried to mobilise working-class support by exploiting these homologies: by collapsing the two issues into the single evil of unfair 'dumping' – of cheap goods and destitute aliens – by 'the foreigners'.[35]

Too often restrictionist prescriptions have been presented by historians as an expression of prejudice: a minority opinion, outside the mainstream of social policy discussion, which could not be supported by any reasonable observer. But this was not so. The case for statutory restriction was widely notable for its capacity to address weaknesses in the arguments of opponents, for its ability to absorb fashionable themes in social policy, for its coherence and for the widespread assent it received. Our recognition that an unfavourable view of Jewish immigration was commonplace and extended beyond the ranks of those who supported the anti-alien agitation should make us question anew why these unexceptional views became the subject of political enthusiasm for some but not for others who by no means welcomed the influx. In other words, why did immigration become a significant political issue at the turn of the century?

Immigration and politics

After 1867, and even more so after the Reform Acts of 1884 and 1885, the Conservative Party was faced with the problem of how it would present itself to the newly enfranchised and, through the revision of constituencies, newly empowered urban masses. The most powerful view envisioned the party defending the ramparts of property, allying the landed and county elites with the growing support among the urban villas. Others, however, who were loud in the party organisation but weak where policy was formulated, hoped the party would conform more to the Disrealian myth of 'Tory democracy'. It was from the project of developing a popular Conservative politics and its coalescence with the more statist preoccupations of Unionism that the immigration issue received its political momentum.

Yet the 'alien question' *first* entered political debate in the East End in terms derived from mid-Victorian liberalism and conservatism: from a context in which the participants on one side defended the integrity of the constitution and, on the other, denounced the

---

35. See Joseph Chamberlain's Limehouse speech in 1904: C. Boyd, ed., *Mr Chamberlain's Speeches*, vol. ii (London, 1914), pp. 262–5.

iniquities of privilege. Each year in Tower Hamlets a large number of unnaturalised Jewish immigrants were placed on the electoral register. This occurred as a matter of course if their rates were 'compounded' (paid through the landlord), since the overseers would register their names if their level of rates appeared to qualify them for the franchise.[36] In 1885, 1,800 objections were laid by the Conservative agent against entries on the Whitechapel register. These names, it was alleged, belonged to foreigners without a title to vote.

Local Conservatives demanded the disenfranchisement of the alien vote on two grounds. One argument concerned the rule of law. The chairman of the local Conservative association argued, 'the question is a very simple one, either these persons are qualified or are not qualified'.[37] The other argument was that the aliens' names had been placed on the register by Montagu to turn Whitechapel into a 'pocket borough'.[38] But in the autumn of 1885, Whitechapel Liberals conducted a vigorous defence of the political rights of disenfranchised foreigners.[39] In late August and September 1885 three large and, at times, violent 'indignation meetings' were held in the constituency to protest against the objections. On these occasions the principle of the Conservatives' actions was contested. As with protests against 'coercion' in Ireland and the practice of policing in London, radicals questioned Conservative interpretations of the rule of law when this threatened the birthright of English liberties.[40] Tory objections were denounced as 'unjust, frivolous and vexatious' and the naturalisation law was dismissed as a 'miserable technicality'. The aliens had fulfilled all the duties of citizenship for several years, by serving on juries and by paying rates and taxes. As a result, it was argued, they were entitled to the rights of citizenship. The expense of naturalisation – £7 once inland revenue stamps and an agent's fee were included – was seen as a barrier set up against those who could not afford it. More generally the objections violated 'the spirit of the times', which was to increase the number enfranchised, not the opposite. One speaker placed the Conservatives' action within a political tradition which he traced back to the severance with the American colonies, and then forward in time through

36. On the intricacies of the system of registration, see N. Blewett, 'The Franchise in the United Kingdom', *Past and Present*, December 1965, p. 38.
37. *East London Advertiser*, 5 September 1885, p. 3.
38. *East London Observer*, 21 November 1885, p. 6.
39. Thereafter they shifted ground and argued merely that the aliens were not placed on the register by design.
40. Samuel Montagu's scrapbook's, AJ/1, *Eastern Post*, 25 June 1886; *East London Observer*, 26 November 1887.

opposition to Catholic and Jewish emancipation and repeal of the Corn Laws, up to support for the Confederacy in the American Civil War.[41]

After 1885, issues of social policy intruded increasingly into party politics. The aliens question was in the vanguard of this change. From the late 1880s onwards the alien was conceived far less often as an illegal voter but, instead, as a figure who damaged the material and moral well-being of the native working classes. As Jewish immigrants were placed within discussions concerned with sweating and overcrowding, it became possible to place the interests of Jewish immigrants in opposition to the interests of labour and the working man. It was a view which acknowledged the economic effects of Jewish immigration in the East End in ways that were beyond a Liberal political ideology defined in terms of liberty and constitutional integrity.

The immigration question received its political momentum from the project of developing a popular Conservative politics. It was this which divided the restrictionists from their opponents within and outside of the Conservative and Unionist Party.[42] The first general election in which the immigration question played a part in the East End was that of 1892. Statutory immigration restriction was advocated by every Conservative candidate in the East End, with the exception of C.T. Ritchie, the President of the Local Government Board, who lost at St George's in the East. But the way the issue was presented varied. These differences reflected the willingness of candidates to appeal to the working classes through a rhetoric which dissolved for a moment distinctions of social status. At one end of the spectrum was H.H. Marks, a Jew and editor of the *Financial News*, who was the Conservative candidate in Bethnal Green North-east. The constituency included a large number of English boot and shoe makers who were suffering competition from immigrant labour. Marks attacked the Liberals' obsession with Ireland and argued that the more pressing needs of Englishmen should come first: 'Chief among these needs he would instance the placing of a restriction upon the alien paupers who were dumped upon the shores and who, by reason of their dire poverty, were compelled to work at starvation

41. *East London Observer*, 5 September 1885, p. 6; *ibid*, 12 September 1885, p. 6; *ibid*, 19 September 1885, p. 6.
42. Of course, there were exceptions. Some Liberals, such as Sydney Buxton, were consistent advocates of statutory restriction: see Gainer, *The Alien Invasion*, p. 164. Between the late 1880s and the mid-1890s a number of trade unions and trades councils, as well as the Trade Union Congress, called for legislation to prevent the immigration of 'destitute aliens'. This occurred largely in the wake of the failure of new unionist attempts to organise the newcomers.

wages to the detriment of English workers.'[43] Marks also declared himself in favour of a graduated income tax and the taxation of ground rents. These proposals were clearly designed to shift the burden of taxation away from his constituents. Marks aimed to neutralise the Liberals' attacks on privilege in general and land-owners in particular. The particular suggestions were allied to a vision of imperial greatness and, of course, defence of the union with Ireland. Positive connections were made between this and the domestic aspects of Marks' programme: between immigration restriction, protection, and the Union: 'These were questions which appealed to every working man, and which demand an early settle-ment: in a nutshell, the question which they had to decide was whether England shall be great or small.'[44]

The immigration question negotiated the space between the expe-rience of the East End electorate and imperial politics. It seized on a point of immediate experience to which the same patriotic deter-mination of policy could apply: in which the construction of 'us' as Englishmen became an object suitable not only for visceral pride derived from the empire but something which could fashion an understanding of the local economy. It is revealing that Marks had so removed himself from a discourse concerned with the constitu-tion that after the election he proposed that the naturalisation fee be reduced to one guinea.[45]

Most other Conservative candidates in the East End, such as H.S. Samuel in Limehouse and F.W. Isaacson in Stepney, used the immi-gration issue in a way similar to Marks.[46] In contrast, in Whitechapel the Conservative candidate, Colonel Le Poer Trench, continued to direct attention to what he portrayed as a Canute-like struggle against the registration of unnaturalised aliens. His comments on the social and economic effects of immigration were brief in com-parison, though he too did support statutory restriction.[47] As with C.T. Ritchie, the Home Secretary who unsuccessfully defended his seat at St George's in the East, this lukewarm attitude towards statu-tory immigration restriction was linked to an unwillingness to con-

43. *East London Observer*, 2 July 1892, p. 7.
44. *Ibid.*
45. *Ibid*, 23 July 1892, p. 7.
46. Although in these instances the issue was not so prominent and the Tory democrat tendency was not so pronounced. Nevertheless, Benskin presented himself to the electorate as 'one of themselves, a working man in every sense of the word'. If other candidates did not claim to be working men, at least they could present themselves as partisans in their cause. Isaacson emphasised that 'he had done all he could to further the interests of the working classes': *ibid*, 25 June 1892, p. 7; *ibid*, 2 July 1892, p. 6.
47. *Ibid*; *ibid*, 25 July 1892, p. 6.

ceal social distance. Ritchie was known as a reformer but his talent and inclination was for administrative improvements.[48] His main achievement was the Local Government Act of 1888. Both he and Trench remained determinedly patrician in their conceptions of a correct Conservative politics. They were not drawn to attempts to champion the sectional interests of the working classes and to attempt to dissolve for a moment the ranks of social distinction in an enthusiastic patriotic unity.

After 1900, as the anti-alien movement attracted thousands of supporters in the East End, the rhetoric of patriotism was matched by one of localism. This was the result, in part, of the emergence within the East End of a local leadership for the anti-alien movement. Increasingly the agitation was coloured by the concerns of local politics. This was given impetus by the creation of the London boroughs in 1899, which led to a new tier of local political leadership. It was also encouraged by the London Municipal Society – the Conservatives' organising force in London politics. In December 1901 the Society decided to organise local municipal associations throughout London because 'by that means only can the local interest, patriotism and enthusiasm be awakened'.[49] Anti-alienism was one important element in this cocktail.[50] In the East End, the attempt to ally the local community with a patriotic unity sometimes attained a mock-heroic effect such as when Thomas Dewar, MP for St George's in the East, pledged that 'his constant cry would be "England for the English" and "fair play for St George's and Wapping"'. But this inadvertent comedy expressed the politically serious attempt to combine traditions of localism with a Conservative, imperial and democratic patriotism. In the course of his speech Dewar identified the empire as a people's imperium whose greatness was founded upon statesmen such as Joseph Chamberlain who had risen from the 'rank and file'.[51]

48. P. Marsh, *The Discipline of Popular Government: Lord Salisbury's Domestic Statecraft 1881–1902* (Hassocks, 1978), pp. 161–2.
49. London Guildhall, records of the London Muncipal Society, MS 19526/1, minutes of annual general meetings, 16 December 1901.
50. *Ibid*, 17 and 14 December 1903. The LMS was rarely presented with political resolutions but in December 1903, one in favour of immigration restriction was carried and the previous year a similar resolution had been withdrawn pending the outcome of the Royal Commission on Alien Immigration. The emergence of this political project within the London Municipal Society coincided with a purge of free traders from its councils: a move which had been led by the Hon. Claude Hay, the anti-alien Conservative MP for Hoxton. On the change in the Society see K. Young, *Local Politics and the Rise of Party* (Leicester, 1975), p. 27. On Hay's view of the immigration question, see *JC*, 13 November 1903, p. 27.
51. *East London Observer*, 1 March 1902, p. 6. The same elements of localism and patriotism could also produce anti-Jewish comments such as the following

Sustained support for an Aliens Act came from those within the Conservative Party who hoped it would express a new relationship between their party, the working classes and the state. It was only after Salisbury's departure that this challenge to his practice of Conservative politics became seriously disruptive, most notably over tariff reform. But whereas the defeat of tariff reform signalled the defeat of radical Unionism, the Aliens Act represented one of its few victories.[52]

British Brothers and Conservative politicians

How successful was this attempt to use the issue of immigration to fashion a popular Conservative politics? The low rates of enfranchisement in East End constituencies make elections a poor guide to the popularity of any policy. Nevertheless some historians have credited anti-alienism with an important role in the Conservatives' political success in the East End between 1885 and 1900.[53] Paul Thompson, however, discounts its significance, and my own reading of the evidence supports his interpretation.[54] The 'alien invasion' was pressed more widely by Conservative candidates in 1892 than in 1895 in East End constituencies. Nevertheless, the Conservatives were routed in 1892 and regained their lost ground in 1895. In that year, in St George's in the East, H.H. Marks was elected. He perceived his victory as a triumph of the working-class Conservative vote, but like Isaacson in the Stepney constituency he had not raised the aliens issue. At the same time, in Poplar the anti-alien Liberal MP, Sydney Buxton, saw his vote decline by 7.1 per cent. There were exceptions to the overall inconsequentiality of immigration as an election issue. These included the fine showing by H.H. Marks in Bethnal Green North-east in 1892 and by William Evans Gordon and Claude Hay in Stepney and Hoxton respectively in 1906. In each case a Conservative fared unusually well in the face of a general

delivered by the Rev. E.G. Parry to a large gathering of the Whitechapel Primrose League: 'He did not like to be represented in Parliament by a Jew [applause] although he knew Mr Samuel well. He was sure of this, that Whitechapel would gain, very much by another representative [a voice, "An Englishman"]': *ibid*, 19 April 1902, p. 6. Stuart Samuel was Samuel Montagu's nephew and had inherited the seat from him in 1900. He had been born in England of English parents.

52. Marsh, *The Discipline of Popular Government*, pp. 50, 159, 235–6; A. Sykes, *Tariff Reform in British Politics 1903–13* (Oxford, 1979), pp. 1–11.
53. H. Pelling, *Social Geography of British Elections* (London, 1967), pp. 44–5, 58; Gainer, *The Alien Invasion*, p. 59.
54. P. Thompson, *Socialists, Liberals and Labour* (London, 1967), pp. 29–30.

swing to the Liberal Party, and all three campaigned powerfully on the point of alien immigration.[55]

The high points of popular support for an Aliens Act were not marked by electoral contests but by two great public meetings at the People's Palace in January 1902 and November 1903. The first was held under the auspices of the British Brothers League and the Londoners League, the latter organised by the Immigration Reform Association. Both attracted audiences of more than 4,000 people and both were marked by a display of vigorous enthusiasm for the cause. But support for the BBL was more extensive than this. At its first annual general meeting in August 1902, the BBL claimed a membership of 12,000, a figure confirmed later by William Stanley Shaw, the organisation's founder, after he had broken from it. But a petition gathered by the League amassed 45,000 signatures.[56]

The voice of propertied anti-alienism in the East End was articulated most consistently in the pages of the *Eastern Post*. More generally, the newspaper gave voice to one militant constituency among the property owners and small capitalists of the East End. In 1902 it complained that the people of Stepney were 'groaning under their increased burdens of rates and taxes'. In every London borough, rates increased by between 30 and 50 per cent between 1890–1906. In Stepney it was the latter figure which applied. Rates were a regressive tax, first, because the rate base was highest where needs were least, and, second, because the poor spent a higher proportion of their income on rent and hence on rates. The situation was aggravated by the decreasing control over expenditure exercised by the collecting authority.[57] The political responses to this situation were varied. Avner Offer has suggested that it contributed to the Liberal landslide of 1906.[58] But there were other responses: one was the periodic revival of ratepayer unions. A less sober reaction was the anti-alien agitation in the East End.

The rates burden was a constant theme of the *Eastern Post* in these

55. *Eastern Post*, 20 July 1895, p. 6. For the fluctuations of the Conservative and Unionist vote in East End constituencies between 1885 and 1906 see Pelling, *Social Geography of British Elections*, p. 43.

56. The League's own explanation of this disparity was that the poverty of many of its supporters prevented them from paying dues and thus payment was made optional: *Eastern Post*, 18 January 1902, p. 6; *JC*, 13 November 1903, p. 27; *ibid*, 31 October 1902, p. 9; *East London Observer*, 16 August 1902, p. 3.

57. Growing proportions were taken by other bodies: the London County Council, the Metropolitan Police, the Board of Guardians and the London School Board: *Eastern Post*, 25 January 1902, p. 6; *ibid*, 12 April 1902, p. 4; A. Offer, *Property and Politics 1870–1914: Landownership, Law, Ideology and Urban Development in England* (Cambridge, 1981), pp. 283, 288, 291.

58. *Ibid*, p. 241.

years. The newspaper was edited by J.L. Silver from 1892 until his death in 1902. Silver was the leading opponent of Jewish immigration on Stepney Borough Council. The *Eastern Post* advocated radical tax changes in the interest of 'the small tradesman and small professional man. Why cannot we impose a graduated tax such as obtains in Germany, which deals lightly with the small tradesman and small professional man, and becomes heavier in proportion as a man's income runs into plethoric thousands, is just one of those things which no sensible man can understand.'[59] In this context, immigration restriction could be offered as one painless, cheap answer to the problems of overcrowding and the shortage of house accommodation. It was preferable to other solutions proposed in the 1900 general election. These included the creation of a greatly enlarged sanitary inspectorate and the suggestion that councils should provide housing to deal with the predicament of those displaced by more rigorous application of the law, or that controls on municipal borrowing should be abolished. The advantage of immigration restriction was that it was expected to be cheap, and what little cost there was would be financed by the Treasury. A further advantage was that, unlike radical solutions which may have led to the creation of rent courts or the taxation of land values, immigration restriction did not bring into question the rights and privileges of property owners.

The support which anti-alienism attracted within the East End in these years came from among the working classes as well as from the shopkeepers and small manufacturers of the district.[60] The BBL was established in May 1901 to campaign for legislation to stem the tide of pauper aliens. Its first public meeting attracted 'a crowded working class attendance' which was 'enthusiastic and unanimous' in its opposition to immigration.[61] Similar reports can be found for other large anti-alien meetings. Before the People's Palace meeting in January 1902 the organisers prepared by enrolling 260 stewards, 'big brawny stalwarts, dock labourers, chemical workers from Bromley, and operatives from Bow, Bethnal Green and Mile End'.[62] It is difficult to go beyond this impressionistic assessment of working-class support. There was a tendency to identify support for the

---

59. *Eastern Post*, 19 April 1902, p. 4.
60. The rating question may have underpinned this. Rates had an immediate knock-on effect for tenants as they translated into rent rises where rates were compounded and paid by their landlord. From this point of view, until another way was devised to finance social policy, working-class tenants as much as landlords and businessmen stood to benefit from cheap local government.
61. *Eastern Post*, 11 May 1901, p. 5.
62. *Ibid*, 18 January 1902, p. 2.

League with the roughest elements of the working class. But it was the League's opponents who did this, and their descriptions should be treated with caution since this is how Liberals and most Jews undoubtedly wished to see the movement: as the unreason of the mob stirred up by agitators.[63]

The BBL blamed the immigrants for the housing crisis in the East End. Above all, the immigrants were accused of 'displacing' the native population. Used in this way the term 'displacement' pushed the grievances held against immigrants beyond a narrowly defined economic sphere – as the cause of high rents and overcrowding – to encompass the decline of community and an affront to a respectability that was seen to be peculiarly English. James William Johnson, a Stepney labourer who became chairman of the BBL executive, demonstrated this tendency to convert economic arguments into cultural ones when he gave evidence before the Royal Commission on Alien Immigration. Certainly, he blamed immigrants for high rents which led to the 'displacement' of English workers. But their removal from the East End was a moment of cultural disinheritance as well as of economic hardship: 'This great influx is fast driving out the native from hearth and home. . . . Some of us have been born here, others of us have come into it when quite young children, have been brought up here, educated here; some of us have old associations here of such a nature that we feel it a hardship to be compelled to part from.'[64]

Home and family were prominent also in explanations of the immigrants' success in the labour and housing markets. This was attributed to their willingness to live beyond the pale of values and practices attributed to the English family. This played on ideals and images which crossed class divisions. A shoe manufacturer commented that 'a respectable and honest man that wants to get an honest living and bring up his family could never compete with them', and that it was impossible 'to live decent' on their wages. An employee of his agreed: 'they work so much cheaper than the native workmen do . . . it affects anyone who wants to live decent on the price that these aliens earn for their weekly wage'.[65] James Johnson understood the cause of the immigrants' competitive success in a different way, but here too the family and the duties of a husband were central to his explanation. The alien's advantage, he said,

63. For example the *East London Observer*, 11 March 1902, p. 5 described its following as 'the frequenters of back street taprooms', and *JC*, 23 January 1903, p. 20 warned, 'once popular passion is aroused logical distinctions may come easily to be disregarded'.

64. *RCAI*, q. 8,558.

65. *Ibid*, qq. 1,829, 2,488.

stemmed from his ability to use the labour of his wife, whereas the Englishman kept his wife at home. In fact, Johnson drew on ideals of English working-class masculinity more than the real sexual division of labour in the immigrant household.[66] He expressed the expectation that 'being a husband was synonymous with providing support'.[67]

The unmanly character of the immigrant workers was further marked out by their concentration in occupations which did not require heavy manual labour. The less provident character of English workmen was attributed to the need of manual labourers to eat more.[68] The failures of organisation among immigrant workers were perceived by English trade unionists to express their want of manly virtues.[69] Jewish immigrants were similarly beyond the bounds of the milieu which gathered around the pub. This uncomfortable fact was recognised even by the internationalist Jewish socialists. In *Di Fraye Velt* Karl Liberman observed that the behaviour of 'roughs' and 'street boys' meant that 'there are certain streets in which the Jew cannot show his long nose without being hit and mocked'.[70] A policeman thought that the poor immigrants were peaceable because 'the Jews are not men enough to be rough'.[71] It is surely no coincidence, therefore, that anti-immigrant feeling became focused by the British *Brothers* League.

Among middle-class supporters of the BBL there was the same tendency to slip from an economic to a cultural understanding of the evils of immigration. A.T. Williams explained that casual and dock labourers were being forced out of the East End by landlords buying up property and demanding rents which aliens would pay by overcrowding. However, another cause of 'displacement', according to Williams, was that the immigrants were not neighbourly. Being un-neighbourly meant desecrating the Christian sabbath, storing

66. The census suggests that Jewish immigrant wives were marginally less likely than their English counterparts to work outside the home; I. Hourwich, 'The Jewish Labourer in London', *Journal of Political Economy*, December 1904, p. 92.
67. E. Ross, 'Fierce Questions and Taunts: Married Life in Working-Class London 1870–1914', in D. Feldman and G. Stedman Jones, eds., *Metropolis London: Histories and Representations Since 1800* (London, 1989), p. 224.
68. A belief which was translated into practice in another sphere, through the division of food in working-class households: *RCAI*, q. 8,859; Ross, 'Fierce Questions and Taunts', pp. 228–9.
69. GLRO, LCC, Special Committee on Contracts, presented papers, pp. 13, 28; J. Smith, 'The Jewish Immigrant', *Contemporary Review*, October 1899, pp. 322–5.
70. *Di Fraye Velt*, July 1892, p. 71; see too *RCAI*, q. 5,214.
71. London School of Economics, Booth Collection, B351, George Duckworth's police notes, p. 151.

rags in the yard, making noise from home work and the presence of girls and women on the streets in the evenings.[72] The importance of a quiet Sunday led many middle-class witnesses before the Royal Commission to complain of immigrants selling coke through the streets and moving house on Sundays.[73] However, other complaints were similar to those made by working-class anti-alienists. The affront to respectability was a recurring theme. Alderman Silver complained that 'every house seems to vomit forth hordes of people' and that 'no decent self-respecting Englishman would live under such conditions'. A tee-total midwife averred that 'they were not fit to be among English people'.[74]

Popular hostility to Jewish immigration drew on powerful representations of daily life, in the home, the family and the locality, and by extension in the nation as well. Historians have noted the importance of neighbourhood ties in determining patterns of working-class residence, and also of a high degree of endogamy within neighbourhoods.[75] This may have nurtured the rhetoric of family and localism. These communities were threatened by the 'alien invasion'. By representing the desecration of the home, a fount of working-class and middle-class respectability, as the immigrants' offence, the ground was defined on which diverse social groups – landlords, shopkeepers, skilled and casual workers – were able to coalesce in the anti-immigrant agitation.[76] This local agitation presented a vision of the nation that was located in the habits and *mores* of daily life. It emphasised the location of the nation in culture and community, something from which the immigrants were necessarily excluded.

The view expressed from the top of the Conservative Party was different. An identification of the political nation with home, family and community did not find a leader in the Conservative Party. The view in the East End was that Jewish immigrants were necessarily an alien and unwelcome element within the nation. But all attempts by militant anti-alienists to have the British-born children of immigrants categorised as anything other than British were rejected by

72. *RCAI*, qq. 1,641, 1,724.
73. *Ibid*, qq. 2,194–6, 2,423–8, 9,187, 10,174, 10,247.
74. *Ibid*, qq. 2,627, 9,418.
75. H. McLeod, *Class and Religion in the Late Victorian City* (London, 1974), table 4, pp. 296–7; E. Ross, 'Survival Networks: Women's Neighbourhood Sharing in London before World War One', *History Workshop Journal*, Spring 1983, appendix, p. 27.
76. On family ideals which crossed class boundaries see J. Lewis, 'The Working Class Wife and Mother and State Intervention, 1870–1918', in J. Lewis, ed., *Labour and Love: Women's Experience of Home and Family, 1850–1940* (Oxford, 1986), pp. 102–6.

the government. In this sense the Conservative leaders abstained from using culture and race as determinants of national identity. Conservative politicians advocated contingent rather than necessary exclusion: it so happened, they argued, that the immigrants damaged the nation's health and efficiency. During the debate on the second reading of the 1905 Aliens Bill, the Prime Minister, Arthur Balfour, told the Commons that in his view 'we have a right to keep out everybody who does not add to the strength of the community – the industrial, social and intellectual strength of the community'.[77] Similarly, William Evans Gordon called for 'a standard of health, character and efficiency for those we accept'.[78]

As these different evocations of the nation indicate, the elements brought together in the aliens agitation did not comprise a stable unity, and the popular element could not be manipulated at will.[79] The force of democratic patriotism was most clearly expressed at the great anti-alien meetings. The *East London Observer* noted that the response to the patriotic singing before the 1902 meeting was enthusiastic 'almost to excess'. Evans Gordon represented the meeting as one of 'the English people of East London . . . of all classes, of all creeds, of all shades of political opinion'.[80] This was a patriotism which elided distinctions between property-owners and the property-less, and between political parties: the question was represented as one of home and country – both of which they all possessed. Yet social and ideological differences within the anti-alien movement could not be repressed. This challenge was expressed through a form of populism which opposed the people to the political system. This stood in contrast to the leadership's political aim to incorporate the people within the Conservative Party. The disruptive impetus came from the grievances held by the League's extra-parliamentary leadership, above all from Silver, Shaw and the *Eastern Post*.[81] The political upshot of these attitudes and their conflict with the parliamentary support for immigration restriction became clear at the first demonstration at the People's Palace: 'Mr H. Robertson MP. . . . suggested that power should be given to the Home Secretary to

---

77. *Hansard*, 4th series, CXLV, col. 803, 2 May 1905.
78. *Hansard*, 4th series, CXXXIII, 1086–7, 25 April 1904. Akers Douglas complained 'we only get the refuse, if I may use that expression': *ibid*, CXXXII, col. 989, 29 March 1904.
79. The reverse is suggested in Garrard, *The English and Immigration*, p. 55; also in L. Gartner, *The Jewish Immigrant in England 1870–1914* (London, 1973 edn), p. 278. For a useful discussion and critique of the term 'social imperialism' see G. Eley, 'Defining Social Imperialism', *Social History*, May 1976, pp. 265–91.
80. *East London Observer*, 18 January 1902, p. 2.
81. *Eastern Post*, 4 January 1902, p. 2; *ibid*, 1 February 1902, pp. 4–5.

restrain anyone whom he did not think fit from coming into the country, but met with loud protests, and eventually he satisfied the audience by promising to support restrictive legislation.'[82] The popular element, far from stabilising right-wing politics, threatened to push it in more radical directions.[83]

On the part of the East End MPs, one response to the impolitic and potentially disruptive elements in the League was to try to take over the organisation. When he resigned from its presidency, William Stanley Shaw complained that 'the opposition and methods of my colleagues were too much for me. In the first place the politicians refused to support me unless I became a tool in their hands.'[84] But the appointment of the Royal Commission on Alien Immigration was the main way in which the vigour of the anti-alien movement was constrained. This removed the agitation indoors. Without going so far as to question the legitimacy of the parliamentary system, the anti-alienists were forced to bide their time while the Commission sat and deliberated.

Nevertheless, the popular agitation had an important influence on the chain of decisions that led to the passage of the Aliens Act in 1905. Throughout 1901, ministers assured restrictionist MPs that existing laws gave adequate powers to deal with the housing difficulty in the East End. Notwithstanding these statements, at the start of 1902, Gerald Balfour, the Secretary to the Board of Trade, advised the cabinet that 'the time has arrived when a further inquiry is desirable'. He pointed out that the government was pledged to act 'through the mouths of several of its most prominent members'.[85] Of course, this was a longstanding commitment which had hitherto been comfortably left unfulfilled. What made it pressing was the popular agitation, which gave legitimacy and urgency to the restrictionist enthusiasts within the Conservative Party, as well as the government's waning popularity.

The enormous meeting at the People's Palace on 14 January 1902 dramatised the government's problem. Several Conservative MPs and candidates spoke. S.F. Ridley, the member for Bethnal Green South-West, proposed the resolution which called upon the government to fulfil the pledges given by Lord Salisbury, Mr Ritchie, Mr Chamberlain and other Ministers of the Crown to prevent the immigration of undesirable aliens.[86] The government's response was to

82. *East London Observer*, 18 January 1902, p. 2.
83. F. Coetzee, *For Party or Country: Nationalism and the Dilemmas of Popular Conservatism in Edwardian England* (Oxford, 1990).
84. *JC*, 31 October 1902, p. 9.
85. PRO, CAB 37/59/146, alien immigration, 7 January 1902.
86. *East London Observer*, 18 January 1902, p. 2.

co-opt the parliamentary leadership of the agitation.[87] A price had to be paid for this, however. The Royal Commission which the government now appointed was weighted towards the restrictionists' cause. It included their most prominent spokesman, the MP for Stepney, William Evans Gordon, and he played an important role drafting its report. This, predictably, recommended legislation.[88]

The ultimate passage of the Aliens Act must be seen in the context of the government's internal divisions and its external unpopularity. Conservative electoral success after 1885 was based on a set of contingent conditions, not on underlying strength.[89] After 1900 the situation deteriorated: Salisbury departed, the 1902 Education Act offended and galvanised Liberal nonconformity and between the general election and May 1903 the government lost eight by-elections. In these circumstances, the Conservatives' electoral dominance in the East End could seem more precious than once it had, and working-class support more widely appeared to be worth courting. Immigration restriction became a matter of practical politics. Contemporaries were well aware that the Act was intended to serve as a piece of 'shop window' legislation for the working classes in the context of an impending election. It was widely assumed that working-class opinion was in favour of statutory restriction. This brought both a direct advantage and an indirect one, since the Aliens Bill evidently caused the Liberals some discomfort and disunity, as East End MPs and candidates urged Campbell-Bannerman not to oppose it.[90]

Apart from its apparent popularity, immigration restriction offered temporary circumvention of the two most pressing questions which divided the Conservative Party: finance and protection. One of the great merits of the Aliens Act was that it was expected to be cheap. The Home Office estimated that it would cost just £24,000 a year.[91] Moreover, immigration restriction allowed the government to

87. *The Times*, 23 January 1902, p. 7.
88. *The Times*, 23 January 1902, p. 7. The members of the Royal Commission were Lord James of Hereford, William Evans Gordon, Henry Norman, Alfred Lyttleton, Lord Rothschild, Sir Kenelm Digby and William Vallance. On the balance of the Commission see Gainer, *The Alien Invasion*, pp. 183–4. On drafting the report see Hereford and Worcester Record Office, Hereford papers, W. Evans Gordon to Lord James of Hereford, 7 June 1903. For the proposals see *RCAI*, pp. 40–3. On the detail of this phase see Gainer, *The Alien Invasion*, pp. 185–97.
89. J. Cornford, 'The Transformation of Victorian Conservatism', *Victorian Studies*, September 1963, pp. 35–66; E. Green, 'Radical Conservatism: The Electoral Genesis of Tariff Reform', *Historical Journal*, September 1985, pp. 674–81.
90. Gainer, *The Alien Invasion*, p. 148.
91. HO 45/10303/117267/51, cost of aliens bill, 4 May 1905.

adopt the language of efficiency and to offer a measure of protection which left trade untouched. Balfour was understandably unwilling to make this connection (though Chamberlain managed to embarass him by doing so).[92] It was legislation which would least inflame internal divisions, from which some credit could be expected in the country, and it sat comfortably with the party's image as the true defender of an empire which could not be entrusted to the Liberal Party.

The Aliens Act of 1905 required immigrants to demonstrate to an immigration officer that they were able to support themselves and their dependents 'decently'. In addition, criminals, the insane and anyone likely to become a charge on the rates through disease or infirmity were also excluded from the country. Immigrants who chose to appeal against the decision had the burden of proof placed upon them. Their appeal, moreover, was not to a court of law but to an Immigration Board comprised of three members.[93] At the last gasp, the Act did provide for asylum for immigrants seeking to evade 'persecution involving danger of imprisonment or danger to life or limb, on account of religious belief'. But this concession did not extend to aliens whose property or liberty, more widely defined, was endangered, as both Liberals and the JBD had proposed. Despite the harrying tactics of some Liberals, notably Winston Churchill, Charles Dilke, C.P. Trevelyan and Walter Runciman, the legislation duly passed into law.[93]

The Act was a victory for those in the Conservative Party who wanted to fashion a new political relation between the working class and the state, as a response to what were perceived to be the needs of an age of democracy and competitive empires. It was an expression of the collectivism of the right which, through the issue of tariff reform, would dominate Conservative Party politics in its years of opposition after 1906. It was an attempt to re-draw the boundaries of the state and the ideology of the nation.

92. *Hansard*, 4th series, CXLV, cols. 763–7, 2 May 1905.
93. The Act allowed for the expulsion of immigrants already resident in the country if they were sentenced to imprisonment by the courts, if they received poor relief within a year of arrival, were found living in overcrowded conditions, or convicted of vagrancy.

Chapter 12

English Jews and the Problems of Immigration

Civilisation and the ghetto

The Aliens Act marked the onset of a period in which an interventionist state transformed the nature of Jewish politics in England. I shall return to this in the last chapter. The following three chapters, however, deal with the years between 1880–1905, when Anglo-Jewish institutions continued to define the terrain of Jewish politics. In the present chapter I shall examine how the leaders and institutions of Anglo-Jewry responded to immigration. To what extent did they react as Jews? Conversely, how far were their responses shaped by opinions and dispositions which were common to the metropolitan propertied classes?

Scholars writing within a tradition of Jewish historiography have emphasised the pressures particular to the Jewish context. They have drawn attention to the confrontation between the East European immigrants and an acculturated and emancipated West European Jewish community. Endelman argues that English Jews feared that the immigrants would arouse anti-Semitism – something the aliens agitation appeared to confirm. Accordingly, English Jews vigorously promoted the immigrants' anglicisation and discouraged immigration.[1] More positively, Black claims that Anglo-Jewry fashioned a sub-culture the aim of which was 'to create patriotic Britons and to preserve Jewish culture'.[2] The key characteristic of these accounts is that Jewish interests provide the dynamic to Anglo-Jewish actions. The Gentile suggestion that immigrants contributed to social distress is seen to have been significant in this context not because it

1. T. Endelman, 'Native Jews and Foreign Jews in London, 1870–1914,' in D. Berger, ed., *The Legacy of Jewish Migration: 1881 and its Impact* (New York, NY, 1981), pp. 109–29.
2. E. Black, *The Social Politics of Anglo-Jewry 1880–1920* (Oxford, 1988), p. ix.

was shared but because it presented Jews in a critical light. Here, as in the case of labour history, accounts which emphasise the particularity of Jewish history have been challenged by historians writing in a marxist tradition. The goals of anglicisation and the practice of communal philanthropy have been seen to conceal motives rooted in class aspiration and class conflict. Writing about Manchester Jewry, Williams claims that the immigrants' anglicisation 'served most of all the class ambitions of the Jewish bourgeoisie'.[3] In his study of Rothschild Buildings, a block of model dwellings built in Whitechapel for the Jewish working classes, Jerry White characterised the rule book as 'a detailed programme of class control'.[4]

Even in the most favourable circumstances the enormous influx of East European Jews would have presented a challenge to the existing structures and practices of communal governance. But conditions were less than favourable. The onset of mass immigration immediately followed a period in which the patriotism of post-emancipation Jewry had been brought sharply into question. Further, by the late 1880s Jewish immigration had been instated as one key element in debates on sweated labour and overcrowding in London. The Jewish immigrants were seen as irritants to Jewish integration and as contributors to social distress.

In 1881 the *Jewish Chronicle*, surveying the community's poor immigrant population, reflected that 'our fair fame is bound up with theirs'. The problem it set Anglo-Jewish institutions was 'to aid these brethren of ours towards the higher stage of culture offered by English life'.[5] The anxiety which immigration excited in English Jews in the early 1880s reflected the post-emancipation debate on the Jewish problem. In the late 1870s Jews had defended themselves against accusations that they could neither be disinterested citizens nor free themselves from the narrowness of the *Talmud* and 'rabbinism'. The influx of East European immigrants threatened this representation of Judaism as progressive and of Jews as patriotic.

Even before 1882, Jewish life in Eastern Europe was comprehended in the shadow of the Jewish question at home. Some English Jews conceded that one cause of the pogroms was friction between Jewish money lenders and the Russian peasantry.[6] Moreover, according-

3. B. Williams, 'The Anti-Semitism of Tolerance', in A. Kidd and K. Roberts, eds., *City, Class and Culture: Studies of Social Policy and Cultural Production in Victorian Manchester* (Manchester, 1985), p. 92.
4. J. White, *Rothschild Buildings: Life in an East End Tenement Block, 1887–1920* (London, 1980), p. 54.
5. *JC*, 12 August 1881, p. 9.
6. See the comments of Serjeant Simon at the Anglo-Jewish Association on this point: *JC*, 1 July 1881, p. 6. F.D. Mocatta expressed disagreement with him, but

ing to the *Jewish Chronicle*, the Talmudic temper of Jewish scholarship in Russia meant that 'superstition . . . too often forms the ingredient of the mind of a Russian Jew'.[7] These criticisms of Russian Jewry were immediately deflected on to the imperial government. It was the legal restrictions on Jewish life in Russia which had stunted its economic and intellectual development. If the Tsar's Jews had their faults, the remedy was to accord them civil and legal equality. Nevertheless, the image of Russian Jewry as usurious and steeped in Talmudism was distinctly unhelpful in view of the criticisms of the financial interests and exclusiveness of English Jews. 'Half our race' lives in Russia and Poland, and 'whatever they are we are thought to be', the *Jewish Chronicle* commented in an editorial.[8] Russian Jews were advised 'to become less narrow and more cultured' and to replace 'the spectacles of the Talmud' with 'science' and 'common sense'. Six months later, once the raw 'Polaks' began to arrive in Britain in unprecedented large numbers, the desire to reform them, not only for their own sakes but for the sake of English Jews, became far more intense.

The conception of Judaism which Anglo-Jewish leaders had promoted presupposed another, traditional Judaism from which Anglo-Jewry was seen to have since evolved.[9] Inevitably the immigrants inhabited this 'other' Judaism. The point was made clear every time the Jewish East End was referred to as 'the ghetto': whether used as a pejorative term or as a sentimental one to evoke an authentic Jewish culture in contrast to the imitative materialism of Anglo-Jewry, the 'ghetto' represented a form of social life which was assuredly pre-modern. 'Russia today is like Spain of the sixteenth century,' commented the minister of Dalston synagogue.[10] In the eyes of their English co-religionists, East European Jews brought with them the 'almost oriental shackles' of the ghetto. Their language, Yiddish, was denigrated as 'a nondescript jargon of Hebrew and low German' – an unsuitable medium for western thought. Worse, 'un-English habits and thoughts' were nurtured even in Lon-

only insofar as he wanted to emphasise the view that Jews entered these trades not from choice but because other avenues were closed to them. A eulogistic assessment of Russian Jewry delivered by the Rev. A.L. Green in a letter to *The Times* was not typical of Anglo-Jewish opinion; the letter was reproduced in *JC*, 1 July 1881, p. 11.

7. *Ibid*, 21 October 1881, p. 9.
8. *Ibid*.
9. Montefiore, 'Is Judaism a Tribal Religion?', *Contemporary Review*, September 1882, p. 361.
10. Booth Collection, London School of Economics, B 197, p. 45. For a characteristic view of Russia see E. Lanin, 'The Demoralisation of Russia', *Fortnightly Review*, October 1891, pp. 463–86.

don by the institutional and associational life created by the immigrants: 'by the *khevras* or minor congregations where Pole meets
Pole and becomes more Polish than ever'.[11]

The ghetto signified a form of society that was 'tribal' and narrowly exclusive as well as backward. It was incompatible with emancipation. Insofar as Jewish immigrants bore the marks of the ghetto
they presented a problem of political integration. The point was
made forcefully in 1887 in the *St James Gazette*.

> Take the colony as it stands. Eliminate the idea that it represents an
> invasion and treat its members neither as foreigners nor as paupers. Look
> at them as citizens, ratepayers, heads of families and tradespeople. Inquire
> how far they fulfil the ordinary duties of civilised life as members of a free
> and independent community. The answer to that question might be given
> in a sentence: they never forget that they are Jews and that other people are
> Gentiles. They are a people apart. Long as they may live among us they will
> never become merged in the mass of the English population.[12]

At the same time as immigration was presented as a problem of
social policy there was a continuing perception of the problem of
immigration as one of political integration. In 1900, in his study
of *The Jew in London*, Charles Russell portrayed the Jewish East End
as 'a state within a state', a phrase which inevitably recalled earlier
controversies over emancipation.[13]

At the very least, civil equality demanded that Jews should obey the
laws of the country, even where these contradicted religious law. But
even this simple requirement presented problems. There was a fundamentally different relation between Jewish law and civil authority
in states which had granted Jews civil equality and those which had
not. In the Russian empire, where Jews were not regarded as equal
subjects, it was possible for Jewish law and self-government to retain
greater force than in a state such as Britain, in which Jews were equal
before the law and Parliament.[14] This difference underpinned conflict over the force of Jewish law. Anglo-Jewish communal leaders
attempted to prescribe the boundaries of Jewish law within the
British state. The JBD faced in two directions. It possessed close
connections with the state and it could use these to discipline immigrant behaviour which threatened to undermine emancipation. But
as the representative body of Jewry it could also attempt to win
concessions which would render that behaviour legitimate. As a

11. *JC*, 17 November 1876, p. 518; *ibid*, 16 February 1883, p. 9.
12. *St James Gazette*, 4 April 1887, p. 4.
13. C. Russell and H. Lewis, *The Jew in London* (London, 1900), p. 9.
14. I. Levitats, *The Jewish Community in Russia, 1844–1917* (Jerusalem, 1981).

result, disputes over the relation of Jews to British law not only brought some Jews into conflict with the state, it also threw into question the nature of authority within the Jewish community.

This was exemplified by controversy over the rules governing marriage and divorce. Jurisdiction over marriage and divorce was crucial to the authority exercised by the Chief Rabbinate and the JBD; it was the intersection of private life and public authority, and the basis of Jewish affiliation. The JBD had policed marriages for the state since 1835 and, at the same time, had used this position to consolidate its communal power. In 1880 the Board stated its interpretation of the official and unofficial scope of its powers and also made clear the intimacy of its relation to the state.

> Although the parliamentary powers of the Board in connection with marriages are confined to certifying secretaries as Jewish registrars it has always exercised a surveillance over these officers advising them on all cases of difficulty and doubt, and correcting abuses when the same have been brought to light, the Registrar-General readily avails himself of the agency of the Board for these purposes.[15]

In 1900 the Law and Parliamentary Committee of the JBD reported on individual cases of bigamy and desertion: '[They] are not isolated ones and indicate a system, adopted by numbers of foreign Jews, of living in defiance of their marital obligations and thus creating a scandal which reflects on the whole of the Jewish community.'[16] An unknown but apparently increasing number of immigrant Jews ignored the civil law when they married and divorced. One cause of the problem was that Jews who had married abroad but who wanted to divorce in Britain were generally unable to afford the legal costs, even if they sued *in forma pauperis*. In many cases the certificate which could prove their first marriage was lost and this created further obstacles. To evade these difficulties, foreign Jews would go to one of their own rabbis who would assist in acquiring a *get* – a divorce. These rabbis were sympathetic to the predicament of uprooted Jews and sanctioned divorce in cases of mutual consent, or when a husband had left the country and it was reasonable to assume that his wife had been permanently deserted. Unlike English law, Mosaic law regarded desertion as a legitimate cause for divorce.[17] These divorces led to re-marriages that were equally beyond the

---

15. Cited in GLRO, JBD A/13, minute book, meeting of the Law and Parliamentary Committee, 28 February 1892.
16. JBD, B2/13/2, *Report of the Law and Parliamentary Committee as to Jewish Marriages and Divorces*, 27 May 1900.
17. *Royal Commission on Divorce and Matrimonial Causes*, PP 1912–13, XX, qq. 41,428, 41,384, 41,447.

English law, as Jews either lied to registrars and presented themselves as bachelors or widowers, or failed to inform the registrar and underwent a religious ceremony only.[18]

These practices were brought to the notice of the 1912 Royal Commission on Divorce and Matrimonial Causes by the Chief Rabbi and the JBD. The Board's representatives perceived the *get* as an inducement to desertion rather than a sympathetic method of dealing with the problem once it had arisen. But the JBD gave greatest weight to the challenge posed by the recusant rabbis to the terms of Jewish emancipation. David Lindo Alexander, President of the Board, explained as follows:

> The position taken up by these rabbis is that it is their duty to administer the Jewish matrimonial law and that where the English law conflicts with Jewish law the former must give way. As regards Jewish divorces these foreign rabbis continue to grant them in spite of their knowledge of their want of legality. Every year cases of these so-called divorces are brought to the attention of the Board and their number is definitely on the increase.[19]

The Chief Rabbi admitted that 'to prevent the idea from going forward that we are not happy to uphold the law as it stands', the Jewish authorities had decided not to request desertion be recognised as sufficient grounds for divorce.[20] Where Jewish law and English law came into conflict he was content for the former to give way.

In fact, the legal situation was unclear. Opinion taken by the JBD when the 1857 Divorce Act was passed unanimously returned the view that the Act did not affect the status of divorces granted by the Jewish ecclesiastical authorities. It was only in 1866, when the Registrar-General no longer recognised these divorces, that they ceased to hold legal force. But as Judge Tindall Atkinson observed, if the opinion given by counsel in 1857 was correct then the rabbis in question were doing nothing illegal.[21] From the legal point of view at least, the JBD could have adopted an argument which defended the principle of rabbinical divorce.

The controversy was underpinned by the different relationship between the state and the Jewish population in East and West Europe. In both Russia and Poland, divorce needed only rabbinical authority to be valid. In Poland, civil approval for marriages was required only if transfers of property were involved. In Russia, responsibility for registration lay with the 'Crown Rabbi' and his failure

18.   *Ibid*, q. 41,384.
19.   *Ibid*, q. 41,467.
20.   *Ibid*, q. 41,447.
21.   *Ibid*, qq. 41,500, 41,482.

to comply with the law did not affect the validity of a marriage 'if the partners were *bona fide*'. [22] In Britain, however, one of the principal battles fought by the emancipationists had been to integrate Jews within the civil system of marriage and divorce on equal terms with non-Jews. A Jewish marriage became one instance of a particular religious ceremony. It was no longer part of a system governed by its own rules. [23]

The figure within the Jewish leadership who stood out against Adler and the Board on this issue was Moses Gaster, the *haham*, ecclesiastical head of the *Sephardi* community. He wrote to the Board's solicitor and secretary justifying his stand.

> The Board is there to vindicate the right of Jewish law and to defend the principles of our sacred faith . . . This question of giving a divorce is absolutely a religious question, in as much as according to Jewish law only a qualified rabbi is capable of granting [it] . . . no rabbi should be declared guilty of doing wrong when in the first place they do that which is commanded by the law of God. [24]

Gaster was born in Roumania and only came to Britain as an adult. His defence of the rights of the rabbinate and of God's law against the claims of the state probably expressed the opinion of the lesser rabbis in the East End who were granting illegal divorces. Gaster went on to advocate a different view of relations between Jews and the state, and another role for the Board: '[The function of the Board] is to safeguard the Jewish law and to protect observant Jews against the operation of hostile legislation which might interfere with the free exercise of their religious duties, to approximate the English law to the Jewish and to seek the recognition of the latter by the state.' [25]

Another area of difficulty, one which affected a more varied section of the Jewish population, arose from infractions of the laws regarding Sunday labour and trading. In the most practical way, these laws raised the question of what provision could be made for the beliefs and practices of Jews in a Christian society. The Factory and Workshop Act of 1878 allowed Jewish occupiers who kept their own sabbath to compensate for the loss of Friday evening and Satur-

22. *Ibid*, q. 41,384. See too Levitats, *The Jewish Community in Russia*, pp. 85–8.
23. G. Bartholomew, 'Application of Jewish Law in England', *University of Malaya Law Review*, July 1961, pp. 92–3; I. Finestein, 'An Aspect of the Jewish and English Marriage Law During the Emancipation: The Prohibited Degrees', *Jewish Journal of Sociology*, June 1965, p. 4.
24. University College London, Gaster papers, bound vol. 18. M. Gaster to C.H.L. Emmanuel, 17 January 1911.
25. *Ibid*.

day as working days. But although Jewish occupiers were able to open their premises on Sundays they were forbidden to open for 'traffic'.[26] Jewish masters objected that the law penalised them for observing their sabbath. The JBD took a sympathetic view of their complaint but its policy was to wait for a favourable opportunity to press for concessions.[27]

Employers, however, were not content to wait and they chose to break the law. Moreover, fierce competition led them to work seven days a week and in this way to abuse the provisions for Sunday labour. Their offences were publicised by the factory inspectorate in 1884 and again in 1895. In 1884 the Board's response was mild: it expressed regret and ventured to hope that publicity in the Jewish press would prevent further violations.[28] This contrasts sharply with the reaction in 1895. In that year J.B. Lakeman, the factory inspector who most came into contact with Jewish employers in London, was interviewed by the *Jewish Chronicle*. He complained that 'lately, some masters have got into the habit of engaging Gentile as well as Jewish workers – the former to work on Saturday, and the latter on Sunday. . . . They secure an unfair advantage over the Gentile master, who can only have his shop open on Saturday and must close entirely on Sunday.'[29] The Law and Parliamentary Committee of the Board responded decisively. It obtained a list of the names and addresses of Jewish factory and workshop occupiers in London from the Home Office and addressed a warning to them. This leaflet was then printed in English, Yiddish, German and Dutch and distributed by the factory inspectorate.[30] The circular concluded with a threat that those who violated the law would receive the punishment they deserved, and that the Board would not deny the inspectorate any assistance.[31]

The origins, distribution and content of the circular clearly reveal one set of linkages between the JBD and the state. Its terminology highlighted the nature of the relationship between the two and the threat which law-breaking employers presented. The concessions given by the 1878 Act were described as 'privileges', not as 'rights'; privileges which might legitimately be withdrawn by the state should

26. JBD A/12, minute book, meeting of the Board, 20 May 1879.
27. JBD, B2/18/1, statement of the law of England as to Sunday observance, 28 January 1890.
28. JBD A/12, minute book, meeting of the Board, 16 July 1884.
29. *JC*, 8 June 1895, p. 15.
30. JBD C13/1/4, minute book of the Law and Parliamentary Committee, 11 December 1895; JBD A/13, minute book, meetings of the board, 19 January 1896, 17 February 1896, 15 March 1896.
31. A copy of the circular can be found in *ibid*, 19 January 1896.

they continue to be 'so shamefully abused'.[32] The state could take
care of itself. But the behaviour of the immigrants also threatened
the Board's claims to represent Anglo-Jewry: 'The privileges having
been obtained by this Board as the representative body of the Anglo-
Jewish community, the good faith and honour of the community
were pledged to the state that the conditions attached to those
privileges should be loyally and faithfully observed.'[33] By working
seven days a week Jewish occupiers were doing more than breaking
sabbatarian legislation: they also threw into question the political
relations within the Jewish community and between it and the
state.

The concept of 'privileges' which the immigrants disregarded
served to place the entire Jewish community in a subordinate position in a Christian state. At the same time, it served to entrench the
position of the elite within the Jewish community. Whereas 'rights'
could be demanded by a democratic or popular movement, 'privileges' were granted by the sovereign power. The concessions of 1878
were presented as 'a gracious and generous act on the part of our
legislators.'[34] The ability of the Anglo-Jewish notables to approach
the government as members of the same governing class and to
obtain concessions for the Jewish community was one basis of their
communal rule. In this way the politics of the Jewish question not
only dealt with the interaction of Englishmen and Jews: it also concerned the articulation and distribution of power *within* the Jewish
community.

Paupers and refugees

Jewish immigrants rapidly came to be seen in the context of pauperism and poverty as well as Jewish emancipation. The consensus
within the immigration debate noted in the last chapter extended to
the leaders of Anglo-Jewry. Indeed, until the passage of the Aliens
Act it was the communal relief agencies rather than the state or
popular movements which represented the greatest threat to an
immigrant's continued residence in London.

It was in the form of the JBG that immigrants were most likely to
encounter Anglo-Jewry. Charitable relief made up a part of the
income of at least one quarter of Jewish families in London.[35] The

32. *Ibid.*
33. *Ibid.*
34. *Ibid.*
35. In 1882 Joseph Jacobs estitmated that 24 per cent of Jewish families in London
   came into this category: J. Jacobs, *Studies in Jewish Statistics: Social, Vital,
   Anthropometric* (London, 1891), p. 14.

burden of the Jewish poor fell almost exclusively on the Jewish community and not on the parish.[36] It was the JBG, above all other institutions, which provided relief for the Jewish poor. In practice this meant that it was the elite of metropolitan Jewry which took financial responsibility for the communal poor; as with the other main London Jewish charities, most of the JBG's income came from forty leading families.[37] In this way the leaders of Anglo-Jewry affirmed and displayed their allegiance to the Jewish community, demonstrated their social responsibility and hoped to prevent the Jewish poor from becoming a burden or an issue within the larger society.[38] In this sense poor relief was a Jewish activity. But in other respects this was not the case.

The JBG was the instrument through which progressive principles of poor relief were applied in a particular denominational instance. The Board's practices were distinguished from those of the parish Boards of Guardians because, in the first instance, its functions were defined more widely than theirs. The JBG carried out programmes of apprenticeship, of emigration and of loan provision, as well as the operations of non-Jewish voluntary bodies such as the Charity Organisation Society which concentrated on 'the deserving poor'. Moreover, unlike the parish authorities the JBG could not resort to the workhouse; its work was necessarily directed to outdoor relief. In the 1860s the Board had been a pioneer among those who developed a practice of poor relief which rejected the absence of a curative component from the 1834 Poor Law.[39] These principles were re-stated in the Board's annual report for 1887: 'A system of repression of pauperism by means of starvation will continue to be cast aside in favour of guiding the humbler classes to self-helpfulness; aiding them to cope with their difficulties instead of leaving them ruthlessly to overcome them.'[40] But the Board's responsibility for the undeserving poor prevented it from implementing this principle thoroughly. In periods of economic depression it adopted a more disciplinary stance.

36. The only exception was the provision of medical relief: Black, *The Social Politics of Anglo-Jewry*, p. 158.
37. *Ibid*, p. 97.
38. V.D. Lipman, *A Century of Social Service, 1859–1959: The Jewish Board of Guardians* (London, 1959), pp. 8–10; T. Endelman, 'Communal Solidarity and Family Loyalty among the Jewish Elite of Victorian London', *Victorian Studies*, Spring 1985, pp. 505–7.
39. Lipman, *A Century of Social Service*, pp. 27–31. This is the basis of the argument made in Stallard, *London Pauperism amongst Jews and Christians* (London, 1867).
40. JBG, *29th Annual Report* (London, 1888), p. 10; see also JBG, *24th Annual Report* (London, 1882), p. 7.

It is perhaps necessary in some instances to draw a line which may appear somewhat harsh. In order to force some people to labour who otherwise would be only too willing to exist on charity . . . [while this is mitigated in cases where women and children would suffer] no such sentiment applies to single able bodied men, these have, during the past year, more than ever been forced to become independent of charity.[41]

Before 1882 the Board regarded immigration as just one source of the Jewish poor in London. Understandably, the unprecedented levels of immigration in late 1881 and 1882 were received as a temporary emergency by Jews and non-Jews alike.[42] The Mansion House Russo-Jewish Relief Fund was administered as a separate committee of the Board and in this way a formal distinction was established between the refugees and the majority of the Jewish poor. Those classified as 'refugees' were offered extraordinary treatment. As a deterrent to immigration, the remainder were ineligible for any relief until they had been in the country for six months. In contrast, some 'refugees' were taught a trade, others were given tools, and families were supplied with clothing, furniture and utensils with which to set up home. There was a greater preparedness to allow disbursements to take the form of gifts, rather than the loans which the Board preferred for anything other than weekly or special allowances. Generally, the Board hoped that its help would be of a once-and-for-all sort, but in the case of the refugees its officials accepted that 'they will for some time require careful watching and from time to time assistance'.[43]

But other considerations meant that the distinctive category of 'refugee' could not be maintained so clearly. In view of the legal disabilities under which all Russian Jews lived, any definition of who was or was not a refugee contained an arbitary element.[44] This was heightened by attempts to distinguish between the deserving and undeserving poor. The Russian-Jewish poor were assumed to be susceptible to the same moral failings as the poor in general. The administrators of the Mansion House Fund were anxious to discover imposters who had not left 'disturbed districts' but who evidently had been attracted to London by a large fund being 'generously

41. JBG, *29th Annual Report* (London, 1887), pp. 16–17.
42. JBG, *23rd Annual Report* (London, 1882), p, 7; JBG, *24th Annual Report* (London, 1883), p. 7.
43. *Ibid*, pp. 62, 65–6.
44. In 1890 the report of the Russian-Jewish Fund conceded that in many parts of Russia Jews were not subject to open persecution; conditions were such that it was 'difficult, even if not impossible for the poor Jews of the district to live in peaceful effort to earn their livelihoods'. JBG, *31st Annual Report* (London, 1890), p. 67.

dispensed'.[45] In 1892 the Board complained that there were 'numerous helpless cases which have wandered to London but which need not, and should not have left places in Russia where they were living unmolested, even if only in a struggling condition'.[46] Immigrants who failed to satisfy the Russo-Jewish Committee that they were refugees inevitably applied to the Board and so confirmed their categorisation as 'paupers'.[47] Even the treatment of immigrants who were deemed to be genuine refugees was predicated upon a wider view of the social problem. In 1891 the Fund's trustees reported that their constant concern had been 'as far as possible to prevent any increased congestion in the overcrowded districts of London'.[48] Clearly, there had been a desire to bring uniquely sympathetic practices of relief to the Russian Jewish refugees. But the principles of Jewish obligation were eroded by assumptions concerning the capacity of the poor for demoralisation in the face of a large fund, and further broke down in the face of the principles of poor relief generally held among the philanthropic classes in the capital.

Anglo-Jewish agencies did more than cajole and discipline applicants for poor relief into a state of independence. They returned thousands to Eastern Europe. How are we to assess the policies of repatriation and emigration pursued by the Jewish Board of Guardians, the Russo-Jewish Committee and by another Jewish philanthropic institution, the Poor Jews' Temporary Shelter? The men who administered these institutions presented the policies as central to their practice throughout the period. The Shelter was from its early days an agent of repatriation as well as a refuge. As a house of first call for thousands, whose officials met boats and trains laden with Russian Jews, it was well placed to act in this way. In 1888, before a House of Commons Select Committee, the Shelter's vice-president, Hermann Landau, took credit for the institution as 'the means of preventing a great number of people remaining here ... and of assisting them to return to their home country'.[49] The JBG's honorary secretary was not to be outdone; he claimed, 'it is one of our largest operations sending people back who, having wandered here,

45. JBG, *24th Annual Report* (London, 1883), p. 66.
46. JBG, *33rd Annual Report* (London, 1892), pp. 9–10.
47. JBG, *27th Annual Report* (London, 1886), pp. 12–13.
48. This was achieved by a programme of emigration and repatriation: YIVO, New York, NY, Mowshowitch Collection, 10,804–7, Mansion House Fund for the Relief of Russian Jews, *Report of the Trustees*, 1886–91. Between 1882–90 the Russian Jewish Committee spent £2,105 on cases remaining in London, whereas £13,580 was spent on repatriation and emigration. These are figures compiled from JBG, *Annual Reports* for 1882–90 and from the *Royal Commission on Alien Immigration*, PP 1903, IX, q. 15,914.
49. *Select Committee on Emigration and Immigration*, PP 1888, XI q. 2,183.

prove themselves to be useless or helpless, and to those whom we did not think fit to send forward we refused any other relief than that of sending them back to their home'.[50] Fifteen years later, when the President of the Board gave evidence to the Royal Commission on Alien Immigration, he argued that there was little need for the government to intervene in the work of immigration restriction since the Board had the matter in hand.[51]

It might be objected that the representatives of Anglo-Jewry were likely to emphasise this aspect of their work before an audience convened to examine immigration as a problem. Nevertheless, the propaganda was also fact. Between 1881–1906 the Board returned over 24,000 Jewish immigrants to Eastern Europe; the Russo-Jewish Committee repatriated over 7,000 between 1882 and 1906.[52] One gauge of the relative significance of these figures is that together they comprise 56 per cent of the increase in the total number of Russians and Russian Poles in London between 1881 and 1911.

All agencies insisted that repatriation was undertaken with the consent of those who made the journey. The choices available, however, were constrained by poverty and dependence, as L.L. Cohen explained to the Royal Commission on Alien Immigration: 'He [the applicant] tells us he cannot succeed without charity. He has been here say nine months. We say: "if you cannot succeed here, and as you had nothing to bring you here you had better go back". He rather demurs the first time, but the second time he agrees and goes.'[53] According to N.S. Joseph those chosen for repatriation were 'starved' out of the country.[54] They were often single, without skills or relatives; they seem to have been powerless to resist.[55]

In many respects the aid given to Jewish migrants to travel on to Australia, the Cape, Canada and above all the United States of America must be distinguished from repatriation. Yet the operations

---

50. *Ibid*, q. 3,553.
51. *RCAI*, q. 15,390.
52. The figures are compiled from JBG annual reports for 1881–1906. For the Russian-Jewish Committee see JBG, *47th Annual Report* (London, 1907), p. 106; the figures for the Board itself are taken from the annual returns of the relief committee giving the number of individuals emigrated and their destinations. Very few of the cases handled by this committee were sent anywhere other than Eastern Europe.
53. *RCAI*, q. 15,691.
54. *Ibid*, q. 16,234.
55. Their isolation is indicated by the small number of individuals per case repatriated by the JBG relief committee as compared to the number of individuals per case assisted onwards to the United States, the Cape or Australia by the emigration committee. The former figure varied between 1.4 and 1.8 in this period, the latter between 1.9 and 3.2: JBG, *Annual Reports* for 1881–1906.

were similar insofar as both were chiefly concerned to remove immigrant Jews from the labour and housing markets. The JBG emigration committee assisted over 17,500 individuals to emigrate between 1881 and 1906; the Russo-Jewish Committee assisted a further 7,500.[56] Emigration and repatriation were two of the foundations of Anglo-Jewish social policy in these years. The percentage of 'new cases' treated in this way was never lower than 30 per cent and in 1900 the figure was as high as 61 per cent.[57]

The leading figures in the provision of Jewish poor relief were also involved in philanthropy for the non-Jewish poor.[58] This institutional and personal integration extended to policy as well. Repatriation was undertaken for similar reasons to those which led non-Jews to oppose immigration – although, as we shall see, these were not the only reasons.[59] The JBG responded to public debate in the 1880s with mimetic speed. In 1884 the re-appointment of a sanitary committee by the Board was their contribution to the panic-stricken apprehension of London slum life which also led to the appointment of the Royal Commission on Housing in March of that year.[60] After 1884, as the depression continued, and was compounded by severe winters, it was London's overcrowded labour market which came to focus the social problem in the capital.[61] In 1885 the effects of immigration on the East End labour market emerged as a point of concern. In that year the JBG announced it would discourage immigration until empolyment was more easily available. In March 1886 it observed ominously that 'the state of our poor already here must not and cannot be ignored'.[62]

The Board placed the problem of immigration in the context of a contracting labour market.[63] The immigrants were the most tractable if not the most significant element of the crisis; efforts could be

56.   *Ibid.*
57.   *Ibid.* In this usage the JBG included among those emigrated the numbers of new cases who returned to Eastern Europe.
58.   Lipman, *A Century of Social Service*, appendix IV. For example, F.D. Mocatta was a member of the Charity Organisation Society, Sir Leonard Lionel Cohen represented the JBG on that body and Sir Benjamin Louis Cohen was President of the London Orphans Asylum.
59.   JBG, *29th Annual Report* (London, 1888), p. 17. Repatriation was not a policy invented to deal with the difficulties of mass immigration after its onset in 1881–2 and had been practised throughout the Board's existence.
60.   The report published in *The Lancet* on the sanitary conditions in which 'Polish tailors' lived and worked in the East End added a particular urgency to the question: JBG, *26th Annual Report* (London, 1885), p. 9; G. Stedman Jones, *Outcast London* (Oxford, 1971), pp. 222–3.
61.   *Ibid*, pp. 291–4; J. Harris, *Unemployment and Politics: A Study in English Social Policy, 1886–1914* (Oxford, 1972), pp. 51–8.
62.   JBG, *27th Annual Report* (London, 1886), pp. 12–13.
63.   *Ibid*; JBG, *28th Annual Report* (London, 1887), p. 15.

made to discourage them from coming and they were packed off elsewhere in increasing numbers. In 1888 the Board's honorary secretary explained that the six-month rule was being disregarded, 'in order to get rid of surplus foreign labour'.[64] This formulation, which echoed the analysis of those non-Jewish observers and politicians who favoured statutory restriction, was not an isolated one. In the following example, from the Board's report for 1894, commonplace restrictionist arguments are applied to the specific conditions of the Jewish poor.

> The conclusion which is irresistibly forced upon it [the Board] is that the extent of recent immigration has been out of proportion to the volume of those trades in which Jews are mainly engaged; the result being a severe struggle for existence in which native Jews hold their own but which presses acutely on both settlers and foreigners.[65]

At the turn of the century responses to the housing crisis among Anglo-Jewish observers illustrate that the restrictionists' concern with the effects of immigration was, once again, shared by many people who did not support statutory restriction. The arrival in Britain in 1900 of thousands of Roumanian Jews made the Anglo-Jewish community aware more acutely than ever of the problem of numbers. The JBG wrote a memorandum to an international relief agency, the Jewish Colonisation Association, asking them to prevent immigration to Britain, so far as was possible. 'Anybody with eyes to see must know that there are limits to the receptive capacity of this country,' they pleaded.[66]

The debate over immigration was, in reality, not between restriction and unlimited immigration but over whether the state or the institutions of Anglo-Jewry should be the instrument of regulation. The JBG report for 1887 argued that its own efforts in repatriation and emigration made legislation unnecessary.[67] In 1902 the President of the Board did concede there should be legislation to prohibit the entry of 'undesirables', and within this category he included those with a physical incapacity, the criminal and those involved in immoral trades.[68] But in addition there was another category, that of 'failures', who were repatriated by the Board and who should remain outside of any legislation, he argued. It would remain the task of the JBG to police these.[69]

64. *Select Committee on Emigration and Immigration*, q. 3,509.
65. JBG, *36th Annual Report* (London, 1895), p. 13.
66. *JC*, 26 June 1900, p. 15.
67. JBG, *29th Annual Report*, p. 13; see also *Select Committee on Emigration and Immigration*, q. 3,509.
68. *RCAI*, q. 15,661.
69. *Ibid*, qq. 15,319, 15,720–3. Both civil servants and supporters of statutory

Historians have shrunk from suggesting there was any connection between the actions carried out by the JBG, among other organisations involved in repatriation, and the measures advocated by proponents of an Aliens Act.[70] Jewish institutions are seen to have acted from peculiarly Jewish considerations: from fear of anti-Semitism, not from a consensus of opinion regarding the social consequences of immigration. But it should be clear that the policies of the JBG shared the assumptions of the propertied classes concerning the provision of poor relief, the organisation of charity and the consequences of unlimited immigration.

The Jewish question and the social problem

Although Anglo-Jewish responses to immigration held many beliefs in common with the more general understanding that Jewish immigration was a misfortune, it increasingly came to be inflected by Jewish considerations. In 1891 a new surge of immigration and a severe winter took the numbers dealt with by the JBG and the Russo-Jewish Committee to record levels.[71] The Board's income was barely equal to the situation. In the summer of 1893 it went into debt and was forced to borrow £1,000 from its own bankers.[72] This was the immediate background to the 'new departure' which quickly dominated the policy of Anglo-Jewish poor relief.

The main proponent of these changes was N.S. Joseph.[73] Joseph criticised the Board's methods as old-fashioned and, in particular, he argued that the rota committee was incapable of differentiating between the deserving and undeserving poor. In part, the 'new departure' was an attempt to re-draw this line more clearly. The reforms were a more complex formulation of an older policy. Joseph spoke in the name of expertise and called for a more highly calibrated classification of the poor.[74] The first function of the new

restriction were quick to point out that the Jewish authorities themselves were engaged in repatriating thousands to Eastern Europe: PRO, HO 45/10303/117267/18, memorandum on Jewish deputation to the Home Secretary, 17 May 1904; *Hansard*, 4th series, CXXXIII, cols. 1086–8, 25 April 1904.

70. Most recently Black, *The Social Politics of Anglo-Jewry*.
71. Lipman, *A Century of Social Service*, table 1, p. 280.
72. JBG, *35th Annual Report* (London, 1894), p. 18.
73. Joseph was an architect and longstanding communal worker. Born in 1834 he became brother-in-law to the Chief Rabbi: *JC*, 16 December 1904, p. 10.
74. 'The first difficulty arises from the heterogenous nature of the refugees . . . it is clear that numerous classes must not be treated in the same manner all alike as paupers; and that the first step must be sufficient investigation and . . . to classify the refugees under fairly defined categories and then to deal with each category on settled principles': *ibid*, 10 March 1893, pp. 15–16.

categories was to determine the destination of immigrants who appeared before the Russo-Jewish Committee. Joseph explained the new procedure:

> All fit subjects for emigration – the sturdy hearty workmen with families, not too large or too young, would be promptly, very promptly assisted to emigrate, so long as America will continue to receive immigrants. All those whose physical, mental, or trade incapacity is such as to yield no hope or chance of achieving self-support in this country, all the indolent loafers and parasites, must be promptly, very promptly, returned to their native country and in the event of a refusal must be denied all help. This principle which will be the true deterrent to further influx has long been recognised by the Russo-Jewish and Conjoint Committees, but its practice has not always been rigidly enforced.[75]

The counterpart to a more disciplinary stance towards the 'impossibles' was a greater effort to incorporate the majority. The new role given to personal contact with the poor was the most significant innovation in the organisation of relief. Hitherto, the Russo-Jewish Committee did not have a visiting committee and the JBG's volunteers had confined their activity to periodic visits to those in receipt of weekly allowances. Under the new system the visitors were placed between an applicant for relief and the adjudicating committee.[76] Wherever possible there was to be continuity of visitation by the same worker. Joseph instructed the Russo-Jewish Committee's visitors to impress their 'influence and personality on each of your protégés so that they may regard you as a personal friend whose counsel they will prize, whose approval they will court and whose censure they will strive to avoid'.[77] Women were seen to have a special role here, instructing and consoling the poor and providing the foot soldiers for this army of volunteers.[78]

These innovations – visitation, feminisation, case work and a more rigid classification of the poor – drew on trends in social policy and social throught outside of the Jewish community.[79] But the 'new departure' was not only an illustration of Anglo-Jewry following philanthropic fashion. It also expressed their heightened apprehen-

75. *Ibid*, 3 February 1893, p. 15. The emphasis upon 'a sustained system of repatriation' was repeated in subsequent years: JBG, *36th Annual Report* (London, 1895), p. 14; JBG, *38th Annual Report* (London, 1897), p. 14.
76. JBG, *35th Annual Report* (London, 1894), p. 63.
77. *JC*, 3 February 1893, p. 15.
78. Black, *The Social Politics of Anglo-Jewry*, p. 92.
79. J. Fido, 'The Charity Organisation Society and Social Casework in London', in A. Donajgrodski, ed., *Social Control in Nineteenth Century Britain* (London, 1977), pp. 207–30; F. Prochaska, *Women and Philanthropy in Nineteenth Century England* (Oxford, 1980); Stedman Jones, *Outcast London*.

sion as Jews at the consequences of immigration. Joseph warned, 'in ten or fifteen years, the children of the refugees of to-day will be men and women, constituting in point of numbers the great bulk of the Jews of England. They will drag down, submerge and disgrace our community if we leave them in their present state of neglect.'[80] In 1893 the same point was made more soberly in the Board's report, in which it explained why the principles of the 'new departure' had been adopted: 'The reputation of the community is obviously a subject which touches vitally and directly on all classes, and it is certain that the fair fame of the Jews in England is intimately bound up with, if not dependent upon the manner in which they apply themselves to grapple with this problem of the care of their poor.'[81]

The sharpened fears of Anglo-Jewish policy makers were due to the combination of increasing levels of immigration with an ominous turn to the debate on social policy. The 'new departure' reflected the perception that immigration was a long-term problem and no longer a temporary emergency. In the 1880s it was still possible for English observers, Jewish and non-Jewish, to believe that the flow of immigration was a short-term phenomenon that could be attributed to the extraordinary events of 1881–2.[82] The unprecedentedly high levels of immigration at the start of the 1890s left this view untenable. It became increasingly apparent that the immigrants were to be a growing and permanent component of the Jewish population in England. Measures had to be taken to deal with the increasing numbers, as Joseph argued with characteristic urgency, 'to convert such of them as are destined to remain with us into good useful British citizens, as speedily as possible'.[83] Similarly, in 1894 the Russian-Jewish Committee reported that 'their great aim has been by direct influence to improve and Anglicise them and to render them self supporting'.[84]

But the new priority given to anglicisation did not reflect rising numbers alone. It was also a response to the new place of Jewish immigration in discussions of the social problem. Increased immigration in 1890 and 1891 coincided with the splintering of the disparate reformers who had coalesced to face the threat of the residuum and the 'bitter cry of outcast London'. The career of Lord Dunraven illustrates the process. A Tory democrat, Dunraven was

---

80. *JC*, 3 February 1893, p. 16.
81. JBG, *35th Annual Report* (London, 1894), p. 11. On the adoption of Joseph's ideas, see *JC*, 16 December 1904, p. 10.
82. *Select Committee on Emigration and Immigration*, q. 3,643.
83. *JC*, 3 February 1893, p. 15.
84. JBG, *35th Annual Report* (London, 1894), p. 67.

political mobilisation

instrumental in establishing the House of Lords Select Committee on Sweating in 1888. To his dismay, the Committee came to the view that a sweating system did not exist, and he dissented from its recommendations, which were limited to sanitary reform. The report, Dunraven argued, gave the impression that the people themselves were to blame for the conditions in which they worked, 'and that such matters as the abuse of sub-contracting, intense competition of capital and the influx of a certain class of foreign labour, and other matters of that kind have little or nothing to do with the sweating system'.[85] In the spring of 1891 he established the Association for the Prevention of Immigration of Destitute Aliens.[86] The immigration question had emerged as a separate focus for political mobilisation.

The more responsibility taken by native Jewry for the immigrants, or the more responsibility they were forced to take by the anti-alien campaign, the more important it was that Russian Jews should conform to Anglo-Jewry's representation of them as law-abiding, industrious refugees who rapidly underwent anglicisation. The first step was to encourage the immigrants to speak English. It was only at this stage that the Russo-Jewish Committee began to hold English classes, and in 1894 it published a Yiddish-English manual. A Location and Information Bureau was also established. Optimistically, it was hoped that it would ease the congestion of the local labour market through its operation as a labour exchange and also draw applicants away from the East End.[87] Allied to the policy of dispersal was the goal of anglicisation. The Chief Rabbi observed that 'in the country foreign Jews become anglicised far more rapidly than in London and it is desired to make London conditions approximate to country conditions as much as possible'.[88]

Whatever deficiencies remained in the adult immigrants had to be eradicated in their children.[89] Of course, one task of the elementary schools of the East End was to render Jewish children truly English. The headmaster of Deal Street Board School believed his pupils would 'develop into intelligent, capable and patriotic English citizens, giving of their best to their adopted country'.[90] But from the

85. *Hansard*, 3rd series, CCCXLV, col. 285, 9 June 1890.
86. B. Gainer, *The Alien Invasion: The Origins of the Aliens Act of 1905* (London, 1971), pp. 61–4; J.A. Garrard, *The English and Immigration 1880–1910* (London, 1971), pp. 30–1.
87. JBG, *34th Annual Report* (London, 1893), p. 67; L. Gartner, *The Jewish Immigrant in England, 1870–1914* (London, 1973 edn), p. 239.
88. London School of Economics, Booth Collection, B197, religious influences (Jews), p. 9.
89. JBD, B2/1/1, 'The Aliens Bill, 1905'; RCAI, q. 16,332.
90. *Ibid*, q. 18,868.

mid-1890s the work of the schools was supplemented by the efforts of clubs. A Jewish Girls' Club had existed since 1888 but it was not until a decade later that a rash of boys' clubs were established.

The scope of anglicisation inevitably changed as the content of English identity developed. It became decreasingly adequate for anglicisation merely to mean obeying the law and adopting a sanitised form of Judaism. By the late 1890s the project of anglicising the immigrants was being coloured by visions of the imperial nation.[91] In this respect, the principal hopes of communal workers were placed in the children of adult immigrants. The anti-alien movement was confronted by glowing reports of the progress made by 'the second generation'. In the 1890s a number of youth clubs and a Jewish Lads Brigade were established with the aim of nurturing the proper virtues among the young: the JLB in 1895, the Brady Street Club for Jewish Boys in 1896, the Stepney Lads Club in 1900, the Victoria Working Boys Club a year later and, in 1905, the Hutchinson House Club. At a parade of the Jewish Lads Brigade the Chief Rabbi affirmed that he was 'a profound believer in muscular Judaism. . . . For unhappily our fathers have for many hundreds of years been pent up within darkened ghetto walls and had but scant opportunity given to them for developing their bodies. This has tended to make us somewhat lacking in stamina and nerve, rather limp and narrow chested.'[92] Physical and moral well-being were, of course, seen to be complementary qualities. The commander of the Brigade explained that its aim was 'to instil into the rising generation all that is best in the English character, manly independence, honour, truth, cleanliness, love of active health giving pursuits, etc. . . .'.[93]

*

Anglo-Jewish leaders responded to immigration both as members of the propertied classes and as English Jews. Historians have made sweeping claims for the salience of one interest at the expense of the other.[94] This assumes that Anglo-Jewish actions and identity were determined by their social interests and that their interests were unitary. But the Jewish elite were subject to multiple ties and interests. Attention to chronology shows that it was not social origin

---

91. On another aspect of this see L. Marks, 'Dear Old Mother Levy's: The Jewish Maternity Hospital and Sick Room Helps Society 1895–1939', *Social History of Medicine*, April 1990, pp. 61–88.
92. *JC*, 29 June 1900, p. 25.
93. *Ibid*, 23 August 1901, p. 6.
94. See above, pp. 7–10, 291–2.

alone – whether Jewish or bourgeois – which determined which of these was uppermost, but the contingent unfolding of events and of political argument as well. The principal dynamic of the period was that as the size of the immigration popuation rose, as immigration appeared as an issue in national politics and as the forms of national ideology changed, so Anglo-Jewry were forced to respond more and more as Jews.

The recommendations of the Royel Commission on Alien Immigration and the 1905 Aliens Act were thus opposed by the JBD. It published reports which denied that Jewish immigrants either lowered the standard of life of English workers or significantly aggravated the problem of overcrowding. The encomia on the immigrants' social attitudes – their 'sobriety, thrift, industry, ability, determination to rise, perfect family life' – suggested their presence would be a perfect boon to society.[95] State intervention thus drove many in Anglo-Jewry to revise their stance towards Jewish immigration. But as the supporters of statutory restriction pointed out, the Jewish authorities themselves had repatriated thousands to Eastern Europe.[96] However, state intervention also created divisions. In 1903, for the first time, voices were raised at the JBG against the practice of repatriation. At the JBD, the grandees argued over whether to try to mobilise the Jewish MPs against the Aliens Act. Samuel Montagu strongly favoured this policy but B.L. Cohen feared that 'ill-considered and imprudent action' would arouse anti-Semitism.[97] These were markers for the future: state intervention would greatly disrupt the established lines of Jewish politics.

95. JBD B2/1/1, 'The Aliens Bill, 1905', pp. 4–5, 8.
96. PRO, HO 45/10303/117267/18, notes on a deputation from the Jewish Board of Deputies on the Aliens Bill, 19 May 1904.
97. *JC*, 27 March 1903, pp. 12, 17; *ibid*, 12 May 1905, p. 13.

Chapter 13

Association and Communal Politics

Patterns of association

Jewish immigrants were, of course, actors in their own right as well as the objects of policy. They created a plethora of associations in the East End of London. These too were concerned with the disposition of communal authority and forestalling poverty. But their understanding of what these goals meant was, in many cases, different from those promoted by the leaders of Anglo-Jewry. The resulting conflicts were the stuff of politics in the Jewish East End. Before turning to this, however, I shall map the pattern of associational life in the Jewish East End. It was from this milieu that the responses and challenges to Anglo-Jewish interventions developed.

Synagogues and *khevras*, as well as a multitude of friendly and benefit societies, were the institutions that thrived in the Jewish East End. They registered the long-term effects of earlier waves of Jewish immigrants as well as the one after 1882. In 1876 at least three of the small synagogues of the Jewish East End were over a hundred years old.[1] Beatrice Potter, in 1887, described the *khevras* as 'self-creating, self-supporting and self-governing communities; small enough to generate public opinion and the practical supervision of private morals, and large enough to stimulate charity, worship and study by communion and example'.[2] She found that there were between thirty and forty places of worship, study groups and benefit societies in the Jewish East End.[3] These institutions defined a sphere of fellowship, mutuality and financial and religious rectitude that was self-consciously Jewish in composition and almost exclusively male.

1. *JC*, 17 November 1876, p. 518.
2. C. Booth, *Life and Labour of the People of London*, 1st series, vol. iii (London, 1902), p. 172.
3. *Ibid*, vol. ii, p. 169.

In the Jewish East End religious observance did not place individuals beyond the normal parameters of working-class sociability. Among Christians in London it was only Catholics of Irish descent who integrated formal religious observance within the mainstream of working-class life. But whereas among Irish Catholics attendance at mass and participation in the life of the Church was feminised to a considerable extent, synagogue attendance and religious study among Jews were overwhelmingly male activities.[4] When Mudie Smith enumerated those attending London synagogues in 1903, he discovered that only 16 per cent of those present were female.[5] The sabbath was poorly observed, however, and societies formed to correct this achieved little success. Indeed, one of the objections made by the *khevras* to a 'monster synagogue' planned for the East End was that each Saturday there were many seats left vacant in the existing accommodation. Sabbath observance was discouraged by the rhythms of the workshop trades. In tailoring many contractors demanded that work be returned to them on Saturdays before noon. Shopkeepers and street traders also felt economic pressure leading them towards sabbath desecration, particularly if their customers were not Jews. Nevertheless, there were regular expressions of religious ritual in households whose male head attended synagogue only irregularly: most commonly prayers and a sabbath meal on Friday night.[6] Moreover, men who were customarily unobservant did worship on high holydays; on these occasions large halls such as the Paragon Theatre, Shoreditch Town Hall and the Jews' Free School were hired to accommodate the extra numbers.[7] Harry Lewis, a Jewish worker at Toynbee Hall, suggested that orthodox forms of observance bore a cultural resonance for many immigrants which extended beyond their religious meanings: 'However unobservant a foreign Jew may be, he cannot entirely forget the time when the synagogue was his only haven or refuge from an unfriendly world. The English Jew of the East End has no such associations and the service of the synagogue seldom wakes in him any real interest.'[8] Anglicised styles of worship were of no use in this respect. In 1891, when fewer people than anticipated attended the free services at the

---

4. H. McLeod, *Class and Religion in the Late Victorian City* (London, 1974), p. 72; L. Lees, *Exile of Erin; Irish Migrants in Victorian London* (Manchester, 1979), p. 184.
5. R. Mudie-Smith, *The Religious Life of London* (London, 1904), p. 265.
6. On Friday night rituals see J. White, *Rothschild Buildings: Life in an East End Tenement Block, 1887–1920* (London, 1980), pp. 86, 90–1.
7. GLRO, United Synagogue, minute book, 6 November 1894; C. Russell and H. Lewis, *The Jew in London* (London, 1900), p. 123.
8. *JC*, 20 February 1903, p. 15.

Jewish Working Mens Club, the organisers attributed this to the engagement of an English *khazn*.[9]

Many benefit societies were attached to a synagogue but a growing number were not. In 1898 there were 150 Jewish benefit societies in the East End.[10] By 1911 there were 300 Jewish friendly societies and lodges in London with a total membership of 39,000. Their accumulated funds stood at between £80–100,000.[11] The practice of joining more than one society makes it impossible to estimate accurately the number of individuals who were members; in 1898 two figures were suggested – 6,000 and 9,000.[12] The most illuminating information came from a survey of some streets in Spitalfields which found that between a half and two-thirds of adult males were members of at least one society.[13] Membership appears to have been more dense than among the English working class as a whole. In his study of Kentish London, Geoffrey Crossick found that between 35 and 40 per cent of occupied male adults were friendly society members between 1864 and 1872.[14] Paul Johnson emphasises that friendly society membership was concentrated among members of skilled trades.[15] But the workers who were least likely to be members of a society were thin on the ground in the Jewish East End. The continuity and stability of organisation of these societies contrasts vividly with the history of Jewish trade unionism. In fact, the success of the benefit societies was encouraged by some of the same forces which discouraged trade union activity. The inevitability of seasonal unemployment meant that the security of a benefit society could appear more attractive than organisation through the more ephemeral workplace.

There were many gradations among the myriad benefit societies. Different societies accommodated the differing abilities of individuals to spare a few pennies a week. Most societies required a weekly

9. United Synagogue, minute book, 27 October 1891.
10. *Ibid*, report on the East End Scheme, 10 November 1898.
11. *JC*, 26 May 1911, p. 31.
12. United Synagogue, minute book, report on the East End Scheme, 10 November 1898. A survey in 1901 suggested that there was a male membership of over 15,500 individuals in Jewish friendly societies in London: *JC*, 8 November 1901, p. 29.
13. United Synagogue, minute book, report on the East End Scheme, 10 November 1898.
14. G. Crossick, *An Artisan Elite in Victorian Society: Kentish London 1840–80* (London, 1978), p. 182; see too P. Johnson, 'Credit, Thrift and the Working Class', in J. Winter, ed., *The Working Class in Modern British History* (Cambridge, 1983), pp. 160–4.
15. *Idem, Saving and Spending: The Working Class Economy in Britain, 1870–1939* (Oxford, 1985), pp. 55–61.

subscription of between 6d and 10d per week, or an equivalent quarterly subscription, and offered sickness benefit of 12s to 15s for the first 13 weeks and half the original payment for a second period of 13 weeks. The payments on a member's death ranged between £5 and £10.[16] To be competitive, societies asked for contributions that were simply proportionate to their benefits and many, thus, provided benefits they were unable to meet except through levies.[17]

Some of these associations, such as the Tailors Mutual Friendly and Benefit Society, were restricted to employers. In 1901, when the society ceased to be restricted to the trade, its members preserved its exclusive character by barring anyone who had not been resident in the United Kingdom for two years.[18] There were also trade unions that acted as benefit societies by default, partly because of their inability to act effectively against either the masters or the warehouses. Likewise, there were social distinctions between synagogue congregations. A rough indication of this is that in 1889, when the annual donation for the Jewish Board of Guardians was raised, Spital Square Synagogue contributed £8 6s and Princes Street £5, while the *khevras* in Newcastle and Windsor Streets could muster only 10s each.[19]

Despite these tendencies towards organisations distinguished along lines of income or occupational status, synagogues and benefit societies typically were associations of workers and employers. Even though there were distinctions of status and class between and within these institutions, there were other points of differentiation which united their members and separated them from others above and below them in society. The entrance fees into benefit societies were high, between 2s 6d and 5s, and discouraged the poor and 'greeners'. But once members were accepted and the fee paid, societies endeavoured to give members every opportunity to remain within them, even during prolonged periods of sickness or unemployment. Distress funds were used to sustain contributions or give more substantial help. These funds were administered in ways designed to avoid shame being attached to the applicant, whose identity was generally kept secret from all but the chairman and secretary, who were disqualified from adjudicating on the case. Any-

16. The rule books of many of these societies can be found among the materials in PRO, FS 3. Some societies offered a further thirteen-week period of sick benefit at one quarter of the original rate. See too GLRO, Federation of Synagogues, letter book, 1 July 1897.
17. *JC*, 26 May 1911, p. 31.
18. FS 3/234/554, rules and amendments.
19. Federation of Synagogues, minute book, 16 June 1889.

one who divulged the name of an applicant was fined heavily.[20] In this way the practice of the societies was crucially different from that of the JBG. Their members set themselves apart from both the poor and their philanthropists. Life insurance, one of the principal services of these societies, was a badge of respectability, a public declaration that dependants would not be forced to plead with the JBG.[21] The payments for a funeral ensured that members and their families would not suffer the indignity of a charity burial. These values and practices could unite masters and workers within the same society.[22]

Not only did members of these societies and synagogues set themselves apart from others above them in the social scale: the same process worked in the other direction. The Order Achei Brith encountered indifference when it tried to attract members from the growing Jewish population in Dalston and Hackney by establishing a lodge in North London. In its first 5 years it attracted only 37 members. The level of sickness benefit at 15s per week was too low to attract the Jews who lived in this district. But 25 years later, a member reflected that the lodge itself was seen as an unwanted intruder in these more prosperous surroundings.[23] A similar divide is indicated by the claim made by Samuel Montagu, in his capacity as President of the Federation of Synagogues – a combination of synagogues whose affiliates were concentrated in the East End – that 'we cater, if I may call it, for the working classes among the Jews'.[24] The members of some federated *khevras* included employers and they possessed sufficient means to collect several hundred pounds among themselves so as to rebuild their synagogues. Nevertheless, these savings could appear less grand, the differences between synagogues less bold and Montagu's statement more comprehensible, when placed alongside the fact that the fee to join one of the established English synagogues in the City of London was £3 10s.[25] This was a measure of the economic gulf which lay between the milieu of the petty producers of the Jewish East End and the prosperous commercial foundations of the Jewish middle classes beyond.

20.   *JC*, 27 October 1911, p. 18.
21.   The practice of belonging to more than one society was a way of increasing the sum which would be paid upon death.
22.   Even one as exclusive as the Hebrew East London Friendly Benefit Society elected a tailor's presser and a boot finisher among its trustees: FS 3/237/649, rules and amendments.
23.   *The Leader*, December 1923, p. 4.
24.   *RCAI*, q. 16,773.
25.   Gartner, *The Jewish Immigrant in England, 1870–1914* (London, 1973 edn), p. 201.

The benefit and friendly societies provided the immigrants with fellowship and with a public life. B.A. Fersht, by the early twentieth century a leading figure in this milieu, commented on its role: 'there he [the member] has friends. All share his sorrows and joys. In the society the foreign Jew feels himself an entity, a man who counts.'[26] The societies' rule books suggest they were proudly self-governing institutions. They regulated their membership; newcomers had to be voted into the society. Fines were imposed for failing to attend meetings and members took on other duties such as visiting the sick.[27] The Brothers of Suwalki Benefit Society stipulated that members could not be interrupted while speaking so long as they were 'dispassionate' and kept to a limit of ten minutes. Fines of between 3d and 5s could be levied on anyone who interrupted business by 'swearing, cursing, uttering opprobrious or indecent expressions or causing any disturbance'.[28]

These institutions, along with the small synagogues of the district, were the principal institutions through which the Russian and Polish Jews created public prestige and manufactured status. According to one observer the 'backbone' of the *khevras* was supplied by 'master tailors, bootmakers, carpenters, etc., who employ hands'. The most prosperous tradesmen and shopkeepers of the East End worshipped at the English synagogues in the City, leaving to the small masters 'the pleasure at playing *shul* business on a small scale, sharing honorary offices and *aliyos* and other *mitzvos*'.[29] Mark Moses was one of the largest master tailors in the East End, who employed forty hands. He led the Masters Association in the 1889 tailors' strike and was also a prominent Whitechapel Liberal, a treasurer of the Federation of Synagogues from 1889 to 1921 and an honorary officer of several benefit societies and charities.[30] But concentration of power and status to this degree was unusual. East End Jewry was characterised by a fragmentation of leadership and prestige. This was reflected by the proliferation of societies and *khevras*, and their resistance to suggestions that they should amalgamate or unite in some other way. One current within this history amounts to attempts to achieve recognition on the part of the aspiring and contending local Jewish

26. *JC*, 26 May 1911, p. 31.
27. For instance, see FS 3/238/700, Kaylor Watchers Benefit Society, rules and amendments.
28. FS 3/232/490, Brothers of Suwalki Benefit Society, rules and amendments.
29. *Jewish World*, 1 January 1892, p. 3. For an account of this milieu elsewhere see B. Williams, ' "East and West": Class and Community in Manchester Jewry, 1850–1914', in D. Cesarani, ed., *The Making of Modern Anglo-Jewry* (Oxford, 1990), pp. 15–33.
30. See his obituary, *JC*, 27 May 1921, pp. 10–11.

leaders. One reason, therefore, why there was such a profusion of Jewish benefit societies was, as one early twentieth-century critic expressed it, 'due to the desire to form a society, whether needed or not, for certain people to be at the top'.[31] The progress of the 'fathers and founders' was thus open to caricature and ridicule by the second generation: 'Form your society; promise anything you like so long as you get your members; get nice heavy gold laced regalias: get yourself photographed, so that they may see "at home" that you are some personage; carry on for a few years: get your testimonial. . . .'[32] Society officers fought tenaciously to keep their positions if they were threatened with amalgamation or democracy. In an attempt to prevent their society from amalgamating with another, the secretary and chairman of one refused to sign the documents required by the Registrar of Friendly Societies. In the Achei Ameth the founders constituted themselves as life members of the Grand Lodge.[33]

But as well as the self-aggrandising rule of the founders there was a contervailing tradition of democracy, and the membership of many of the societies was very active in these early years. The King Solomon Lodge of the Order Achei Brith was dominated by its two founders, who kept personal possession of all its monies and books. Nevertheless, its meetings were attended by 'almost all members on each occasion', there were frequent discussions about employment, wages and politics, and there was a 'keen competition' for office. In the Order Achei Ameth the democratic current was sufficiently strong to demand a plebiscite in 1901, which resulted in the defeat of the founding oligarchy.[34]

Unlike the synagogues, benefit societies had neither an historic tradition nor a religious claim within the East End upon which to base their claims to prestige nor, unlike the Zionists, did they possess a political programme. Their response was to invent a lineage in which to place themselves. In 1896, the Hebrew Order of Druids was formed and named after 'the earliest known spiritual guides of the

31. *Jewish Friendly Societies Magazine*, October 1926, p. 4. Zionist societies were used in the same way to generate places and prestige. Radicals in the movement criticised the creation of societies with only a paper membership. Kalman Marmor, a left-wing zionist, polemically explained that 'the reason why so many [zionist] *khevras* exist is simply because there are ten people who want to be president and in one *khevra* there can only be one president': *Der Yudishe Frayhayt*, Iyar-Sivan, p. 15. See too *Der Yidisher Ekspres*, 5 November 1902, p. 4.
32. *Jewish Friendly Societies Magazine*, January 1926, p. 4.
33. *Ibid*, October 1926, p. 4; FS 3/238/680, Brethren of Vlotslovak and Poltusk Friendly Benefit Society, rules and amendments.
34. University of Southampton, AJ 291/1/8, Reference Book of the United Jewish Friendly Society, chapters 1–3.

country'.[35] The increasing separation of prayer and thrift, which had been held together within the *khevras*, led to the introduction of the masonic paraphernalia of regalia, passwords and handshakes in many societies: 'In the early days of the Achei Ameth, members were initiated in the dark, with the officials masked, with long beards, etc. At the crucial moment a lucifer was struck – and Moishe arise.'[36] Societies named after Baden Powell and Prince George were only the most outrageous of several titled after royal or imperial themes. Leading figures in Anglo-Jewry were also honoured by societies in this way. An identification with Britain or British Jews provided a powerful symbol against which rival *landsmanshaftn* and *khevras* could appear 'green' and backward-looking. Ironically, the *landsmanshaftn* themselves were post-migration inventions. In Grodno or Plotsk, men would not have organised themselves in societies based merely on residence in the town. It was only after migration that this became a significant form of differentiation and association.

The vital associational life of the Jewish East End reflected the limited wealth of the area and its diffuse distribution. Whereas the economic insecurity of enterprises vitiated attempts to establish alliances of masters and workers at the workplace, the same conditions allowed the two to come together in another context. The fluidity of economic relations meant that divisions of income, security and geographical location, which might have been translated into an associational life that enhanced divisions between workers and employers, were mitigated in the Jewish East End. Economic and social experience was not unitary. The opposition of master and worker could not be translated successfully into institutional forms but there were other social relations that could be. The *khevras* and benefit societies of the Jewish East End emphasised their independence from philanthropy, they distinguished themselves from those who could not afford to save and they identified themselves as separate from the surrounding non-Jewish population.

Orthodoxy, Liberalism and communal politics

Synagogues and benefit societies were not only local institutions. They occupied a place within a larger political arena, one which encompassed the Jewish community as a whole. The intervention of Anglo-Jewish communal institutions in the East End produced conflicts through which the immigrants and, more particularly,

35. *Jewish Friendly Societies Magazine*, August 1926, p. 4.
36. *Ibid*, October 1926, p. 4.

those who claimed to represent them challenged the rule of the communal elite. One crucial issue was how the concept of the Jewish community and the practice of communal institutions would take account of the immigrants' presence. The JBG, the JBD and the United Synagogue presented one set of answers to this question. But, at times, they were subject to fierce challenge. The successful containment of immigrants within the established communal organisation was of great significance for the long-term development of Anglo-Jewry. To contemporaries, however, the threat of schism sometimes reached critical proportions.[37]

Criticism of Anglo-Jewish social policy was an abiding theme in the immigrant press. In the winter of 1884–5 *Di Tsukunft* turned its attention to the theories and assumptions governing Anglo-Jewish philanthropy. The philanthropists were likened to the sun in winter: they shone but they warmed nothing. Specifically, they were afraid that their benevolence would flood London with poor Jews: they did not build a Jewish hospital fearing that all would go there to be sick, nor a shelter because they were afraid it would attract all the homeless Jews, nor a kitchen to feed the poor in the slack time because it would only draw to London everyone who was hungry and needed to be fed.[38] The newspaper's heavy irony reflected the belief that in adhering to the principles of English philanthropy the communal leaders were ignoring their obligation to help the Jewish poor.

This belief was focused in May 1885 when the JBG forced the closure of a shelter for homeless immigrants which had been established in the heart of Whitechapel by a master baker, Simon Cohen. At a meeting held at the Jewish Working Mens Club, F.D. Mocatta, an influential figure in the Charity Organisation Society as well as the JBG, argued that the shelter was attracting Jewish paupers to London and should be closed. In fact, the meeting resolved to appoint a committee to examine the situation but the JBG prevailed on the local authority to close the premises for sanitary reasons.[39] Cohen's refuge was replaced by the Poor Jews Temporary Shelter, sponsored by Anglo-Jewish philanthropy and the Rothschilds in

---

37. On similar conflicts in New York see A. Goren, *New York Jews and the Struggle for Community: The Kehillah Experiment, 1908–22* (New York, NY, 1970).
38. *Di Tsukunft*, 23 January 1885, p. 195.
39. *Ibid*, 1 May 1885, p. 305; Gartner, *The Jewish Immigrant in England*, p. 52. Cohen's description of the shelter was that 'the first and second floors consist of two large rooms, each over four feet long by about seventeen feet wide. . . . On weekdays, both halls are used for study and several hundred persons go in and out daily. . . . On the ground floor there is a *mikvah*. It is open from six a.m. to midnight.' Cited in J. Jung, *Champions of Orthodoxy* (London, 1974), p. 128.

particular. But the practice of the new institution was significantly different from the old. It was a business as well as a charity. It leased beds to shipping companies who needed temporary accommodation for transmigrants in London. Moreover, the Shelter authorities actively encouraged many migrants to move on to other countries rather than remain in England.[40]

A view which counterposed Jewish tradition and obligation to the practices of Anglo-Jewry recurred throughout this period. Most ferociously, the JBG was attacked for its conduct in the face of the large influx of Jews from Roumania between 1899–1901.[41] The Board had responded to this emergency by discouraging fund-raising for the relief of Roumanian immigrants. It reported to its subscribers that 'from the very outset the Board made known both here and abroad . . . the only relief it could offer to applicants arriving here in a helpless condition would be to assist them to return to the countries they had left with such deplorable absence of foresight'.[42] In an editorial entitled 'Who Should Help Whom?', *Der Yidisher Ekspres* replied bitterly.

> So you see we have all been mistaken, we and you too believed that the situation of Jews in Russia and Roumania is so bad that we must try to help them. We all thought that since Jews in the countries of Western Europe are better off it is particularly their duty to come to the help of these Jews. But someone said you live and learn. We have discovered that we made a mistake. It is from the Roumanian Jews that help is required. True, the Roumanian Jews possess nothing in this world apart from their lives but this makes no difference, they are required to lay down their lives. They can drown themselves, they can die with whatever death comes to hand, only they should die quietly, because the interests of English Jews demand it.[43]

It was not only the response to the emergency which drew a sharp retort. 'The truth is the whole system of the Boards of Guardians is rotten,' the newspaper argued. It went on to criticise that system in terms derived from both Judaic prescription and the ideals of social independence represented by the synagogues and benefit societies of the Jewish East End.

> This is not the form of charity our learned men have prescribed; the donor should not know to whom he gives, and the recipient should not know

40. *RCAI*, p. 573, table A. Also see the earlier discussion of the Poor Jews' Temporary Shelter, p. 302.
41. On this see J. Kissman, 'The Immigration of Roumanian Jews up to 1914', *YIVO Annual*, 1947–8, pp. 160–79.
42. JBG, *42nd Annual Report* (London, 1901), p. 16.
43. *Der Yidisher Ekspres*, 12 June 1901, p. 4.

from whose hand he takes. . . . The charity of our prominent men is given with noise, alarms and advertisement and it is divided amid uproar, openly and humiliatingly. No one but a professional beggar can accept it with a light heart, anyone who has not sunk so low cannot without it leaving a permanent stain on his conscience.[44]

Some East End societies did try to alleviate the misery of the Roumanian immigrants. They provided food and shelter, and one society tried to find work for immigrants who would otherwise have been forced to apply to the JBG – with repatriation the inevitable result. But ventures such as these did not have the resources to achieve a broad or sustained impact. One society was able to supply bread and tea to just forty or fifty immigrants a day.[45] The *Jewish Chronicle* conveyed the scale and nature of this effort. Roumanian Jews, it reported, were sleeping in the streets. They were provided with food by 'poor working men (tailors and bootmakers principally) . . . denying themselves a meal in order to alleviate the suffering of their starving co-religionists'.[46] The criticisms of Anglo-Jewry in *Der Yidisher Ekspres* must be read as appeals too, which recognised the real capacities of both East and West End Jewries. The challenge to West End philanthropy was necessarily more powerful in invective than in deed.

It was through the Federation of Synagogues that the associational life of the Jewish East End cohered sufficiently to present a significant challenge to the communal regime. This was possible only because the Federation of Synagogues received the substantial patronage of Samuel Montagu. As a result, it was the orthodox Judaism promoted by the Federation which became the focus for one challenge to communal authority. Plans to establish the organisation were developed at meetings between Montagu and leading members of a number of *khevras* and synagogues in October and November 1887.[47] At the first meeting in December 1887, sixteen synagogues and *khevras* accounting for over 1,200 members were represented. They included some of the older synagogues of the East End, such as the Sandys Row and Prescott Street Synagogues, frequented by Dutch, German and English Jews, as well as others established by more recent immigrants. In January 1888 the

44.   *Ibid*, 11 May 1900, p. 4.
45.   *Ibid*, 23 March 1900, p. 5.
46.   *JC*, 27 June 1900, p. 24.
47.   All congregations in the East End with fifty members or more were invited to elect representatives to the proposed federation. The fullest account of the organisation's history will be found in G. Alderman, *The Federation of Synagogues* (London, 1987).

new organisation drew up a list of aims; these were to obtain representation on all of the main communal bodies, to secure the services of an orthodox minister or a *dayan*, and to negotiate with the United Synagogue to reduce the cost of funerals and thereby reduce the number of charity funerals.[48]

This list reflected the different interests which came together in the new organisation. The self-governing *khevras* appealed to Montagu's liberalism, their orthodoxy appealed to his own practices and beliefs, and the organisation itself provided an arena in which he did not have to play second fiddle to Lord Rothschild, as well as a position through which he could cultivate his parliamentary constituency.[49] But Montagu faced two ways. He not only saw the Federation as a means of promoting orthodoxy: he also saw it as a way of forestalling a breakaway *kehila* in the East End. Among observant immigrants there was a great deal of dissatisfaction with the autocratic position of the Chief Rabbi and with the relaxed quality of the Judaism he promoted.[50] By funding the Federation, Montagu ensured that orthodox opposition would be consolidated in the East End but he also ensured that it would remain within the existing communal structure.[51] When the Federation appointed a minister, Montagu made it a condition of his employment that he should be acceptable to the established ecclesiastical authorities. In practice, any synagogue which did not accept the authority of the Chief Rabbi was not able to join the Federation and so would not benefit from Montagu's patronage.[52] Indeed, some congregations joined to secure their own existence as well as traditional practices. They took loans from Montagu which ranged in value between £30 and £700. The interest, generally at 3 per cent, accrued to the Federation. Montagu used these loans to foster mutual recognition between the Federation and the ecclesiastical authorities. In 1899, when he advanced £500 to the Cannon Street Road Synagogue, Montagu made it a condition that the Chief Rabbi should be invited to consecrate the new building he was financing.[53]

Nevertheless, for representatives of the *khevras* the Federation was an avenue through which they could remedy their exclusion from communal institutions and a force through which they might

48. Federation of Synagogues, minute book, 4 December 1887, 16 January 1888.
49. L.H. Montagu, *Samuel Montagu: First Baron Swaythling, A Character Sketch* (London, 1913).
50. See *ibid*, chapters 3, 4.
51. J. Blank, *The Minutes of the Federation of Synagogues* (London, 1912), p. 18.
52. Federation of Synagogues, minute book, 4 December 1887, 12 November 1889.
53. Federation of Synagogues, minute book, 19 November 1899.

improve the religious standards of the *kehila*.[54] The Federation's
first requests for representation on communal bodies received an
encouraging response. In March 1888 it was invited to elect a representative to sit on the JBG, and after 1889 the Federation had a *de
facto* presence at the Board of Deputies through the representation
of Spital Square Synagogue. But although the *Sephardi* synagogue
favoured the enlargement of the Board of Shechita to include the
Federation, the United Synagogue decided to block the application.[55] The Board of Shechita oversaw the slaughter of animals and
the sale of meat according to Jewish law. Representation here was a
financial issue as well as a matter of institutional recognition. The
Board imposed a tax on the meat it passed as *kosher* and the surplus
left from this income was divided annually between its constituent
synagogues. The Federation had asked for a modest fraction of the
booty – just one fifth of the surplus – in view of the fact that the East
End consumed up to 90 per cent of all *kosher* meat in London.[56] The
levy on *kosher* meat was a system of communal taxation, and the
Board's refusal to allow the Federation a portion of the proceeds
was, in effect, an invitation to it to secede from the community. But
Montagu effectively deflected the challenge. Until the Federation
was finally admitted to the Board of Shechita in 1901, he donated
annually the sum it would have received had it been a member, a
figure roughly equal to its running expenses.[57] This was of crucial
importance in ensuring the immigrants' integration within the
established structure of communal authority.

The United Synagogue also rejected the Federation's request for
a reduction in funeral charges. It was prepared to reduce the fees for
adults but not for children.[58] The existing level of charges meant
that there were a large number of charity funerals in the Jewish East

conflict!

54. University of Southampton, Samuel Montagu's scrapbook's, AJ/1, *JC*, 6 July
     1889.
55. Blank, *The Minutes of the Federation of Synagogues*, p. 18.
56. *Der Yidisher Ekspres*, 2 March 1900, p. 4.
57. This was between £60–80 each year: Federation of Synagogues, minute book,
     19 February 1888, 18 November 1888, 17 February 1889.
58. Federation of Synagogues, minute book, 18 November 1888; *Jewish World*, 20
     February 1891, p. 7. But the age structure of immigration meant that children
     comprised an unusually large proportion of all deaths in the Jewish East End.
     In 1905 Rosenbaum calculated that the 'age at which 50 per cent of all deaths
     has been reached, is in the case of Jews as low as 1.88 years among males and
     2.67 years among females, while among the general population it is as high as
     26.2 years for males and 33.5 years for females': S. Rosenbaum, 'A Contribu-
     tion to the Study of the Vital and Other Statistics of the Jews in the United
     Kingdom', *Journal of the Royal Statistical Society*, 1905, p. 534. The intransigence
     of the United Synagogue was, therefore, felt with particular force.

End. These funerals were a stigma on East End Jewry; they implied a position of dependence on the part of East End Jews. It was this relationship, in which the East End was supposed to assume a position of powerlessness and an attitude of thankfulness to Anglo-Jewish philanthropists, which the Federation intended to challenge. The annual collections for the JBG made by the federated synagogues not only gathered funds: they were also declarations that the Federation was to be treated on an equal basis, because it, and by extension the East End, were donors as well as recipients of charity. The paradox was that the Federation was only able to make these claims and strike this pose of independence because Montagu's generosity allowed it to do so. In the case of the Board of Shechita, Montagu had ensured the continued existence of the Federation; now he secured it an independent position by purchasing two acres, at the cost of £1,000, on which the Federation established its own burial grounds. Montagu also subsidised the burial society which the Federation established, until it became self-supporting in 1893. Through the burial grounds and society the Federation established its independence without challenging the unity of the *kehila*.[59]

The rhetoric of the Federation's campaign against its treatment by the United Synagogue brought together orthodox Judaism and Liberalism. Montagu was the foremost spokesman for this current in communal politics but it ran deeper than his leadership alone. English Jews formed a portion of the Federation's East End membership. Mark Moses, a treasurer of the Federation, could also be found on Liberal platforms. Moreover, since the mid-1880s, at least, the political preferences of some prominent English Jews had been a source of immigrant discontent. Support for the Conservative Party and the established Church was presented by *Di Tsukunft* as one step towards apostasy. 'The Germans have a saying that shoemakers should remain by their lasts! A pity that our Jewish Tories did not stay in their loan offices,' one editorial suggested. The sight of a placard in the King's Cross and St Pancras constituency asking voters to support Saul Isaacs and 'the Church! the Altar!', was too much: 'Soon our Jewish Tories will think they are Jesus himself.'[60] In 1885 and 1886 *Di Tsukunft* vigorously supported Montagu's candidacy. This was despite, or perhaps because of, the disenfranchisement of alien voters and the Liberals' defence of them. The newspaper stressed the support due to the Liberals as the party which had fought against lords and bishops in favour of Jewish emancipation.

59. Federation of Synagogues, minute book, 18 June 1889; Blank, *The Minutes of the Federation of Synagogues*, pp. 30–2.
60. *Di Tsukunft*, 20 November 1885, p. 153. See too *ibid*, 6 November 1885, p. 137.

Moreover, in 1886 it argued that Jews of all peoples ought to sympathise with the oppressed Irish. It also pointed out that Polish Jews had a special debt to Samuel Montagu, who had done so much for them.[61] This Liberal current in immigrant politics lay alongside the ardent Liberalism of the English Jews in Whitechapel. In 1885 Montagu estimated that he had won between 500 and 700 votes from among the members of the Jewish Working Mens Club and 'had been assured that not half a dozen had voted against him'.[62] At the Brick Lane polling booth, in the heart of the Jewish quarter, he received twice as many votes as his Conservative opponent.[63]

Montagu's patronage in the Federation effected a union between Liberal politics and orthodox Judaism in the Jewish East End. When Nathan Adler, the Chief Rabbi, died in 1890 it was a foregone conclusion that he would be succeeded by his son who had already been appointed Delegate Chief Rabbi. Nevertheless, a conference had to be convened to elect Hermann Adler into office. Lord Rothschild, as President of the United Synagogue, invited the Federation to send eight delegates to the conference but this number was later reduced to two. The principle of representation was calculated on the basis of the amount contributed to the Chief Rabbi's Fund.[64] In 1891, at the annual general meeting of the Federation, Montagu conceded that the forthcoming election would proceed without difficulty. At the same time, he predicted that subsequent elections would be disputed when 'the danger of a money system of representation would be seen, as the money-bags have it entirely in their power to thrust a Reform Chief Rabbi on the community'. He argued that the smallness 'of the representation of the working classes' meant that they were only able to protect their interests by 'combination' – by which he meant the Federation.[65] This was the language of radical Liberalism applied to the Jewish community.

The United Synagogue responded to the pretensions of the Federation with a scheme to build a large synagogue in Spitalfields. It planned to let 800 seats at 3d per week and undercut the synagogues in the Federation. It also aimed to engage a minister acceptable to the foreign Jews, to establish a provident society and to locate the *Beth Hamedrash* on the same site. It would offer facilities the

61. *Ibid*, 20 November 1885, p. 153; *ibid*, 1 July 1886, pp. 1, 6.
62. *JC*, 11 December 1885, p. 12.
63. *East London Observer*, 13 March 1886, p. 2.
64. Federation of Synagogues, minute book, 29 April 1890, 7 April 1891.
65. *Jewish World*, 17 April 1891, p. 6.

Federation could not match and so crush it as a force. The centre was to promote the ideal of a community expanded to embrace the immigrants. The executive committee of the United Synagogue reported:

> The main problem to the solution of which the executive committee have applied themselves is to attract the Jews of all classes in the East of London, whether foreign or native, within the fold of the body politic; and thus to afford them in a way alike conducive to the welfare of these institutions and creditable to themselves, that share in the government and administration of the great communal establishments which attachment to the community should properly confer and which it is believed the poorer Jews desire and would appreciate, so to give a tangible expression living expression to the sacred maxim 'ALL JEWS ARE BRETHREN.'[66]

But the East Enders were not to be included on equal terms:

> As it may take some time to familiarise the members of the new synagogue, many of whom will be foreigners, with the required formalities, it has been deemed necessary that the election of salaried officers shall in the first instance be vested in the council [of the United Synagogue] and that the officers chosen shall hold office for a term of three years.[67]

At a general meeting of the Federation in 1889, Montagu claimed that that institution represented the real Jewish community in London, and he defended orthodoxy and self-help against the religious backsliders and pauperising philanthropists of the West End.[68] The Federation called a meeting to ask the United Synagogue to reconsider its plans. The audience was reminded by one resolution, passed unanimously, that 'the working classes' had made sacrifices of thousands of pounds in improving their buildings and that the proposed scheme would 'so reduce their incomes as to cripple any further attempt on their part for self improvement'. The scheme was regarded as an example of pauperising philanthropy which also required the political subordination of the East End.[69]

In contrast to the description of the East Enders by the United Synagogue as 'poorer Jews' and thus as fitting objects for charity, the term 'working classes' denoted a group that was respectable, independent, clearly distinguished from the residuum and, increasingly, enfranchised. The resolution that described the members of the Federation of Synagogues as the 'working classes' was proposed

66. United Synagogue, minute book, 18 February 1890.
67. *Ibid.*
68. *JC*, 6 December 1889, p. 11.
69. Federation of Synagogues, minute book, 6 May 1893.

by J. Singer and seconded by S. Strelitskie: Singer was a fur and skin merchant, Strelitskie was the President of the Netherlands Club, the most prestigious club in the Jewish East End, and the leading representative of the Dutch Jews living in London. In their conflict with the West Enders they could join and represent themselves as the 'working classes'. It was a self-description which owed much to Liberal political discourse. It echoed the distinction between the producing and non-producing classes, the faithful and the corrupt. The lines of class division were construed in communal terms so that the whole Jewish population in the East End became synonymous with the Jewish working class. Their ideology was not socialist but formed around the defence of traditional Judaism, both for itself, but also as a symbol of the independence of the East End Jews.

The representation of political conflict within the Jewish community as a polarisation of East against West, the independent against the pauperisers, the honest and religiously faithful masses against the backsliding elite, reinforced the associational life of the Jewish East End in which masters and workers collected together. It drew strength from the gulf between, on one side, the small producers and workers of the Jewish East End and, on the other, the Jewish middle classes of north and north-west London: of Dalston and Islington, let alone Maida Vale and Kilburn. The challenge to the Anglo-Jewish elite from the Jewish East End and the political language in which it was presented, tended to consolidate a politics which crossed the boundaries between employer and worker. Employers and workers formed religious and secular organisations based on the practice of independence and self-government. They were offended by a great deal of what they saw in the Anglo-Jewish elite: by its quality of Judaism, by its parsimonious and bureaucratic philanthropy, and by its patronising and unrepresentative political practice. This lay the ground for a political alignment which crossed divisions between master and worker and which, indeed, could refer to both as 'the working classes'. But the key social and political division, as it was conceived within this milieu, was between 'East End' and 'West End'. It was the great irony of the Federation of Synagogues that its claim to champion the interests of East End Jews could only be made because it received patronage from within the West End elite. At the same time as it made claims for its independence, the Federation demonstrated the limits to politics under West End tutelage.

Chapter 14

The Politics of Anglicisation

Revolutionaries

By the mid-1890s the leaders of Anglo-Jewry had set about anglicising the immigrants and their children with some urgency and foreboding. How successful were they? Historians have given two sorts of answer to this question. Gartner's classic study played down their impact. Migration was seen here as a process of uprooting, as in histories of immigration to the United States written in the 1950s.[1] In the case of the Jewish immigrants, Gartner argued, their origins in the small towns and villages of Lithuania, Poland and the Ukraine were circumscribed by 'a traditional way of life' which they tried vainly to sustain in London. But their 'enlightenment' was 'simply . . . an inevitable consequence of migration to a western country'. The immigrants' anglicisation was similarly inexorable and 'would have happened with or without the diligent efforts of native Jewry'. In this view, cultural change is seen to have been as natural as the change of seasons and as little subject to human agency: a process of transition from the traditional to the modern world.[2] More recent work has taken a different view. This has placed great emphasis on the intentions and effects of Anglo-Jewish intervention. Some historians have seen this as an exercise in 'social control', in which class goals were uppermost.[3] Most recently Eugene Black has preferred the term 'socialisation' and, though he does not ignore the role of class in forming Anglo-Jewish attitudes, he argues that 'what Anglo-

1. O. Handlin, *The Uprooted* (New York, NY, 1951).
2. L. Gartner, *The Jewish Immigrant in England, 1870–1914* (London, 1973 edn), pp. 166, 241–2, 268.
3. J. White, *Rothschild Buildings: Life in an East End Tenement Block, 1887–1920* (London, 1980), p. 54; B. Williams, 'The Anti-Semitism of Tolerance', in A. Kidd and K. Robert, eds., *City, Class and Culture: Studies of Social Policy and Cultural Production in Victorian Manchester* (Manchester, 1985), p. 92.

Jewry sought to create and in many ways succeeded in doing, was to establish a [Jewish] sub-culture within English society'.[4] In one view, then, immigrant culture was shaped largely by impersonal social forces in another it was moulded by Anglo-Jewish philanthropy. What is missing from all this is any substantial role for the immigrants themselves. But once their own activity is acknowledged we shall have to reconsider these other explanations of cultural change.

Jewish immigrants were presented with more than one vision of anglicisation. Whereas one project of cultural transformation was pressed on them by the acculturated leaders of native Jewry, radically different visions of cultural and political progress were developed by Jewish anarchist, social democrat and zionist propagandists in the Jewish East End. The first Yiddish newspaper to propound these ideas, *Di Poylishe Yidel*, appeared in July 1884.[5] For a period it retained an undogmatic stance to all Jewish radicals: socialists, nationalists and assimilationists. The pogroms of 1881–2 and their aftermath stimulated a nationalist turn among sections of the radicalised Russian-Jewish intelligentsia. A minority saw colonisation in Palestine as a solution to the problems of Russian Jewry and, parallel to this, many Jewish socialists were briefly friendly to Jewish nationalism.[6] Accordingly, *Di Poylishe Yidel* announced to its readers that it would address them 'as man, as Jew and as worker'.[7] Between 1886–92 the spirit of ecumenism between Jewish radicals turned to sectarianism. First socialists and nationalists and then anarchists and socialists divided from each other and were locked in bitter feuds.[8]

Despite their endemic disputes, Jewish revolutionaries held a number of ideas in common; one of these was that the Jewish masses were steeped in ignorance. Their activity was informed by a view of the cultural under-development of the East European Jewish masses just as sharp as any within native Jewry. From the outset, the founders of the radical press presented themselves as pedagogues as well as agitators. *Di Poylishe Yidel* encouraged its readers to learn English and equip themselves to read scientific and other literature which was rarely available in Hebrew and never in Yiddish. Although he defended Yiddish against its detractors, the editor, Morris Vinchevsky, looked forward to a time when the newspaper could be

4. E. Black, *The Social Politics of Anglo-Jewry, 1880–1920* (Oxford, 1988), p. ix.
5. After seventeen issues it was renamed *Di Tsukunft*.
6. J. Frankel, *Prophecy and Politics: Socialism, Nationalism, and the Russian Jews, 1862–1917* (Cambridge, 1981), pp. 81–97, 114–17.
7. *Di Tsukunft*, 14 November 1884, pp. 117–18. On the ecumenical character of Jewish radicalism in the early 1880s, see Frankel, *Prophecy and Politics*, pp. 123–32.
8. *Ibid*, pp. 129–31; W.J. Fishman, *East End Jewish Radicals 1875–1914* (London, 1975), pp. 191–209.

produced in English.[9] In his memoirs Avram Frumkin, editor of the anarchist newspaper *Der Arbayter Fraynd* between 1896–8, recalled the faith he and his comrades had placed in the press: 'the belief in the people in its struggle towards freedom was deep and sharp. But the people remained in darkness, in ignorance . . . we had to awaken it.'[10] It was typical of this perspective that readers of *Der Veker*, a social democrat newspaper, were encouraged to support a recently established reading room and library, 'to give the Jewish immigrant something he lacked in the old country, namely development and education'.[11] The name of the paper itself, meaning 'the awakener', gives a sense of what its editors understood their role to be. In 1910 the anarchist leader Rudolf Rocker presented trade unionism within an historical and anthropological scheme of social evolution that would eventually create 'new living conditions and a higher culture'.[12] Accordingly, the stock in trade of the socialist and anarchist clubs and their connected associations was not only political propaganda but also libraries, lessons in English and arithmetic, and lectures on scientific and literary subjects such as astronomy and drama.[13]

The identification of revolutionary politics with the idea of progress was particularly evident in the propaganda of social democrats. In 1893 Moishe Baranov proclaimed, 'our principles are the only progressive principles, our struggle is the aspiration of all humanity, our wish is the wish of the whole proletariat'.[14] Statements such as this drew on a social evolutionist tendency widespread within revolutionary movements influenced by Marx as well as the liberal tradition. In the Jewish case this perspective also drew on the self-image of the *maskil* as the voice of radical enlightenment amid the ignorant and backward-looking East European Jewish masses.[15] Trade union-

9. *Di Poylishe Yidel*, 8 August 1884.
10. A. Frumkin, *In Friling fun Yidishn Sotsializm* (New York, NY, 1940), p. 71.
11. *Der Veker*, 6 January 1893, p. 3; see too *Di Fraye Velt*, June 1891, pp. 1–2.
12. *Der Yidisher Trayd Yunionist*, 1 June 1910, pp. 2–3.
13. *Di Tsukunft*, 7 November 1884, p. 112; M. Vinchevsky, *Gezamelte Shriftn*, vol. ix, (New York, NY, 1927) pp. 106–7; R. Rocker, *In Shturm* (Buenos Aires, 1952) pp. 310–12; A. Gorelik, *Shturmedike Yorn* (New York, NY, 1946), p. 127; S. Osipov, *Mayn Lebn: Deringerungen un Iberlebungen fun a Yidishn Sotsialistn* (Boston, Mass, 1954), pp. 125–7; T. Eyges, *Beyond the horizon* (Boston, Mass, 1954) p. 84; E. Tcherikower, *Geshikhte fun der Yidisher Arbayter Bavegung*, vol. ii (New York, NY, 1945), pp. 110–11; W.J. Fishman, *East End Jewish Radicals, 1875–1914* (London, 1975), chapter 2.
14. *Der Veker*, 6 January 1893, p. 1.
15. An image of the enlightened socialist intellegentsia labouring among the ignorant masses is portrayed in *Di Fraye Velt*, July 1892, pp. 71–2. The *maskilic* perspective was, of course, not necessarily one committed to revolutionary politics: see for example *Der Vunderer*, 13 February 1903, p. 1; *ibid*, 6 March 1903, p. 1.

ism, cultural progress and the solution of the Jewish question were yoked together, with the first placed as the foundation for the others. For Baranov, anglicisation meant unity with the English working class.

> Don't stand off from your English comrades. Don't make a separate state within the state in which you live. Throw away the asiatic customs you have brought from Russia. Throw away your barbaric language and learn the language of the country in which you live. Unite in unions, or – better – join, when possible, English unions. Don't allow yourselves to be sweated by your bloodsuckers. Live like human beings and demand human wages. In a word – become men (at present you are half wild) and citizens. Don't consider all other peoples to be lesser than you, because you are not better than others only, perhaps, a little more unfortunate. Look on your English comrades as brothers in work and suffering, go with them hand in hand, fight together with them. Here lies your help, only in this way can the Jewish Question be resolved.[16]

A revealing sign of the influence of this modernising perspective among Jewish social democrats in the early 1890s is that only rarely did they appear to recognise the economic causes of trade union weakness in the Jewish East End. The disarray of workers' organisations was seen to reflect the cultural and political ignorance of the workers themselves. Baranov complained that 'at the same time as workers in all countries are joining unions and are organising themselves, when the unskilled workers in England have already united and organised . . . the Jewish worker is like a wildman; he is quickly enthused and cools even faster'.[17] Like other critics of East European Jewish backwardness, many socialists believed that the immigrants possessed a lower standard of life than English workers. Thus trade unionism became charged with an educational and moral significance beyond bargaining over wages and conditions. Baranov believed, 'a union frees the workers, unslaves him in his own eyes, awakens in him the feeling of self worth . . .'.[18]

Both anarchists and social democrats regarded religion as an obstacle to enlightenment and political self-consciousness.[19] From its early issues, *Der Arbayter Fraynd* insisted on the connections between sweaters, capitalists and the religious leaders of the Jewish community. The Chief Rabbi in particular was abused as someone 'who

16. *Der Veker*, 23 December 1892, p. 1; see also *ibid*, 24 February 1893, p. 1.
17. *Ibid*, 20 January 1893, p. 1.
18. *Ibid*, 3 February 1893, p. 1.
19. Typically, the orthodox Jew was portrayed as someone whose ignorance was reflected in personal uncleanliness: for example *ibid*, 20 January 1893, p. 1.

believes in the sweating system more than God'. Likewise, the honorary officers of the East End synagogues were identified as sweaters.[20] The high point of this propaganda was the parade by 2–3,000 'Jewish unemployed and sweaters victims' who marched to the Great Synagogue on Saturday 16 March 1889.[21] The demonstration was organised by a Committee of Jewish Unemployed led by the trade unionist Lewis Lyons and the editor of *Der Arbayter Fraynd*, Philip Krantz. Its ostensible intention was to challenge Adler to deliver a sermon on behalf of the victims of the sweating system; but the strategic aim, as Benjamin Feigenbaum explained at the rally which followed the parade, was to demonstrate to 'our still deluded brothers'

> ... that they cannot expect any improvement in their condition, either from the rich or from religion; only from their united strength, together with all the workers of the whole world, by once and for all introducing another system to the world, a system in which workers themselves enjoy the entire fruit of their labour and are no longer robbed by sweaters and capitalists.[22]

Enlightenment and the workers' struggle were connected, since sweating was the product of ignorance as well as the unjust condition of society.[23] The ties and beliefs of religion led immigrant proletarians to place their hopes in philanthropists and their faith in God, rather than in their collective strength. Writing in *Di Fraye Velt*, Karl Liberman argued that 'before becoming a progressive, a socialist, even a nationalist, simply a civilised person, a European equal with other men, he [a Jew] must first become anti-religious'.[24]

The threat the revolutionaries presented was not, therefore, one which followed only from their role as agitators in the trades. Their work in the trade unions was part of a wider challenge to the sources of institutional and cultural authority in the Jewish East End. Their opponents acknowledged as much. Following the synagogue parade a member of the Federation of Synagogues executive committee 'called attention to certain socialist disturbances the previous Saturday and said that the Federation representing as it did the Jews of East London should disclaim any connection or sympathy with the socialists'.[25]

20. *AF*, 2–9 March 1888, p. 7; *ibid*, 23 March 1888, p. 2; *ibid*, 20–27 April 1888, p. 2.
21. On the parade see Tcherikower, *Di Geshikhte fun der Yidisher Arbatyer Bavegung*, vol. ii, pp. 124–5; Fishman, *East End Jewish Radicals*, pp. 164–8.
22. *AF*, 22–29 March 1889, p. 2.
23. *Ibid*, 25 May 1888, p. 1.
24. *Di Fraye Velt*, July 1892, p. 72; see too Eyges, *Beyond the Horizon*, pp. 75–6.
25. GLRO Federation of Synagogues, minute book, 19 March 1889.

In the aftermath of the 1889 tailors' strike Montagu proposed to counter 'the influence of a few atheists over Jewish working men' by giving the Federation funds with which to employ a minister or *maged*.[26] At the end of January 1890, Rabbi Dr Mayer Lerner was appointed to the position of minister. Lerner's energetic promotion of Sabbath observance in the Jewish trades was an attempt to present the antagonism between masters and men as an obstacle in the way of Jewish communal unity, rather than as a symptom of the need for a community of a different sort in which 'mine' and 'thine' did not exist.[27] In 1894, after Lerner's resignation, once again it was the threat presented by 'Jewish socialists' and 'demagogues' which led the Federation to employ the popular preacher Chaim Maccoby – the Kammenitzer *maged*. This step was taken in the immediate aftermath of further public demonstrations by unemployed Jewish immigrants. Montagu argued that these outbreaks placed the public reputation of Jewish immigrants in jeopardy: 'not a minister but a lecturer or *maged* was required immediately both to replace Dr Lerner and to counteract the evil work of those who were responsible for the recent disturbances in the East End'.[28] This was a shrewd decision. Anti-religious propaganda excited some immigrants but it also generated misgivings, even within the revolutionary circles.[29] It presented an easy opportunity to portray the socialists and anarchists as beyond the Jewish community. *Der Yidisher Ekspres* wrote, 'for the Jewish comrades socialism means free marriage, *Yom Kippur* balls and sabbath demonstrations outside Duke's Place Synagogue; an ugly low charlatanism . . . it is no wonder that the Jewish masses look on them [socialists] as trash'.[30]

The sabbath demonstration of 1889 had been staged at a time of growing socialist influence, but the defeats of the labour movement and the departure of the best writers and speakers to the United States damaged the prestige and influence of the movement. By the turn of the century the *Yom Kippur* balls were no longer aggressive proselytising occasions but the defiant gathering of a sect. On the Day of Atonement in 1904 the socialists were so beleaguered that the police had to rescue them from orthodox youths who attacked their club. Predictably, the East London Jewish branch of the Social

26. *Ibid*, 27 October 1889.
27. On Lerner see J. Jung, *Champions of Orthodoxy* (London, 1974), chapter 1. The 'election' was not repeated when Lerner's successor as minister was appointed in 1901.
28. *Jewish World*, 18 February 1894, p. 6.
29. Eyges, *Beyond the Horizon*, pp. 75–6; Osipov, *Deringerungen un Iberlebungen*, p. 140.
30. *Der Yidisher Ekspres*, 23 February 1900, p. 4.

Democratic Federation responded to these disturbances with a pamphlet portraying the orthodox of the East End as fanatical, uncivilised and unfit to enjoy the benefits of freedom in England.[31]

Orthodoxy and modernity

There was a striking convergence in the propaganda of immigrant revolutionaries and the responses of Anglo-Jewish philanthropists on the low level of cultural evolution attained by Jewish immigrants and on its expression in forms of religious orthodoxy. In fact, these views tell us more about the tendencies of social comment than the attitudes of the religious orthodox to the technological, cultural and political demands of their new environment. It was not only the revolutionaries who contested the meaning of modernity and progress.

The institution which most focused the opinion of the militant orthodox was the Machzike Hadath. The society, whose name means 'Upholders of the Law', was formed in 1891 by the combination of an East End *khevra*, Machzike Shomrei Shabbat, and a group of German Jews from the North London *Beth Hamedrash*.[32] During 1891–2 it initiated a dispute over the ritual cleanliness of the meat passed as *kosher* by the Board of Shechita. In effect, the Machzike Hadath demanded that there should be two tiers of *shechita*, the higher level to be supervised by themselves but financed by the established authorities. The Chief Rabbi could not compromise with this challenge to his authority. The militants responded by establishing their own slaughterhouse and in February 1893 they constituted themselves as a separate *kehila* and repudiated the authority of the Chief Rabbi.[33] The ostensible issue which precipitated the split was succinctly expressed by one member of the Machzike Hadath: 'Jews who do not obey the Jewish laws have no religious principles.'[34]

Adler dismissed the schismatics as 'a small section of Russian and Polish Jews' who were 'uncultivated and uncivilised', and who, therefore, could not be relied upon to make humane arrangements for the slaughter of animals.[35] The Board of Shechita's investigating officer, Morris Van Thal, took a different view. He believed the Machzike Hadath would receive the sympathy of most of the Jewish

31. Social Democratic Federation (East London Jewish Branch), *Yom Kippur Pogrom un di Sotsialistn* (London, 1904).
32. B. Homa, *A Fortress in Anglo-Jewry* (London, 1953), pp. 8–9.
33. *Jewish World*, 20 November 1891, p. 6.
34. *Ibid*, 18 August 1892, p. 3.
35. Homa, *A Fortress in Anglo-Jewry*, p. 34.

East End. The conflict spilled out of the synagogues and *khevras* on to the streets of the Jewish quarter. Rival butchers informed on each other and spread rumours that competitors sold unclean meat.[36] There was a price war between the rival Boards of Shechita. Each side solicited and received letters of support from eminent European rabbis, copies of which were placarded all over the Jewish East End.

The support which gathered around the Machzike Hadath was due only in part to its rigorous standards of observance. Harry Lewis argued that the secession was a protest 'against the government of the foreign Jews, who are the most numerous section of the community, by the English Jews who are in imperfect sympathy with them'.[37] From within the immigrant milieu, *Der Yidisher Ekspres* attached the same wider significance to the breakaway; it was a protest against the treatment of Russian Jews as 'ignorant beggars, as barbarians, who must be civilised through Sabbath sermons, soup kitchens and such like'.[38] Alongside and beyond the issue of *shechita* lay a conflict over anglicisation.

In fact the leaders of the Machzike Hadath did embrace a programme of 'anglicism'. At one of its earliest meetings the chairman assured his audience that the 'defenders of the law' aimed to be fully patriotic citizens.

> We ourselves, our own consciences, ought to learn us [sic] that with a true heart we must be thankful to the English government, and it is our sacred duty to pray for long life to our Queen, and all the royal family, and I cannot understand how real Judaism should be against anglicism, the contrary, the Jew who prays everyday and keeps the dietary laws, that very Jew knows the traditions, 'thou shalt pray for the welfare of the Kingdom'. And we are certain that the government does not require us to throw out our religion on the other side of the sea, and therefore we will try with all our might to reach our Holy project. Be true to your God and to your Queen.[39]

This view was affirmed by the synagogue's religious leader, Rabbi Aba Werner.[40] Even on the side of militant orthodoxy there was a willing identification with England. It was not the goal of anglicisation that was rejected but its meaning that was disputed.

36. *Ibid*, p. 39; Gaster papers University College London, M. Van Thal to Gaster, 27 January 1892; *ibid.*, 16 November 1891; *ibid.*, 20 November 1892.
37. C. Russell and H. Lewis, *The Jew in London* (London, 1900), p. 211.
38. *Der Yidisher Ekspres*, 24 July 1901, p. 4.
39. University of Southampton, AJ/121, minute book of the Machzike Hadath, 7 Adar 5651.
40. *JC*, 9 February 1911, p. 20.

For social revolutionaries as much as for Anglo-Jewish philanthropists, the immigrants' anglicisation was a matter of their westernisation and cultural development as well as their political orientation. But here too we should see that the Machzike Hadath and its supporters did not represent the force of unreflective traditionalism – although this is how they were portrayed by their opponents. They did not oppose the advance of secular knowledge in itself but merely anything which prevented men from obeying Jewish law. Rabbi Werner believed that 'there is no reason why secular education should alienate Jews from their own literature'.[41] Similarly, *Der Yidisher Ekspress* argued that the association of strict orthodoxy with ignorance was unwarranted and that works of geography, geology and anthropology, which were at variance with the Biblical account of creation, were read by pious Jews. It was 'materialism' not science which was seen to be the enemy of orthodoxy.[42]

Controversy over religious education in the East End allows us to explore more closely the debate over the union of modernity, 'anglicism' and religious observance. The background to this conflict was the low-level, or non-existent, Jewish religious education available in the voluntary and board schools of the East End. Even at the Jews' Free School religious education was given a low priority. Here there was a half-hour instruction each day for the lower standards and one hour for the higher ones, and there were additional classes for two hours on Sunday mornings. But the weekday lessons, the first of the morning, were those most often 'cut' by pupils, and one third of the school did not attend on Sundays. Elsewhere the situation was even less satisfactory. In 1896, 1,416 Jewish children of foreign parents attended London board schools at which there was no Jewish religious instruction at all. But at other board schools some provision was made for teaching Hebrew and the Old Testament during and after normal school hours. The amount of religious instruction varied between one and a half and seven hours per week, as different schools adopted different practices.[43] The additional hours were organised and paid for by the Jewish Association for the Diffusion of Religious Knowledge. In 1894 this body was re-formed and re-named the Jewish Religious Education Board. But the fundamental problems of underfunding and teachers ill-qualified to instruct children in the Jewish religion remained. In some cases the lessons were given by Jewish teachers but in others the task fell to Christians. Still

41. *Ibid.*
42. *Der Yidisher Ekspres*, 23 February 1900, p. 4; *ibid*, 9 March 1910, p. 3.
43. Federation of Synagogues, minute book, 7 April 1891; J. Jacobs, ed., *The Jewish Year Book; an Annual Record of Matters Jewish, 5657* (London, 1897), pp. 54–5.

less satisfactory was the predicament of the Jewish children who attended Christian voluntary schools. By the turn of the century 1,628 Jewish children attended Anglican schools in East London.[44]

Immigrant parents looked elsewhere for their children's religious education. In 1891, 2,000 of the 7,000 children who attended Jewish voluntary schools in the East End or board schools that provided Jewish religious instruction also attended one of 250 *khadorim*.[45] These figures appear in their proper light when we consider that this education was reserved, almost exclusively, for boys. In 1903, 1,308 boys out of the 2,184 who attended the Jews' Free School also attended extra religious classes outside of school.[46] At board schools the proportion of boys attending a *kheyder* or *Talmud Torah* was still higher.[47]

In a *kheyder* the weekly charges were between 6d and 1s 6d for one pupil. One hostile observer described the classrooms in this way:

> An East End *kheyder* consists usually of one, sometimes two rooms, in a very small dwelling house. The rooms are usually low pitched and of dimensions accommodating less than a dozen pupils, but receiving any number between twelve and thirty. The furniture consists mainly of benches or forms, mostly without backs and there is no accommodation for writing.[48]

Over the period the number of children receiving their Jewish education in a *Talmud Torah* increased dramatically. In the early 1890s there was just one such school in the Jewish East End, teaching 300 pupils. In 1895 the Machzike Hadath opened its *Talmud Torah* which, within ten weeks, had enrolled 500 pupils. By 1907 this had expanded to 800 children organised in 16 classes. Alongside it there were 4 other schools, 2 of which took roughly 200 children each; 1 took 500 and the other 600. Here children spent between $1\frac{1}{2}$ and 3 hours after school each weekday.[49] Despite this expansion, the de-

44. Federation of Synagogues, minute book, 7 April 1891; Gartner, *The Jewish Immigrant*, pp. 227–9.
45. Federation of Synagogues, minute book, 7 April 1891. In the late 1890s the proportion of boys at board schools attending *khadorim* had declined; but this signified a shift to education in the new large *Talmud Torahs*. In 1898 there were two of them in the East End: one taught between 550 and 650 pupils and conducted its classes in English, the other was connected to the Machzike Hadath and there instruction was in Yiddish.
46. Of the 1,164 girls at the school, only 24 attended extra classes. *Ibid.*
47. *JC*, 6 November 1903, p. 23.
48. *JC*, supplement, 1 July 1898, p. 5.
49. Homa, *A Fortress*, p. 51; Federation of Synagogues, minute book, report of the *Talmud Torah* Committee, 19 July 1905; *JC*, 15 March 1907, p. 32; *ibid*, 26 April 1907, p. 22.

mand for places continued to exceed their supply. Lack of finance was the main obstacle to further growth.[50] Although a minority of children did pay fees, the schools were principally charitable institutions whose main aim was to give a religious education to poor children. In 1898, 499 children at the Great Garden Street *Talmud Torah* either paid nothing or up to 6d per week, 98 pupils were charged 6d and just 10 paid more than this.[51]

It was as part of an attempt to effect a synthesis between orthodoxy and one view of modernisation that the Federation delegated an enquiry into the *khadorim* in 1891. The leaders of the Federation wanted to combine modernity and orthodoxy. Just as Rothschild's Four Per Cent Dwelling Company provided 'model dwellings' for the immigrants, so the Federation of Synagogues promoted 'model synagogues'.[52] In 1891 members of the Crawcour and the Sons of David *khevras* were informed by the Federation's architect that their premises were unfit for public worship and 'induced to close them'. In their place the first 'model synagogue' was built.[53] During the first nine years of the Federation's existence it had assisted in the erection or improvement of fourteen synagogues. The significance of sanitary progress in the moral and material improvement of the immigrant colony was not an idea limited to Anglo-Jewish reformers. It was an issue around which Montagu and the federated synagogues were able to cooperate. Literally and figuratively they strove to remove orthodox observance from its connotations with Russian medievalism and physical impoverishment. In 1892 the annual report explained that congregations which had once worshipped in synagogues little better than rooms now did so in buildings 'thoroughly worthy of their holy purpose'.[54]

The Federation's report on the *khadorim* recognised the weakness of the Hebrew and religious education given at board and voluntary schools, and appreciated that 'this desire of our working classes for further instruction on these subjects for their children should be respected'. Its objection to the *khadorim*, however, was that 'the surroundings are of the most insanitary description and the teachers in the most abject poverty'.[55] The report advised that the *khadorim*

50. *Ibid*, 4 January 1907, p. 27.
51. *JC*, 28 March 1898, p. 28.
52. On the Dwellings Company see White, *Rothschild Buildings*.
53. Federation of Synagogues, minute book, 20 November 1891.
54. Federation of Synagogues, minute book, 6 November 1892; *ibid.*, 22 November 1896.
55. Lerner believed that a *melamed* could gather together an income of just 15s a week. Little wonder that one confided that although he had plans to improve his schoolroom, 'sometimes I get tired of it, it ain't good business. I think one day I will go into *geshaft* [business].' In the *Talmud Torah* teachers could be

should be supervised by the federated synagogues and that the *melamdim* should be encouraged to transfer their classes to accommodation made available at Stepney Jewish schools. The apparent concern was with sanitation but this could also lead to a more significant gain – a change in the language of instruction from Yiddish to English.[56] Even among a large section of observant Jews in the East End the *khadorim* and the *melamdim* represented all that was backward and undesirable about East European Jewish culture. It was the aim of one part of the Federation's leadership to wrench orthodox Judaism from this context.[57] But the inadequacy of the other sources of Jewish education ensured that they made meagre progress.[58]

Controversy over religious education, and the role of the *khadorim* in particular, came to a head in June 1898 during and after the Anglo-Jewish conference on elementary education at the Central Synagogue in the West End of London. The *Jewish Chronicle* reported that 'chief interest was aroused in the subject of the *khadorim* and *Talmud Torah* schools'. The principal paper on these schools was given by Mrs N.S. Joseph. She described them as the peculiar products of Russian and Polish conditions in which other places of education were closed to Jews.[59] Presented in this way, rather than as the necessary nursery of religious knowledge, they were fit only to be swept away.[60] By 1898 the *khadorim* had become the scapegoats for the failure to achieve a more complete physical as well as moral anglicisation of the immigrants.

> In these times when so many praiseworthy efforts are being made by the more fortunately placed members of our community to improve the stunted growth and sickly appearance of the Jewish school children, the question naturally arises why, notwithstanding annual country holidays, notwithstanding brigade drills, notwithstanding cricket, football and swimming clubs, the boys still retain their unhealthy appearance.[61]

paid more; there wages ranged between 15s and 27s per week: *JC*, 22 July 1898, p. 24; Federation of Synagogues, minute book, report of the *Talmud Torah* Committee, 19 July 1905.

56. Federation of Synagogues, minute book, 7 April 1891. Lerner informed Samuel Montagu that of the 250 *melamdim* only 11 taught in English and 'the remainder in the jargon'.
57. Federation of Synagogues, minute book, 20 November 1891; *Jewish World*, 10 April 1891, p. 6; *ibid*, 13 November 1891, p. 6. See the comments of Samuel Montagu, *ibid*, p. 11.
58. The reformers themselves acknowledged this problem. Federation of Synagogues, minute book, 7 April 1891.
59. *JC*, supplement, 1 July 1898, p. v.
60. *Ibid*, p. vi.
61. *Ibid*.

The blame was placed on the 'strain' caused by long hours in the *khadorim*. These anxieties were seen to be sufficiently pressing to override conventions of parental control. Since the parents were irremediable and 'probably regard it as a supreme virtue that their children should suffer physical ill in acquiring their religious education', Mrs Joseph argued the Public Health Act should be extended to regulate the *khadorim*.[62]

Other speakers concentrated on different facets of the criticisms brought by Mrs Joseph. Some were anxious that young children were being 'overworked'. According to Dr Schorstein, excessive brain work caused disease and so East End children became 'pale and washed out and nervously unstable'. The principal concern of the Chief Rabbi was modernisation. He described the discipline and instruction in the Great Garden Street *Talmud Torah* as 'thorough and efficient' and urged that it should be 'energetically upheld'. This, he feared, could not be said for the Brick Lane *Talmud Torah*, where the teaching was in Yiddish. He declared, 'it was not correct to speak of a *kheyder* in Booth Street Buildings as being only twenty yards from the nearest board school; the fact was that two hundred years lay between them'.[63]

The proceedings at the Central Synagogue provoked a protest meeting, held three weeks later at the Jewish Working Mens Club. The *Jewish Chronicle* conveyed both the scale and the intensity of the gathering.

> The hall of the Jewish Working Mens Club has been the scene of many a striking meeting but seldom has such a spectacle been seen as on Sunday last when the spacious hall was not only filled to overflowing but the passages leading to it were also thronged. The speakers were decidedly aggressive and every point made against the 'West Enders' was cheered to the echo, the wildest enthusiasm prevailing when the resolution 'that we East Enders do not recognise the West End Jews as authorities upon Hebrew and Religious Education' was carried. Men and women stood upon their seats, hats, sticks and handkerchiefs were waved and it was some time before the meeting calmed down again. The watchword of the meeting was 'Freedom from the West' and one speaker went so far as to call upon the East to emancipate itself from the yoke of the West.[64]

Among the speakers were Eliazer Laizerovitch, a journalist who wrote for *Der Yidisher Ekspres*, and the chairman of the Union of

62. *Ibid.*
63. Only one speaker at the conference defended the *chedarim*: the Rev. W. Esterson, who wanted to defend the autonomy of the family and a father's right to determine his child's education.
64. *JC*, 22 July 1898, p. 25.

Melamdim, Joseph Cohn-Lask. Theirs was not a simple defence of traditionalism. Laizerovitch called for better accommodation and shorter hours and Cohn-Lask claimed that critics had under-estimated the extent to which these changes, in fact, had been introduced. He claimed that only 'greeners' taught in cellars. Children were not overworked, he explained, since not all of their time at *kheyder* was spent studying. He presented the Union of *Melamdim* as a force for self-regulation and improvement, one which did not require the interference of English Jews.[65]

At the same time as Cohn-Lask and Laizerovitch advocated the progressive reform of the schools, they defended their programme of religious education uncompromisingly and condemned the sort of anglicisation pursued by English Jews. Cohen-Lask suggested that if children were overworked then they should spend less time in board schools. Against the denigration of Yiddish and religious education in immigrant institutions, Laizerovitch denounced English Jews for striving after social status and materialism. The Anglo-Jewish clergy had capitulated to the 'golden calf that rules in the stock exchange' and he punned that although English Jews claimed their concern was with ethics it was really etiquette which worried them.[66] The West End reformers were deserting God and ignoring the lessons of Jewish history. The attack on the *khadorim* was a futile attempt to escape the consequences of anti-Semitism by assimilation. But only the assimilators needed to fear anti-Semitism, according to this argument, for they were not prepared for it. For the rest it would only strengthen their Jewish feeling.[67]

This was not an atavistic revolt against the pressures of modernity but it did envision an accommodation of Judaism to modernity different from one foreseen or desired by the leaders of native Jewry. The commitment of Laizerovitch, Werner and *Der Yidisher Ekspres* was to political zionism, and thus to a radical transformation in Jewish life: a negation of the ghetto rather than a desire to recreate it in London.

Zionism

In late nineteenth- and early twentieth-century Britain the political uses of national identities were becoming ever more promiscuous. Further, as we have seen, there was a growing tendency for national ideologies to invoke cultural and racial communities. Jews could

65. *Der Yidisher Ekspres,* 22 July 1898, p. 4; *ibid,* 29 July 1898, p. 3.
66. *Ibid,* 22 July 1898, p. 4.
67. *Ibid.*

respond to these circumstances in a number of ways; for instance, the voluble anti-alien sympathies of Jewish Conservative MPs such as H.S. Samuel and H.H. Marks might be seen to express one sort of reaction. Zionism was a very different sort of response. Through Zionism some Jews chose to make claims for their own national identity.

As we have seen, the idea that Jews were connected by cultural and spiritual bonds was not new. However, with zionism, Jewish national identity became territorial and political. The innovatory point of Herzl's project, and its institutionalisation through the First Zionist Congress at Basle in August 1897, was the constitution of the Jewish people as a political entity. Herbert Bentwich told a zionist audience in the East End in December of that year, 'the mere holding of such a Congress by Jews, two thousand years after the dispersion made an impression on all our generation which could not be effaced'.[68] Political zionism intended to solve the Jewish problem by securing for the Jews a legally recognised territory. Emancipation and assimilation, it argued, could neither provide defences from anti-Semitism nor establish the conditions in which Jewish culture could flourish.[69] The answer to the problems of exile was to end this unnatural condition. Equally significant was the intention of the World Zionist Organisation to negotiate with governments to secure this goal.[70] This ambition contrasted vividly with the practice of Choveve Zion, the predecessor of political zionism.

In 1890 a Choveve Zion Association was established in London 'with the avowed object of fostering the national idea in Israel and of establishing agricultural colonies in the Holy Land'.[71] The concept of Jewish nationality expressed by the Choveve Zion journal, *Palestina*, was conceived as an historical-religious bond, not a political aspiration for statehood.

> We want to provide for numbers of our co-religionists homes and sustenance by agricultural labour in a country eminently suitable for that purpose. The practicability of such efforts is surely not impaired by the circumstance that the country is the cradle of our race, and that those who will benefit materially, will be at the same time spiritually raised above the common drudgery of a peasant's life by such noble sentiments as love of their race and devotion to their national traditions.[72]

68. *Jewish World*, 3 December 1897, p. 162.
69. Where the emphasis should lie between these goals was subject to debate: see D. Vital, *Zionism: The Formative Years* (Oxford, 1982), pp. 348–64.
70. On the significance of the Basle Congress and of Herzl's initiative see D. Vital, *The Origins of Zionism* (Oxford, 1975), pp. 297–8, 354–70.
71. *Palestina*, October 1892, p. 7. On the pre-history of zionism in London see the same article.
72. *Ibid*, October 1892, p. 2.

The idea of creating a Jewish polity was not present here; the aim was to promote the 'Love of Zion' and colonisation in Palestine. The movement's origins lay in Russia, in the response to the pogroms of 1881–2. The founding conference was held in Katowice in November 1884.[73] The English Choveve Zion contained several different currents: the nationalist faction among the East European Jewish radicals in London, some of the pious masses attracted to the movement by the Kammenitzer *Maged*, and English Jews eager to find expression for those ties between Jews which seemed to reach beyond the bonds of a common religion.

The Association's highpoint came in 1891, in the face of greatly increased emigration from Russia. In May of that year a mass meeting of 4,000 Jews was held at the Great Assembly Hall, Stepney, with Montagu as chairman. At the time, it was the largest meeting of Jews ever held in England. Its object was to publicise a petition to the Sultan, asking him to allow further Jewish colonisation in Palestine. However, the support given to Choveve Zion by the Anglo-Jewish elite was never large enough to allow significant results in the practical work of purchasing land and settling Jews upon it. Just 24,000 acres of land in the Golan were purchased and two Jewish colonies were 'adopted'. Calls to the East Enders to support the work were pathetically impractical. The result was impatience and dwindling enthusiasm.[74]

Herzl's intervention eclipsed Choveve Zion and transformed the Zionist agenda. By November 1897 the English Choveve Zion Association had voted to identify itself with the Basle declaration. The issue was no longer the revival of identification with the Holy Land combined with a philanthropic effort to aid some East European emigrants. The aim had become the political reconstitution of Jewish political nationality after 2,000 years of dispersion, through an organisation which owed its only loyalty to Jewish interests, as it construed them.

Political zionism radically challenged the customary ways of combining Jewish and English identities. Inevitably, the new movement was anathematised by the leaders of Anglo-Jewry. The subject was dismissed from discussion in all the main Anglo-Jewish institutions.[75] In claiming that a Jewish territory was the only defence against anti-Semitism, zionists rejected the programme of political emancipa-

73. Of the thirty delegates, all but three came from Eastern Europe but two of these others travelled from London: Vital, *The Origins of Zionism*, pp. 163–4.

74. *Palestina*, December 1894, p. 2; *ibid*, June 1895, p. 1; *ibid*, December 1895, p. 23; *ibid*, September 1896, p. 1.

75. S. Cohen, *English Zionists and British Jews: The Communal Politics of Anglo-Jewry, 1895–1920* (Princeton, NJ, 1982), pp. 47–9.

tion, education and westernisation that the communal leaders prescribed not only for Jews in England but for those in Russia as well. Most straightforwardly, political zionists were an embarrassment because they appeared to claim a political identity for Jews beyond the one they had as subjects or citizens in the states in which they lived.[76] Montagu lectured the executive of the Federation of Synagogues: 'in his opinion for a Jew to espouse political zionism made him unfit to be a member of the British parliament... and [would] bring trouble upon the loyal and patriotic Jews of England'.[77]

For zionists, however, this did not indicate a rejection of political integration and anglicisation but a conception of it which did not require the effacement of Jewish interests. The responses of *Der Yidisher Ekspres* to the Boer War illustrate the way in which these views were combined. The newspaper urged its readers that 'Jews now have the opportunity to show thanks to the country which has taken them in and given them freedom. Jews should not let this opportunity slip.'[78] But it claimed that the patriotism of Jews was not evidence of anti-zionism. It claimed that hearts were not so small that they were unable to sympathise with two causes at one time. Zionism was defended in the light of evidence of growing anti-Jewish feeling. The newspaper responded vigorously and unapologetically to the increasing anti-Jewish attitudes expressed both by pro-Boers and anti-aliens in the English press. 'The question is not whether Jews think of Palestine or England as their fatherland but how England will later regard its Jews, as its own people or as foreigners.'[79] This was a bold statement which rejected the conditional acceptance of English Jews within the nation.

But despite the hopes and fears it excited, political zionism did not become a popular and radical force in Anglo-Jewish life in this period. Zionists failed to transform the enthusiasm expressed on occasions such as a visit by Herzl into a bedrock of organised support. Although the English Zionist Federation, established in January 1899, grew rapidly – an individual membership of 4,000 in 1899 had grown to 7,155 in 1902 – since many individuals were members of more than one society, these figures overestimate affiliation.[80] In 1909–10 the organisation was threatened by bankruptcy. When the Zionist Congress was held in London in 1900, Joseph Cowens warned delegates not to be misled by the large public

76. *Ibid*, pp. 163–83.
77. *JC*, 2 November 1900, p. 22.
78. *Der Yidisher Ekspres*, 5 January 1900, p. 2.
79. *Ibid*, 2 February 1900, p. 4.
80. Cohen, *English Zionists and British Jews*, p. 56.

meeting which had gathered to hear and see leading personalities. 'Our experience is that although it is comparatively easy to obtain any amount of "shouting" for zionism, it is of the utmost difficulty to get any real "working" for zionism.'[81] The situation had not improved by the end of our period. In 1914 Cowens wrote to the Zionist Actions Committee: 'You state that you have received a number of letters from England proving that there is great enthusiasm for our cause here. Perhaps you would put me in touch with your correspondents, as I have not been able to find much sympathy.'[82]

The significance of the English Zionist Federation in this period does not lie in any progress it made towards transforming the conditions of Jewish life. Instead, the English Zionist Federation became a site, not a solvent, of cultural and political conflict. The conflict between East End and West End Jewry, native and immigrant, was reproduced within the zionist movement. This was articulated with particular force by the socialist zionists in the East End. They went so far as to accuse the English Zionist Federation executive of introducing their own 'Aliens Bill' when it disqualified persons not permanently resident in England from being elected to the World Zionist Congress.[83]

The English Zionist Federation's fundamental tactical dilemma contributed to this internal division. How was the movement to maintain support in the present when its success appeared so distant? Many individual zionist societies acted merely as fund-raising organisations. Kalman Marmor described this sort of zionist activity in this way: 'In London there are not a few zionist societies, that is societies which have a chairman, a couple of vice-chairmen, a certain number of committee men, collectors and, above all, a thick book in which the names and addresses are written of several men who give a penny when they are asked and often without knowing to whom and for what.'[84]

This kind of zionism generated a paper membership but little enthusiasm. Marmor's alternative was for the zionists to undertake more agitation, issue more propaganda and open more libraries.[85] But the result was internal strife, as each current in the Jewish East End, each vision of the Jewish future, from the socialists to religious orthodoxy, was represented within the zionist movement: from the free-thinkers of the Herzl-Nordau Cultural Society to Rabbi Aba

81. *JC*, 17 August 1900, p. xv.
82. Cited in Cohen, *English Zionists and British Jews*, p. 126.
83. G. Shimoni, 'Poale Zion: A Zionist Transplant in Britain, 1905–45', *Studies in Contemporary Jewry*, 1986, pp. 228–9.
84. *Der Koysl-Maarovi*, November 1902, p. 2.

Werner of the Machzike Hadath. In January 1903 a despairing correspondent to *Der Yidisher Ekspres* argued that the local movement should devote all its energies to fund-raising for a national home. Cultural activities only divided Jews from each other; they weakened zionism, he said.[86] Even as it strove to negate it, zionism was a growth of the diaspora and, with the major exception of anti-zionism, contained within itself all the contending visions of the Jewish future.

Accounting for change

The forms of anglicisation pressed on Jewish immigrants by philanthropists and zionists, revolutionaries and orthodox Jews shared certain features; each welcomed Jewish emancipation, and each sought a positive use for new forms of knowledge. Beyond this common ground, however, the meaning of anglicisation, the shape of the modern world and the position of Jews within it were all subject to debate from widely different positions. Acknowledging the diverse ways in which cultural change was conceived has important consequences for the way we understand those changes which did take place.

A contextualised understanding of anglicisation must take acount of the different ways in which this goal was defined. In contrast to the view that immigrant life was characterised by traditionalist concerns, I have drawn attention to the variety of modernising ideologies and projects in the Jewish East End. In this light an opposition between immigrant traditionalism and western modernity does not make sense. The immigrant colony was the site of conflict, not between traditionalism and modernity, East European habit and English innovation, but between diverse and contending conceptions of what anglicisation and modernity actually meant. It is not enough for us to say that anglicisation was inevitable; this merely raises the question, 'Which form of anglicisation?'

Accounts couched in terms of 'social control' and 'socialisation' offer one sort of explanation of the eventual outcome. Yet the influence of Anglo-Jewry was more broad than it was deep. Anglo-Jewish institutions not only provided relief for the communal poor; they also intervened offering, *inter alia*, secondary education, religious education, youth clubs, apprenticeship schemes, model dwellings, soup kitchens, clothing, maternity care, care in old age, care for the disabled and a shelter for newly arrived immigrants.[87] Fund-

85. *Ibid.*
86. *Der Yidisher Ekspres*, 7 January 1903, p. 6.
87. Black, *The Social Politics of Anglo-Jewry* provides the fullest account.

ing these operations was a constant problem. The oft-projected East End Scheme – a Jewish Toynbee Hall – never materialised, for lack of finance. Lack of money also hobbled Anglo-Jewry's attempts to dominate religious education in the Jewish East End.[88] The club life created for boys and girls once they left school could accommodate but a slender minority of the cohort at which it was aimed. Just before the First World War, there were fewer than 3,000 boys' club places in the Jewish East End. This represented an impressive amount of activity, particularly on the part of the Jewish Lads Brigade which provided half the number. Nevertheless, this must be placed against the fact that there were club places for fewer than half of the Jewish boys between the ages of fourteen and eighteen in the East End.[89]

Testimony to the effectiveness of Anglo-Jewish efforts, if we examine it, invariably comes from the men and women who were responsible for these initiatives.[90] But these voices should not be our only guides. By the 1920s their successors were mourning the march of religious indifference among East End Jewish youths; hardly evidence of the security of a Jewish 'subculture' as Anglo-Jewish leaders would have defined it.[91] East End Jews were able to resist the influence of institutions and messages they disliked. Reformers met with a response that was, at best, selective. Efforts to disperse the Jewish East End foundered on the need of Jewish workers to live near their workplaces and the street labour markets through which opportunities could be found. The immigrants did not constitute a decorous and politically submissive population. At the end of this period, far from waning, anarchist influence in the Jewish East End was at its peak and prominent in the 1912 strike of ladies' tailors. *Der Arbayter Fraynd*, after its reappearance in 1903, was soon being printed in batches of over 4,000 each week. The anarchists' literary journal, *Germinal*, published after 1905, had a circulation of 2,000. Rudolf Rocker, who edited both publications, claimed their readership far exceeded the number of copies sold.[92] In January

88. Out of 37,500 Jewish children in London in 1910, 10,500 received no formal religious education: *ibid*, p. 128.
89. *Ibid*, pp. 141–7; Rosenbaum, 'A Contribution to the Study of the Vital and Other Statistics of the Jews in the United Kingdom', *Journal of the Royal Statistical Society*, 1905, p. 540.
90. This a problem with Black, *The Social Politics of Anglo-Jewry* in particular: see for example, pp. 109–11, 134–8, 138.
91. See, for instance, papers on 'Religious Work among Adolescents' and 'The Disruptive Influences on Jewish Life', presented by Rabbi H. Cohen and Rev. E. Drukker at the Conference of Jewish Preachers in 1923. *JC*, 13 July 1923, pp. 26–30.
92. Rocker, *In Sturm*, pp. 345, 351–2.

1917 Lucien Wolf, a leading member of the JBD, conceded wearily that the majority of immigrants remained in sentiment a part of their countries of origin.[93]

A further difficulty with the social control or socialisation model is that responses to the problem of aligning Jewish and English identities among the Anglo-Jewish middle and upper classes were not uniform. These divisions created opportunities for dissenting forms of political and religious organisation in the Jewish East End. Political zionism had this effect, for example, though its middle-class leaders were unwilling to appeal to the East End masses.[94] More significant, however, was the Federation of Synagogues. Under Montagu's patronage, East Enders could carry out improvements to their synagogues and find a voice within the Jewish community, urging the community to become more orthodox in its religious practice and more democratic in its governance. Moreover, the leaders of Anglo-Jewry pursued goals which, at times, contradicted a policy of vigorous anglicisation. One such goal was communal unity. This was felt with particular keenness as the campaign for an Aliens Act neared fruition in 1905. This provided the background to the concessions which persuaded the Machzike Hadath to return to the official community when Lord Rothschild and Samuel Montagu cleared its debts of £5,000. In another instance, it was not pressure for communal unity but fear of the influence of Jewish revolutionaries that led Montagu and others to employ the Kammenitzer *Maged* even though, normally, his *droshes* were regarded as a prime example of East European Judaism's retrograde characteristics.

Concepts such as socialisation and social control introduce agency into explanations of cultural change – as opposed to an impersonal process of 'modernisation' – but they do so in a one-sided way. The choices of immigrants and other East End Jews must also be taken into account. The plurality of cultural and political projects was testimony to the vigour with which Jews responded to their freedom from both state and religious controls in Eastern Europe. At the same time, this plenitude was indicative of weakness. None of these projects possessed either the financial resources or the coercive force capable of dominating cultural life in the Jewish East End. It was, perhaps, the scant economic and institutional resources available to immigrant institutions which provided the structural determinant of cultural and political change.

The decline in Jewish religious observance in London, for

93. YIVO archives, New York, NY, David Mowshowitch Collection, papers of Lucien Wolf, folder 47, memorandum, 31 January 1917.
94. Cohen, *English Zionists and British Jews*, p. 63.

example, can be accounted for, in the first place, in terms of the attenuated opportunities to sustain orthodox beliefs and practices following emigration. As the emigrants moved away from Eastern Europe, their Judaism was taken from a context in which it was closely integrated with the sources of economic and political power. In the Russian empire the synagogue had enjoyed compulsory financial support from the Jewish community; in London affiliation became voluntary. It was transplanted to a society in which rabbis had to compete, not only with the *maskilim* and Jewish revolutionaries, but with other institutions supported by the state and Anglo-Jewry. From this point of view, the problems confronting Judaism were one variant of the difficulties the churches faced in the same period, as their role was challenged by other institutions in fields such as politics, education, philanthropy and leisure.[95]

In Russia and Poland the rabbinate and the communal authorities, despite encroachment by the Russian state, still wielded significant legal and coercive powers. In London, in comparison to the legal powers and financial resources available to day schools, which aimed to turn the immigrants' children into 'good English subjects', the resources of Jewish synagogues and educational ventures were puny. It is in the contested and specific relations between religious institutions, society and the state that we can locate the dynamic leading to the decline of traditional Jewish observance. The persistence of orthodox belief is thus comprehensible, not as an eccentric phenomenon running in the face of social trends, but as a reflection of the capacity of minorities to erect structures of social and cultural independence.[96] But in London the resources did not exist for orthodox institutions to survive on any scale without compromise. The sharpest example of militant independence, the Machzike Hadath, returned to the communal fold.

In the most literal sense native Jewry had to pay a price for communal unity but financial necessity had tamed the political and cultural challenge of the 'Upholders of the Law'; the implications of their orthodoxy were contained. This outcome is all the more telling since among the members of the Machzike Hadath were individuals drawn from the wealthiest stratum of the immigrant community: traders and merchants who had risen above the milieu of the workshop trades.[97] Poverty took its toll on other independent initiatives.

95. For this interpretation see J. Cox, *The Churches in a Secular Society: Lewisham 1870–1930* (Oxford, 1982).
96. S. Poll, *The Hasidic Community of Williamsburg: A Study in the Sociology of Religion* (New York, NY, 1969 edn), p. 254.
97. GLRO Records of the Great Synagogue, A/SGS 26, 14 February 1898, lease of Spitalfields Great Synagogue.

The Great Garden Street *Talmud Torah,* for example, helped secure its survival by pledging to conduct lessons in English.[98] Among the orthodox the reputation of London was exceedingly low. The worst fate that could befall a rabbi or teacher, we are told, was that he should find himself in that city.[99]

Signs of the weakness of immigrant institutions in this early period are legion. For most of these years the newspapers and clubs established by revolutionary groups endured a hand-to-mouth existence.[100] In the 1880s London had been regarded as the 'Jerusalem' of the Jewish labour and revolutionary movements, and for a period some of its greatest propangandists – Morris Vincehvsky, Phillip Krantz, Benjamin Feigenbaum, Saul Yanofsky and others – settled there. By the mid-1890s, in the wake of the retreat of the immigrant labour movement in London, all had gone to the United States.[101] The greater number of East European Jews in New York could better support them. What is striking is that in London they could not be replaced from within the Jewish immigrant colony. The leaders of the anarchist and social democrat groups in the East End in the early twentieth century were both non-Jews: Rudolf Rocker and Adolf Beck respectively. Jewish revolutionaries attained heights of influence in 1889–90 and the anarchists did so again between 1910–14. But on the first occasion the defeats of new unionism led to a powerful reversal of fortunes and on the second the movement was broken by repression and dissension after the outbreak of war. In 1903 *Der Vunderer* mourned the Jews' decrepit spiritual life in London. It looked back on the years between 1889–93 as a golden age in which agitators had educated the Jewish masses and there had existed a theatre with fine actors.[102] This image of decline is confirmed from other sources: from Morris Meyer, for example, who related that in 1902, when he arrived in London, the capital's immigrant colony was unable to support a Yiddish theatre.[103]

In short, the dynamic of cultural change in the Jewish East End can be located in the interaction between contending ideologies of modernity, their capacity to thrive and reproduce themselves institutionally and the decisions of the immigrants themselves as they

98. P.L.S. Quinn, 'The Jewish Schooling System of London, 1656–1956' (University of London doctoral thesis, 1958), vol. ii, p. 611.
99. M. Berlin, *Fun Voluzin biz Yerushalayim,* vol. ii (New York, NY, 1933), pp. 415–16.
100. In the secondary literature this story is well told in Fishman, *East End Jewish Radicals,* chapters 7, 8.
101. Frankel, *Prophecy and Politics,* pp. 119–23.
102. *Der Vunderer,* 13 February 1903, p. 1.
103. M. Meyer, *Yidish Teater in London, 1902–42* (London, n.d.), pp. 29–31.

confronted a multitude of choices in their new environment. The process of anglicisation was framed by the financial and institutional resources available to contending groups. This allows for the possibility that, in favourable circumstances, the scope of Jewish affiliation and the opportunities to exercise it would expand. Explanations derived from concepts such as 'socialisation', 'social control' and 'modernisation' all agree that the process of Jewish integration in English society led to a linear attenuation of Jewish identity. But as will be seen in the final chapter, in the early twentieth century, as the state became a stronger presence in the Jewish East End, immigrants were provided with a new resource. In the years preceding the First World War, Jewish immigrants forced themselves in unprecedented ways and with conspicuous success into the arena of English politics.

Chapter 15

The State, the Nation and Jewish Politics

Enforcing the Aliens Act

The Aliens Act was the first of a series of bills and Acts of Parliament which, in the decade before the First World War, encroached on the particular interests of Jews and immigrants. New legislation and the debates surrounding it reshaped the problem of Jewish integration. As the state intervened more extensively in economic and social life so, in many cases, the status of Jews and immigrants under new legislation had to be defined. The supporters of state intervention buttressed their policies with appeals to new sorts of national community. In the case of Conservative collectivism these were focused on empire. In the case of the Liberal government after 1906 it was the concept of citizenship which played a central role. The relation of Jews and immigrants to the idea of the nation, as well as the state, thus became problematic in new ways. This chapter, therefore, returns to the subject of the relation of Jews to the state and to the nation. Addressing new developments from this perspective, it will be possible to ask to what extent, and with what consequences, new conceptions of the nation took hold within political argument and displaced older formulations.

The second section of this study analysed the infirm condition of the labour movement among Jewish workers in London. But it left unanswered what the shape of politics was in the Jewish East End in the absence of a vigorous labour movement. The discussions of associational life, communal politics and the conflicts over anglicisation have gone some way to providing an answer. But at present this account of immigrant politics remains incomplete. Between 1900–14, through a series of legislative initiatives and administrative practices, the advance of the collectivist state presented a series of challenges to both immigrant and native Jews. It will be argued here that state intervention gave rise to new and vigorous forms of politics in the Jewish East End which mobilised large numbers of Jewish immigrants to achieve considerable practical results.

Before looking at new legislation some of these themes can be addressed by examining the way the Aliens Act was administered. The Liberal Party won heavily in the general election of January 1906. The Aliens Act had not been brought into force before the election and its Conservative supporters feared that Herbert Gladstone, the new Home Secretary, would undermine the Act and render it ineffective. At the same time, the Act's most active Liberal and Labour opponents demanded that this was what he should do. Gladstone found he 'occupied the unhappy position of knowing that whatever he did or said on the subject of the administration of the Act would draw fire upon him from all quarters of the House'.[1]

The Aliens Act did not provide any clear guidelines for determining who was or was not a refugee. Each case was judged on its particular merits. The burden of proof, however, was placed on anyone appealing against rejection. Liberal and Labour opponents of the Act claimed that genuine refugees were being excluded by the Immigration Boards. The rhetorical terms of their argument are significant. Liberal and Labour critics such as C.P. Trevelyan, Sir Charles Dilke and Ramsay Macdonald attacked the legislation as a departure from national traditions. Trevelyan urged the Home Secretary to administer the Act in a way that would render it 'as little onerous and as little discreditable to Englishmen as it was possible to be'.[2] Drawing on the same conception of national identity, Leif Jones condemned the early conduct of the Immigration Boards as 'unworthy of the reputation of a humane and free people, and it did violence to the strong and hereditary sympathy of the people of this country, in regard to the poor and oppressed of every land'.[3] The campaign against the Aliens Act is one sign of the continuing vitality of a conception of the nation rooted in indigenous freedoms.

The campaign against the Act in Parliament and the press reached its crescendo as pogroms, which accompanied the counter-revolution in Russia, swelled the number of refugees trying to enter

1. *Hansard*, 4th series, CLIII, col. 155, 5 March 1906.
2. The Home Office issued the following instruction: 'the Board appears to the Secretary of State to be perfectly right in rejecting immigrants unless they are satisfied that it is reasonably certain that the immigrant will proceed out of this country or are satisfied (in the absence of such certainty) that he is not an undesirable in the meaning of the Act': PRO, HO 45/10327/132181/11, memorandum [regarding a] letter from London Immigration Board Clerk, February 1906.
3. *Hansard*, 4th series, CLIII, cols. 134, 143, 5 March 1906.

the country.[4] In March 1906 Gladstone issued instructions that, in view of the 'disturbed conditions' in parts of Europe, immigrants were to be given the benefit of the doubt if they came from these areas and claimed to be refugees. Gladstone also made the Act easier to evade. He directed Immigration Boards to consider whether rejection of an alien would cause hardship to women and children and he relaxed the definition of an immigrant ship.[5] Back-bench Conservatives were indignant. Evans Gordon accused the government of effectively repealing the Act's main provisions.[6] The new instruction gave free licence to any immigrant misrepresenting himself as a refugee.[7] In fact, Conservatives need not have worried, and Liberal and Jewish satisfaction was premature: as soon as the wave of pogroms came to an end so too did the impact of the March instruction. The number of immigrants entering the country as refugees declined precipitously after 1906. The exemption for political and religious refugees allowed by the 1905 Act was being narrowly interpreted.

The Aliens Act forced the JBD into a new and abrasive relation with the state. Between 1906–10 the JBD kept up a vigorous correspondence with the Home Office and the Prime Minister, repeating the same complaints against the harsh operation of the Aliens Act. For the first time since the debate on Jewish emancipation the

Table 13   Numbers of refugees admitted to the United Kingdom between 1906 and 10[8]

1906	505
1907	43
1908	20
1909	30
1910	5

4. On the press see J. Garrard, *The English and Immigration 1880–1910* (London, 1971), p. 111.
5. Under the original rules, vessels with more than twelve alien passengers in steerage class were designated immigrant ships; now the figure was raised to twenty. HO 45/10326/131787/9, Aliens Act. Secretary of State's directions as to administration, March 1906; *Hansard*, 4th series, CLIII, cols. 916–17, 12 March 1906.
6. Although front-bench disarray and demoralisation meant that Gladstone was not greatly harrassed on the point: J.R. Vincent, ed., *The Crawford Papers* (Manchester, 1984), pp. 93–4.
7. *Hansard*, 4th series, CLIII, cols. 1,312–13, 14 March 1906; W. Evans Gordon, 'The Attack on the Aliens Act', *National Review*, November 1906, pp. 460–71.
8. *Aliens Act 1905. Fifth Annual Report of Her Majesty's Inspector for the Year 1910*, PP 1911, X, p. 36.

relation between Jews and the state took on a new form. This no longer concerned the constitutional position of Jews or the rights of Jews as a religious minority; the question now arose of how the state, as it promoted the material well-being of large sections of the population, impinged on the interests of a group composed primarily of Jews.

The JBD protested that the proceedings of Immigration Boards did not allow immigrants a 'fair trial'. Immigrants faced the Boards without legal representation and had no right of appeal against their decisions.[9] The JBD also criticised the system of gathering and presenting evidence. Immigration officers had a dual role: they were the officials who prevented an alien from landing but they were also the individuals responsible for making enquiries for an appeal. This double responsibility was incompatible with the interests of justice, the JBD argued. For instance, when an immigrants' friends or relatives wanted to offer evidence on his or her behalf, the immigration officer was not bound to inform them of the time of the hearing.[10] These were the complaints about the machinery of exclusion as it was set up; others dealt with the way it operated in practice. Despite the presence of six Jews on the panel of twenty-six Immigration Board members in London, the JBD was dissatisfied with many of the appointees. Some of them, it claimed, had taken part in the agitation for the Aliens Act and so were incapable of adjudicating impartially.[11] The steamship companies' refusal to erect a receiving house for aliens landing at the Port of London was also a cause of complaint. The absence of any accommodation for immigrants awaiting appeal meant that their right of appeal was lost if the ship to which they were confined left port before evidence could be secured.[12] The JBD concluded that the decisions of Immigration

9. GLRO, JBD B2/1/7, the London Committee of Deputies of the British Jews to Sir Henry Campbell Bannerman, 28 January 1908; PRO, HO 144/1014/151705/17, the London Committee of Deputies of the British Jews to H.H. Asquith, 26 May 1908; HO 45/10519/135998/13, the London Committee of Deputies of the British Jews to W.S. Churchill, 4 April 1910.

10. JBD, B2/1/7, the London Committee of Deputies of the British Jews to Sir Henry Campbell Bannerman, 28 January 1908; HO 45/10519/135998/13, the London Committee of Deputies of the British Jews to W.S. Churchill, 4 April 1910. The standard of interpretation at Immigration Board hearings was another source of complaint.

11. HO 144/1014/151705/17, the London Committee of Deputies of the British Jews to H.H. Asquith, 26 May 1908.

12. For the same reason the provision which allowed hearings to be adjourned so that enquiries could be made – for instance, into whether relatives were expecting the immigrants and could provide them with work – were 'practically ignored': HO 144/1014/151705/17, London Committee of British Jews to H.H. Asquith, 26 May 1908; HO 45/10347/143271/3, the

Boards were inconsistent and that the provision for refugees made in the Aliens Act was being ignored.

The representations made by the JBD to the Home Office between 1906–9 were notably unsuccessful. The JBD and the Home Office regarded the Aliens Act from quite different perspectives: the JBD wanted to ensure 'justice' for refugees and to secure a wide definition of this term, whereas the Home Office sought to administer the Act efficiently and to fulfil its statutory duty to exclude undesirables.[13] Relations between the two bodies were not friendly and John Pedder, the civil servant most closely responsible for the operation of the Aliens Act, was especially hostile to the JBD.[14] Churchill's arrival at the Home Office in 1910 did result in a friendlier tone and some concessions. The new Home Secretary established a departmental committee to investigate the possibility of creating a receiving house in the port of London.[15] More significantly, he allowed appellants before Immigration Boards to receive legal assistance.[16] But the Home Office continued to argue that immigration officers were impartial agents and that the actions of Immigration Boards were administrative, not judicial.[17]

From the point of view of the Home Office, the Board's persistent

London Committee of Deputies of the British Jews to H. Gladstone, 5 March 1907.

13. J. Pellew, 'The Home Office and the Aliens Act, 1905', *Historical Journal*, June 1989, pp. 369–85.

14. It is equally clear that Gladstone did nothing to promote a more flexible approach: HO 45/10347/143271/2, Pedder memorandum, February 1907; JBD, C13/1/5, minutes of the Law and Parliamentary Committee, 10 March 1907.

15. The difficulty here was not that the Home Office opposed the idea but that there was no question of public funds being used to maintain a receiving house. The burden would have to fall on the shipping companies who, in turn, would have passed it on to the immigrants. But one effect of the Aliens Act had been to reduce the volume of immigrants trying to enter London, and the administration of the Act, by placing the definition of an immigrant ship as high as twenty steerage passengers, reduced the number coming within the Act still further. In view of the fact that a toll of sixpence per head was seen as the maximum the immigrants could bear, the receipts would not meet expenditure on a receiving house: HO 45/10347/143271/3, the Jewish Deputies and the Aliens Act, 5 March 1907; *Report of the Departmental Committee Appointed to Advise the Secretary of State as to the Establishment of a Receiving House for Alien Immigrants at the Port of London*, PP 1911, X.

16. HO 144/1014/151705/62, instruction by W.S. Churchill, 11 May 1910. Churchill's other concession was to invite the JBD to submit any names it would like considered for appointment to the Boards.

17. HO 144/1014/151705/61, E. Troup to the Jewish Board of Deputies, 4 May 1910; see too HO 45/10347/143271/2, draft reply to the Secretary to the London Committee of Deputies of British Jews, 30 January 1907.

complaints were an ominous sign of the Jews' failure to identify themselves with the general interest of the community. In a minute written in June 1908, Pedder contrasted the disinterested work of immigration officers, members of Immigration Boards and inter- preters – who were pursuing the public good – with the opposition of the Jews: 'Special agencies, a special press and a body claiming authority as representatives of a special interest, all conspiring together in dishonest attitudes – whether from ignorance or fabrica- tion'.[18] This emphasis on the Jews' singular interests and, implicitly, their conflict with the common good, presents a vivid illustration of how the particular claims of Jewish institutions and interests raised difficulties for the growing collectivist state.

How did Anglo-Jewish leaders and institutions respond to this new situation? In the first decade of the century, the JBD remained a body whose constitution and practice reflected its domination by the Anglo-Jewish patriciate. Its members were elected on a narrow franchise, from which immigrant bodies were excluded, and the Board itself was dominated by a handful of members who manned its leading committees.[19] The armoury of the JBD consisted of letters, reports and informal contacts with the government through sympa- thetic MPs; it did not include meetings of public protest. Its idea of consultation was to deliberate with Anglo-Jewish grandees but not to take account of wider currents of Jewish opinion. For instance, in December 1907, the JBD, having decided to write to the Prime Minister, Campbell Bannerman, to request repeal of the Aliens Act, not merely its reform, quickly withdrew from this position once it became clear that it did not have the support of Lord Rothschild. Rothschild was not a member of the JBD but any memorial signed by English Jews which did not include his signature 'would certainly be considered as a sign of want of unanimity on the part of the Jews themselves'.[20] In effect Rothschild exercised a veto over JBD policy.

This patrician style of politics had survived successfully into the twentieth century. It had not given way before Jewish immigration even though this had rendered communal leaders still less repre- sentative of Anglo-Jewry socially, culturally and politically than they had been hitherto. Moreover, the organised Jewish community was resisting successfully the democratic tendency of English politics.

18. Pedder found them hopelessly biased and advised that their letters should be discouraged by the simple device of ignoring them: HO 144/1014/151705/ 17, London Committee of Deputies of British Jews, minute by J. Pedder, 18 June 1908.
19. S. Cohen, *English Zionists and British Jews: The Communal Politics of Anglo-Jewry, 1895–1920* (Princeton, NJ, 1982), pp. 134–7.
20. JBD, B2/1/1, report of the Alien Immigration Committee, 23 December 1907.

But the growth of collectivism intensified the impact of these pressures for change and it also created some new ones. The impact of the state on Jewish interests no longer arose mainly in the constitutional area of religious and political liberty. Now government policy touched on issues such as where Jews were able to live and how they would maintain themselves.[21] Whereas legislation which dealt with the principle of religious equality had implications, or could be presented as having implications, for the whole Jewish population, social policy affected only sections – albeit large ones – of the Jewish population. Moreover, it impinged most immediately on those elements of the Jewish population who were not directly represented at the JBD. This undermined the capacity of the JBD to speak on behalf of the whole Jewish population. Inevitably, what Jewish interests were in the face of this newly energetic state could be defined and interpreted by those who were directly affected by it and not only by the unrepresentative Jewish Board of Deputies. In 1911 there were a series of episodes which brought these incipient conflicts to the fore.

The criminal alien

After 1906, more than the alien pauper it was the alien criminal who seemed to embody the corrosive consequences of the immigrant presence. The experts' interest in categorising criminals, and in the 'professional criminal' in particular, contributed to a growing awareness of 'alien crime'.[22] But the Aliens Act itself fed these fears. It empowered the Home Secretary to expel foreigners convicted of imprisonable offences, and this led to controversy. Some Conservatives feared that Liberal leniency was allowing the country to become overrun with foreign criminals.[23]

Impressions of alien criminality were brought sharply into focus in the winter of 1910–11. On 16 December 1910 four burglars were disturbed while breaking into a jeweller's in Houndsditch, just east of the City of London; as they escaped they shot three policemen. Literature in Yiddish and Russian was discovered in a flat where some of the men had stayed, and on the strength of this evidence

---

21. This is a contrast which stands in need of qualification. Clearly, sabbatarian legislation and legislation such as the Factory and Workshops Acts had also impinged on the Jews' ability to pursue their trades. See above, pp. 297–9.
22. V.A.C. Gatrell, 'Crime, Authority and the Policeman-State', in F.M.L. Thompson, ed., *The Cambridge Social History of Britain 1750–1950*, vol. iii (Cambridge, 1990) pp. 306–10.
23. For instance *Hansard*, 4th series, CLXXIII, col. 530, 29 April 1907.

the burglars were identified as a gang of immigrant anarchists. The episode ended famously on 3 January. The police were informed that two suspects had taken a room at 100 Sidney Street. Shots were exchanged, two squads of the Scots Guards were called up, and the Home Secretary, Winston Churchill, arrived on the scene. The siege ended as the flat caught fire. Two dead bodies – two of the suspected burglars – were found inside.

Journalists investigated the milieu in which these alien criminals found a home.[24] The Conservative press especially drew an alarming picture. Although innocent individually, collectively the immigrants constituted a danger to English society. Notwithstanding the law-abiding character of most Jewish immigrants, the inscrutability of the Jewish East End to English eyes rendered it dangerous, for here the police could not distinguish the criminal from the foreigner.[25] In the period between the Houndsditch incident and the Sidney Street siege, the image of the immigrant quarter as a closed society led commentators to doubt whether the murderers would be traced.[26] The immigrant anarchists, moreover, were portrayed as representatives of a foreign criminal type. They refused to acknowledge the legitimacy of the state, personified by the policeman's authority. They were contrasted with English criminals who, however rough, accepted the role of the police even as they tried to circumvent it. For instance, *The Times'* reflections on Houndsditch included a testimonial to the native law breaker.

> One of the curious things about the regular criminal is the absence of any grudge against the police who are regarded as doing their duty and engaged in a fair match of wits and nimbleness. A savage delight in taking life is the mark of the modern Continental anarchist criminal. We have our ruffians but we do not breed that type here and we do not want them.[27]

It was the English criminal's acceptance of the apparatus of law enforcement which marked him out as English. Once again we see the relation of the individual to the state was central to the image of English identity.

The Houndsditch murders revived the complaint that the government had 'deliberately crippled' the Aliens Act. Criminals masquerading as refugees had been allowed to settle in England.[28] Proper

24. *Pall Mall Gazette*, 5 January 1911, p. 1; *Daily Mail*, 23 December 1910, p. 4; *The Times*, 20 December 1910, p. 10.
25. *Daily Mail*, 23 December 1910, p. 4.
26. *The Times*, 23 December 1910, p. 9.
27. *The Times*, 19 December 1910, p. 12.
28. *Pall Mall Gazette*, 28 November 1910, p. 7; *Daily Mail*, 20 December 1910, p. 4; *The Times*, 5 January 1911, p. 8; *ibid*, 9 January 1911, p. 7.

administration of the Aliens Act would be a step forward but the solution was seen to lie in new legislation that would compel aliens to register with the police, forbid them to carry firearms and provide the courts with powers to expel them from the country *before* they committed an offence.[29] Stepney Borough Council passed by 31 votes to 7 a resolution which called for the Aliens Act to be tightened and for foreigners to be registered for five years after their arrival in England. The resolution was moved by A.H. Castle. He complained that the borough had been 'inundated by people who had been called the scum of Europe'.[30] Stepney received the support of nine other London borough councils and of fourteen Boards of Guardians.[31] The call for legislation was justified in collectivist terms. The *Pall Mall Gazette* claimed that 'no other policy will accord with a rational conception of social well-being or the duty which the state owes to its weaker members'.[32] The *Daily Mail*, like many other newspapers, took the opportunity to reconsider the whole question of alien immigration: 'We cannot consent longer to admit these thousands of undesirables to the cruel injury of our own people or permit indefinitely the scum of Europe to be poured into our country to replace the very cream that has been skimmed off by emigration. That way lies the moral and spiritual death of our race.'[33]

Parliament was in recess while the press outcry was loudest. Nevertheless, Churchill prepared new legislation. He proposed to strengthen the procedure for expelling aliens convicted of imprisonable offences. Instead of applying to the Home Secretary for an expulsion order, a court would have to explain its action to the Home Secretary only if it chose not to recommend expulsion. The Bill, Churchill confessed to the Cabinet, contained two 'naughty principles': 'First, a deliberate differentiation between the alien, and especially the unassimilated alien, and a British subject, and second, that any alien may, in certain circumstances, be deported before he has committed an offence'. What Churchill meant was that his Bill empowered courts to demand sureties for good behaviour from aliens and, if these were not given, to expel them.[34] By attempting

29. *Pall Mall Gazette*, 5 January 1911, p. 7; *Daily Mail*, 6 January 1911, p. 4; *The Times*, 9 January 1911, p. 7; W. Evans Gordon, 'The Stranger Within our Gates', *Nineteenth Century and After*, February 1911, pp. 214–16; R. Anderson, 'The Problem of the Criminal Alien', *ibid*, pp. 220–4.
30. *JC*, 13 January 1911, pp. 17, 26.
31. But the resolution was also met with a protest from seven Jewish friendly societies, representing 12,000 members: *ibid*, 24 February 1911, p. 25.
32. *Pall Mall Gazette*, 10 January 1911, p. 7.
33. *Daily Mail*, 10 January 1911, p. 6.
34. Specifically, if a complaint was made to a court of summary jurisdiction that an alien who had been in the country for less than five years was consorting with

to introduce a law which made an alien uniquely vulnerable to the courts, the Bill embodied the idea that murderous crime was essentially un-English.

Churchill's Aliens Bill did not pass into law. In part, this was because the criminal alien scare passed away. But another reason for its failure was its unpopularity in the Liberal Party. Josiah Wedgwood wrote to Churchill immediately after the siege of Sidney Street appealing to English liberties against the clamour for legislation.

> Please do not be rushed into exceptional laws against anarchists. It is fatally easy to justify them but they lower the whole character of the nation. You know as well as I do that human life does not matter a rap in comparison with the death of ideas and the betrayal of English traditions. Rebelling against civilisation and society will go on anyhow. It is only a new form of the disease of '48; so let us have English rule and not Bourbon. Yours with apologies but frightened by *The Times*.[35]

Churchill's Liberal opponents were particularly displeased by the Home Secretary's preparedness to cooperate with the sponsors of a private bill introduced by the Conservative MP Edward Goulding. In many respects Goulding's proposals were similar to the government's own. But they also included the dirigiste solutions advocated by newspapers such as the *Daily Mail* and *Pall Mall Gazette*. Goulding proposed to make all aliens entering the country in 'steerage class' register their address and, in an effort to resuscitate immigration as an issue that appealed to the working-class electorate, to compel employers to pay immigrants a minimum wage.[36] Pressure of parliamentary time led Churchill to try to use Goulding's Bill to carry his own proposals into law. Accordingly it received ministerial support and was given a second reading in the House of Commons. But aside from members of the government, more Liberals voted against the Bill than for it, and all but one of the Labour MPs who voted opposed the measure.[37] Liberal and Labour dissent was presented as

---

criminals or suspected persons, or living in circumstances which made it likely that his continued stay in the country would lead to crime, the court could require sureties, from two English citizens, for good behaviour of up to five years. In addition, it required aliens to obtain special permission before carrying or possessing pistols and it gave wide powers of search, on a magistrate's warrant, if there were reasonable grounds to believe an offence under the Act was being committed: HO 45/10643/207426/8, Aliens (Prevention of Crime) Bill, 15 May 1911; *Hansard*, 5th series, XXIV, cols. 624–8, 18 April 1911.

35. R. Churchill, *Winston S. Churchill*, vol. ii, companion part 2, (London, 1969), p. 1,239.

36. HO 45/10641/206332, Aliens Bill 1911 introduced by Mr Goulding; *Hansard*, 5th series, XXIV, cols. 2,112, 2,170, 28 April 1911.

37. Churchill, *Winston S. Churchill*, pp. 1,254–5.

a defence of English liberties. For Atherley Jones the legislation 'savours of the very worst days of old régimes, and which has been repudiated during the last two hundred years'. Ramsay Macdonald attacked the Bill in similar fashion: 'This colossal system of police registers, this troublesome provision compelling law abiding, decent aliens to go in hundreds to the nearest police station to register their names, is a proposal absolutely alien to the most fundamental conceptions of English civic liberty and the obligations of English civic law.'[38] As with opposition to the Act of 1905 and its administration, opposition to the bills of 1911 was rallied by a conception of the nation rooted in a set of individual liberties guaranteed by law.

The JBD contributed weakly to opposition to the 1911 Aliens Bills. Churchill's plan to expel individuals if they could not find sureties met with a limp request that he should add a right of appeal to the Home Secretary.[39] The Board decided that it was an inopportune moment to campaign more vigorously. Statistics collected by the Board seemed to reveal the low and declining level of Jewish criminality in England. These were sent to the Home Office but they were not publicised more widely.[40] In other words, the JBD pursued a traditional policy of public quietness and private contacts.

The JBD's unwillingness to consult widely and to campaign before the Jewish or non-Jewish public contrasted sharply with the activities of an East End organisation that was established early in 1911 – the Aliens Defence Committee. The origins of the ADC lay in the Jewish Protection Society. This organisation was established at the start of February 1911 in response to the rise of anti-Jewish opinion in general and the resolution passed at Stepney Borough Council in particular. According to *Der Yidisher Zhurnal* the leaders of the JPS were East End *'balebatim'* – householders. Its aims were to protect Jews from anti-Semitic attacks, to raise the immigrants' social and political condition and to promote their naturalisation as citizens.[41] The question of how to translate this programme into a plan of action led to a split in the young organisation. The men who had emerged as its initial leaders favoured a protest-meeting at the Great

38. *Hansard*, 5th series, XXIV, cols. 2,146, 2,170, 28 April 1911.
39. HO 45/10643/207426/8, D.L. Alexander to W.S. Churchill, 15 May 1911.
40. JBD, B2/1/9, alien statistics prepared by the Jewish Board of Deputies in February 1911 in reply to published and misleading statements; B2/1/1, report of the alien sub-committee on attacks on the Jews, Feburary 1911; *JC*, 3 February 1911, pp. 20–1.
41. *Der Yidisher Zhurnal*, 5 January 1911, p. 1; *JC*, 10 February 1911, p. 17. One of the men who spoke at the meeting, Reuben Cohen, was prominent also in the Jewish shopkeepers' agitation against the threat of Sunday closing legislation.

Assembly Hall, at which Jews would make a stand against their attackers and show they were 'honest citizens'.[42] Others led by Morris Meyer – a social democrat in politics and a journalist – argued that the new organisation should collect and publicise statistics and information. It was this group of socialists, trade unionists and radicals which took control at the second meeting of the JPS.[43]

The *balebatim* who had established the JPS dropped away.[44] The organisation took a new name – the Aliens Defence Committee – and a new chairman – Meyer.[45] The ADC constituted itself as a standing body whose task was 'to protect the immigrant population in England against all unjust attacks made against them; and also to educate the people about everything that can avert collisons with the laws and customs of the land'.[46] This was the role – mediating relations between Jews and the state – which the JBD had long claimed to occupy. Moreover, the ADC invited a range of bodies to join it which had no place at the JBD and whose roots were in the immigrant colony. By the beginning of June 1911, thirty-five bodies – benefit societies, trade unions and political organisations – were represented within it. The ADC presented the broadest coalition of forces ever assembled in the Jewish East End.[47] *Der Yidisher Zhurnal*, whose owner and editor, L.A. Jouques, was a member of the ADC's executive committee, reported its activity and deliberations in detail. Access to the Yiddish press enabled the ADC to stake its claim to represent the immigrant population in a way the JBD did not. The Aliens Bills of 1911 not only engendered a new sort of conflict between Jews and the state: they also generated dissatisfaction with the way Jewish interests were being defended in the face of the state.

The ADC addressed itself to the threat of new legislation against aliens and, in particular, 'the tendency to turn the alien into a criminal just because he is an alien'.[48] Its opposition to the government's proposals was more far-reaching than anything the JBD offered. The ADC attacked Churchill's Bill for aiming to create one system of justice for aliens while it left English citizens untouched.

42. *Der Yidisher Zhurnal*, 5 February 1911, p. 1; *ibid*, 13 February 1911, p. 1.
43. *Ibid*; *AF*, 24 March 1911, p. 4.
44. Their defeat over tactics may account for this; but, in addition, the government's Shops Bill, which sought to strengthen legislation against Sunday trading, threatened the interests and attracted the energies of prominent shopkeepers who had helped establish the JPS.
45. *Ibid*, 24 April 1911, p. 1.
46. *Ibid*.
47. *Ibid*; *Ibid*, 1 June 1911, p. 3; *AF*, 24 March 1911, p. 4. It is remarkable that none of the published works on the history of the Jewish East End has mentioned the Aliens Defence Committee.
48. *Ibid*, 8 May 1911, p. 1.

Further, it criticised the powers allowed to magistrates to expel aliens, first because the impartiality of magistrates could not be relied on where aliens were involved, and second, because it would lead to expulsions for trivial offences.[49]

The ADC's campaign was a major departure in the history of immigrant politics. This can be seen more clearly if, briefly, we look back at the feeble reactions in the Jewish East End to the earlier anti-alien movement. In September 1902 a Jewish Defence Committee was formed in the East End with the intention of collecting evidence to present to the Royal Commission on Alien Immigration, but the organisation quickly vanished from the record and never appeared before the Commissioners. As a result, newspaper evidence remains one of the few indications we have of opinion among the immigrants at this time. A recurrent complaint made by *Der Yidisher Ekspres* was that the Jewish Board of Deputies was not fulfilling its role of defending the 'interests' and 'honour' of Jews.[50] The emergence of a competitor newspaper in 1905, *Der Yidisher Zhurnal*, in this respect, meant only that the same view was now broadcast from another source.[51] It is striking, however, that this current of opinion did not find any organised expression.

In 1911 the ADC eschewed public meetings but its approach presented a vivid contrast both to the quietism of the JBD and the evanescence of earlier East End protest. A memorandum criticising Churchill's Bill, written by a committee of five, was sent to all MPs. In addition, the executive obtained interviews with four local Liberal MPs – Stuart Samuel, Edward Pickersgill, William Glyn-Jones and William Benn – to enlist their support, and met with a committee from the Labour Party dealing with the Aliens Bill.[52] Not only did the ADC campaign vigorously, through *Der Yidisher Zhurnal*, it also ensured that its East End constituency knew it was doing so.

The growing appetite of the state to intervene in the organisation of society not only produced a danger to Jewish interests; it also provided the motive and the opportunity to develop new forms of politics independent of Anglo-Jewish tutelage. The motive arose because the JBD did not consult with representatives of any immigrant institutions and because Jewish interests, in the face of the 1911 Aliens Bills, were interpreted differently in the Jewish East End. The opportunity was there because the intervention of the state

49. *Ibid*, 31 May 1911, p. 1.
50. For example *Der Yidisher Ekspres*, 13 November 1901, p. 4; *ibid*, 22 January 1902, p. 4.
51. *Der Yidisher Zhurnal*, 27 May 1905, p. 2.
52. *Ibid*, 8 May 1911, p. 1; *ibid*, 10 May 1911, p. 1; *ibid*, 11 May 1911, p. 1; *ibid*, 30 May 1911, p. 1.

introduced a new arena of political activity. It presented an opportunity to bypass the Anglo-Jewish grandees, to act independently of them and develop a more democratic organisation and a more vigorous campaign. As the aliens issue faded in the summer of 1911, so too did the ADC. But, in a more general sense, the developments to which it had responded – the emergence of an activist state seeking to act upon the Jewish population – took new forms.

Shopkeepers, sabbatarians and social reform

The Shops Act of 1912 was one of the Liberal government's least successful ventures in the field of social reform. Yet, as Herbert Gladstone made clear, the shopworkers' predicament was conceived in similar terms to the wretched plight of sweated labour, which the more celebrated Trades Boards Act of 1908 had been intended to ameliorate: 'About a million and a half people are employed, and a great mass of them work excessively long, wasteful, uneconomic hours. The remedy is only to be found by state action, and it is a case where limitation of hours could be secured without any loss to the business done, and will lead to a great saving of time, expense and health.'[53] Ultimately, the 1912 Act secured for shopworkers one half-day holiday each week. But the original intention had been to ensure, in addition, that shop assistants did not work seven days a week. This would have been achieved by revising and strengthening the law resticting Sunday trading.

By the turn of the century the existing law on Sunday trading was badly in need of reform: the fines for breaking it were too low to be effective and it was rarely enforced.[54] But in attempting to legislate against Sunday trading the government had to reconcile a number of conflicting interests, among them the sabbatarians' and the Jews'.[55] Effective enforcement of the laws on Sunday trading would have limited an orthodox Jew who kept his own sabbath to trading five days a week. He would, Jews claimed, have to choose between his religion and his livelihood. Churchill attempted to take account of the Jews' religious interests and this led him into trouble.

When, in November 1910, the government announced that the Shops Bill would be left over until the following year it also revealed that there would be a substantial change in the way it dealt with

53. Churchill, *Winston S. Churchill*, p. 1,140.
54. *Report of the Joint Select Committee on Sunday Trading*, PP 1906, XIII, p. vi.
55. See the comments of C. Masterman in *Hansard*, 5th series, XIII, col. 1,686, 31 March 1911.

Jewish shopkeepers and stall holders. Originally, Churchill had proposed to restrict Sunday opening by Jewish shops to areas 'largely inhabited by Jews'; but now the Bill would allow Jewish shops in any district to remain open until 2 p.m. on Sunday – though only for the purpose of serving Jewish customers, and subject to the conditions that only Jewish shop assistants would serve on that day and that shops were closed during the Jewish sabbath.[56] This extraordinary provision revived the pre-emancipation idea that Jews would be governed by a separate body of laws which applied to them alone. Equally extraordinary was the fact that it was inserted at the request of the JBD. In May 1911 Churchill explained, 'the proposal in the Bill was agreed to by the Jewish representatives who came to him as a deputation'.[57]

The fact that the JBD brought forward this proposal at all may reflect its confusion in the face of the activist state. Even an apparently familiar problem, such as legislation on Sunday trading, was now being confronted in a new way as it was promoted by the government principally as an instrument of social policy. The extension of government regulation in society was leading the JBD to consider new ways of defending Jewish interests. The clause it had proposed to Churchill would have given Jews a statutory right to trade on Sundays if certain conditions were met, and this, initially, made it attractive to the JBD.[58] Very quickly, however, the members of the Law and Parliamentary Committee realised that this solution would be 'unworkable' and that it would leave Jewish traders vulnerable to persecution at the hands of informers. Fundamentally, the Board's proposal ran contrary to the emphasis of Anglo-Jewish policy since the struggle for civil and political equality. The Board wrote to Churchill telling him it was now opposed to the exemptions it had originally requested.[59]

The JBD was not the only body which claimed to represent the interests of Jewish traders. The Whitechapel and Spitalfields

56. *JC*, 18 November 1910, p. 27.
57. *JC*, 19 May 1911, p. 25; for mention of the deputation see *ibid*, 28 October 1910, p. 22. The difficulty of enforcing this clause was raised in Parliament in the course of the debate on the Bill's second reading. Edward Goulding, who objected to the great indulgence shown 'to the chosen people', had a point when he confessed that he did 'not know how on earth the right hon. Gentleman's inspectors are going to carry out the provision that they must only supply gentlemen who have uncommonly large proboscises': *Hansard*, 5th series, XXIII, col. 1,731, 31 March 1911.
58. On this see JBD, B2/10/8, report of the Law and Parliamentary Committee, 4 October 1909; C/13/1/6, minutes of the Law and Parliamentary Committee, 21 May 1911.
59. *JC*, 3 March 1911, p. 16.

Costermongers and Street Sellers Union had 500 members, mostly Jews. Formed in 1894, its task had been to represent the interests of Jewish street traders to local government and to the police. Of all the Jewish organisations in the East End it had the most experience of negotiating with a regulatory state. The union contained a large number of English-born Jews and it was one of the components in the coalition of forces which returned a Liberal MP for Whitechapel at every election between 1885–1918. This background shaped the Whitechapel costers' response to Churchill's Bill in 1911. First, the union's proposals did not take an exclusively Jewish standpoint: it argued that Christians as well as Jews should be able to sell in Sunday markets. Second, the union approached the Home Office independently of the JBD. Drawing on the rhetoric of populist radicalism, in the course of their interview with Churchill, the costers' leaders attacked the deputies' hypocritical support for sabbatarian legislation: 'there were among them men who drove in Hyde Park on Saturday and motored through the country on Sunday, and yet had the effrontery to endeavour to bar persons of a humble calling earning a few shillings a week on both days'.[60] At the end of the year the president of the Whitechapel and Spitalfields Costermongers and Street Sellers Union reflected on the JBD's handling of the Shops Bill – its failure to consult with the Jewish traders, its blunder in proposing a new clause and then, once it was accepted, urging its withdrawal. He concluded, 'thank heaven our organisation does not require to go to the Board of Deputies for help'.[61]

Criticism of the Board for not taking account of the interests of Jewish traders came from shopkeepers as well as the costermongers. But unlike the street sellers this group did approach the question solely as a Jewish interest group. A meeting of Jewish shopkeepers in January 1911 objected to the idea – which the JBD had now come to adopt – that trading on Sundays should stop at 2 p.m. The shopkeepers wanted Jews to be exempt from the law on Sunday closing in areas where they comprised over 50 per cent of the total population.[62] Reuben Cohen, who presided at the meeting, explained its purpose.

> Perhaps it would be right to call the meeting a protest meeting against the Jewish Board of Deputies. . . . The Board of Deputies had thereby enforced upon them a half-holiday which they could ill-afford. The Board

60. *Ibid*, 28 October 1910, p. 22.
61. *Ibid*, 10 November 1911, p. 16; *ibid*, 24 November 1911, pp. 17–18.
62. *Ibid*. Later, however, their position was that they wanted all Jews to have the freedom to trade on Sunday if they closed on their own sabbath: see *ibid*, 12 May 1911, p. 35.

had acted against the interests of the Jews who stood most in need of its services. The Board had compromised with the Government on a Bill that concerned the welfare of many thousands of Jews without having previously consulted the Jewish public.[63]

The shopkeepers did not pursue a course independently of the Board. Instead they tried, with some success, to induce it to campaign more vigorously on their behalf. A deputation asked the JBD to mobilise the Jewish MPs on the question, issue a pamphlet and organise a public meeting. In contrast to its position on other issues, the Board responded positively on all the points.[64] Although sabbatarian legislation was now being pursued by the government primarily for social rather than religious ends, the issue remained a congenial one for the JBD. The Board was able to construe the Bill as an attack on the religious liberties of a respectable constituency. Moreover, a public meeting offered the Board's leaders an opportunity to regain the confidence of Jewish traders on an issue which had been egregiously mishandled. The public meeting, held at the Great Assembly Hall, was enormous. According to the *Jewish Chronicle*, 6,000 people gathered inside the hall and two large overflow meetings for another 4,000 were held outside.[65] The Liberal legislation was portrayed as an attack on the Jewish religion. The tone of the protest was caught when Dayan Feldman described the Shops Bill, as it stood, as 'a fatal blow to the observance [of sabbath] by the middle-class Jew'.[66]

The Home Office tried to take account of the Jews' objections. Churchill offered a new solution: he revived the idea that the Home Secretary could select certain areas of London in which Jews and non-Jews could trade on Sunday until 2 p.m.[67] Although there was room for bargaining over precisely which areas would be included in the schedule, the JBD and the shopkeepers eagerly agreed to this solution as the best they would get.[68] In fact, legislation on Sunday trading did not pass into law. Sabbatarians objected to the breach of the principle of Sunday closing. Shopkeepers objected to the opportunity offered to pious Jews to trade on Saturday evenings in winter, when the sabbath ended early, as well as Sunday. With good reason,

63. *Ibid*, 27 January 1911, p. 29.
64. The deputation comprised representatives of the Jewish butchers, bakers, grocers, drapers and the East London Jewish Shopkeepers Protection Association: *ibid*, 2 June 1911, pp. 22–3; JBD, C13/1/6, minutes of the Law and Parliamentary Committee, 8 June 1911; *ibid.*, 16 June 1911.
65. *JC*, 14 July 1911, p. 17.
66. *Ibid*, 9 June 1911, p. 14.
67. *Ibid*, 7 July 1911, p. 7.
68. *Ibid*, 14 July 1911, p. 17.

they also suspected that many Jews would abuse their allowance and trade seven days a week.[69]

Finally exasperated, in October 1911 Churchill abandoned those parts of the Shops Bill which dealt with Sunday trading. But the episode is significant, nevertheless. First, the government's willingness to conciliate Jewish interests is striking. In this regard, the claims of religious liberty remained powerful. Second, the Shops Bill provides an illustration of how intervention by the state could generate new forms of Jewish politics. It spurred both criticism of the JBD and independent forms of political organisation in the East End. But it also had an impact on the politics of the Jewish elite. Dealing with respectable allies in the East End, over the congenial issue of religious liberty, the JBD pursued a persistent and, ultimately, a conspicuous campaign.

National insurance and citizenship

National insurance was the crowning achievement of the Liberals' social reform programme and introduced a totally new form of state intervention. The scheme had two parts: the first dealt with health, and applied to all wage earners, the second with employment and, initially, was confined to workers in a small number of industries. It was part one which affected immigrant workers. The health insurance scheme was introduced to the House of Commons in May 1911. Wage earners would be compelled to contribute 4d each week to finance health benefits, their employers would have to contribute 3d per week and the state 2d. In return, insured male workers would be entitled to free medical treatment from a doctor and a cash benefit of 10s per week for the first 13 weeks of illness and 5s per week for a further 13 weeks.[70] The administration of the scheme would be undertaken by voluntary institutions – benefit societies and trade unions – but the scheme itself was compulsory and the state would supervise its operation.

The National Insurance Bill expressed a mutual relationship of duties and obligations between the state and its citizens. Wage earners were compelled to save but, in return, they received the support of the state. Here was the doctrine of citizenship, a new development of the national community, operating through the

---

69. Churchill, *Winston S. Churchill*, p. 1,261; *Select Committee of the House of Lords on the Sunday Closing (Shops) Bill*, PP 1905, VII, p. 2,158; *Select Committee on Sunday Trading*, pp. 586–7, 591.
70. B.B. Gilbert, *The Evolution of National Insurance* (London, 1966), p. 344.

practice of health insurance.[71] As Andrew Vincent and Raymond Plant have shown, for 'new Liberals' the concept of citizenship not only prescribed that the state should consciously promote a better life for its citizens, and thereby promote freedom; it also placed requirements on the citizens themselves. 'Part of this freedom was the actual performance of the duties of citizenship, and actively and intelligently participating in the functions of social life.'[72]

As with all communities there were boundaries, and one way of drawing them was to exclude those incapable of participating as citizens. Accordingly, 'the riff-raff of the population' were excluded from the health insurance scheme.[73] The 'approved societies' who administered health insurance were permitted to reject applicants on grounds such as ill-health and low character. In other words, those people who were excluded came from the poorer strata of the working population, apparently beyond the penumbra of respectability.[74] Their weekly contributions would be paid into the Post Office; they would not be insured, they would merely be saving. If sickness kept them away from work, they received benefit only for so long as their Post Office savings allowed. Taking into account the charge for administration, this would probably amount to 7s 6d a week for three weeks.[75]

How did immigrants stand in relation to the criteria of citizenship? The answer to this question rested on the terms under which an alien could become a naturalised British subject. In 1905 the criteria for judging applications for naturalisation were altered. In that year a Home Office circular determined that naturalisation should be withheld from aliens who could not 'speak, read or write English reasonably well'.[76] This was a major departure. Previously it had been sufficient for an applicant to pay taxes, obey the law and submit the fee. The new procedures were reviewed and renewed under Herbert Gladstone and Herbert Samuel after the Liberals came to power in 1906. The rationale for the new system under a

---

71. The legislation was intended to promote among the workers a sense of belonging 'to an organic community bonded by a network of reciprocal rights and duties': P. Thane, 'Government and Society in England and Wales, 1750–1914', in Thompson, ed., *Cambridge Social History of Britain*, vol. iii, p. 56.
72. A. Vincent and R. Plant, *Philosophy, Politics and Citizenship* (Oxford, 1984), p. 77.
73. PRO, PIN 3/3/27, Scope of [National Insurance] Scheme.
74. Gilbert, *The Evolution of National Insurance*, pp. 351–2.
75. *Ibid*, p. 352; *JC*, 3 November 1911, p. 14.
76. JBD, C13/1/6, minute book of the Law and Parliamentary Committee, 5 April 1905; HO 45/10687/226279/6, applicants for naturalization and knowledge of English, 27 December 1912.

Liberal government was explained in a Home Office memorandum in 1912.

> The practice is founded on the principle that, save in very exceptional circumstances, a person can have no claim to be invested with the full rights of British nationality in the United Kingdom if he has not identified with the life and habits of the country to the extent of becoming reasonably proficient in the language; and a man can hardly be said to be reasonably proficient if he cannot read the language. . . . Mere conversational facility when he meets a Gentile does not suffice to show that a Jew is identifying himself with English life. On the contrary, if the only newspapers he can read are the Jewish ones the likelihood is that his ideas are kept widely apart from those of the ordinary English citizen.[77]

The literacy test was administered by the police and in their hands it was used to obstruct applications. Until instructions to the contrary were issued in 1912, the ability to read was tested, in many cases, with handwritten not printed material.[78] But irrespective of the way it was applied, the new practice indicates a broader definition of national identity. In order to become a British citizen it was now necessary for Jewish immigrants to pass a cultural test.

Once the state began to make welfare provisions for its citizens it was clear that it would have to determine what, if anything, the entitlement of immigrants, of unnaturalised immigrants in particular, would be. When the National Insurance Bill was published it became clear that the government intended to exclude 'aliens' along with the 'riff-raff'. A memorandum explained the thinking behind this: 'Aliens over the age of 16 are excluded from the benefit of the Government grant and from the right to join approved societies. There is no reason why the government should contribute, for to do so would be to encourage the immigration of aliens.'[79] Workers who were insured for the first time would be provided by a state credit, with a 'reserve' to take into their approved society. In all, the government gave the insurance scheme a credit of £66 million and this was to be redeemed by diverting a portion of the workers' weekly contributions.[80] The Treasury view was that in the case of immigrants neither the state's contribution to the reserve value nor its weekly contribution was warranted.

77. *Ibid.*
78. *Hansard*, 5th series, XXX cols. 1,094, 1,098, 2 November 1911; HO 45/10687/ 226279/4, naturalization work in Manchester, 31 July 1912.
79. PIN 3/4/349, National Insurance Bill, part 1 (health insurance), notes on clauses.
80. Gilbert, *The Evolution of National Insurance*, p. 344.

If societies are allowed to insure aliens over the age of 16 they can only do so by obtaining a reserve value under clause 40 appropriate to the age of the person insured. These credits are being given at the cost of the whole insurance and paid for, as there provided, by deduction from all contributors, and it is unfair to charge the British subject with the cost of insuring foreigners.[81]

But additionally, larger social and political ideals were called upon to explain government policy; these concerned citizenship and the national community. Reginald McKenna, the Home Secretary in 1911, asserted, 'I do think we are entitled to ask that he [an alien] should become a British subject before he receives the special assistance which the state offers.'[82]

The Insurance Bill not only discriminated against immigrants as individuals; it also threatened their benefit societies as institutions. Since payment into the Post Office was to be compulsory for all uninsured workers, it was likely that the state scheme would lead to a fall-off of membership from Jewish societies. Poorer members would be unable to contribute to a voluntary organisation as well as maintain their compulsory payments to the Post Office.[83]

Through a series of three conferences held in May and June 1911, the Jewish benefit societies and orders gathered their disparate forces to combat the way the National Insurance Bill dealt with aliens.[84] The JBD twice offered its assistance and twice its help was refused. The societies' leaders feared the JBD would ignore their view of what their own interests were and how they should be defended.[85] Instead, they approached Stuart Samuel. Samuel had inherited the Whitechapel constituency from his uncle, Samuel Montagu, in 1900. Of all West End Jews his political prestige was highest in the East End owing to his staunch opposition to the Aliens Act and his criticism of the JBD's handling of the Shops Bill.

The Jewish benefit societies were divided over what they should

---

81. PIN 3/4/349, National Insurance Bill, part 1 (health insurance), notes on clauses. On the problem of aliens and the reserve value see the comments of Lloyd George, *Hansard*, 5th series, XXX, cols. 1,119–20, 2 November 1911, and of W.J. Braithwaite, *JC*, 30 June 1911, p. 13.
82. *Hansard*, 5th series, XXX, col. 1,093, 2 November 1911. This was significant, not least because McKenna's department was responsible for administering new regulations which made it more difficult for aliens to become British subjects.
83. *JC*, 16 June 1911, p. 11.
84. *Der Yidisher Zhurnal*, 19 May 1911, p. 1; *JC*, 16 June 1911, p. 11; *ibid*, 23 June 1911, p. 12.
85. JBD, B2/10/10, report of the Law and Parliamentary Committee on the National Insurance Bill, 3 July 1911; *JC*, 14 July 1911, p. 21.

ask for. One party favoured contracting out. If this solution were adopted, the employers' 3d and the workers' 4d would be paid to the Jewish orders – not the Post Office – and the orders would then administer the fund for the government. The Jewish societies would secure their existence; Jewish immigrants would be in an insurance scheme and not just a saving one, but they would not receive any support from the state.[86] This path created a separate enclave for Jewish immigrants within the state; it penalised them; it diminished the disadvantage which new legislation brought them but it did not eradicate it.[87] In this respect the proposal was similar to the idea that Jewish traders could trade on Sundays if they served and employed other Jews only. When W.J. Braithwaite – the civil servant responsible for drafting the insurance legislation – met with the friendly societies' representatives this was the concession he was prepared to consider and raise with Lloyd George.[88] But there was another, bolder, way of combatting discrimination against aliens: this was to propose that they should be entitled to become members of approved societies and that, if they had been members of a society for five years, they should be entitled to the state's 2d and a reserve value. This was the solution the Jewish friendly societies decided to pursue.[89] On 25 July their standing conference decided not to pursue 'contracting out' since it would 'create another dividing line between alien and native-born'.[90]

The benefit societies embarked on a vigorous campaign. Their representatives wrote to Lloyd George; they lobbied Braithwaite; they organised a 'huge meeting of protest' at the Great Assembly Hall in mid-July and, crucially, took their case to Charles Masterman, who fought a by-election for the East End constituency of Bethnal Green South-West having been appointed Secretary of State at the Treasury. They also approached other Liberal MPs, as well as the leading Conservatives Austen Chamberlain and Sir Henry Forster. Once again we find that as the state took a place alongside Anglo-Jewry as the focus for political organisation, new forms of independent politics developed in the Jewish East End.

The Jewish friendly societies supported their request for equal treatment for aliens with a barrage of arguments. One dwelt on the physical and moral respectability of Jewish immigrants, the low death rate among them, the virtuous respectability evinced by their benefit societies and the 'ignominy' of forcing them into the Post

86. *Der Yidisher Zhurnal*, 19 May 1911, p. 1.
87. See above, p. 367.
88. *JC*, 30 June 1911, p. 13; *ibid*, 14 July 1911, p. 21.
89. *Ibid*, 23 June 1911, p. 11.
90. *Ibid*, 14 July 1911, p. 21; *ibid*, 4 August 1911, p. 21.

Office scheme. I. Solomon, the President of the Order Achei Brith, objected that it would be 'a brand of physical or moral deficiency'.[91] A second argument focused on the injustice of the Bill. Aliens would be bound to bear the burdens of compulsory national insurance but would not be eligible for any of its benefits. Moreover, against the argument that aliens would be free-riders, enjoying a reserve value paid by native workers, the friendly society leaders pointed out that alien as well as native contributions would repay the state credit.[92]

However, the argument most commonly brought forward in the immigrants' defence dealt with their relationship to the state and their effective membership of the national community. The Conference of Jewish Friendly Societies wrote to Lloyd George suggesting that after five years' residence or membership of an approved society an alien should be 'entitled to all the benefits under the Act'.[93] Five years was a significant interval because this was the period after which an alien became eligible to apply for naturalisation as a British citizen and it was because they had not taken this step that aliens were being excluded from the benefits of national insurance. Speaking at the Great Assembly Hall, Stuart Samuel argued that many alien residents were too poor to pay up to £7 for naturalisation. This already deprived them of the vote and under the National Insurance Bill they would suffer further. In Samuel's view, 'The alien had the right to say that whilst he lived in this country under its laws and by its laws, he looked to its laws to protect him.'[94] At the same meeting, speaking in Yiddish, Adolf Lewinstein set out the obstacles in the way of an immigrant seeking to naturalise: the expense, the new requirement to read and write in English and the difficulty of finding English-born sponsors.[95] These arguments were taken up by representatives of all political parties to the extent that the government finally gave way and made concessions far beyond those it had anticipated.

The first set of concessions came as a result of the approach to Masterman during the Bethnal Green by-election in July 1911. He adopted the cause of the Jewish Friendly Societies, giving them a voice in the Treasury.[96] When, at the end of October, Lloyd George finally met with a deputation from the Jewish Friendly Societies

91. *Ibid*, 23 June 1911, p. 12; *ibid*, 21 July 1911, p. 11; *Der Yidisher Zhurnal*, 18 July 1911, p. 1.
92. *JC*, 23 June 1911, p. 11; *ibid*, 30 June 1911, p. 13.
93. *Ibid*, 23 June 1911, p. 11; *ibid*, 30 June 1911, p. 13.
94. *Ibid*, 21 July 1911, p. 11.
95. *Der Yidisher Zhurnal*, 18 July 1911, p. 1.
96. *JC*, 4 August 1911, p. 21; *ibid*, 3 November 1911, p. 13; *ibid*, 10 November 1911, p. 14.

he agreed that aliens should be allowed to become members of approved societies.[97] This would take them out of the Post Office and place them in an insurance scheme. Moreover, a Jewish society could act as the approved society as long as it had a minimum of 10,000 members. But with regard to the state's 2d per week contribution, Lloyd George would not move. He argued, 'There would be a great deal of criticism if that exceptional benefit were given to a man who did not care to take over the full responsibility of citizenship.'[98] Citizenship, it seemed, represented a commitment beyond keeping the law and paying taxes; it was a more substantial commitment to the state, in return for which the state offered its benefits.

When in November 1911 the treatment of aliens under the National Insurance Bill was debated in the House of Commons, this extended conception of citizenship, and its role in determining the extent of the state's obligation to an individual, was disputed from all sides. The Liberal MP, Richard Holt, argued that the Insurance Bill should be extended to anyone who had made their permanent home in the country regardless of whether he had undergone naturalisation: 'Such a man is, just as much as any British citizen, paying his taxes and contributing to the government share of the money to be paid under this bill . . . I cannot see on what ground of justice it can be pretended that this person ought not to receive the full benefits of the Bill.'[99] He was supported by Sir Henry Forster, the Conservative Chief Whip, who also wanted to extend the benefits of the Bill 'to the alien who has thrown in his lot with us to all intents and purposes although he has not become naturalised. . . . Why should aliens who have lived among us five years or more, who pay the same taxes we pay, and discharge all the duties of citizenship we discharge, not be included in the full membership this bill proposes to create?'[100]

Support for the Jewish benefit societies extended from the leading tariff reformer, Austen Chamberlain, to the Labour MP Will Crooks. Repeatedly, it was expressed through an account of the relation between the state and those who lived in it which was bereft of any bond located in culture or race. It was untouched by those tendencies which had broadened the national idea. It was a relationship articulated in terms of the rights of the tax-paying, law-abiding individual under the law. The support offered to the immigrants was sufficiently broad and tenacious to lead Lloyd George and McKenna to concede. McKenna provided an assurance that 'an additional

97.   *JC*, 3 November 1911, p. 13.
98.   *Ibid.*
99.   *Hansard*, 5th series, XXX, col. 1,092, 2 November 1911.
100.   *Ibid*, cols. 1,094–5.

provision will be introduced recognising the special case of aliens who have been settled in the country for five years at the time of the Bill and who are already members of an approved society'.[101]

The victory won by the aliens and their societies cannot be attributed to any material power they held. Rather, it was due to their appropriation of an image of the national community which suggested that aliens were, *de facto*, citizens and as such were entitled to receive support from the state. This image, and its bearing on the aliens' position, received such widespread assent that the government was persuaded to withdraw. The broad-based and successful support mobilised on behalf of Jewish immigrants over national insurance indicates the partial degree to which more expansive, cultural conceptions of the national community took hold within British political culture. Certainly, such conceptions were evinced in the suggestion that the children of immigrants should be categorised as aliens, in the racial arguments brought in favour of the extension of aliens legislation in 1911, as well as in the changing rules for naturalisation and the attempt to exclude aliens from the benefits of health insurance.[102] But in each of these cases we find that the exclusionary project was, at best, partially successful. The realisation of more organic or racial conceptions of the national community was obstructed. Resistance was repeatedly expressed in terms of a countervailing conception of the nation, one located in a set of liberties held by individuals in the face of the state. New ideologies of national identity made ground, but they were unable wholly to displace conceptions of the national community which eschewed racial or cultural criteria.

In 1911 the aliens and their benefit societies won a signal victory. They did so, in part, through their own efforts of lobbying. British political culture allowed the immigrants and their representatives to approach MPs and, moreover, to win their support.[103] It was not only

---

101. *Ibid*, col. 1,114. In fact, to qualify, five years' membership of a benefit society was also necessary: *JC*, 10 November 1911, p. 14.
102. On the attempt to categorise English-born children as aliens see, for instance, Evans Gordon's comments on the English-born children of immigrants: *RCAI*, q. 642.
103. Compare the relation of Jewish immigrants to the state described in J. Wertheimer, *Unwelcome Strangers: East European Jews in Imperial Germany* (New York, 1987), especially chapter 3. Unfortunately, studies of Jews in France have not dealt with a similar range of issues. However, a great deal of work on Jewish history in France emphasises the inhibitions Jews had, in that political culture, in establishing a self-conscious Jewish presence in public life: see M. Marrus, *The Politics of Assimilation* (Oxford, 1971); P. Hyman, *From Dreyfus to Vichy: the Remaking of French Jewry* (New York, NY, 1979); J. Berkovitz, *The Shaplng of Jewish Identity in Nineteenth Century France* (Detroit, 1989).

the growth of state intervention but also the dominant political culture in which it developed that created circumstances in which new and strikingly successful forms of Jewish politics were forged in the years before the First World War.

Conclusion

In concluding I shall return to the three themes set out in the introduction to this book: first, the relation of Jews to the nation and to the institutions which comprised the state; second, the changing ways in which Jews tried to establish a collective identity and pursue collective interests in England; and third, the economic, social and political history of Jewish immigrants and especially of the Jewish working class.

Over the whole period covered by this book the Jews' position within the state and the nation was a cause for political controversy. At the beginning of the period the problem of integrating Jews within the state arose in the context of a conflict between proponents of the confessional state and those who wanted to reform or dismantle it. But the difficult relationship between Jews and the state, and between Jews and the nation, was not brought to a close by Jewish emancipation. In the aftermath of emancipation there were attempts to redefine the national community according to new criteria. Some Liberals and radicals, as well as nonconformists, advanced religious, cultural or racial definitions. In the political circumstances of the late 1870s, these more stringent conceptions of the nation led Disraeli's opponents to wonder whether Jews could be patriots. By the turn of the century the problem of integrating the Jewish minority within the state and within the national community had undergone a further change. Now it was re-shaped by the collectivism promoted by a Conservative imperial ideology and by the ideology of 'new Liberalism'. Throughout the period between 1840–1914, therefore, the Jewish issue was inserted consistently within debates which not only encompassed the Jewish problem but also extended beyond it. Attitudes to Jews are thus better understood if we acknowledge the significance of these other and broader contexts. Similarly, responses to the Jewish minority can illumine our understanding of political argument and of government in nineteenth- and early twentieth-century England.

In particular, this book has examined the extent to which different institutions and collectivities were able to accommodate the Jewish minority. It has focused on the relation of Jews to institutions which comprised the state and to collectivities such as the nation. If we take this perspective, the weakness of political anti-Semitism no longer leaves us with the limiting problem of explaining why something did not happen, or with the temptation to give disproportionate significance to a minor phenomenon. Instead of an absence we find a substantive problem, namely, why it was that in England the state and the predominant political conception of the nation were, comparatively, able to accommodate the Jewish minority. Seen from this angle, attitudes to the Jewish minority illumine a part of the character of political culture and government in nineteenth- and early twentieth-century England. Above all, they highlight the significance in political argument of contending accounts of national identity and competing visions of the national community.

The widely diffused belief in freedoms guaranteed to law-abiding, tax-paying individuals in England, extended to Jews and immigrants. To a degree, this confirms the traditional interpretation that the strength of liberalism in England ensured that Jewish integration was relatively benign and unproblematic. But this is only part of the story. If we concentrate on it alone we stand in danger of overlooking both the importance of ideas regarding the nation to which Jews were being admitted and the difficulties which the advance of democratic government created for the Jewish minority. The rights which the individual was guaranteed in England belong to a history of the nation as well as a history of liberalism. The extension of these rights to the Jews was thus more ambivalent than has been acknowledged. The development of representative government in the nineteenth century provoked new and more extensive conceptions of the national community. Initially, in its attack on the confessional state, the extension of representative government promoted pluralism. But the new conceptions of the national community which accompanied it, held dangers for the Jewish minority. These dangers became apparent in episodes such as the Bulgarian agitation and the subsequent political attack on Disraeli's statecraft. They became still more clear in the opposition to Jewish immigration orchestrated by East End Conservative MPs and the British Brothers League which mobilised populist and democratic conceptions of national identity. The standards of conformity demanded from a minority such as the Jews became more far-reaching. At the start of this period Jews were excluded from Parliament because they could not swear a Christian oath. By the early twentieth century the cultural competence of Jewish immigrants was being investigated as one criterion for citizenship.

But, despite these changes and dangers, in political argument the symbolic centre of the nation remained the institutions of state which guaranteed individual freedoms. The focus of the nation was not 'the people': it was Parliament, the constitutional monarchy and the liberties they ensured. To be sure, less restrained conceptions of national identity were promoted in the early twentieth century. The English countryside, folklore, literature and race were each called into service as a repository of English national identity.[1] The East End agitation against immigration, and the newspaper response to the Houndsditch murders and to the Sidney Street siege, indicate how some of these themes could be brought to bear on the subject of Jews and aliens. Nevertheless, from what can be seen of the treatment of Jews and aliens, it is striking how little these coinages were converted into the currency of party political argument and policy. The abiding strength of a conception of the nation based on the relation of individuals to institutions was a significant barrier to more culturally oriented or racial definitions. National identity at the constitutional level could be acquired by an accident of birth, by residence or by conscious selection. The legal and political significance of this view of national identity was noted by the 1901 Inter-Departmental Committee on Naturalisation: 'To the Common Law belongs the fundamental principle that any person who is born within His Majesty's Dominion is from the moment of his birth a British subject, whatever may be the nationality of either or both of his parents, and however temporary or casual the circumstances determining the locality of his birth may have been.'[2] Qualities which have been associated exclusively with English liberalism should also be regarded as part of the debate on English national identity. It was not the absence of a debate on national identity but the dominant form it took in political argument which determined the terms of Jewish integration in England.

1. C. Baldick, *The Social Mission of English Criticism 1848–1932* (Oxford, 1983); S. Collini, *Public Moralists, Political Thought and Intellectual Life* (Oxford, 1991); R. Colls and P. Dodd, eds., *Englishness: Politics and Culture 1880–1920* (London, 1986); G.R. Searle, *Eugenics and Politics in Britain 1900–14* (Leiden, 1976).
2. *Report of the Inter-departmental Committee in Connection with the Acts Relating to Naturalisation*, PP 1901, LIX, p. 7. Nevertheless the treatment of gypsies, whose wandering style of life appeared to disqualify them from citizenship and membership of the national community, was exceedingly severe and resulted in their collective deportation. See C. Holmes, *John Bull's Island: Immigration British Society, 1871–1971* (London, 1988), pp. 64–5.

The collective life of the Jews in England developed in a context provided by the debates on national identity and Jewish integration. The history of the Jews' collective life in this period is often understood as a process of socialisation or of adaptation to modern society. These terms are generally intended to account for an attenuation of Jewish identity and its retreat from public life to the synagogue, the communal association and the home. But, in significant ways, in England in the early years of the twentieth century the tendency of development was in the opposite direction. Jewish immigrants entered the British political arena to pursue their interests as Jews and immigrants, not as part of a flight from them. The more the processes of British politics encroached on immigrants and other East End Jews, the greater was their active participation within them. This was a major departure in the history of emancipated Jewry in England. It illustrates vividly that anglicisation was not a linear process of change and that, to this extent, some models of socialisation and modernisation do not capture its dynamic.

Instead, the case of English Jewry illustrates how forms of collective Jewish identity developed within a contested field. First, Jews and Judaism were subject to hostile commentary which ranged from critique to calumny. This, of course, was an ancient problem. However, from the early nineteenth century it took on new significance as the removal of the Jews' civil and political disabilities entered the realm of political possibility. Jews had not only to justify the persistence of Judaism within a Christian society but also to show themselves worthy of inclusion within the nation. The conditions within which Jewish culture and politics developed in the mid-nineteenth century were shaped by the idea that the nation was a Christian nation, by contending versions of patriotism and by the Protestant critique of Judaism. It is important not to underestimate the constraints which this placed on English Jews and their leaders in particular. The development of Reform Judaism as well as the innovations introduced within the orthodox community in the 1840 and 1850s were, in part, a response to the critique of Judaism as a religion which hobbled the spirit and which had been developed by and for the benefit of rabbinical authority. The passive response among Anglo-Jewish leaders to the pogroms of 1881–2 provides a further illustration of their deference to what they perceived to be the requirements of English society. Their subsequent attempts to repatriate, anglicise, raise and reform the immigrants were influenced not only by assumptions regarding the causes and treatment of poverty that were commonplace within the metropolitan propertied classes but also by particular anxieties which arose from their positions as Jews. As Jewish immigration became the subject of political controversy and mobilisation, Anglo-Jewry's interventions in the Jewish East End became inceasingly defensive and, at moments, desperate.

At the same time, Jewish institutions and movements were engaged in a fight for cultural and political dominance within Jewry. The outcome was heavily influenced by the distribution of political and financial resources. This is evident in the mid-Victorian period in the difficulties encountered by pious Jews who wanted to establish a seminary in London. It can also be seen in the attempts made by the orthodox establishment to place the Reform movement beyond the bounds of communal association. But it can be demonstrated most clearly in the decades after 1880. The immigrants' anglicisation and the shape of Jewish culture in the East End were shaped not only by the immigrants' own choices but also by the resources available to competing groups and institutions. The longevity of the Federation of Synagogues and the vitality of the Jewish friendly societies, for instance, present vivid contrasts with the decrepitude of Jewish trade unions and the erratic fortunes of the socialist and anarchist movements. The Federation's strength was underpinned by Samuel Montagu's financial and political patronage, and one reason for the longevity of Jewish benefit and friendly societies was that, unlike trade unions, they existed at one remove from the economic turbulence of the workshop trades.

Of course, the strongest institutions were among those created and financed by Anglo-Jewry. But the effectiveness of Anglo-Jewish efforts at socialising the immigrants should not be overestimated. The end of this period witnessed a marked departure in Jewish politics which owed nothing to the institutions of Anglo-Jewry. Jewish immigrants, in pursuit of their interests as Jews and as immigrants, forced themselves in unprecedented ways and with conspicuous success into the arena of English politics.

The government's activity and the JBD's failures created openings for other organisations to claim to represent Jewish interests. Jewish politics was transformed in the decade before the First World War by the growth of the collectivist state. The Aliens Act not only announced the end of free immigration; it also heralded a new phase in Jewish politics in Britain. The threat of new legislation against aliens, the protracted struggle to revise the law on Sunday trading and the introduction of national insurance gave rise to challenges which the JBD was unable to meet. Each episode led to the formation of new and independent political organisations in the Jewish East End. None of these groups went on to establish a permanent organisation which would represent generally the interests of East End Jews or immigrants. In this respect, it was a limited challenge to the JBD which emerged from the Jewish East End. But some of these pressure groups, particularly the friendly societies, won significant concessions. By freeing East End Jews from the tutelage of the Anglo-Jewish elite, state intervention provided opportunities as well as challenges for Jews and immigrants. Parliament, political parties and the government itself constituted a new political arena within which East End representatives could act independently of established Anglo-Jewish institutions and leaders. The eruption of a self-conscious Jewish presence in English public life suggests that Jews were not passing down a road to a predetermined resolution of English and Jewish identities. Instead, acculturation is better conceived as the outcome of a series of conflicts. Government intervention provided immigrants with a new challenge and a new resource; in these circumstances anglicisation developed in fresh directions.

The conflicts between East End and West End Jewry, and the friction between Jewish interests and those of the state, did not eclipse other social and political relations which generated other sorts of conflicts among Jewish immigrants. In the workplaces and labour markets of the East End, Jews were called upon by revolutionaries to identify themselves with the whole of the exploited proletariat. English trade unionists cajoled them to respond to what, they claimed, were the interests of their trade as a whole. Master tailors, sabbatarians and zionists urged them to identify themselves with the Jewish sector of their trades. Divisions of labour, moreover, generated conditions in which other, still more specific interests, such as those of under-workers, persisted. Above all, attempts to organise workers across the Jewish sector of trades, vilification of the 'sweating system' and the doctrine of class conflict were continuing presences which, in June and July of 1912, gave rise to a massive and bitter strike in the tailoring trade.

This plethora of institutions and movements, the practices they promoted and the identities they offered and formed, presented Jews with a series of choices as they confronted particular situations. Nevertheless, it is important to remember that these multiple affiliations could converge in the biographies of single individuals. Someone such as S. Kopelovitch, a tailor by trade, was, in a short space of time, a member of the Herzl-Nordau Zionist Society, the Under Pressers, Plain Machinists and Plain Hands Union which opposed all sub-contracting and was dominated by Jewish Socialists, and the East London Jewish Branch of the Amalgamated Society of Tailors. In this light, it would be imprudent to claim that any of the movements or organisations of the Jewish East End indicate the single category, whether 'class' or 'Jewish' or some other, within which individuals acted and which can be seen as a crystallisation of their social identity.[3] Social experience in the Jewish East End encompassed diverse patterns of social relations.

Therefore, when contemporaries strove to elevate one or other of these identities as the determining centre of social and political identity, they were engaged not merely in an attempt to describe the world; they were also seeking to change it. English Jews, immigrant trade unionists and revolutionaries, English trade unionists and social investigators all had particular goals which heavily influenced their characterisation of Jewish immigrants. When historians simply adopt these characterisations at their face value they do so at a considerable cost. An emphasis on the peculiarly Jewish character of immigrant enterprise, on one side, or on the progress of trade unionism, radical politics and class-consciousness on the other, have both served to create distortions in the history of Jewish immigrants; misrepresentations which also confirm a particular and partial interpretation of the English working class.

In important respects the problems that Jewish immigrants faced and their responses to them, in fact, resembled the difficulties which beset groups of English workers and the strategies which they pursued. But these resemblances fall outside the parameters of orthodox interpretations of the working class. As such, they contribute to a more complex and variegated history of work, workers and class. For example, the conflicts of interest within the immigrant labour force and the attempts by some immigrants to achieve independence through petty enterprise were variations on patterns that were diffused widely among English workers. Indeed, in significant ways the unorganised majority of English workers, as they struggled to maintain or improve their living conditions without the aid of trade unions, may have had more in common with Jewish immigrants than with the minority of English workers who were members of trade unions. The most widespread form of association among Jewish workers, benefit and friendly societies, also conformed to the more general pattern of working-class saving. As Paul Johnson has shown, this pattern was determined by low and uncertain levels of income. The small and irregular sums which were available for saving meant that working-class families generally chose to pool their funds with others' in mutual insurance organisations.[4] There was much that was distinctive in

---

3. YIVO, New York, NY, English Territorial Collection, zionist materials, membership cards of S. Kopelovitch.
4. P. Johnson, *Saving and Spending: The Working Class Economy in Britain 1870–1939* (Oxford, 1985), pp. 219–20.

the attitudes of Jewish immigrants. But even here we should be cautious before depicting them as *sui generis*. For instance, the support given to the British Brothers League, and the view of the immigrants taken by many native trade unionists and workers, suggest that national identities were significant among English as well as Jewish workers.

If we turn to the history of popular politics in the Jewish East End, here too we find that its dynamic not only reflected factors that bore upon immigrant and Jewish interests in particular. It too bore the impress of developments which were transforming popular politics more generally. The emergence of independent patterns of popular politics in the Jewish East End was one response to changes which, elsewhere, were generating support for the Labour Party. These resemblances have previously been obscured by the tendency to explain the fortunes of the Liberal and Labour Parties before 1914 as a political concequence of the emergence of a more homogeneous and self-conscious working class. But the force of this argument has been recently undermined by our growing awareness of the continuing economic fragmentation and cultural diversity of the working class. Some historians have argued that the gains made by Labour should not be explained by a rising tide of class-consciousness but can be accounted for by the specifically political content of Labour's appeal in particular locations. It was often interventionist policies by the state, both at national and local levels, which offered Labour opportunities to address experiences, mobilise sentiments and propose solutions which other more established institutions and parties failed to confront.[5]

This is a pattern of change into which the rise of independent popular politics in the Jewish East End, albeit outside of the Labour Party, fits very well. The authority of Anglo-Jewish patrons in the Jewish East End diminished as Jews responded to the challenges brought by the growing appetite of governments for state regulation and intervention. In particular, that network of influence which had circulated around Samuel Montagu and the Federation of Synagogues dwindled. By 1912 the costermongers' union threatened Montagu's parliamentary successor, Stuart Samuel, that it

5. D. Tanner, *Political Change and the Labour Party, 1900–1918* (Cambridge, 1990); A. Reid and E. Biaggini, 'Currents of Radicalism, 1850–1914'. See too in the same volume P. Thane, 'Labour and Local Politics: Radicalism, Democracy and Social Reform, 1880–1914', pp. 244–70. On the local state and Labour politics in the East End after the war see J. Gillespie, 'Popularism and Proletarianism: Unemployment and Labour Politics in London, 1918–34', in D. Feldman and G. Stedman Jones, eds., *Metropolis London: Histories and Representations since 1800* (London, 1989), pp. 163–88.

would desert him for a Labour candidate.[6] Of course, before the First World War few East End Jews could vote. Before 1918 most were doubly disqualified from voting: the property and residence qualifications shrunk the enfranchised population in the East End of London without regard to national origin and, on top of this, few immigrants were naturalised. Inevitably, the Jewish East End was a barren territory for the Labour Party before 1914; however, by the early 1920s it was providing a large labour vote. Indeed, the strength of the Stepney Labour Party in the inter-war period was based on a coalition between Jews and Irish Catholics.[7] The origins of this new political alignment in the Jewish East End can be traced to the pre-war years.

The themes pursued in this book – Jewish emancipation and its legacy, Jewish acculturation, and the social and political history of Jewish immigration – are interconnected. But two connections in particular require comment here. First, the liberal conception of the nation, which was central to the emancipation and immediate post-emancipation debates on Jewish integration, continued to have a vital significance after 1880 when it informed aspects of the response to Jewish immigration. Indeed, the abiding strength of a vision of the nation that was rooted in a set of constitutional freedoms stands as one of the main conclusions of this study. An understanding of the debate on Jewish integration in the pre-immigration period is thus vital to our full comprehension of responses to Jewish immigration until 1914 at least. This leads us to a second connection, for the predominant English response to Jewish immigration had a formative influence on the history of acculturation and the development of politics among Jewish immigrants. The dominance of a liberal conception of the nation within political culture enabled new and independent forms of political organisation to emerge in the Jewish East End in the years before the First World War. As we have seen, this vision of the national community could generate hostility to Jews and did so, for example, between 1876–8 and again during the Boer War. But it did also mean that, when threatened by the growth of state intervention, Jewish immigrants and their representatives were not powerless. It enabled Jewish immigrants, in the years before the First World War, to fashion a new and independent relationship of English public life.

These considerations serve to highlight the overarching claim of

6. House of Lords Records Office, S.M. Samuel scrapbook, *East London Observer*, 4 May 1912. In 1919 the costers' president, Alfred Vallertine, was one of the Labour candidates for a seat on Stepney Borough Council.
7. K. Harris, *Attlee* (London, 1982), p. 46; G. Alderman, *The Jewish Community in British Politics* (Oxford, 1983), pp. 105–27.

this book: namely, that some of the central issues in modern English history, such as the nature of Victorian liberalism, the growth of the collectivist state and the history of the working class can be seen in a new light by closely examining their relation to the Jewish minority. Similarly, abiding themes in Anglo-Jewish history, such as the problem of anti-semitism and the history of acculturation, can be examined in new ways if they are treated, as they developed, in dynamic interaction with the English context. Even more than the particular arguments which are developed here, it is this approach which I believe is valuable and which, I hope, will present a stimulus and a challenge to others.

Index